Teaching Elementary Students through Their Individual Learning Styles

Practical Approaches for Grades 3-6

RITA DUNN
St. John's University

KENNETH DUNN
Queens College

ALLYN AND BACON
Boston London Toronto Sydney Tokyo Singapore

Portions of this book first appeared in *Teaching Students through Their Individual Learning Styles: A Practical Approach,* by Rita Dunn and Kenneth Dunn, copyright© 1978 by Allyn and Bacon.

Unless specified differently, photographs credited to the Center for the Study of Learning and Teaching Styles, St. John's University, and to the Amityville Public Schools and Sacred Heart Seminary in New York were taken by Dr. Kenneth Dunn.

Library of Congress Cataloging-in-Publication Data

Dunn, Rita Stafford, 1930–
    Teaching elementary students through their individual learning
styles : practical approaches for grades 3-6 / Rita Dunn, Kenneth
Dunn.
         p.   cm.
    Portions of this book first appeared in Teaching students through
their individual learning styles, ©1978.
    Includes bibliographical references (p.   ) and index.
    ISBN 0-205-13221-9
    1. Individualized instruction. I. Dunn, Kenneth J. II. Dunn,
Rita Stafford, 1930–   Teaching students through their individual
learning styles. III. Title.
LB1031.D818 1992
372.13'94—dc20   91-40523
                                          CIP

Printed in the United States of America

10 9 8 7 6 5 4   95 94

DEDICATION

To those scholars and researchers at more than seventy institutions of higher education throughout the world, and to those administrators and teachers in hundreds of elementary schools across the United States who have reported results and provided feedback:

We thank you, with the deepest appreciation, for your consistent energy and willingness to experiment, accept difficult challenges, persist, test this model of learning style, improve it, and share what you learned for the benefit of children everywhere. We recognize your valuable contribution and dedicate this book to you.

Among those outstanding professionals are the following who have made particularly unique contributions:

Researchers

Dr. Marie Carbo, St. John's University, New York*
Dr. Corinne Cody, Temple University, Pennsylvania
Professor Gene Geisert, St. John's University, New York
Professor Josephine Gemake, St. John's University, New York
Professor Shirley A. Griggs, St. John's University, New York
Dr. Sheila Jarsonbeck, University of South Florida, Florida
Dr. Angela Klavas, Center for the Study of Learning and Teaching Styles, St. John's University, New York
Dr. Jeffrey Krimsky, St. John's University, New York*
Dr. Harold MacMurren, St. John's University, New York
Dr. Maureen Martini, St. John's University, New York*
Dr. Barbara Miles, St. John's University, New York*
Dr. Janet Perrin, St. John's University, New York*
Dr. Jeanne Pizzo, St. John's University, New York*
Professor Gary E. Price, University of Kansas, Kansas
Professor Louis Primavera, St. John's University, New York
Professor Peter Quinn, St. John's University, New York

*Research award recipients.

Professor Richard Sinatra, St. John's University, New York
Dr. Donald Treffinger, State University College at Buffalo, New York
Professor Jennie Venezzia, St. John's University, New York
Dr. Joan Virostko, St. John's University, New York*
Professor Robert Zenhausern, St. John's University, New York

Practitioners

Duane Alm, principal, C. C. Lee Elementary School, Aberdeen, South Dakota

Roland Andrews, principal, Brightwood Elementary School, Greensboro, North Carolina

Carolyn Brunner, coordinator, International Learning Styles Center, Erie 1 Board of Cooperative Educational Services, Depew, New York

Dr. Vincent Coppola, superintendent, West Seneca Central School District, West Seneca, New York

Dr. Joan DellaValle, principal, Otsego Elementary School, Dix Hills, New York

Dr. Mary Cecelia Giannitti, Sacred Heart Seminary, New York

Phyllis White Hamilton, principal, Ethridge Elementary School, The Colony, Texas

Dr. Jeff Jacobson, assistant superintendent, Converse County School District #1, Douglas, Wyoming

Dr. John M. Jenkins, director, P. K. Yonge Laboratory School, University of Florida, Gainesville, Florida

Patricia Sue Lemmon, principal, Roosevelt Elementary School, Hutchinson, Kansas

Ms. Carol Marshall, Education Director, Center for Success in Learning, Dallas, Texas

Dr. Timothy O'Neill, superintendent, Amherst Central School District, Amherst, New York

Joe Rice, principal, Sherwood Elementary School, Edmonds, Washington

Mary Ann Ritchie, principal, Christa McAuliffe Elementary School, Lewiston, Texas

CONTENTS

PREFACE

Research on the Dunn and Dunn model of learning styles is more extensive and more thorough than the research on most previous educational movements. As of 1992, that research had been conducted at more than seventy institutions of higher education, at grade levels from kindergarten through college, and with students at most levels of academic proficiency, including gifted, average, underachieving, at risk, dropout, special education, vocational, and industrial arts populations. Furthermore, the experimental research in learning styles conducted at the Center for the Study of Learning and Teaching Styles, St. John's University, New York, received two regional, twelve national, and two international awards/citations for their quality between 1980 and 1990 (see Appendix A).

That wealth of well-conducted research verifies the existence of individual differences among students—differences so extreme that the identical methods, resources, or grouping procedures can promote achievement for some and inhibit it for others.

This book is designed to assist teachers, administrators, college professors, and parents to discover the learning style of each youngster and then to suggest practical approaches for teaching students through their individual learning style strengths. Each chapter presents practical, tried and tested ideas and techniques that can be used as quickly as the personnel in a given school can absorb them and put them into practice. The ideas and strategies include the following:

- A thorough analysis of each of the 21 elements of learning style and an instrument and observational methods for recognizing them
- Detailed blueprints for redesigning elementary school classrooms to accommodate a wide variety of learning style differences
- Step-by-step guidelines for creating instructional spaces for elementary students, such as Interest Centers (for global students), Game Tables (for tactual/kinesthetics), Media Corners (for youngsters with specific perceptual strengths), a Reading Corner (for people who cannot concentrate on printed text in an environment with classmates' movements, sounds, or other distractions
- Descriptions and examples of small-group instructional strategies for

peer-oriented students, such as Team Learning, Circle of Knowledge, Brainstorming, and Case Study

- Detailed explanations for designing Programmed Learning Sequences, Contract Activity Packages, Multisensory Instructional Packages, and tactual and kinesthetic instructional resources—different methods for teaching the identical information to elementary students with different learning styles
- Sample individual printouts that permit readers to test their developing ability to diagnose and prescribe for individuals with diversified learning styles
- An instrument for identifying the teacher's learning style and another for identifying the teacher's teaching style to determine the degree to which each teacher teaches the way he or she learns—or the way he or she was taught
- An instrument for identifying the teacher's learning style and each of his or her students' learning styles to determine the degree of match between the two

In a practical sense, these tried and tested techniques, all based on valid and reliable research findings (see Appendix A), may be used by all people concerned with the instructional process at the elementary level.

- Teachers can use the text as a how-to guide to respond to the learning style requirements of individual students.
- Administrators can use the descriptions of methods and approaches as supervisory tools when assessing and aiding teachers to respond to the idiosyncratic characteristics of their young charges.
- Central office personnel can use the separate chapters as a basis for staff development to build instructional skills among faculty.
- Colleges and university professors can use the text as a basis for a course in theory and its practical translation into responsive methods for the preparation and retraining of teachers—who increasingly are being required to diagnose and prescribe on the basis of individual learning style differences.
- Parent groups can use this text to understand, monitor, and support improved instructional programs and to assist their own offspring at home.
- School districts can protect themselves against the increasing number of educational malpractice suits by accurate identification of student learning differences and provision of instructional prescriptions based on accurate data.
- Motivated elementary students can use the strategies included herein to teach themselves how to: (a) do their homework through their learning style strengths; (b) translate their textbooks and other printed materials into instructional resources through which they can teach themselves new and difficult information; and (c) cope with their teacher's style if it happens to be dissonant from how they learn.

This book, then, was written to translate accepted research theory into practical techniques that any teacher, administrator, professor, or parent can use and try immediately. It also includes the first guidelines for teaching elementary students how to teach themselves based on their unique learning style patterns. The acquisition of new skills, the redesign of conventional classroom areas, and the provision of varied and style-responsive resources and approaches will, in a relatively short period of time, build an instructional process that will respond directly to the individual learning styles of all students.

Previous Books by Rita and Kenneth Dunn

- *Practical Approaches to Individualizing Instruction: Contracts and Other Effective Teaching Strategies* (1972)
- *Educator's Self-Teaching Guide to Individualizing Instructional Programs* (1975)
- *Administrator's Guide to New Programs for Faculty Management and Evaluation* (1977)
- *How to Raise Independent and Professionally Successful Daughters* (1977)
- *Teaching Students through Their Individual Learning Styles: A Practical Approach* (1978)
- *Situational Leadership for Principals: The School Administrator in Action* (1983)
- *Teaching Students to READ through Their Individual Learning Styles* (1986)
- *Bringing Out the Giftedness in Every Child: A Guide for Parents* (1992)

Previous Prentice-Hall Books by Rita and Kenneth Dunn
Translated into Foreign Languages

- *Procedimentos Practicos para Individualizar la Enseñanza* (1975)
- *Programmazione Individualizzata: Nuove Strategie Practiche per Tutti* (1977)
- *La Enseñanza y el Estilo Individual del Aprendizaje* (1978)

Previous Book by Rita Dunn

- *Learning Styles: Quiet Revolution in American Secondary Schools* (with Shirley A. Griggs) (1988)

Previous Book by Kenneth Dunn

- *Using Instructional Media Effectively* (with Jack Tanzman) (1971)

ACKNOWLEDGMENTS

Rita and Ken Dunn wish to express loving appreciation for the valuable word-processing expertise, attention to detail, willingness to revise the manuscript consistently, and ever-present sunshine emanated by Madeline Larsen, Executive Secretary, Center for the Study of Learning and Teaching Styles, St. John's University, New York.

We are indebted to Dr. Lewis Grell, Executive Director, Association for the Advancement of International Education (AAIE), who graciously permitted us to incorporate articles written by Rita Dunn, and previously published in that association's newsletter, into several chapters. We also wish to thank Patricia Broderick, editor and associate publisher of *Teaching K–8,* for permitting us to include the essence of "Presenting Forwards Backwards" (October 1988) in Chapter 4 of this book. In addition, Miss Broderick has been a continuing advocate of our learning style concept for more than a decade. She has provided a forum in which elementary teachers throughout the nation have been exposed to the theory and related practices of individualization through learning style and could, if they were so inclined, learn how to implement through many series of articles on this topic. It is our belief that she and *Teaching K–8* have contributed ongoing excellence to elementary education by providing practical instructional know-how unavailable in many teacher education courses.

1

Understanding Learning Style and the Need for Individual Diagnosis and Prescription

The research on learning styles explains why, in the same family, certain children perform well in school whereas their siblings do not. It demonstrates the differences in style among members of the same class, culture, community, profession, or socioeconomic group, but it also reveals the differences and similarities between groups. It shows how boys' styles differ from girls' and the differences between youngsters who read well and those who read poorly.

More important than the documentation of how conventional schooling responds to certain students and inhibits the achievement of others, the research on learning styles provides clear directions for either how to teach individuals through their style patterns or how to teach them to teach themselves by capitalizing on their personal strengths.

Everybody has strengths, although parents' strengths tend to differ from each other's, from their offspring's, and from their own parents'. Thus, mothers and fathers often learn differently from each other and from their children. Nevertheless, a common parental practice is to insist that children study and do their homework as those adults did when they were young. That is not likely to be effective for at least some of the siblings because, in the same family, members usually learn in diametrically opposite ways.

What Is Learning Style?

When a child is ill, a competent physician examines more than merely that part of the anatomy that hurts—such as the throat, the eyes, or the chest. Professionalism requires that the child be examined thoroughly to determine what might be contributing to the health problem; thus doctors get at the *cause,* not just the symptoms. So it is with learning style. Although some pioneers identified style as only one or two variables on a bipolar continuum (Dunn, DeBello, Brennan, Krimsky, & Murrain, 1981; DeBello, 1990), style is a combination of many biologically and experientially imposed characteristics that contribute to learning, each in its own way and together as a unit.

Thus, learning style is more than merely whether a child remembers new and difficult information most easily by hearing, seeing, reading, writing, illustrating, verbalizing, or actively experiencing; perceptual or modality strength is only one part of learning style. It also is more than whether a person processes information sequentially, analytically, or in a ''left-brain'' mode rather than in a holistic, simultaneous, global ''right-brain'' fashion; that, too, is only one important component of learning style. It is more than how someone responds to the environment in which learning must occur or whether information is absorbed concretely or abstractly; those variables contribute to style but, again, are only part of the total construct. We must not look only at the apparent symptoms; we need to examine the whole of each person's inclinations toward learning.

Learning style, then, is the way in which *each* learner begins to concentrate on, process, and retain new and difficult information. That interaction occurs differently for everyone. To identify a person's learning style pattern, it is necessary to examine each individual's multidimensional characteristics to determine what is most likely to trigger each student's concentration—maintain it—respond to his or her natural processing style—and cause long-term memory. To reveal that, it is necessary to use a comprehensive model of learning style because individuals are affected by different elements of style and so many of the elements are capable of increasing academic achievement for those to whom they are important within a short period of time—often within six weeks. Only three comprehensive models exist, and each has a related instrument designed to reveal individuals' styles based on the elements included in that model (DeBello, 1990). It is *impossible* to obtain reliable and valid data from an unreliable or invalid assessment tool, and the instrument with the highest reliability and validity and the one used in most research on learning styles is the Dunn, Dunn, and Price *Learning Style Inventory* (LSI).

Teachers cannot identify correctly all the elements of learning style (Dunn, Dunn, & Price, 1977; Marcus, 1977; Beaty, 1986); some aspects of style are not observable, even to the experienced eye. In addition, teachers often misinterpret behaviors and misunderstand symptoms. Chapter 2 explains which instruments are appropriate at different age levels and how to prepare students to answer their questions. Chapter 2 also describes how to administer a learning style instrument to obtain accurate information.

The Dunn and Dunn Learning Styles Model

Evolution of the Model

In 1967 Professor Rita Dunn was invited by the New York State Department of Education to design and direct a program that would help "educationally disadvantaged" children to increase their achievement. Freed from teaching responsibilities and thus able to focus on how individuals were responding to alternative instructional approaches, she observed the widely diverse effects of exposure to identical methods and teaching styles on same-age and same-grade youngsters. She and Dr. Kenneth Dunn then scrutinized the educational and industrial literature concerned with *how* people learn. They found an abundance of research accumulated over an eighty-year period that repeatedly verfied the individual differences among students in the way each begins to concentrate on, process, absorb, and retain new and difficult information or skills.

Initially, the Dunns identified 12 variables that significantly differentiated among students (Dunn & Dunn, 1972); three years later they reported the existence of 18 (Dunn & Dunn, 1975); by 1979 they had incorporated hemispheric preference and global/analytic inclinations into their framework. Over the past two decades, research conducted by the Dunns, their colleagues, doctoral students, graduate professors, and researchers throughout the United States have documented that, when students are taught through their identified learning style preferences, they evidence statistically increased academic achievement, improved attitudes toward instruction, and better discipline than when they are taught through their nonpreferred styles (*Annotated Bibliography,* 1991; *Learning Styles Network Newsletter,* 1980–1991).

Currently, research is being focused on additional variables, such as the amount and kind of space that people need when concentrating on new and difficult information or the effects of color. By 1990, however, the Dunn and Dunn model included 21 elements that, when classified, revealed that learners are affected by their (1) *immediate environment* (sound, light, temperature, and furniture/seating designs); (2) *own emotionality* (motivation, persistence, responsibility [conformity versus nonconformity], and need for either externally imposed structure or the opportunity to do things in their own way); (3) *sociological preferences* (learning alone, in a pair, in a small group, as part of a team, or with either an authoritative or collegial adult; and wanting variety as opposed to patterns and routines); (4) *physiological characteristics* (perceptual strengths, time-of-day energy levels, and need for intake and/or mobility *while* learning); and (5) *processing inclinations* (global/analytic, right/left, and impulsive/reflective) (see Figure 1–1).

Theoretical Cornerstone of the Dunn and Dunn Model

Learning style is a biological and developmental set of personal characteristics that make the identical instruction effective for some students and ineffective for others. Although initially conceived of as an outgrowth of practitioners' observations combined with university researchers' studies, this learning style model traces its roots to two distinct learning theories—cognitive style theory and brain lateralization theory.

Cognitive style theory suggests that individuals process information differently on the basis of either learned or inherent traits. Many previous researchers investigated the variables of field dependence/independence, global/analytic, simultaneous/successive, and/or left- or right-preferred processing. As we conducted studies to determine whether relationships existed among these cognitive dimensions and students' characteristics that appeared to be more or less responsive to environmental, emotional, sociological, and physiological stimuli, we found that selected variables often clustered together. Indeed, relationships appeared to exist between learning persistently (with few or no intermissions), in quiet and bright light, in a formal seating arrangement, and with little or no intake, and being an analytic Left processor (Dunn, Bruno, Sklar, & Beaudry, 1990; Dunn, Cavanaugh, Eberle, & Zenhausern, 1982). Similarly, young people who often requested breaks while learning and who learned more, more easily in soft lighting, with sound in the environment, seated informally, and with snacks, often revealed high scores as Right processors. Field dependence versus field independence correlated in many ways with a global versus analytic cognitive style and, again, seemed to elicit the same clustering as left- and right-preferred students did.

In some cases, more attributes allied themselves with global/right tendencies than with their counterparts'. Thus, although global/rights often enjoyed working with peers and using their tactual strengths, analytic/lefts did not reveal the reverse, nor did their sociological or perceptual characteristics evidence consistent similarities.

As the relationships among various cognitive style theories were evidenced, brain lateralization theory emerged, based to a large extent on the writings of the French neurologist Paul Braco, whose research had led him to propose that the two hemispheres of the human brain have different functions. Subsequent research by the Russian scientist Luria and the American scientist Sperry demonstrated that the left hemisphere appeared to be associated with verbal and sequential abilities, whereas the right hemisphere appeared to be associated with emotions and with spatial, holistic processing. Those conclusions, however, continue to be challenged. Nevertheless, it is clear that people

FIGURE 1-1 Learning Styles Model
Designed by Dr. Rita Dunn and Dr. Kenneth Dunn

5

begin to concentrate, process, and remember new and difficult information under very different conditions.

Thus, the Dunn and Dunn model is based on the following theoretical assumptions:

1. Most individuals can learn.
2. Instructional environments, resources, and approaches respond to diversified learning style strengths.
3. Everyone has strengths, but different people have very different strengths.
4. Individual instructional preferences exist and can be measured reliably (see Appendixes A and B).
5. Given responsive environments, resources, and approaches, students attain statistically higher achievement and attitude test scores in matched, rather than mismatched treatments (see Appendix A).
6. Most teachers can learn to use learning styles as a cornerstone of their instruction.
7. Many students can learn to capitalize on their learning style strengths when concentrating on new/or difficult academic material.

Assessing the Elements of Learning Style

What Do We Know about Processing New and Difficult Information?

The terms *analytic/global, left/right, sequential/simultaneous,* and *inductive/ deductive* have been used interchangeably in the literature; the descriptions of these variables tend to parallel each other (Dunn, Beaudry, & Klavas, 1989). Analytics learn more easily when information is presented step by step in a cumulative sequential pattern that builds toward a conceptual understanding. Globals learn more easily when they either understand the concept first and then can concentrate on the details, or are introduced to the information with, preferably, a humorous story replete with examples and graphics. What is crucial to understanding brain functioning, however, is that both types reason, but by different strategies (Levy, 1979; Zenhausern, 1980); each strategy "is a reflection of a trend toward optimalization of efficient use of neural space" (Levy, 1982, p. 224).

Thus, whether youngsters are analytic or global, left or right, sequential or simultaneous, or inductive or deductive processors, they are capable of mastering identical information or skills if they are taught through instructional methods or resources that complement their styles. That conclusion was documented in mathematics at the elementary (Jarsonbeck, 1984), high school (Brennan, 1984), and community college (Dunn, Bruno, Sklar, & Beaudry, 1990) levels; in high school science (Douglas, 1979) and nutrition (Tanenbaum,

1982); and in junior high school social studies (Trautman, 1979). Processing style appears to change; the majority of elementary school children are global. However, the older children get and the longer they remain in school, the more analytic some become.

What is fascinating is that analytic and global youngsters appear to have different environmental and physiological needs (Cody, 1983; Dunn, Bruno, Sklar, & Beaudry, 1990; Dunn, Cavanaugh, Eberle, & Zenhausern, 1982). Many analytics tend to prefer learning in quiet, well-illuminated, formal settings; they often have a strong emotional need to complete the tasks they are working on, and they rarely eat, drink, smoke, chew, or bite on objects *while* learning. Conversely, globals appear to work with what teachers describe as distractors; they concentrate better with sound (music or background talking), soft lighting, an informal seating arrangement, and some form of intake. In addition, globals take frequent breaks while studying and often prefer to work on several tasks simultaneously. They begin a task, stay with it for a short amount of time, stop, do something else, and eventually return to the original assignment.

This student is most productive in bright, natural daylight. He also requires conventional seating and sound to screen out distracting noises while completing a reading assignment. (Photograph courtesy of Center for the Study of Learning and Teaching Styles, St. John's University, New York.)

Although this student also requires natural daylight, he prefers to stand while doing difficult academic work and is not disturbed by normal classroom activities. (Photograph courtesy of Center for the Study of Learning and Teaching Styles, St. John's University, New York.)

Neither set of procedures is better or worse than the other; they merely are different. Globals often prefer learning with their peers rather than either alone or with their teacher, and also often prefer to structure tasks in their own way; they tend to dislike imposed directives. What is interesting is that most gifted children with an IQ of 145 or higher are global (Cody, 1983). On the other hand, most underachievers also are global. The difference between the high-IQ and underachieving global students tends to be motivation and perceptual preferences.

It is understandable that the motivation levels of underachievers would be lower than those of achievers, but what may separate the two groups is the biological development of their auditory, visual, tactual, and kinesthetic senses. Although we currently do not know how to intervene in their biological development, we have been successful in teaching them through their existing perceptual preferences (Bauer, 1991; Carbo, 1980; Gardiner, 1986; Ingham, 1989; Jarsonbeck, 1984; Kroon, 1985; Martini, 1986; Urbschat, 1977; Weinberg, 1983; Wheeler, 1983).

Beginning Steps for Practitioners
Teachers need to know how to teach both analytically and globally. Chapter 4 describes that process and will help develop beginning skills in teaching both

In most instructional environments, some students require extra clothing because they feel cool. At the same time, others feel comfortable whereas their classmates remove sweaters or jackets because they are warm. (Photograph courtesy of Center for the Study of Learning and Teaching Styles, St. John's University, New York.)

ways. However, global students often require an environment very different from the conventional classroom. They also appear to need more encouragement and short, varied tasks because of their lower levels of motivation and persistence. Most children learn more easily when lessons are interesting to them, but globals *require* that new and difficult information be interesting, be related to their lives, and permit active involvement. Hart (1983) insists that these are requirements for all youngsters; without doubt, they are necessary if globals are to master academic requirements.

What Do We Know about Students' Environmental Needs?

Although many children require quiet while concentrating on difficult information, others literally learn better with sound than without (Pizzo, 1981, 1982). For the latter group, music without lyrics provides a more conducive-to-concentrating atmosphere than melodies with words, and baroque music appears to cause better responsiveness than rock (DeGregoris, 1986). Similarly, although many people concentrate better in brightly illuminated rooms,

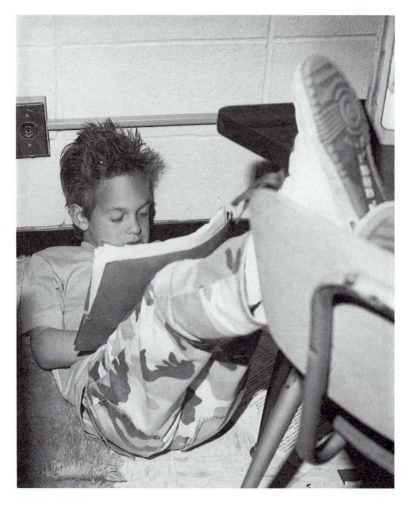

The positions in which youngsters learn best vary from upright and formal seating in chairs to diverse, informal reclining on couches, carpeting, beanbags, soft chairs, and/or cushions. (Photograph courtesy of the Northwest Elementary School, Amityville, New York.)

others think better in soft light than in bright light. Indeed, fluorescent lighting often overstimulates certain learners and causes hyperactivity and restlessness (Dunn, Krimsky, Murray, & Quinn, 1985).

Temperature variations affect individual students differently. Some achieve better in warmth and others in cool environments (Murrain, 1983). Similar differences are evidenced with varied seating arrangements. Some prefer studying in a wooden, plastic, or steel chair, but many others become so uncomfortable in conventional classroom seats that they are prevented from learning.

Few educators are aware that, when a person is seated in a hard chair, fully 75 percent of the total body weight is supported by four square inches of bone (Branton, 1966). The resulting stress on the tissues of the buttocks causes fatigue, discomfort, and frequent postural change—for which many youngsters are scolded on a daily basis. Only people who, by nature, happen to be sufficiently well padded exactly where they need to be can tolerate conventional seating for long periods of time.

Everywhere that teachers teach, they testify to the fact that boys tend to be more hyperactive and restless than girls, and seating arrangements contribute to this phenomenon. However, when students were permitted to learn and/or take tests in seating that responded to their learning style preferences for either a formal or an informal design, they achieved significantly higher test scores when matched, than when mismatched, with their design preferences. That occurred in high school English (Nganwa-Baguma, 1986; Shea, 1983) and mathematics (Orsak, 1990), in junior high school mathematics (Hodges, 1985), and in elementary school reading and mathematics (Lemmon, 1985) (see Table 1–1.)

Beginning Steps for Practitioners

Redesign conventional classrooms with cardboard boxes and other usable items placed perpendicular to the walls to permit quiet, well-lit areas and, simultaneously, sections for controlled interaction and soft lighting. Permit children who want to to work in chairs; on carpeting, bean bags, or cushions; and/or seated against the walls, as long as they pay attention and perform as well as or better than they have previously. Turn the lights off and read in natural daylight with underachievers or whenever the class becomes restless. Establish rules for classroom decorum as you feel comfortable (e.g., no feet on desks, no shoes on chairs, do not distract anyone else from learning). You also may require better test performance and behavior than ever before. You will be surprised at the positive results that occur (Dunn, 1987).

For easy-to-follow suggestions for redesigning classrooms without any cost and in a minimum of time, see Chapter 3.

What Do We Know about the People with Whom Students Learn Most Easily?

For years, many teachers taught their students whatever had to be learned rather directly. When youngsters had difficulty in acquiring knowledge, teachers believed that their charges had not paid attention. Few realized that despite the quality of the teaching, some children were incapable of learning directly from an adult. These young people were uncomfortable when under pressure to concentrate in either teacher-dominated or authoritative classes. They were

TABLE 1–1   Experimental Research Concerned with Learning Styles and Instructional Environments

Researcher/ Date	Sample	Subject Examined	Element Examined	Significant Effects	
				Achievement	*Attitudes*
DeGregoris, 1986	Sixth-, seventh-, eighth-graders	Reading compre-hension	Kinds of sound needed by pref-erents	+ [a]With moderate talking	Not tested
DellaValle, 1984	Seventh-graders	Word recognition memory	Mobility/ passivity needs	+	Not tested
Hodges, 1985	Seventh-, eighth-graders	Mathematics	Formal/informal design prefer-ences	+	+
Krimsky, 1982	Fourth-graders	Reading speed and accuracy	Bright/low light-ing preferences	+	Not tested
Lemmon, 1985	Third–sixth-graders	Reading and mathematics	Design and time	+	Not tested
MacMurren, 1985	Sixth-graders	Reading speed and accuracy	Need for intake while learning	+	+
Miller, 1985	Second-graders	Reading	Mobility/ passivity needs	+	Not tested
Murrain, 1983	Seventh-graders	Word recognition/ memory	Temperature preference	*[b]	Not tested
Nganwa-Baguma, 1986	High schoolers	English	Formal/ informal design	+	Not tested
Pizzo, 1981, 1982	Sixth-graders	Reading	Acoustical pref-erences	+	+
Shea, 1983	Ninth-graders	Reading	Formal/informal design prefer-ences	+	Not tested
Stiles, 1985	Fifth-graders	Mathematics testing	Formal/informal design prefer-ences	0	Not tested

Source: Adapted by permission from "Survey of Research on Learning Styles" by R. Dunn, J. Beaudry, and A. Klavas, March 1989, *Educational Leadership, 46*(6), p. 51, copyright © 1989 by the Association for Supervision and Curriculum Development.

Note: Price (1980) reported that the older students became, the less they appeared able to adapt to a conventional setting. Thus, design may be far more crucial to secondary students' ability to concentrate than to that of fifth-graders, who may be better able to adjust to this element (Stiles, 1985). Dunn and Griggs (1988) described the importance of design to high schoolers throughout the United States.

[a] + represents significant positive findings at $p < .01$ or greater; 0 = no differences or slight trend.

[b]*represents trend toward significant findings at $p < 1.00$.

fearful of failing, embarrassed to show inability, and often too tense to concentrate. For such little ones, learning either alone or with peers is a better alternative than working directly with their teachers in either an individual or a group situation. Indeed, research demonstrates that when students' sociological preferences were identified, and the youngsters then were exposed to multiple treatments—both congruent and incongruent with their identified learning styles—each achieved significantly higher test scores when taught in congruent patterns (Dunn, Beaudry, & Klavas, 1989). Four studies also examined the effects of sociological preferences on attitude toward learning and found statistically higher attitude scores when students were taught in matched situations (DeBello, 1985; Dunn, Giannitti, Murray, Geisert, Rossi, & Quinn, 1990; Miles, 1987; Perrin, 1984) (see Table 1–2). Indeed, gifted students strongly prefer to learn by themselves rather than with others (Cross, 1982; Griggs & Price, 1980; Kreitner, 1981; Price, Dunn, Dunn, & Griggs, 1981). These research data were supported in schools throughout the United States when site visitations, observations, and evaluation collection documented that adolescents achieved more, behaved better, and liked learning best when they were permitted to learn through their sociological preferences as revealed through the *Learning Style Inventory* (Andrews, 1990; Dunn & Griggs, 1988; Lemmon, 1985; Harp & Orsak, 1990; Sinatra, 1990). Since 1984, schools have been experimenting with teaching students to teach themselves by capitalizing on their sociological and other learning style preferences (Dunn, 1984); the results to date are very promising (Clark-Thayer, 1987, 1988; Dunn, Deckinger, Withers, & Katzenstein, 1990; Griggs, 1990; Knapp, 1991; Miller & Zippert, 1987).

Beginning Steps for Practitioners

It is easy for teachers to post an assignment with specific objectives and/or tasks and say to the entire class, "You may work on this alone, in a pair, in a team of three, or with me. If you wish to work alone, sit wherever you will be comfortable in the room. If you wish to work in a pair, take a moment to decide where you want to work, but allow privacy to classmates who need to be by themselves." After a momentary pause, those students who want to work cooperatively may move together quietly. After that, those who wish to work directly with the teacher or an aide may move to a specifically designated area of the room.

We strongly recommend, however, that Team Learning and Circle of Knowledge—specific small-group strategies to *introduce* and to *reinforce* difficult information—become an integral part of the class repertoire *prior* to permitting many sociological choices. Those strategies enable students to work efficiently with a tape recorder and printed illustrated materials, either alone or in a small group, for a lengthy period. Thus, once youngsters are familiar with these strategies and can function independently, or with a peer or two, teachers find themselves with sufficient time to teach the smaller group while others are engaged in Team Learning or independent study. These small-group instructional strategies, as well as others, can be found in Chapter 5.

When learning is difficult, some children prefer to work alone. (Photographs courtesy of the Northwest Elementary School, Amityville, New York.)

What Do We Know about Triggering Concentration and Increasing Retention through Perceptual Strengths?

When students were *introduced* to new material through their perceptual preferences, they remembered significantly more than when they were introduced through their least preferred modality. That was true for primary (Carbo, 1980; Urbschat, 1977; Wheeler, 1980, 1983) elementary (Hill, 1987; Weinberg, 1983), *and* secondary (Bauer, 1991; Kroon, 1985; Martini, 1986) students, as

well as for adults (Ingham, 1989). Furthermore, when new material was reinforced through students' secondary or tertiary preferences, they achieved significantly more than when they merely were introduced correctly—an additional .05 (Kroon, 1985) (see Table 1–3).

Considering that most elementary children are not auditory, (they rarely
remember at least three-quarters of what they hear in a normal 40- or 50-
minute period), lectures, discussions, and talking are the *least* effective way
of teaching. Few teachers, however, know how to *introduce* difficult new ma-

Some students learn best with one partner, whereas others are most productive in groups or teams of threee, four, or five. (Photographs courtesy of the Northwest Elementary School, Amityville, New York.)

terial tactually or kinesthetically—the sensory preferences of most young or underachieving students. Easy-to-make tactual resources are described in Chapter 6 and should be used *before* discussing new content.

1. Using all four modalities without a matched sequence does not insure that each youngster is *introduced* to difficult material correctly (through his or her perceptual strength/preference); neither does it insure that each will

be *reinforced* correctly—and that is what caused achievement gains and/or retention in the studies cited earlier.

2. Young children or underachievers are almost exclusively tactual/kinesthetic learners (Crino, 1984; LeClair, 1986; Keefe, 1982; Price, 1980). Teaching them new and difficult information auditorially at the onset almost guarantees confusion and/or difficulty for many. If their auditory skills are to be developed, we must *reinforce* that way and patiently wait for the day when, as usually happens, their modalities mature and they are "ready" to learn our way. In the meantime, only a small percentage of what we say is absorbed and understood. As a general guideline, it is better to teach underachievers tactually and experientially first and then speak to emphasize and reinforce.

3. Underachieving, at-risk, and dropout students almost exclusively are tactual/kinesthetic learners; when they have auditory preferences, they usually are only tactual/kinesthetic/auditory—missing the visual, which often is a typical "learning-disabled" or "LD" profile. So-called Learning-Disabled students often are tactual/kinesthetic or tactual/auditory, but it is easier for them to learn tactually than in other ways. Introducing them to new material with Flip Chutes, Pic-A-Holes, Multipart Task Cards, and/or Electroboards (see

TABLE 1–2 Experimental Research Concerned with Sociological Preferences

Researcher/Date	Sample	Subject Examined
Cholakis, 1986	106 underachieving, inner-city, parochial school seventh- and eighth-graders	Vocabulary development was provided through three strategies—by the teacher, alone by themselves, and in a peer group treatment.

Findings: Those who preferred learning alone scored significantly higher (.01) than those who preferred learning either with peers or the teacher. However, all students attained significantly higher achievement (.001) and attitude (.01) scores when learning with an authority figure.

DeBello, 1985	236 suburban eighth-graders	Students wrote social studies compositions and then experienced revision strategies that were congruent *and* incongruent with their sociological preferences.

Findings: Peer learners scored significantly higher when matched with the peer-conferencing technique (.01). Authority-oriented learners, when revising through the teacher-conference, achieved statistically higher (.01) than when revising either through peer conferencing or self-review. And those who preferred to learn alone scored significantly higher (.01) when matched, rather than mismatched, with self-review. No learning style group achieved better than any other, but a significant interaction occurred between individual sociological style and the matched method of revision (.001). In addition, the attitudes of students who preferred to learn alone or with an adult were significantly more positive (.01) when they were assigned to approaches that matched their styles.

Giannitti, 1988	104 suburban, parochial and public school sixth-, seventh-, and eighth-graders	Social studies was taught through both a mini–Contract Activity Package (CAP) and a small-group strategy, Team Learning.

Findings: Peer-oriented students achieved significantly higher test and attitude scores when learning through Team Learning than through the mini Cap (.01). Learning-alone preferents attained significantly higher test and attitude scores (.01) through the mini-CAP than with their peers. Nonpreferenced students achieved better through the mini-CAP than through the Team Learning and liked working alone better than in groups. A significant interaction occurred between learning alone and peer-preferenced learning and the method of learning (mini-CAP and Team Learning).

Miles, 1987	40 inner-city fifth- and sixth-graders	Twenty-two who preferred to learn alone and 18 who preferred to learn with peers were assigned randomly to two instructional groups that taught career awareness and career decision-making concepts in conditions both congruent and incongruent with their preferences.

Findings: The matching of sociological preference with complementary grouping patterns increased achievement significantly on career awareness (.01) and career decision making (.01). In addition, students' attitude scores were statistically higher when they were taught career awareness (.01) and career decision-making concepts (.05) in patterns accommodating their sociological preferences. With the exception of career awareness achievement, neither sociologically preferenced group achieved better than the other, but learning-alone preferents scored higher (.05) than peer-preferenced individuals.

Perrin, 1984	104 gifted and nongifted, suburban first- and second-graders	Problem solving and word recognition were taught through both individual and peer-group strategies. Learning

TABLE 1–2 *Continued*

Researcher/Date	Sample	Subject Examined
		with the teacher was eliminated as a strategy when not a single gifted child preferred to learn that way.

Findings: Analysis of the mean gain scores revealed that achievement was significantly higher (.05) whenever students were taught through approaches that matched their diagnosed sociological preferences. Although the gifted tended to prefer to learn alone in their heterogeneously grouped classes, a small group of seven gifted, who previously had known each other from participation in a special, part-time program for the gifted, actually performed best when learning in isolation with other gifted children.

Source: Adapted from "Survey of Research on Learning Styles" by R. Dunn, J. Beaudry, and A. Klavas, March 1989, *Educational Leadership, 44*(6), p. 54, copyright © 1989 by the Association for Supervision and Curriculum Development. Adapted by permission.

TABLE 1–3 Experimental Research Concerned with Perceptual Learning Styles

Researcher and Date	Sample	Subject Examined	Perceptual Preference Examined	Significant Achievement
Bauer, 1991	Junior high school underachievers	Mathematics	Auditory, visual, tactual, kinesthetic	+
Buell & Buell, 1987	Adults	Continuing education	Auditory, visual, tactual	+[a]
Carbo, 1980	Kindergartners	Vocabulary	Auditory, visual, "other" (tactual)	+
Ingham, 1989	Adults	Driver safety	Auditory/visual; tactual/visual	+
Jarsonbeck, 1984	Fourth-grade underachievers	Mathematics	Auditory, visual, tactual	+
Kroon, 1985	Ninth-, tenth-graders	Industrial arts	Auditory, visual, tactual, sequenced	+
Martini, 1986	Seventh-graders	Science	Auditory, visual, tactual	+
Urbschat, 1977	First-graders	CVC Trigram Recall	Auditory, visual	+
Weinberg, 1983	Third-grade underachievers	Mathematics	Auditory, visual, tactual	+
Wheeler, 1980	Learning-disabled second-graders	Reading	Auditory, visual, tactual, sequenced	+
Wheeler, 1983	Learning-disabled second-graders	Reading	Auditory, visual, tactual	+

Source: Adapted by permission from "Survey of Research on Learning Styles" by R. Dunn, J. Beaudry, and A. Klavas, March 1989, *Educational Leadership, 46*(6), p. 51, copyright © 1989 by the Association for Supervision and Curriculum Development. Adapted by permission.

Note: It is important to note that the Carbo (1980), Ingham (1989), and Martini (1986) studies won national awards for the "best research" during the year each was published. Each demonstrated the statistically higher test scores that occurred when students *initially* were introduced to new and difficult academic information through their perceptual preferences—rather than through their less preferred modalitites (see Appendix B).

[a] + represents significant positive findings.

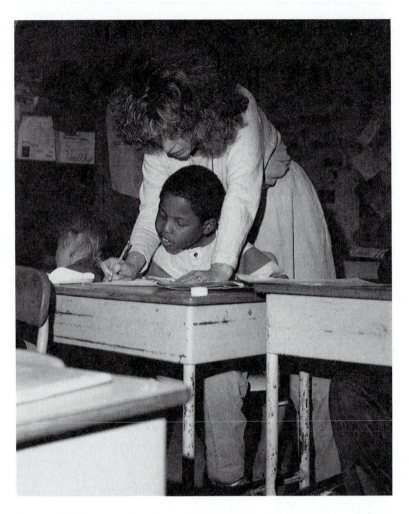

Some children need to learn directly from their teacher. (Photograph courtesy of the Northwest Elementary School, Amityville, New York.)

Chapter 6) and then reinforcing with auditory and visual supplements is likely to help them achieve almost at grade level and in approximately the same amount of time that most average achievers require.

4. A system for introducing each student to new material through his or her perceptual strengths and reinforcing through his or her secondary or tertiary modality is available (see Chapters 6 and 11), is easy to use, costs little or nothing, and does not require repetition through various forms of whole-class instruction provided at different times in four different ways.

Only 10 to 12 percent of elementary school students remember approximately 75 percent of what they hear *during a 40- to 50-minute period; those who do are called* auditory *learners. (Photograph courtesy of the Northwest Elementary School, Amityville, New York.)*

Beginning Steps for Practitioners

Identify students' primary perceptual preferences with the *Learning Style Inventory* and use the sequence for introducing new material through individuals' strengths and reinforcing through their secondary and tertiary modalities whenever you teach by talking or discussing (see Chapter 11). *Before* you lecture, introduce tactual students to the new content tactually—with Electroboards, Flip Chutes, Pic-A-Holes, Multipart Task Cards, and so on as described in Chapter 6. If you need help remembering which youngster needs what, obtain or design your own "Homework Charts," available from St. John's University's Center for the Study of Learning and Teaching Styles (see Chapter 12). Use Programmed Learning Sequences to *reinforce* for essentially tactual children. Tape record the printed material for poor or slow readers (see Chapter 7).

Forty percent of elementary students are visual; *they remember what they* see *or* read. *(Photograph courtesy of the Northwest Elementary School, Amityville, New York.)*

What Do We Know about Time-of-Day Preferences?

Task efficiency is related to each person's temperature cycle (Biggers, 1980); thus, it is related to *when* each student is likely to learn best. For example, junior high school math underachievers became more motivated and better disciplined, and produce a trend toward statistically increased achievement, when they were assigned to afternoon math classes that matched their chronobiological time preferences—*after* they had failed during their energy lows (Carruthers & Young, 1980). One year later, Lynch (1981) reported that time preference was a crucial factor in the reversal of chronic initial truancy patterns among secondary students.

Later, the matching of elementary students' time preferences and instructional schedules resulted in significant achievement gains (.001) in both reading and math (Dunn, Dunn, Primavera, Sinatra, & Virostko, 1987). The following year, teachers' time preferences were identified and inservice sessions

Most young children learn by manipulating objects such as Electroboards or Pic-A-Holes. Such youngsters are called tactual *learners. (Photograph courtesy of the Northwest Elementary School, Amityville, New York.)*

were conducted in both matched and mismatched sessions (Freely, 1984). Interestingly, teachers implemented innovative instructional techniques significantly more often (.01) when they were instructed at their preferred times. Then Lemmon (1985) administered the *Iowa Basic Skills Achievement Tests* in reading and math to elementary school students whose time preferences matched their test schedule—either morning or afternoon. She reported significantly higher test gains in both subjects compared with each youngster's previous three years' growth as measured by the same test.

Most students are *not* alert early in the morning. Primary school children experience their strongest energy highs between 10:00 A.M. and 2:00 P.M.: Only approximately 28 percent are "morning" people (Price, 1980). Approximately one-third of junior high schoolers are alert in the early morning when academics are accented but, again, the majority first "come alive" after 10:00 A.M. In high school, almost 40 percent are "early birds"; a majority, however, continue to be late morning/afternoon preferents and, for the first time since

Another large group of children are kinesthetic; *they remember new and difficult material best through whole-body activities and real-life experiences. (Photograph courtesy of the P. K. Yonge Laboratory School, Gainesville, Florida.)*

infancy, 13 percent are "night owls" (Price, 1980). There are exceptions to these data, but test *your* pupils to determine their individual style patterns.

Beginning Steps for Practitioners

Advise students to do all their studying during their energy highs at their best time of day. Offer demanding subject material at varied times of the school day and assign underachieving, at-risk, and dropout students to their most important subjects when they are most alert. Time is one of the most crucial elements of learning style and demands attention—particularly for potential underachievers (Gardiner, 1986; Gadwa & Griggs, 1985; Griggs & Dunn, 1988; Johnson, 1984; Thrasher, 1984), for whom learning at their energy high increases achievement.

What Do We Know about Restlessness and Hyperactivity?

Most students referred to psychologists for "hyperactivity" are not clinically hyperactive; instead, they often are normal youngsters in need of mobility (Fadley & Hosler, 1979). The less interested the children are in what is being

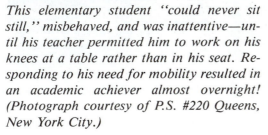

This elementary student "could never sit still," misbehaved, and was inattentive—until his teacher permitted him to work on his knees at a table rather than in his seat. Responding to his need for mobility resulted in an academic achiever almost overnight! (Photograph courtesy of P.S. #220 Queens, New York City.)

taught, the more mobility they need. A disquieting point is that such youngsters are "almost always boys" (p. 219).

Restak (1979) substantiated that "over 95 percent of hyperactives are males" (p. 230) and that the very same characteristic, when observed in girls, is correlated with academic *achievement*. He deplored the fact that boys are required to be passive in school and are rejected for aggressive behaviors there, but are encouraged to engage in typical male aggressions in the world at large—a situation that Restak suggested might lead to role conflict. He added that conventional classroom environments do not provide male students with sufficient outlet for their normal movement needs and warned that schools actually cause conflict with societal expectations that boys not be timid, passive, or conforming.

Tingley-Michaelis (1983) corroborated Restak's warnings and affirmed that boys labeled "hyperactive" in school often were fidgety because their teachers provided experiences for them "to think about something"; instead, those young people needed "to do something" (p. 26). Tingley-Michaelis also chastised educators for believing that activities prevented—rather than enhanced—learning!

Redesigning the classroom to create Interest Centers and Learning Stations simultaneously provides for students' need for movement and positive activity. (Photograph courtesy of the Northwest Elementary School, Amityville, New York.)

When researchers began redefining hyperactivity as students' normal need for mobility, they experimented with providing many opportunities for learning while engaged in movement. Reports then began to document that, when previously restless youngsters were reassigned to classes that did not require passivity, their behaviors were rarely noticed (Fadley & Hosler, 1979; Koester & Farley, 1977). Eventually, teachers began indicating that, although certain students thrived in an activity-oriented environment that permitted mobility, others remained almost exclusively in the same area—despite frequent attempts to coax them to move (Hodges, 1985; Miller, 1985). That led to Fitt's (1975) conclusions that no amount of persuasion increased selected students' interest in movement, whereas others found it impossible to remain seated passively for extended periods. "These are cases of a child's style . . . governing his interactions with and within the environment" (p. 94).

Add to all that the knowledge that almost 40 percent of youngsters require informal seating while concentrating, and it is not difficult to understand why so many—particularly boys—squirm, sit on their ankles and calves, extend their feet into aisles, squirrel down into their seats, and occasionally fall off their chairs.

DellaValle (1984)* documented that almost 50 percent of a large, urban junior high school's students could not sit still for any appreciable amount of time. Twenty-five percent could remain immobile if interested in the lesson, and the remaining 25 percent preferred passivity. Della Valle, whose research won three national awards (see Appendix B), clearly demonstrated the importance of the mobility/passivity dimension of learning style. When students' preferences and their environment were matched, they achieved significantly higher test scores (.001) than when they were mismatched. Students who required mobility moved from one part of the room to another in order to master all the information in the lesson and performed better than when they sat for the entire period. On the other hand, students who disliked moving performed worse when required to learn while walking and significantly better when permitted to sit quietly and read. Table 1–4 reports the post hoc analysis used to determine exactly where the interaction occurred. This analysis was conducted after the initial repeated measures design indicated a significant interaction at the .001 level.

Beginning Steps for Practitioners

Establish varied areas in the classroom so that mobility-preferred youngsters who complete one task may move to another section to work on the next. See Chapter 3 for easy-to-follow guidelines for redesigning a conventional classroom so that it responds to multiple learning style characteristics.

Whenever possible, incorporate kinesthetic activities into each lesson so that, while demonstrating points, acting, role-playing, brainstorming, interviewing (whether simulated or real), or observing phenomena, students may move. Permit those who can be trusted to behave *and* who require mobility (as revealed through their behavior and/or the LSI) to move to the varied areas you have established in the classroom. Some may need only the space

TABLE 1–4 Analysis of Preference × Environment Interaction

	Means	
	Passive b_1	Active b_2
Passive a_2	8.70	5.45
Active a_2	7.15	9.10

Source: Adapted by permission from "Survey of Research on Learning Styles" by R. Dunn, J. Beaudry, and A. Klavas, March 1989, *Educational Leadership,* 46(6), p. 51, copyright © 1989 by the Association for Supervision and Curriculum Development.

Note: a = preference; b = environment, N = 20.

Although some *children can sit passively and concentrate on difficult material for long periods of time, others require frequent intermittent breaks. Being able to move and relax permits them to return to their studies with renewed vigor. (Photographs courtesy of the Northwest Elementary School, Amityville, New York.)*

available in their own "office" or "den"; others may require movement to one classroom area (such as a Library Corner, an Interest Center, a Media Section, or a sectioned-off space near the door in a hall). One or two responsible students might be permitted to work in the corridor immediately outside the classroom under the supervision of a volunteer parent, older student, or aide. Children become increasingly trustworthy when they see that you recognize their needs and are aware that they will lose a privilege if they abuse it. Many of the most difficult-to-contain youngsters are precisely those who cannot sit and, thus, require opportunities to stretch (Dunn, DellaValle, Dunn, Geisert, Sinatra, & Zenhausern, 1986; Miller, 1985).

In addition, do not forget to experiment with a form of independent study such as Programmed Learning Sequences (see Chapter 7) or Contract Activity Packages (see Chapter 8), where students may move as they concentrate without disturbing others. Finally, be certain to experiment with the

small-group techniques such as Team Learning for *introducing* new and difficult material and Circle of Knowledge for *reinforcing* it (see Chapter 5). Peer-
oriented learners who need mobility will function well with these instructional
strategies because of their responsiveness to both the sociological and physiological characteristics.

What Are Some Important Ramifications of Style?

Both Restak (1979) and Thies (1979) ascertained that three-fifths of learning
style is genetic; the remainder, apart from persistence, develops through experience. Individual responses to sound, light, temperature, seating arrangements, perceptual strengths, intake, time of day, and mobility are biological,
whereas sociological preferences, motivation, responsibility (which correlates
with conformity), and structure versus need-for-providing-self-direction are

thought to be developmental. The significant differences among the learning styles of students in diverse cultures tend to support this theory (Dunn, 1990b; Dunn, Gemake, Jalali, Zenhausern, Quinn, & Spiridakis, 1990; Dunn & Griggs, 1990; Guzzo, 1987; Jacobs, 1987; Jalali, 1989; Lam-Phoon, 1986; Mariash, 1983; Roberts, 1984; Sims, 1988; Vazquez, 1985).

The one variable that may provoke disagreement concerning whether its origin is biological or developmental is persistence. Analytics tend to be more persistent than globals; globals tend to concentrate on difficult academic studies for relatively short periods of time, need frequent breaks, and work on several different tasks simultaneously. Once strongly analytic students *begin* a task, they appear to have an emotional need to complete it.

Within each culture, socioeconomic stratum, and classroom there are as many within-group differences as between groups. Indeed, within each family, some members are analytic and others are global—each with many of the learning style traits that tend to correlate with one processing style or the other.

Every person has a learning style pattern and every person has learning style strengths. People tend to learn more when taught with their *own* strengths than when taught with the teacher's strengths (Buell & Buell, 1987; Cafferty, 1980).

No learning style pattern is better or worse than another. Each style encompasses similar intelligence ranges. Students tend to learn and remember better, and to enjoy learning more, when they are taught through their learning style preferences. More than fifty studies documenting that statement exist (see *Annotated Bibliography,* 1991; *Learning Styles Network Newsletter,* (1980–1991).

Beginning Steps for Practitioners
Ask the teachers and administrators in your building or district to take the *Productivity Environmental Preference Survey* by Dunn, Dunn, and Price (1979, 1985, 1991; see Chapter 2) to identify their learning styles. Compare your style and the learning style of the teacher you like best—and least—or wish most or least to emulate. Notice where the two individual printouts differ.

Decide to learn a little more about learning style. Administer the appropriate test to those children about whom you are most concerned. Examine their styles. Discuss their individual printouts with them. Ask questions about how they believe their styles have affected their attitudes toward school and why. If possible, visit a learning styles school (Andrews, 1990; DellaValle, 1990; Dunn & Griggs, 1988, 1989a, 1989b, 1989c, 1989d, 1989e; Orsak, 1990; Sinatra, 1990).

Next, decide which students are of most concern to you. If you are *visual,* read the chapters in this book that help you work with the styles of those youngsters. For example, if you want to attend first to bright, achieving children and enhance their ability to teach themselves more rapidly than could occur in a heterogeneous class, read Chapters 1, 2, 8, 11, and 3, in that order—and you will be able to help those little ones. However, if you are more concerned with an at-risk and potential dropout population, read Chapters 1, 12, 11, 2, 3, 4, 6, 7, 9, and 10, in that order. If you are global or nonconforming, pay no attention to *our* sequence; we know you will design your own! If you prefer a structure for learning and can identify a specific type of student you wish to help, you probably will adhere to our suggested pattern (see Table 1–5). It really does not matter where you start and how you proceed; what is important is that you *do* start and experiment with the suggestions so that you can determine for yourself whether, in fact, students achieve higher tests scores when taught through their styles than when not.

   If you are *not* a visual learner, examine Chapter 11's resources and purchase one of the Teacher Inservice Packages (TIPs) available for learning tactually or auditorially. You will learn kinesthetically as you begin to implement the methods you choose. Study in an environment that complements *your* style for sound, light, temperature, and design. Examine your sociological preference and decide to work either by yourself, with a friend or colleague (or two), or with an authority—another teacher, an administrator, or a college professor.

   If you have no strong primary perceptual preference, you can use this book *if you are motivated;* if not, you are likely to learn better with one of the videotapes described in Chapter 11 or through an on-site visitation.

   Table 1–5 may be a good guide for involving you in learning styles–based instruction. Once you decide with which children you are most concerned, find that group in the table and then follow its itemized chapter sequence.

   In the meantime, if you want to begin *tomorrow* and have little time to

TABLE 1–5 A Guide to Reading This Book for Visual Learners

Students with Whom You are Concerned	Chapters to Read in Indicated Sequence										
	One	Two	Three	Four	Five	Six	Seven	Eight	Nine	Ten	Eleven
Slow learners	1	2	3	6	4	7	8	—	5	9	10
Gifted but under-achieving learners	1	2	7	4	5	10	9	3	6	8	11
Fidgety children who do not concentrate	1	2	3	10	5	4	7	6	8	9	11
Dropouts and the turned-off	1	2	5	3	4	6	8	—	9	7	10
Behavior problems	1	2	4	9	3	5	6	8	7	10	11
Bright, achieving Learners	1	2	4	5	8	6	7	3	9	11	10
All	1	2	3	4	5	6	7	8	9	10	11

read and absorb today, experiment with those of the following suggestions *that most appeal to you.* Almost any effort to complement students' learning styles produces positive effects. Try—and encourage your colleagues to experiment with—one or more of the following suggestions. Look for improvements in students' behaviors, attitudes, and test scores.

- Tell them what is "important." As you mention the items you want remembered, give them clues: "Make note of this!" "Write this down!" "This is important!" "This could be on your test!" This provides *structure* for those who need it.
- When you mention important items, walk to the chalkboard and, in big print, write a word or two that synthesizes that content so that *visual* learners can see it and others can copy it onto their papers.
- When you write on the chalk board, illustrate important information; stick figures will do. If you can't draw, ask students to do it for you. Encourage *global* students to illustrate their notes. *Visual left* processors seem to respond to words and numbers; *visual rights* pay attention to drawings, symbols, and spatial designs. *Global rights* often are strongly *tactual;* they are the doodlers who pay attention better if they use their hands while they are listening. Use colored chalk on blackboards or colored pens on overhead transparencies for global learners.
- Give strongly *visual* children a short assignment to read to introduce new and difficult material. Then they should listen to you speak or participate in a discussion of the topic. Strongly *auditory* students should hear your explanation first and then read materials that will reinforce it. Visual children should copy notes while they listen; auditory learners should copy notes while they read.
- When working with youngsters who read poorly, read in natural daylight. If necessary, turn off the classroom lights or darken a section of the room. Low light relaxes and permits better concentration for 8 out of 10 children who do not read well.
- Write a three- or four-word illustrated outline of the lesson on the chalk board at the beginning of each period. That overview helps the *visual* learner who cannot focus well to keep track of the lesson's emphasis. From time to time, draw attention to the outline and say, "Now we're moving into this part of the topic."
- Laminate 30 or 40 numbered, colored footprints and 6 or 8 handprints. With masking tape folded against itself to provide two sticky surfaces, place the prints into a Twister Game pattern in a less busy part of the classroom so that walking on it in sequence requires body contortions. When youngsters with short attention spans lose interest in a task they should be doing, give them a chance, one at a time, to "walk the footprints." *Kinesthetic* youngsters, or those in need of *mobility,* will benefit greatly. After just one minute, they will be able to return to their seats

and concentrate—for another ten minutes or more. These kinesthetic prints can be designed to incorporate educational games as well.

- Encourage highly *kinesthetic* children to walk back and forth while they are reading their assignments. Somehow, this helps them understand better.
- Encourage youngsters to study at their best time of day, whether it is early in the morning *before* they leave for school, during lunch or free periods, immediately after school, or in the evening before they go to bed.
- Permit children who need *intake* while they are concentrating to bring raw vegetables to school. Establish firm rules: They cannot make noise while eating (you need quiet!); the custodian must never know what you are permitting; no leftovers should remain in the classroom; whatever they don't want must be placed into wastebaskets; and they must get better test grades than they ever have before—otherwise it's not helping!
- Begin reading this book tomorrow, if you can't possibly begin today! Experiment with the suggestions made in each of the chapters you read.

2

Identifying Students' Individual Learning Style Characteristics

Why Use an Identification Instrument?

Learning style encompasses at least 21 different variables, including each person's environmental, emotional, sociological, physiological, and cognitive-processing preferences. Thus, a comprehensive instrument that measures all, or at least *most,* of those elements has a distinct advantage over more limited instruments such as those used for bipolar models (see DeBello, 1990). The very variable *not* examined by a limited instrument may fail to identify an element or style pattern crucial to the successful learning of an individual.

Teachers cannot correctly identify all the elements of a student's learning style pattern through observation. Some elements of style are not observable even to the experienced eye, and the behaviors associated with other elements often are misinterpreted (Dunn, Dunn, & Price, 1977; Marcus, 1977; Beaty, 1986). For example, children who do not sit quietly in their seats often are seen as hyperactive, immature, troubled, or troublesome; few adults ever consider that these youngsters may have an unusually high energy level throughout the day (a sign of good health!) or may require an informal seating design, a great deal of mobility, or opportunities to move from one area of the room to another *while* learning. Those characteristics can be dealt with easily once a knowledge of learning style exists by permitting the student to sit on a pillow or carpet and/or to move from one section of the instructional environment to another as tasks are completed (see Chapter 3).

It is important to identify learning style with a comprehensive instrument, and it is *crucial* to use one that is both reliable and valid. An unreliable or invalid instrument will provide incorrect information. The extensive experimental research on learning styles verifies that students *can* tell you their learning style preferences accurately, but the concept of style *should be explained to them clearly before* they are tested.

Preparing Students for Taking a Learning Styles Test

We know that many youngsters cannot remember three-quarters of what they either hear or see, and many of those students do not read well. Such learners cannot possibly feel good about themselves in our auditory/visual-dominated schools. Thus, it is extremely important to identify their learning styles to determine whether—if they *are* low-auditory/low-visual—they have tactual or kinesthetic strengths through which they can be taught. Tactual students taught with tactual instructional resources (see Chapter 6) achieve almost as well and as rapidly as auditory students taught auditorially and visual students taught visually (Carbo, 1980; Kroon, 1985; Martini, 1986; Wheeler, 1983).

Begin by explaining the differences in learning styles that exist among all classes, families, and cultures. Tell the students that their mothers' styles are likely to be different from their fathers' and that their own styles are probably different from one another's and from their sisters' and brothers' styles.

After some discussion, read either *Two-of-a-Kind Learning Styles* (Pena, 1989) (grades 5–8) about Global Myrna and Analytic Victor, two middle schoolers who do most of their leisure-time activities together but who must study separately because their learning styles are so different, or use *Mission from No-Style* (Braio, 1989) (grades 2–6) as a basis for developing understanding of the concept. Both are obtainable from the Center for the Study of Learning and Teaching Styles at St. John's University (see Chapter 11).

As you read the story to the elementary school class, tape record it and explain to the students why you are doing so. Then break the small tab at the top of the tape to prevent accidental erasure of the contents, and glue the plastic box in which the tape came to the back of the story book. Tell the students that any time individuals wish to hear that story read again, they can use the tape attached to the back of the book and hear it as often as they wish. Some young people will choose to hear the tape repeatedly. If the tape was made so that each time a page in the book was turned, the reader indicated that whoever is using the tape should also turn the page, the books will be read and reread repeatedly.

Encourage students to guess the styles of members in their own family and then write why they believe those are their relatives' styles. Eventually, they can graph their family's styles and compare them with those of their classmates' families. They can illustrate their own learning styles and write poems about how they *feel* now that they know about their style.

Explain that it is important for each person to understand his or her style *strengths*. Accentuate that everyone *has* strengths but that each person's are different from his or her friends' and relatives'. Introduce the idea of learning about one's strengths through a series of questions—which each person must answer truthfully, or there is no way to learn how each should be taught, or do homework, or study efficiently. Tell students in advance that one day in the near future you are going to ask all of them many questions about how they prefer to learn new and difficult information. When you get the results back from the computer, you will be able to tell each boy and girl exactly how he or she should study in order to remember anything that ordinarily would be difficult.

Using the Learning Style Inventory

The *Learning Style Inventory* (LSI) (Dunn, Dunn, & Price, 1975, 1978, 1984, 1986, 1987, 1989) is the first comprehensive approach to the assessment of an individual's learning style in grades 3 through 12. This instrument is an important first step toward identifying the conditions under which each person is most likely to concentrate on, learn, and remember new and difficult academic information.

Careful analysis of each student's LSI Individual Printout identifies those elements that are crucial to the individual's learning style. Further, the instrument aids in prescribing the type of environment (see Chapter 3), instructional resources (see Chapters 4, 6, 7, 8, and 9), social groupings (see Chapter 5), and motivating factors that maximize personal achievement. Many of the questions in the instrument are highly subjective and relative—and that, of course, is precisely why they contribute to an understanding of how each student learns in ways that are different from those of his or her peers.

Each student's learning style is based on a complex set of reactions to varied stimuli, feelings, and previously established patterns. Those patterns tend to be repeated when the person concentrates on new or difficult material. Thus, the words *think, learn, read, write,* and *concentrate* are used interchangeably throughout the inventory, and it is not necessary for the respondent to differentiate among their meanings. Comparisons of answers to questions that include these words, and to others that seem to ask the same thing in different ways, contribute to the accuracy of the student's overall profile.

The inventory does not measure underlying psychological factors, value systems, or the quality of attitudes. Rather, it yields information about the patterns through which learning occurs. It summarizes the environmental, emotional, sociological, physiological, and global/analytic processing preferences a student has for learning—not *why* they exist.

Finally, the inventory does not assess the finer aspects of an individual's skills, such as the ability to outline procedures, organize, classify, or analyze new material. Again, it gives evidence of *how* students prefer to learn, not the skills they use (Dunn, Dunn, & Price, 1989, pp. 5-6).

The LSI uses dichotomous items and can be completed in approximately 30 or 40 minutes. It reports a Consistency Key to reveal the accuracy with which each respondent has answered the questions. The National Center for Research in Vocational Education at The Ohio State University published the results of its two-year study of instruments that diagnose learning styles and reported that the LSI had established impressive reliability and face and construct validity (Kirby, 1979). Since examination by that center more than a decade ago, the LSI has evidenced remarkable predictive validity (DeBello, 1985; Dunn, Bruno, Sklar, & Beaudry, 1990; Dunn, DellaValle, Dunn, Geisert, Sinatra, & Zenhausern, 1986; Dunn, Dunn, Primavera, Sinatra, & Virostko, 1987; Dunn, Giannitti, Murray, Geisert, Rossi, & Quinn, 1990; Dunn, Krimsky, Murray, & Quinn, 1985; Dunn, White, & Zenhausern, 1982; Hodges, 1985; Martini, 1986; Miller & Zippert, 1987; Pizzo, Dunn, & Dunn, 1990; Shea, 1983).

In a comparative analysis of the style conceptualization and psychometric standards of nine different instruments that measure learning style instructional preference, the Dunn, Dunn, and Price *Learning Style Inventory* (LSI) was the *only* one rated as having good or very good reliability and validity (Curry, 1987). Of the 18 instruments reviewed in the document, including an additional 9 concerned with information processing, the LSI was one of only 3 with good or very good reliability and validity. The LSI is an assessment that is easy both to administer and to interpret. Perhaps because of that, Keefe (1982) revealed that it "is the most widely used in elementary and secondary schools" (p. 52).

Information Provided by the LSI

The LSI assesses individual preferences in the following areas: (1) immediate environment (sound, light, temperature, and seating design); (2) emotionality (motivation, persistence, responsibility/conformity, and need for internal or external structure); (3) sociological factors (learning alone, in a pair, as part of a small group or team, with peers, with an authoritative or collegial adult, and/or learning in a variety of ways or in a consistent pattern); (4) physiological factors (auditory, visual, tactual, and/or kinesthetic perceptual preferences; food or liquid intake, early morning, late morning, afternoon, or evening time-of-day energy levels, and mobility needs; and, through correlation with sound, light, design, persistence, peer-oriented, and intake scores (Dunn, Cavanaugh, Eberle, & Zenhausern, 1982), indications of global (right) or analytic (left) cognitive/psychological processing inclinations (see Figure 2–1).

The LSI Inventory

- Permits students to identify how they prefer to learn and also indicates the degree to which their responses are consistent.

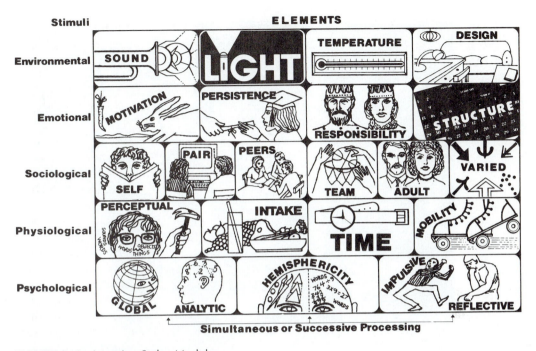

FIGURE 2–1 Learning Styles Model
Designed by Dr. Rita Dunn and Dr. Kenneth Dunn

- Provides a computerized summary of each student's preferred learning style; that summary is called an *Individual Profile* (see Figure 2–2).
- Suggests a basis for redesigning the classroom environment to complement many students' needs for sound, quiet, bright or soft light, warmth or coolness, or formal or informal seating (see Chapter 3).
- Describes with whom each student is likely to achieve most efficiently— for example, alone, in a pair, with two or more classmates, with others with similar interests or talents (peers), with either an authoritative or a collegial teacher, and/or with all, none, or only one or two of these possibilities.
- Explains for whom to provide options and alternatives and for whom direction or structure is appropriate.
- Sequences the perceptual strengths through which individuals should *begin* studying and then *reinforce* new and difficult information and how each student should do his or her homework (see Chapter 12).
- Indicates the methods through which students are likely to achieve well— for example, through Contract Activity Packages (CAPs), Programmed Learning Sequences (PLSs), Multisensory Instructional Packages (MIPs), tactual/kinesthetic manipulatives, or a combination thereof.

The Individual Learning Style Printout provides information about 21 different elements that affect students' preferences and strengths. The young man at the top requires subdued lighting; he frequently shades his eyes and seeks softly lit classroom areas despite a physician's assurance that he has normal vision. Conversely, the young lady in the next photo repeatedly removes the shade from her lamp to obtain brighter illumination. (Photographs courtesy of Center for the Study of Learning and Teaching Styles, St. John's University, New York.)

- Extrapolates information concerning which children are nonconforming, and how to work with those who are.
- Pinpoints the best time during the day for each child to be involved in required difficult subjects, and thus permits grouping students for instruction based on their learning style energy-high strengths.
- Itemizes the types of students for whom snacks, *while learning,* are an integral part of the process.
- Notes the types of students for whom movement, *while* learning, may accelerate the learning process.

- Suggests for whom analytic or global approaches to learning new and difficult material are likely to be important (see Chapter 4).

These questions are sample items from the LSI:

- I study best when it is quiet.
- I study best at a table or a desk.
- I can ignore most sound when I study.
- I like to study by myself.
- When I can, I do my homework in the afternoon.
- The things I remember best are the things I hear.
- I concentrate best on difficult subjects seated on a couch or easy chair.
- I think best when I work on hard tasks with a friend.
- It's hard for me to sit in one place for a long time.
- Music helps me concentrate when I have to learn difficult things.

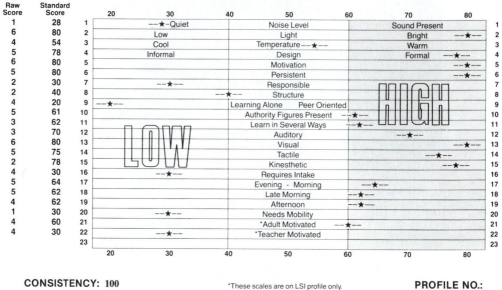

Name: Elizabeth Patrice   Sex: F   Year in School: 6   Date of Birth: 6/80   I.D. No.: 1406

Group Identification: Malverne Public Schools   Special Code: G/T   Date: 1-24-1991   Group No.: 9021

PREFERENCE SUMMARY

Raw Score	Standard Score									
1	28	1	--★-Quiet	Noise Level	Sound Present	1
6	80	2	Low	Light	Bright --★--	2
4	54	3	Cool	Temperature--★--	Warm	3
5	78	4	Informal	Design	Formal --★--	4
6	80	5		Motivation	--★--	5
5	80	6		Persistent	--★--	6
2	30	7	--★--	Responsible		7
2	40	8	--★--	Structure		8
4	20	9	--★--	Learning Alone Peer Oriented		9
5	61	10		Authority Figures Present --★--		10
3	62	11		Learn in Several Ways --★--		11
3	70	12		Auditory	--★--	12
6	80	13		Visual	--★--	13
5	75	14		Tactile	--★--	14
2	78	15		Kinesthetic	--★--	15
4	30	16	--★--	Requires Intake		16
5	64	17		Evening - Morning --★--		17
5	62	18		Late Morning --★--		18
4	62	19		Afternoon --★--		19
1	30	20	--★--	Needs Mobility		20
4	60	21		*Adult Motivated --★--		21
4	30	22	--★--	*Teacher Motivated		22
		23				23

CONSISTENCY: 100   *These scales are on LSI profile only.   PROFILE NO.:

FIGURE 2–2 Individual Profile: Learning Style Inventory

Individual Profile

The Individual Profile (see Figure 2–2 for an example) for the LSI includes the student's name or number, gender, date the inventory was administered, school, teacher, grade, and class number. A Consistency Score, which indicates how accurate the responses are for this particular student, is provided in the lower left-hand corner of each Individual Profile (see Figure 2–2). To interpret an individual's profile, follow these guidelines:

1. Note that the rectangle that constitutes the Preference Summary for each student has numbers beginning with 20 at the upper left-hand side through to 80 at the upper right-hand side.

    a. Bracket the upper section to include everything between 70 and 80. Label that section "Strong Preference." Any learning style element that falls within the range from 70 to 80 on an Individual Profile is *extremely important* to that person. That person will *always* learn new and difficult information more easily and retain it better when

The Learning Style Inventory *reveals which students are self-structured and which require extensive direction from their teacher. This youngster is most productive when permitted to work independently with a Contract Activity Package. (Photograph courtesy of the Grafflin School, Chappaqua, New York.)*

that particular element is responded to. Thus, in Figure 2–2, Elizabeth Patrice will always learn better in *bright* than in low lighting, at a conventional desk and seat than on an easy chair, and when given a variety of resources or methods (Learning in Several Ways) than when following patterns or routines.

b. Bracket the upper section to include everything between 60 and 69. Label that section "Preference." A preference is almost as important as a strong preference, but the person with a preference has some limited options. That learner will *usually* or *often* learn new and difficult information more easily and retain it better when that particular element is addressed. That learner, however, *occasionally* can learn well despite the failure to address that element. It is important to remember that more than three-fifths of learning style appears to be biologically imposed (Restak, 1979; Thies, 1979).

Thus, it is not easy for students to overcome their preferences, and it is very difficult indeed to overcome a strong preference.

c. Bracket the upper section to include everything between 20 and 29. (Restak, 1979; Thies, 1979). A strong opposite preference is just as important as a strong preference, but it responds to the *opposite* of the element printed in the *center* of the Preference Summary. Thus, Elizabeth Patrice (Figure 2–2), who scored 28 on needing quiet, will *always* work better in a quiet rather than in a sound-filled environment. This is not a young person who can work well with music or any kind of sound while she is concentrating on new or difficult academic material.

d. Bracket the upper section to include everything between 30 and 30. Label that section "Opposite Preference." An opposite preference is just as important as a preference and almost as important as an opposite strong preference. The individual *occasionally* can overcome an opposite preference—but not too often.

e. Bracket the entire middle upper section of the Preference Summary and label it "Not Important" or "It Depends." Elements that fall within this middle section suggest that the individual has the *ability* to learn in that way but will use it only when *interested in the topic* or motivated.

Thus, the *Learning Style Inventory* (LSI) Individual Profile for each student represents how he or she responded to the series of questions for each subscale. That information describes how the student should be taught, with whom, in which section of the environment, at what time of day, and with which methods or approaches (Contract Activity Packages, Programmed Learning Sequences, Multisensory Instructional Packages, or tactual/kinesthetic resources). As an example, consider Figure 2–2, the Individual Profile of Elizabeth Patrice.

Interpreting Elizabeth Patrice's Individual Profile: What Is Her Learning Style and How Should She Be Taught?

When "reading" a profile, first scan the student's demographic information to learn age, gender, and how accurate this information is for that individual—the Consistency Score. Elizabeth Patrice is an eleven-year-old girl in the sixth grade. Her Consistency Score (lower left corner) is 100 percent. You may use any data with a Consistency Score of 70 or above; do *not* use information on an Individual Profile with consistency below 70 percent. If that occurs, and you have read *Two-of-a-Kind Learning Styles* or *Mission from No-Style,* retest and send the new Answer Sheet to Price Systems, where it will be reprocessed at no cost.

Environmental Information   Scan the first four elements of the environmental stimulus and determine each student's preferences for either a quiet (40 or below) or sound-filled (60 or above), well-illuminated (60 or above) or softly illuminated (40 or below), cool (40 or below) or warm (60 or above), and formal (60 or above) or informal (40 or below) classroom. Elizabeth prefers quiet; because her LSI score is below 30, that is an opposite strong preference of hers. She also strongly prefers bright light and seating at a conventional desk. Temperature, because her score is in the 41–59 range, is not important to her. When she is interested in what she is learning or doing, she is unaware of temperature except when it is at an extreme; when she is bored, however, she will become aware of temperature discomfort.

Emotional Information   Elizabeth is highly motivated and persistent (scores in the "Strong Preference" range of 70 or above), does not require external structure, and sometimes prefers to provide her own structure. Her low Responsibility score suggests that she is a nonconformist and likes to do things *her* way. When working with nonconforming students, experiment with doing the following three things.

1. Explain why whatever you want the student to do is important to *you.*
2. Speak collegially. Do *not* address the nonconforming student in an authoritative or directive tone. Instead, make believe you are talking with the teacher next door (assuming you respect the teacher next door!).
3. Give the student choices of how he or she can show you that what you requested has been completed,

For example, you might say, "Liz, it is important to me that you translate this chapter into a Contract Activity Package you can use, because I have not had the time to create one on this topic and I do not want to keep you at the class' pace. I know you can progress faster than most students, and I do not want you to become bored. However, if you do not find the material interesting, speak with the librarian, Mrs. Roberts; perhaps she can help you find multimedia related to this topic. Or you might see whether our local museum can add information that we do not have in our school library. Also, if you prefer, you can translate the material into a videotape or another media form that might make the topic more interesting. Which of these alternatives make sense to you?" Once a nonconformist commits to a choice, he or she often will follow through.

Teachers often believe that having motivated, persistent students in their classes makes teaching easy. Liz, however, as you will see when we examine other elements of learning style, is a bright student who remembers easily by listening, seeing or reading, taking notes or using manipulatives, and experiencing. Because she *is* motivated, she enjoys learning; because she is persistent, once she begins an assignment or project, she continues until it has been completed. Thus, she works attentively and finishes tasks before most of her classmates do. Because she is a nonconformist and is motivated, she will not hesitate to tell her teacher that she has done the assignment and requires that it be corrected (high on Authority Figures Present, thus wants feedback from her teacher). If told to wait for the others to complete their work, she will respond that *she* is ready to continue. She is not "fresh," but she does not need social approval for things she believes in. Thus, an Elizabeth Patrice who has completed her assignment, is motivated to learn, and is highly persistent *and* a nonconformist will ask for individual attention. If her teacher either is whole-class-oriented or does not understand that this adolescent's learning style dictates her need for constant involvement, tension is likely to develop both within the two individuals *and* between them. Many gifted students experience such frustration, and many teachers are unaware of why those young people do not perform well in school or become angry with the process of schooling.

Sociological Information   Elizabeth is a strong Learning Alone student (only 20 on the LSI Individual Profile); she is not peer-oriented. Elizabeth may be offered the choice of working with peers when she wishes, but she should be permitted to do difficult assignments on her own if she chooses. Elizabeth is *not* a good candidate for cooperative learning or small-group techniques unless *she* opts for those strategies when permitted to choose.

Despite her high nonconformity score (Responsibility score below 31), Elizabeth wants feedback from the authority or authorities in her life (LSI score of 61). She also likes variety (LSI score of 62 on Learning in Several Ways) and thus becomes bored quickly when required to engage in patterns and routines. Given this information about Liz, her teacher would be wise to permit her to work either alone, with peers, or with media *or adults* when she prefers to do so. The variety of sociological choices is, in and of itself, enticing to her.

Perceptual Strengths   Most people have just a single perceptual strength, as indicated by LSI scores of 60 or higher. Scores between 41 and 59 indicate that a person *can* remember what is learned through that modality, but only if interested in what is being studied. Liz's scores are all above 70, indicating that she remembers easily what she hears, what she sees or reads, what she writes or manipulates, and what she experiences. Thus, Liz has *multisensory* perceptual strengths. Unlike most students, Liz does not need to sequence her perceptual exposures when she is introduced to new and difficult material. She can learn through all senses. That gift contributes substantially to high achievement in school, and thus it is easy to conjecture that Liz performs very well academically, particularly because those high perceptual strengths are combined with high motivation and high persistence.

Other Physiological Information   Liz's low intake score (below 31) indicates no need for snacking while learning. Her chronobiological scores (60 or above on every segment of time of day) suggest a consistently high energy level—which "keeps her going." Most people have only a single energy high each day, but Liz has *three*. Such people often are labeled hyperactive by teachers who do not understand why these youngsters never sit still. The reason is simply that they have so much energy, they *cannot* contain it.

Hypothesize a student with high energy levels, who is motivated and persistent, who completes work quickly because of strong perceptual strengths and a need for variety. It is easy to understand why that student is always "on the go." Because few people experience such energy drive, in contrast with an average level, that youngster *appears* to be hyperactive. Consider, too, Tingley-Michaelis' (1983) admonition that youngsters labeled hyperactive in school often were fidgety because their teachers provided them with experiences "to think about something"; instead, those children needed "to do something" (p. 26). Tingley-Michaelis also chastised teachers for believing that activities prevented—rather than enhanced—learning. Indeed, when previously restless youngsters were reassigned to classes that did not require passivity, their behaviors were rarely noticed (Fadley & Hosler, 1979; Koester & Farley, 1977).

Observe Liz's low mobility score (30 on the LSI); she does not need to be in constant motion. Instead, she needs to learn experientially—through *doing*. Such a youngster should be permitted to choose from among alternative projects of which the teacher approves and should be enabled to complete them through *any* perceptual strength. Thus, she might build, paint, draw, act out or role play, demonstrate, graph or chart, and so forth. The choice of projects should respond to her need for variety, multiple strengths, preference for learning alone, and need to complete many tasks at her own fast pace.

Adult Motivation Scores   Although Liz wants to please *some* adult in her life, it probably is her parent or an other-than-teacher figure. Her low Teacher Motivation score (30 on the LSI) suggests she is not in need of pleasing her teacher—although she *does* want feedback (high on Authority Figure Present).

Analysis of LSI Data from Individual Profile   Let's consider what a teacher looking at Elizabeth Patrice's LSI Individual Profile might do to improve instruction for her. In terms of classroom environment, Liz might be seated near a window or under a direct light. Because of her need for quiet, her desk should be away from the center of activity—perhaps even in a corner of the room. If the floor is uncarpeted, a small rug placed beneath Liz's desk and seat would help to absorb sound.

Contract Activity Packages (CAP) (see Chapter 8) would be an excellent instructional method for Liz. They provide the choices that nonconformists respond to and suggest multisensory materials that a good student like Liz could use easily and well. The teacher should set aside some time to review Liz's work periodically, add comments to her grade to provide the feedback she needs, and permit her a range of choices of ways to demonstrate mastery of objectives. Because Liz is capable of becoming an independent learner, she should be able to design her own Activity, Reporting, and Resource Alternatives after just a few experiences using the CAP system. Eventually she would develop the ability to read textbook information and convert it into a CAP through which she could teach herself anything required by her teachers—or anything else of interest to her.

Determining Global or Analytic Processing Inclinations   Previous studies revealed correlations between individual learning style characteristics and global and analytic processing styles (Cody, 1983; Dunn, Bruno, Sklar, & Beaudry, 1990; Dunn, Cavanaugh, Eberle, & Zenhausern 1982). Global learners tend to prefer learning with what conventional teachers think of as distractions—sound (music, tapping, or conversation), soft illumination (covering their eyes or wearing sunglasses indoors), an informal design (lounging comfortably), peer orientation (wanting to work with a friend), and a need for intake (snacks) *while* studying. Furthermore, globals tend not to be persistent; they begin working with a burst of energy, which lasts for a relatively short period, and then they want a "break." Globals return to their task and work again for another short interval; then they want another break. Globals also dislike working on one thing at a time; they often become engaged in multiple tasks simultaneously and concentrate on several in varying sequences. Thus, globals may begin an assignment in the middle or at the end.

Analytics, on the other hand, tend to prefer learning in silence, with bright lighting, and a formal design—a conventional classroom. They rarely eat, chew, drink, or smoke *while* learning; instead, they do so afterward. Analytics tend to be persistent; they may not always start an assignment immediately, but once they *do* begin, they have a strong emotional urge to continue until the task is done or until they come to a place where they feel they can stop.

These five elements—sound, light, design, persistence, and intake—correlate significantly (.01) with processing style. Many global learners also prefer to learn with peers and have strong tactual perceptual preferences. That is true of many fewer analytics.

It is not necessary to have all five elements to be either a global or an analytic processor; the presence of three of the same group indicates tendencies in that direction. Thus, Liz prefers quiet, bright light, a traditional desk and chair, and no intake; she also is persistent. Liz has five analytic qualities, and thus the teacher would be safe to assume that Liz learns best via step-by-step sequential lessons that begin with the data or details and gradually build up to an understanding (see Chapter 4).

Interpreting a Second LSI Individual Printout

Now examine Figure 2–3, Keith David's Individual Profile. Keith is an eight-year-old third-grader attending Carey Elementary School. His Consistency Score is 88, which is fine.

Environmental Information   Scan the first four elements of the environmental stimulus and determine which learning style elements are important to Keith.

Name: **Keith David**   Sex: **M**   Year in School: **3**   Date of Birth: **1/83**   I.D. No.: **40000000**

Group Identification: **Carey Elementary**   Special Code: Date: **02–05–1991**   Group No: **110**

PREFERENCE SUMMARY

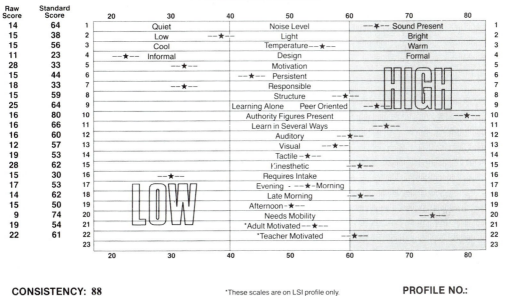

Raw Score	Standard Score		Preference	
14	64	1	Quiet — Noise Level — Sound Present	1
15	38	2	Low — Light — Bright	2
15	56	3	Cool — Temperature — Warm	3
11	23	4	Informal — Design — Formal	4
28	33	5	Motivation	5
15	44	6	Persistent	6
18	33	7	Responsible	7
15	59	8	Structure	8
25	64	9	Learning Alone — Peer Oriented	9
16	80	10	Authority Figures Present	10
16	66	11	Learn in Several Ways	11
16	60	12	Auditory	12
12	57	13	Visual	13
19	53	14	Tactile	14
28	62	15	Kinesthetic	15
15	30	16	Requires Intake	16
17	53	17	Evening - Morning	17
14	62	18	Late Morning	18
15	50	19	Afternoon	19
9	74	20	Needs Mobility	20
19	54	21	*Adult Motivated	21
22	61	22	*Teacher Motivated	22
		23		23

CONSISTENCY: 88   *These scales are on LSI profile only.   **PROFILE NO.:**

FIGURE 2–3   Individual Profile: Learning Style Inventory

In contrast to Elizabeth Patrice, who requires quiet, Keith prefers sound—music or conversation in the background—while learning. He also prefers soft lighting and an informal design. Conventional seating makes Keith physically uncomfortable and unable to concentrate on new and difficult information for any length of time. But when he is permitted to study on a floor, rug, beanbag, or pillow, Keith's attention span increases and his power of concentration is enhanced. Temperature is not important to him.

Emotional Information   Keith is unmotivated (LSI score of 33) and has a low Responsibility score (33), suggesting that he is a nonconformist (Dunn, White, & Zenhausern, 1982). When he is interested in what he is learning, he can be persistent and function with an average amount of structure. But when he is either uninterested or unable to master the material, he reveals a short attention span and does not follow directions.

Sociological Information   Keith is strongly peer-oriented (LSI score of 64), wants feedback from an authority (LSI score of 80), and prefers a great deal of instructional variety rather than patterns or routines (LSI score of 66). Unlike Elizabeth Patrice, he does not enjoy learning alone but, rather, will perform better when permitted to learn with peers.

Perceptual Strengths   Keith has good perceptual strengths. He remembers nicely the things he hears (LSI score of 60) and experiences (LSI score of 62 on Kinesthetic), and his visual and tactual scores (57 and 53, respectively) are good, provided he is interested in what he is being exposed to.

Other Physiological Information   Keith's best time of day for difficult learning is in the late morning (LSI score of 62), but, if interested, he is capable of learning at any time of day. He needs frequent mobility (LSI score of 74).

Adult Motivation Scores   Although he wants to please another adult in his life when he is interested in what he is learning and can do so, Keith is strongly teacher-motivated. When a student's score on Teacher Motivated is 60 or above, also note the LSI score on Authority Figure Present. If both are 60 or above, that youngster may need an authoritative teacher—someone warm but firm. However, if the LSI Teacher Motivated score is 60 or above and the Authority Figure Present score is 40 or below, a collegial rather than an authoritative teacher would appear to be a better match of teaching and learning style.

Analysis of LSI Data from Individual Printout   Keith's low motivation may be reversed if his teacher responds to his learning style characteristics. The conventional classroom itself is unmotivating to students like Keith, who thrive in the midst of activities, variety, peer interaction, and choice. The first step is to redesign a section of the room to permit casual seating arrangements. Obviously, regulations need to be established—for example, students may do their work anywhere they wish as long as they are: (1) responsive to the teacher's directions; (2) considerate of others and not distracting to anyone; (3) able to complete their assignments; and (4) evidencing better grades than they achieved before they were permitted to choose their work places.

   Keith needs soft lighting. Undoubtedly, he will choose a section of the classroom away from the lights and windows, perhaps even underneath or in back of a piece of furniture. Noise not only does not disturb Keith, he probably uses it to block out extraneous sounds (such as classmates breathing or moving in their seats) of which many of us are unaware. The teacher might be willing to experiment with using a listening station or music through earplugs to help him concentrate. Again, the same rules should apply: Keith may use the sound blocks provided he is responsive to his teacher's directions, does not distract or interfere with classmates' learning, completes his work, and achieves better than previously.

   Another way to motivate Keith may be to permit him to study, learn, and complete assignments with classmates, rather than alone. Many young people function poorly cognitively when required to concentrate on difficult tasks by themselves; they simply are not loners. Conversely, they are stimulated by interaction with others. His teacher should experiment with permitting Keith to work with others *providing* all students in the group complete their tasks; function in an orderly, quiet manner; *and* perform as well as or better than they have previously. Normally, we suggest that students must perform *better* than previously; in Keith's case, however, to increase his desire to achieve, working with classmates is just an initial step forward.

In addition to permitting Keith to complete tasks with classmates, his teacher must give him the feedback he needs. He should understand that she is trying to help him perform better than before and is there to assist, question, monitor, and guide him on a frequent basis (because of his need for an authoritative presence).

Keith's perceptual strengths are fine; he is auditory (LSI score of 60) and kinesthetic (LSI score of 62), and his visual and tactual scores are all in the middle of the Individual Profile, indicating that, when interested, he is capable of remembering what he sees or reads and what he writes, draws, or expresses manipulatively. Keith's problems are his low Motivation score, his inability to adjust to traditional classroom settings, and his preference for working with others rather than alone. He also wants a variety of instructional experiences; he becomes bored with patterns and routines.

Keith does not require intake and, if interested, can concentrate at any time of day, but his *best,* most alert period is in the late morning. Thus, he should be scheduled for his most important subject between 10:00 A.M. and 12:00 noon, with some variation to respond to his need for variety.

Keith's strong need for mobility undoubtedly causes problems in school. Teachers often do not understand that, when a person is seated in a wooden, steel, or plastic chair, fully 75 percent of the total body weight is resting on just four square inches of *bone* (Branton, 1966). Only people who are sufficiently well endowed exactly where they need to be can sit for more than 10 or 12 minutes in such seating. Keith's teacher would be wise to experiment with permitting him to sit on a cushion on his chair or on a beanbag, pillow, carpet, or couch (if one is available).

Keith's willingness to please his teacher (LSI score of 61 on Teacher Motivated) will help increase this young man's motivation *and* achievement.

When choosing an instructional method appropriate for Keith, the knowledge that he has good perceptual memory, wishes to learn with peers, likes variety, and is a nonconformist is helpful. Ordinarily we would not recommend Contract Activity Packages (CAPs) for unmotivated learners because successful use of a CAP demands a strong measure of independence. However, Keith is *capable* of learning through this method because he can learn easily when interested (no perceptual strengths below 40), and his problems appear to stem from the mismatch between his learning style and the traditional school environment. A CAP would permit Keith to work anywhere in the classroom where he felt comfortable, with a peer or two, and would provide

TABLE 2-1 Graphic Overview of Interpreting LSI Individual Profiles

Elements	20–29	30–40	41–59	60–69	70–80
Sound while learning	Always needs quiet when learning.	Usually needs quiet when learning. A	It depends on what is being learned; sometimes needs quiet and sometimes does not.	Often works with some kind of sound. Is it radio? Records? TV? Conversation? G	Always/usually works with sound. What is listened to? Radio? Records? TV? Conversation? G
Light while learning	Always works in very low light G	Sometimes works in low light.	It depends on what is being done.	Likes light. It does not have to be extremely bright, but likes more light than less. A+	Always has lights high when learning. Prefers them bright. A+
Temperature while learning	Likes it very cool; is "warm" when others are cool.	Likes it more cool than warm, but can adjust if needs to.	It depends on what is being done, the season, how student feels.	Likes it warm—not very warm, but nowhere near cool.	Feels better in the warmth and loves sunshine. A
Design while learning	Always does best thinking work on a bed, lounge chair, floor, or carpet. G	Often does best thinking in an informal environment.	It depends on what is being done.	Student thinks best on a wooden chair and desk, as in a library, classroom, or kitchen. A	Always works in a formal setting; doesn't do best work unless in "hard" chair. A
Motivation for academic learning	Is not really tuned in to school academic learing in a conventional classroom.	Occasionally enjoys academic learning—but not too often and not conventionally.	It depends on what is supposed to be learned. Sometimes student "turns on," but if he or she is not interested, no one can make him or her do it.	Likes to learn most of the time, especially when interested.	Enjoys learning. Gets a sense of accomplishment from achieving.

Persistence during learning	Starts many things that are not finished; enjoys working on several tasks simultaneously. G	There are things student has started that are still not done—but it does not happen too often, only occasionally. G	Whether or not student completes what he starts depends on his interest in it.	Usually completes the things he begins. A	Always completes the things begun; in fact, it bothers him not to. A
Responsibility for academic learning	Likes to do things that most other people usually don't do; does not respond well to authority but does to collegiality.	Sometimes enjoys doing things that he knows he would be better off not doing; is fairly nonconforming.	Whether or not student does unconventional things depends on what the task is, how he feels, what the circumstances are, etc.	Usually does the things that he believes he ought to do.	Feels best when he does the things he knows he should do, and that is what he does most of the time; is conforming.
Structure versus options while learning	Student can't stand other people telling him what to do or how to do it.	Really likes to do things in own way.	What is being done, with whom and why are what determines whether it gets done the student's way, someone else's way, or cooperatively.	Doesn't mind at all being told what to do or how to do it—as long as student likes the person who's telling him!	Student feels best when told exactly what is required, all the guidelines (including the date it is due), and when he knows exactly how to proceed before starting.
Learning alone	Student works best alone and gets more done that way.	Student prefers doing most things alone.	It depends on what needs to be done—and with whom.	Student really prefers doing things with someone else. G	Should be the chairperson of the committee. G
Learning with an authority	There aren't many things that a teacher suggests that this student will actually do, unless made to. Try a collegial approach; give options.	Often does the opposite of what a teacher suggests. Try a collegial approach; give options.	It depends on whether or not student respects the teacher.	Student likes to do what teacher asks; feels better when he does than when he doesn't. Provide frequent feedback.	Usually does what teacher requests—unless he disagrees on the issue, at which point motivation determines action. Provide frequent feedback.

Continued

TABLE 2-1 Continued

Elements	20–29	30–40	41–59	60–69	70–80
Needing variety	Likes routines and patterns. Does not feel comfortable doing new/different things too often.	Prefers doing essentially the same thing in the same way, but can tolerate some change.	It depends on what is being done, why, how, when, and with whom.	Likes change. Gets bored with the same old routine.	Rarely does the same thing in the same way twice in a row. Needs variety.
Learning by listening (auditory)	Often sits at a lecture and doesn't really know much of what is being said. Finds it difficult to listen for long periods of time.	Sometimes sits at a lecture and "tunes out." Has to concentrate to "stay with" a speaker.	If interested, can learn by listening; if bored, doesn't know what is going on.	Finds it easy to learn by listening.	Remembers things heard, can concentrate and "pull back" people's voices and reconstruct a lot of what they have said.
Learning by reading or viewing (visual)	Often reads a page, comes to the end, and thinks, "I don't know what I've read!" Then rereads the page.	Sometimes needs to reread a page because although it has been read, virtually no meaning has been absorbed.	If interested, can retain a great deal of what has been read; if not, can go through the text without absorbing what the words actually mean.	Remembers a great deal of what has been read.	Can concentrate on things read long afterward; closes eyes, "sees" the open book, the section of the page and the paragraph, focuses on the print—and remembers what was read.
Learning by touching (tactual)	Never/rarely takes notes. Is also not too great at doing things with the hands.	Only takes notes for numerical data or things that can't be remembered easily.	Whether or not student takes notes during a lecture depends on how difficult/interesting the topic is.	Often takes notes either during a lecture or when reading something new or difficult that student wants to learn. Global tactuals often draw or doodle to remember; they enjoy hands-on learning.	If student forgets shopping list, he/she remembers most of the things on it. If hands were not used during a lecture (by note-taking, doodling, knitting or a similar activity) student would find it difficult to listen.

Learning by doing (kinesthetic)	Would rather drive than walk.	Does not often engage in energetic, action-oriented learning.	Student's degree of involvement in doing things is determined by what is being done—and by whom.	Likes being active and involved.	Becomes involved in many energetic activities, and people comment on high energy level.
Needing intake while learning	Never eats, drinks, smokes, chews, or gets involved with intake while studying.	Rarely eats, drinks, smokes, chews, or gets involved with intake while studying.	Whether or not student uses intake when learning depends on what is in the refrigerator. G	Often uses intake when studying. G	Always uses some kind of intake when studying. G
Evening-morning energy levels	Remembers best the things studied at night.	Remembers best the things studied in the evening.	Time of night or day is not important; what is important is what is being done and with whom.	Remembers best the things studied in the morning.	Remembers best the things studied early in the morning.
Late morning energy levels	Not really "alive" just before lunchtime.	Can function, but learning does not come easily late in the morning.	The time is not important; what is important is what is being done and with/for whom.	Can learn very nicely in the late morning.	Learns extremely well in the late morning.
Afternoon energy levels	The afternoon is a terrible time for studying. Avoid making important decisions of any kind at that time!	Can get through an afternoon—but not easily.	The time is not important; what is important is what is being done and with/for whom.	Learns nicely in the afternoon.	Afternoon is an excellent time for learning.
Mobility while learning	Can sit still for long periods of time when interested in what is being learned.	Sitting still is not much of a problem.	If interested, can sit still; if bored, can't.	Finds it difficult to sit still for long periods of time.	Finds it impossible to sit still for long periods of time.

Note: A = Analytic; G = Global.
+Some analytics prefer a softly-lit room with a bright, intense light focused directly on the page they are reading.

the variety (choices of Resource, Activity, and Reporting Alternatives, and even of Objectives) (see Chapter 8). However, Keith also could work well with a Programmed Learning Sequence (PLS), which provides more structure than he necessarily needs but would permit another alternative while learning (see Chapter 7). A Multisensory Instructional Package is unnecessary for someone so capable of learning. Keith could use tactual/kinesthetic materials if he were attracted to them, but could *create* those himself as part of the Activity Alternatives of CAP.

Determining Global or Analytic Processing Inclinations Here is Keith's *real* problem. You may recall that global people prefer to have sound while learning, soft illumination, an informal design, and intake; they also are not persistent learners; they rarely stay on task for any extended period when engaged in difficult academic studies. No wonder Keith is unmotivated. He has five of six possible global characteristics and, in addition, prefers working with peers, is tactual, and requires a great deal of movement rather than passivity. Traditional classrooms respond better to analytics than to globals, and Keith's additional needs for mobility and peer interaction are more than enough to reduce his motivation to learn. Awareness of this will encourage the teacher to begin new units with an anecdote (a short story related to the topic and demonstrating why this subject matter is relevant and interesting), humor, illustrations, and/or symbols—to gain the concentration and attention of global learners.

Graphic Overview of Interpreting LSI Individual Profiles

Global readers will find Table 2–1 an easy-to-follow representation of how to interpret LSI Individual Profiles. Extrapolation to which methods are appropriate for which learners will be addressed directly in each of the chapters concerned with instructional resources—Chapters 5, 6, 7, 8, and 9. You might care to test a few of your students with the LSI at this point and see whether you can identify their learning styles by following the guidelines in this chapter.

_3_

Redesigning the Educational Environment

Building an Instructional Taj Mahal without Cost

The secret of building your own instructional Taj Mahal at no cost (or very little) involves using in new patterns what you already have. The desks, chairs, tables, bookcases, file cabinets, and other furniture are moved to take maximum advantage of the space available and the individual learning styles of students.

Begin slowly, be flexible and receptive to new ideas and approaches, plan carefully, and continually evaluate how well the new design meets your objectives for each of the students in the class.

Room Redesign Based on Individual Learning Styles

Many teachers alter the seating assignments in their classrooms in response to discipline problems. Changing an individual to another seat without changing his or her total learning environment is a little like playing Russian roulette—one never knows what will happen.

For example, a student who likes to work with one or two peers might be moved away from friends because their voices disturb others. That youngster may become very unhappy and, as a result, may not be able to concentrate on his or her studies. How much better it would be to establish ground rules for when, how, and under what circumstances students may teach each other and discuss what they are learning, so that peer-oriented students may have time to learn together.

To begin redesigning your classroom to provide for varied learning styles, you first must identify each of your student's learning styles with the

Teacher Anne Reid redesigns her classroom to respond to students' environmental, socio-logical, and physiological learning style strengths. (Photograph courtesy of the Princess Margaret Public School, Ontario, Canada.)

Learning Style Inventory (LSI) (see Chapter 2). Then, using the following checklist, begin to identify the parts of the room that might lend themselves to each of the following:

- Places where several students may meet to discuss what they are learning
- Well-lit reading areas
- Warmer areas
- Desks or tables and chairs
- Sections that permit responsible students to work without direct supervision
- Sections that permit students to work alone, with a friend or two, in a small group, with an adult, or in any combination thereof, provided they show academic progress
- Essentially quiet and screened study areas for individuals or pairs
- Darker sections for media viewing, photography, or dramatizations
- Cooler areas

- Carpeted informal lounge sections with easy chairs, a couch, bean bags, and/or pillows
- Sections that permit close supervision of less responsible students
- An area where snacking may be available (preferably raw vegetables and fruits, nuts, and other nutritious foods)

Changing the Classroom Box into a Multifaceted Learning Environment

Some teachers can visualize an entire room redesign by closing their eyes. Others must move one seat or section at a time. Still others must try several alternatives before deciding on a relatively permanent arrangement.

Planning Step 1: Locating Dividers

The first planning step is to identify and locate as many things as possible that can be placed perpendicular to walls, unused chalkboards, and spaces between windows. Such items include file cabinets, desks, bookcases, tables, shelves, material displays, screens, charts that can stand unsupported, and cardboard cartons or boxes that may be attractively painted or decorated. Even your desk can be used effectively this way. Do not overlook bookcases that may be partially fixed to a wall or those, such as library stacks, that may seem too unstable to stand out into the room.

The custodians will enjoy the experience and novelty of assisting you in this venture. They are your "design engineer assistants" and will be proud of having helped you. To enlist their support, tell them why you are changing your room and that your room will be easier to move around in and to clean— because it will be. The custodians will also respond positively to the need to build supports and add backings to rickety bookcases. They may have good suggestions and, once involved, might be able to obtain that extra table, too.

Step 1 is the key to providing different types of areas and more space than you realized was possible.

Planning Step 2: Clearing the Floor Area

Look at your room. Walk around. There are likely to be boxes of science equipment, art supplies, reading materials, and other assorted items stacked on the floor (as well as crushed crayons, broken pencils, and such). Temporarily place this material outside the room or in a closet or corner. Later you will place these resources on top of the perpendicular units to provide additional screening and separation of the instructional areas such as the Learning

---

Examples of Dividers Used by Teachers

Cardboard boxes	Cardboard carpentry
Bookshelves	Homosote
Filing cabinets	Closets
Wooden crafts	Colored yarn
Bulletin boards	Fish nets
Coat racks	Fish tanks
Streamers	Yarn or beaded strings
Plastic six-pack holders	Voting booths
Shower sheets	Shower curtains
Wire	Burlap
Plastic wall coverings	Piping
Styrofoam	Wire
Bed sheets	Planters
Drop cloths	Bath or "math" tub
Art easel	Tree house
Cutting boards	Awnings
Real or artificial plants	Couch or chairs
Boards on wheels	Tables
Bunk bed	Book cases
Display cases	Posters suspended on string
	Laminated, stapled-together paper bags

Station, Interest Center, Magic Carpet (reading) Area, Media Corner, Little Theater, Science Center, Game Table, and so forth.

When moving the furniture and developing the physical environment, it is usually wise to do it with the students. They should be aware of what is going to be created and why, and that it will take a while to become acclimated to the change. Their involvement in the development of the design invariably creates a positive attitude of acceptance for the revision and, of greater importance, the youngsters' suggestions and reactions help to correctly place students with specific learning styles.

Planning Step 3: Involving the Students

Should you elect to involve all your students, you might begin your conversation by explaining that, as in their apartments or homes, the way the furniture is arranged in an area should make sense for the people who live there; that some of the boys and girls who "live" in their classroom (and it is living for four or five hours each school day!) may enjoy the arrangement just as it is, but that others might feel uncomfortable because people are different from each other and some need certain things that others do not.

For example (and here begin to personalize with them), everyone in the present arrangement is seated, in a sense, out in the open, even if there are separations between groups. With many students at close range it must be difficult for some of them to concentrate as they see and hear the door opening, chairs and people moving, and materials being used and replaced. Some need a quiet, cozy place to concentrate on their studies; for those people you would like to create small offices, dens, or alcove areas where they can be by themselves, or with a friend or two, to complete their work.

At this point you are certain to have their undivided attention; they will be curious, stimulated, intrigued, and individually motivated to redesign their classroom. You might ask how many students would like to serve as assistant interior decorators to aid you in rearranging the room to create spaces in which they will enjoy doing their schoolwork.

One of the first things you will suggest is the establishment of some areas where small groups of students may literally turn their backs on what is happening in the room and become absorbed in their work. This can be done by facing their chairs toward any available wall space. You may add, "If I told you that you were going to face a wall, you might think, 'Who wants to look at a bare space? *You* might, if I then said that each person facing a wall will be able to create his or her own bulletin board. You could display your work on it—the things you draw, write, paint, or sew; the models that you build; the photographs of your pets—wouldn't you like that?" Most elementary and middle school students enjoy having a bulletin board in their seating area and making it attractive with a personalized decorating scheme.

To promote bulletin board motivation, use sheets of colored construction or drawing paper to form a rectangular wall area as wide as the desk adjacent to it. Scallop a border to complement the paper and vary the colors so that bulletin boards that are next to each other reflect individual decorative preferences. Frequently, there is not enough wall space in the room for each student to have a bulletin board, and some may not want the responsibility for keeping one attractive and current. Establish rules for what may or may not be displayed but, within the confines of good taste, permit wide variation based on student choice.

You can increase bulletin board space by using the backs of file cabinets, bookcases, closet doors (that can be left closed) and rarely used chalkboard sections. Plywood, cardboard, wallboard, and other building materials can be added to one side of bookcases that are open in both directions or to the side of a file cabinet.

Describe how you plan to clear one section of the room at a time; explain the kind of den or office it will be (number of students it can hold, light or shady, warm or cool, open or partitioned); and tell the students that if individuals would like to try locating in that area (either alone or with a friend or two, or occasionally three), they should so indicate by any method you suggest (raised hands, quietly spoken words). Preface any decisions by clearly explaining that students who shout for recognition, call out "Oooooh!," or in any way behave disruptively will slow down the process and will have to wait longer for their turn. (Do not confuse excitement with disruptiveness; be prepared to be flexible.)

It is also necessary to explain that they really have to understand themselves, that some of them work best alone. These students should not volunteer to sit with their friends, for if they do not complete their work, their seats will have to be changed; it's better to diagnose themselves correctly in the beginning. Conversely, if youngsters promise they will work well with a friend (even if they previously played more than they worked and therefore made little academic progress), give them an opportunity to try to do so. Warn them, however, that if they do not show achievement, their seating arrangements will be altered. Students frequently become highly motivated when allowed to share a secluded section of the room with a friend or two, and they often gradually will conform to higher standards of behavior and effort than previously shown.

Mention to your students in this pre-redesign discussion that, just as they are used to the placement of the furniture in their homes, they are currently at home with the placement of the various items in their classroom. Explain that it takes time for people to adjust to new things, but that the more flexible they are, the faster they adjust. (This will encourage many of the pupils to experience positive reactions to the emerging redesign. In turn, they then will assist others to become acclimated to the new arrangement.)

Finally, assure the students that if they do not like the redesigned room, you will help them return to the present arrangement. Ask them, however, to agree to live with the new placement for at least one week before deciding whether to keep it or to revert to the way the room was arranged before the proposed change.

Once the students indicate a willingness to experiment with the classroom furniture and to remain with the change for at least a one-week trial period, you are ready to actually redesign. This is when you (1) distribute the students' Individual Printouts; (2) teach them how to "read" (interpret) their own; and (3) show them how to temper their decisions concerning where they will relocate on the basis of their preferences as revealed by the LSI.

Redesign: Preliminary Considerations

The major objective of changing the placement of furniture in the classroom is to provide different types of areas to permit students to function through patterns that appear to be natural for them and for their learning styles. Some students, however, may not know how they work best or where they prefer to sit; they can only try new placements and determine whether the arrangement is good or appropriate for them on the basis of how they react after the change. Therefore, rather than asking students where they would like to sit, begin by establishing the areas. Then, one by one, explain the advantages and disadvantages of each, describing the responsibilities of those who elect to sit in that den, alcove, office, corner, or section. Next, describe the learning styles that the area will complement and request volunteers. Students need only try the area for a week or so; if they either are dissatisfied or are unable to work there, changes can be made on a flexible basis with your approval.

Step-by-Step to Partial or Total Redesign

A simple way to begin is to clear a section of the room other than a window wall. Then identify all the movable objects in the room that can be used as perpendicular extensions to break up the linear effect and to provide small areas. If there are few movable items such as bookcases, file cabinets, tables, or chests available, low-cost dividers can easily be constructed with cardboard.

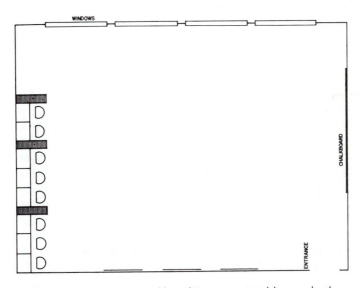

FIGURE 3–1 Bookcases, file cabinets, extra tables, and other movable items may separate desks that have been arranged to face the wall so that students have their backs to the center of the room and thus can turn away from the hub of activity to concentrate on their work. The wall space directly in front of the desk is used for a personal bulletin board. The divider provides privacy for occupants on both sides of it.

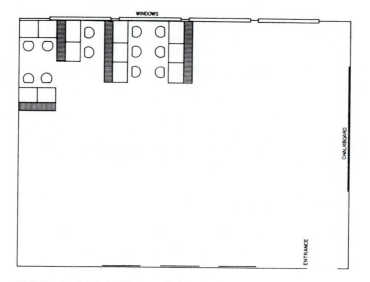

FIGURE 3–2 To create small den areas for two or more pairs of students (selected by student preferences), separate the desks from adjacent groups by placing the movable objects perpendicular to the walls. Face each pair or small group of desks toward the divider so that the paired students have their backs to other pairs. This arrangement is conducive to the development of close peer relationships between the members of each paired group, but not necessarily among the members of the two groups.

The movable objects may be used in a variety of ways in different sections of the room. For example, bookcases of varying lengths and widths may separate pairs of desks to provide privacy and to permit quiet areas (see Figure 3–1). Small groups of desks (three to five) may be isolated in a charming little den or alcove that encourages small-group teamwork (see Figure 3–2). The movable objects may also set apart resource instructional areas such as Learning Stations or Media Corners so that students may conduct their work out of the mainstream of activity (see Figure 3–3). In addition, dividers may be used to separate the motivated, persistent students from those who do not follow through on their prescriptions and who require constant supervision (see Figure 3–4).

When you have cleared the first section of the room, you may begin by saying, "Here is an area that is far from the windows. The lighting will probably be soft and the temperature may be a little cooler in the summer and in the winter" (if that is true). If you think you'd like to work where the lighting is less bright and it's a little less warm than in other areas of the room, you may sit here with one or two friends—if you are certain that you'll work qui-

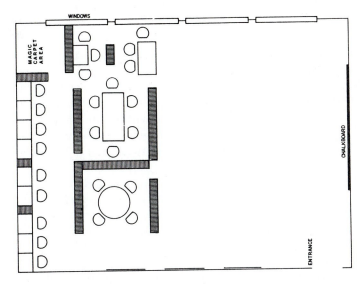

FIGURE 3-3 Cleverly used dividers can separate the active area of the classroom (which frequently centers around Interest Centers and Learning Stations) from the Magic Carpet Corners and other study-reading areas. Such an arrangement provides students with the options of either working in the center with others or studying alone or with a friend at one's desk or den area.

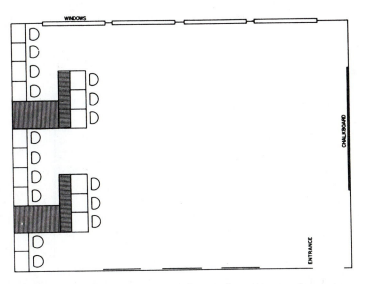

FIGURE 3-4 Dividers also may be used to separate those students who are capable of working independently from those who need constant supervision. The former are provided with den or alcove areas on the periphery while the latter are seated toward the center of the room where the teacher is closer and may work with them more directly.

etly with those friends and learn, too. This area, because it is next to the wall, will have a bulletin board space. Remember, if you accept the responsibility of the bulletin board, you'll have to keep it looking attractive, neat, and interesting. Is there anyone who would like to sit here with a friend or two?''

If one youngster volunteers, ask him with whom he would like to sit. If he names one or two friends, ask them if they would like to sit together with the person who nominated them. If so, ask them each to bring their seats and desks to the area (see Figure 3–2).

Show the students the wall section that will hold their bulletin boards and ask them again if they are willing to assume the responsibility for keeping their bulletin boards attractive, up to date, and interesting. If they respond affirmatively, give them an opportunity to try with your approval. They may immediately obtain the construction paper and masking tape (it does not pull off paint when removed) and begin mounting their boards. Move the first object that will be used as a divider and place it perpendicular to the wall at the end of the grouped desks to form the first private section in the room (see Figure 3–5).

If the divider that you have used to mark off the first den area is long enough to place two side-by-side desks on the other side, you can begin the second den area by describing that arrangement to the class. This would be an area that would tend to be a little lighter than the first and a little warmer,

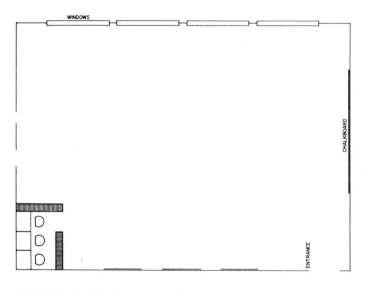

FIGURE 3–5 The first step in classroom redesign is to divide available space into small dens or alcoves to provide privacy and relative quiet for those students who need these elements to function effectively.

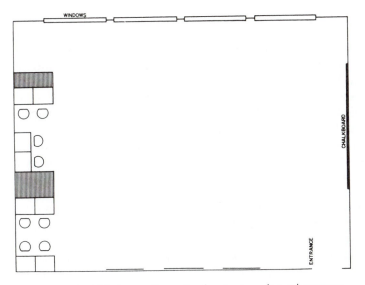

FIGURE 3–6 This is an alternative beginning plan where two pairs of students share the same den areas.

and would, again, offer a relatively secluded space to its occupants. This section also would contain space for individual bulletin boards. Again, request volunteers and, depending on your and their preferences, place their desks either directly against the wall as in Figure 3–5 or in back-to-back pairs (see Figure 3–6). Combinations of the two designs provide increased interior interest, but some people prefer either one or the other pattern. Exact placement is not of prime importance; what is necessary is that small groups of youngsters each have a place of their own in which to escape the activity and accompanying classroom distraction so that they may work effectively alone or with a friend or two.

Some dividers, such as a single file cabinet, aid in isolating an individual youngster who prefers to work alone. Explain that this is an area that permits a person to work quietly and independently, and encourage the students to know themselves and to select a placement that will enhance their learning style.

Establishing Instructional Areas

The Magic Carpet
After the second or third den area has been situated, identify two long dividers that can set off a Magic Carpet corner (a quiet, casual reading-meditating area) of the room where absolutely no discussion is permitted. This should be

close to the windows, a place where students may go to relax, to read in silence, or to rest if they feel the need.

The term *magic carpet* is derived from the notion that the students within the area can "magically" withdraw temporarily from the noise and activities of the class, thus transforming this corner into the quietest area of the room. It is usually carpeted or pillowed. It holds no chairs, desks, or hardware—only many interesting books to be read. There are other places in the room (shelves, bookcases, display cases) that also house interesting books on every subject, but those are easily accessible to all students. The Magic Carpet books are accessible only to the students who are in the area for as long as they choose to remain. The teacher may be flexible, of course, and permit students to take books out of the area to be read elsewhere (perhaps by a pair), but the object of maintaining a current display there is to prevent other students, who may want to browse through or take a book away from the Magic Carpet area, from intruding on the privacy of the youngsters who are actually in that corner at any given time. The authors therefore suggest that a special group of non-movable books (that may be duplicated in other sections of the room) be kept in this special area.

To establish the Magic Carpet area, use two bookcases (or cardboard open-shelf dividers) at right angles to each other in the corner of the room at the other end of the wall on which you began to establish the den areas. This should be a corner near or at a windowed section (to provide light for the readers). Place the two dividers so that each is perpendicular to one of the

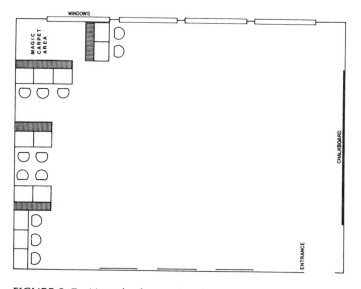

FIGURE 3–7   Note the formation of a Magic Carpet area, a casual, carpeted area where students may read or meditate in silence.

corner walls (as in Figure 3–7), but not touching each other. Leave room for a small entranceway that should be the only means of access to the Magic Carpet area. When established, spread a piece of masking tape on the floor stretching from the near entrance end of one bookcase to the near entrance end of the second. This suggests the line beyond which shoes are not permitted (to enhance its special nature and to prevent the carpeting from becoming soiled and undesirable to sit or lie on).

Merchants who sell carpeting frequently will donate samples and remnants. These squares and rectangles then may be placed end to end inside the area to provide a clean, soft, inviting, and quiet place.

It is wise to establish rules to limit the number of students who may "ride" the magic carpet at one time. The number will vary in accordance with the size of the area, but should allow for at least two or three more than the actual number of students whose LSI printouts indicate the need for an informal design. The percentage will vary with grade level and gender, but will rarely exceed six—unless students in that class are predominantly global. If that is the case, develop *two* Magic Carpet areas—one near and the other away from bright light. Explain that these areas provide privacy and that the students who are using them should not be disturbed or intruded on. Tell the youngsters that if they want to use the Magic Carpet area, there is a good way to determine how many students are currently using it without looking directly into the area. First ask them how they might know this. If they cannot identify a method, remind them that only five or six students may use the area at one time. If there is no response, ask them about the rule concerning shoes. When they understand that they can count the number of shoes on the outside of the masking tape entrance line to compute the number of youngsters on the inside, give them a few examples to help them decide whether an individual may enter the area.

You might pose the questions, "If I wanted to go inside the Magic Carpet area and counted one, two, three, four, five, six shoes, might I go in?" When they respond, ask, "Why?" Explain, if they do not understand, that six shoes indicate that three children already are using the area and that, because as many as six children may use it at one time, three more may still enter.

After one or two additional examples, ask them, "If I counted one, two, three, four, five shoes, what might that mean?" They will offer various solutions—for example, someone is inside with one shoe on or someone lost a shoe. Respond that it could mean that someone did not place shoes together, side by side, in the masking tape area and that another person accidentally kicked one shoe away from the taped line. Ask them what they could do if that ever happened and add that it would be kind to look for the missing shoe, locate it, and replace it next to the other half of the pair.

If you make this preparation for working in the Magic Carpet area gamelike, the students are likely to remember what they have discussed with you. The area (and the classroom) will then function with fewer crises than might otherwise be anticipated.

An appropriate redesigned classroom permits students to learn alone . . .

Expanding the Den Area Concept

Once the Magic Carpet area has been established, you will be able to determine how many desks may be placed against each of the two dividers that were used to mark off its boundaries. Show the students that you plan to place desks snugly up against each of the dividers to begin the formation of additional dens.

If the back of the divider is solid, place this solid part so that it faces the front (or the inside) of the room. When a desk is pushed up against that surface, the back of the divider (if high enough) becomes a bulletin board for each youngster who faces it. If the divider has only one open side (such as a one-sided bookcase), use the bookshelf part on the inside of the Magic Carpet area and the closed shelf part on the outside to form a bulletin board surface. If both sides of the divider are open, place the books in the divider so that the bindings are easily accessible to the students inside the Magic Carpet area.

Explain the attributes of each of the two newly created den areas to the students—for example, "This section is near the windows. It is likely that the light will be brighter than elsewhere in the room. It is also near the heater. If you volunteer for this space, be certain that you like warmth. You'll also be

. . . in pairs . . . (Photographs courtesy of the Northwest Elementary School, Amityville, New York.)

near the Magic Carpet area, so you'll have to be able to avoid socializing with students as they enter and leave that section. Can you work quietly with only the friend you elect, and can you ignore the traffic going in and out of the area? If so, this may be a good location for you. You'll be responsible for keeping the top of the divider attractive and covered with new books, the bulletin board interesting and current, and so forth. If you would like to sit here with a friend or two, raise you hand.''

After each of the two sections behind the two dividers that border the Magic Carpet area have been occupied by their new tenants, survey the entire wall area with which you have been working. Do you have room for an additional pair, a single youngster who wants to work alone, another divider to provide even more privacy? Add whatever appeals to you aesthetically and makes sense educationally. Your first wall should be near completion and may look something like the model in Figure 3-8 or 3-9. If not, do not be con-

. . . in groups of three . . . (Photograph courtesy of Lafayette Academy, Cleveland, Ohio.)

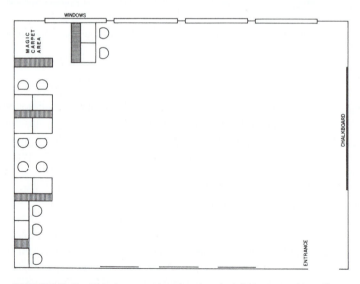

FIGURE 3–8 This is one plan for the development of small den or alcove areas where two to four students may share their efforts toward completing their individual or group prescriptions. On the right, near the window corner, is the Magic Carpet area.

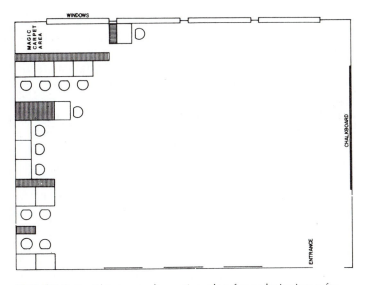

FIGURE 3-9 This is an alternative plan for redesigning a far wall in a traditional classroom. This arrangement also features the Magic Carpet near the windows (to provide light) and on the far, rear wall (to provide quiet).

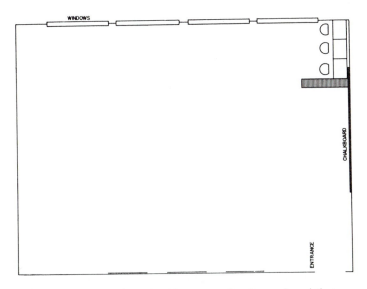

FIGURE 3-10 Students in this corner den have placed their desks so that they face against the interior wall, which provides bulletin board space for its occupants.

cerned. As long as the students are positive about their seating arrangements and you are willing to try the design, further adjustments may be made as the need for them becomes evident.

Once the far wall has been designed to your initial satisfaction, the front wall directly opposite the one you have just completed should be redesigned. Begin with the section of the front wall that is directly opposite the magic carpet area. Establish a den by using two dividers to enclose the corner. Determine if you wish to place two pairs of youngsters, two groups of three students, or some other number. The width and depth of the den will depend on the number of desks and chairs you place there.

Once each of the dividers has been located perpendicular to one of the two right-angled corner walls, the students' desks may be placed so that they either face the interior wall (as in Figure 3–10) or face the back side of either one or both of the dividers (as in Figure 3–11). The latter placement is directly opposite from the way we used the dividers in the Magic Carpet area, where students inside needed to be able to reach whatever occupied the shelves or drawers of the dividers used to form the area; here it will be the students who do not share this area who will need to be able to get to the materials housed in the dividers without intruding on the youngsters inside.

If a bookcase or cabinet is used as a divider on the outside of the corner den, two or three additional students may be placed at right angles to it on the outside of the corner area. These new desks could face the front wall and

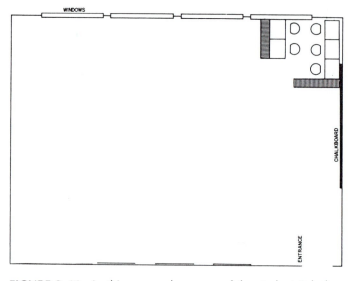

FIGURE 3–11 In this corner den some of the students' desks face against the back of one of the dividers and others face the interior wall.

begin to form the next area. If the divider on the front wall of the corner area has neither side shelf nor side drawer space (such as a file cabinet where the drawers face the center of the room), desks may be placed up against the divider itself. A table may be used as a material resource center and may be flanked on both sides by dividers. This arrangement would permit an additional area where students who do not share a den area may meet to work together during a small-group instructional activity such as a Circle of Knowledge, Simulation, or Case Study (see Figure 3–12).

Any of the techniques for grouping two to five students may be used to continue the pattern of establishing small den or alcove areas. The section nearest the door lends itself well to being a material resource section. Dividers may be placed at right angles to the walls near the entrance to provide an open passageway where books and manipulative materials (games, reading and math equipment, and so forth) may be selected easily without intruding on others (see Figure 3–13).

Behind the bookcases on the side wall near the door, two or three students' desks may be placed to form another den. When a wall includes a clothing closet, it may be feasible to establish only one den area behind the en-

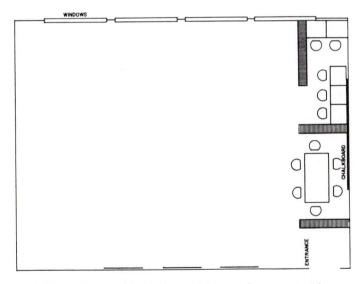

FIGURE 3–12 A table has been designated as a material resource center (for example, a place where mathematics or reading materials may be available) and placed between two dividers to facilitate easy access to the materials and privacy when using them. This area also can be used as a small-group center where students who do not share a den may meet to work together.

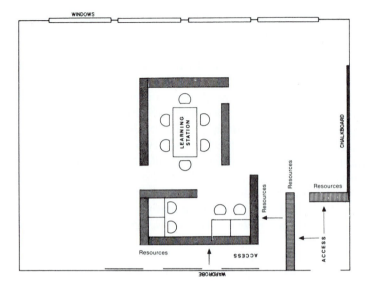

FIGURE 3–13   The entrance to a room serves effectively as a resource center, providing easy access to learning materials without intrusion on working students. Built-in wardrobes or bookcase walls may be made more functional by placing dividers three to four feet in front of them with access to the materials they house from the side away from the middle of the room. Students' desks may then be placed against the dividers on the inside of the room to create new den areas.

tranceway bookcase. The remaining section must be free for access to the closet. In older, traditional buildings, closets frequently have some stationary doors. These may be used for individual youngsters who prefer to work alone. Their desks may be placed against the nonmovable doors that may then be used as bulletin boards (see Figure 3–14).

Where large, old-fashioned heating units are exposed to view, it is possible to cover the surface with a protective, fireproof material and to use the units themselves as areas against which one or two desks may be placed, using the portion of the unit above the desk heights as a bulletin board.

When sections of the room appear to be unusable for desk placement (such as long sections of wardrobe walls, built-in bookcase walls, or sink and other wet areas), it is attractive to leave an aisle between these sections and a series of horizontally placed dividers. This arrangement creates an attractive resource aisle on the periphery of the room and permits small dens to be established toward the inner part. Access to the materials placed in the dividers

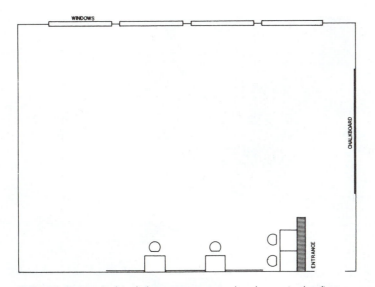

FIGURE 3-14 Behind the entranceway bookcase is the first side wall den area. If this is a clothing closet wall and the closets include some nonmovable doors, individual youngsters may occupy the space directly in front of the stationary doors and may use the doors as bulletin boards. An alternative would be to establish a resource aisle directly in front of the wardrobe area by placing dividers approximately four feet away from the closets and permitting access to materials from the closet side (Figure 3-13).

does not interfere with students engrossed in their studies outside the area (see Figure 3-13).

The various patterns of separating the rear and front walls of the classroom into small den areas to accommodate between two and five students should be extended all around the outer area of the room with the exception of closets or sinks. If sufficient space is available, it may be possible to establish one or more material resource centers or small-group meeting areas within the total design. The outer sections of the room should be maintained as quiet areas for independent, paired, or small-group work. The teacher should move from youngster to youngster and from small group to small group to check each student's progress, respond to questions, guide youngsters in need of assistance, and evaluate the quality of what has been completed.

Initially, redesign efforts should be restricted to the outer perimeter of the room. The center should be reserved for areas where students may work

. . . or four . . . (Photograph courtesy of Sacred Heart Seminary, Hempstead, New York.)

together in more gregarious or mobile activities. The den areas that foster privacy and small-group work will aid in keeping the noise level down and student concentration high. Youngsters may work alone, in pairs, or in small teams in their dens or in the small-group instructional areas that have been established on the outer edge of the room. For more interactive activities, they may work in the center of the room. With this method, youngsters involved in their independent prescriptions can literally turn their backs on the activity in the center and remain with their tasks. Should it be appropriate to join those involved in the center of the room, at a holiday Interest Center for example, they need merely move to the larger area. Basic rules and procedures for moving from one area to another should be established to promote positive learning activities for all.

The center area might include a Learning Station or two, an Interest Center, or a Game Table. If the teacher and class prefer, one of the corner den areas may be used as a Little Theater or a Media Corner. The room arrangement may be as creative as the teacher, but much of the practicality of this kind of redesign will not become apparent until experienced by the group for a week

. . . or directly with the teacher based on individual learning style strengths. (Photograph courtesy of the Franklin Elementary School, Hewlett, New York.)

or more. The room should be revised, especially in the early stages, to meet needs as they emerge.

As you reconstruct your classroom, it is important to teach the students to use it effectively. This necessitates the ability to cooperate with peers; to choose from among appropriate alternatives; to complete assignments or tasks; to locate, use, share, repair, and return resources; and to function independently in an environment that requires increased decision making and student responsibility.

Figure 3–15 depicts a completely redesigned model classroom that provides for different learning styles.

Adding Creative Dividers and Designer Touches
Now that the basic room redesign is complete, you may wish to supplement furniture dividers, such as bookcases and file cabinets, with decorative floor-to-ceiling, see-through partitions to further the illusion of separation and to

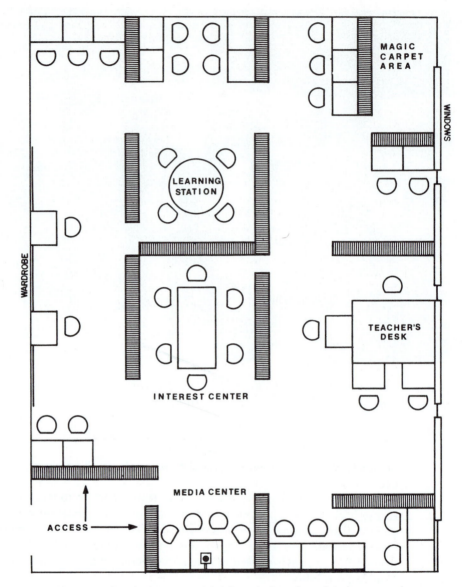

FIGURE 3–15 This depicts a completely redesigned model classroom that provides for different learning styles.

Dens, alcoves, and junior offices are available in each classroom, permitting children to learn identical information through alternative strategies. Thus, at the same time, a few youngsters engage in a Team Learning (if they are peer-*oriented), auditory learners* hear *their teacher's explanation, and a third group is using media to complete the same assignment. (Photographs courtesy of Sacred Heart Seminary, Hempstead, New York.)*

add interest and color. These inexpensive cardboard-box dividers may also be used to display student work or to post rules and objectives for instructional areas.

Colored Yarn   Obtain colored yarn from local merchants as a donation or from parents as a contribution. Stretch floor-to-ceiling lengths between two areas in straight, triangular, or other patterns (see Figure 3–16). This wall of yarn is most attractive and can be used to display student work or to post directions. Thumbtacks, staples, marking tape, or loops around metal ceiling supports can be used as anchors at the top and bottom. Have custodians aid in designing and tying the yarn down. They will know what will work with minimum damage.

Plastic Beverage Tops, Paper Rings   Have the students save the plastic (non-metal) rings from six-pack beverage containers. These may be attached to each other with colored string or wire to form see-through wall dividers similar to the colored yarn partitions. When these are weighted at the bottom, they need not be anchored to the floor, but you will find that they hold their shape better when they are. Colored chains consisting of construction paper rings, such as

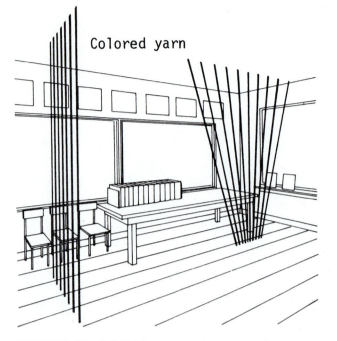

Colored yarn

FIGURE 3–16 Subdividing instructional space into dens, alcoves, offices, and labs with colored yarn permits visibility of everything that happens in the room while simultaneously providing a feeling of privacy for students. The colors brighten the environment and deinstitutionalize the classroom's ambience.

those usually made for holiday seasons, may also be used, although they are not as permanent as the plastic rings. These should be anchored and repaired as soon as they break (see Figure 3–17).

Aluminum Foil, Construction Paper, and Paint Leftover holiday wrappings, colored construction paper, unused paint, clear food wrappings, or aluminum foil can be used effectively to decorate walls, bulletin boards, cardboard dividers, and the backs and sides of file cabinets. Remnant wallpaper, shelf liner, and sections of carpeting, burlap or cut-up old jeans can be used to create montages and attractive backs for dividers, walls, shelves, and mounted objectives. In addition to creating an attractive learning environment, you will promote interest and enthusiasm if you let the students and, occasionally, their parents help in the interior decorating process.

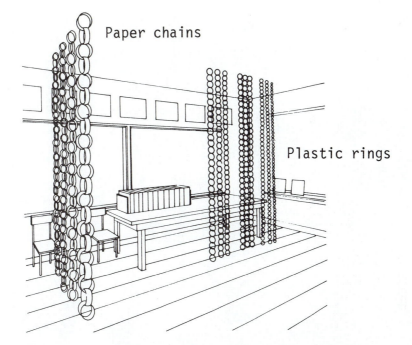

Paper chains

Plastic rings

FIGURE 3-17 Subdividing instructional space with student-made colored-paper chains or the strung-together ring tops from plastic soda pop cans creates small, private areas in which individuals, pairs, or small groups of three or four youngsters can work together quietly to complete their assignments in relative privacy. The fabrics add gaiety and charm to an otherwise unornamented classroom, and the smaller stations and centers produce less frenzy and turmoil among active, energetic children.

Other Instructional Areas

Math Tubs Locate an old, discarded bathtub. Have the students scour and decorate it. Place it in the Math Learning Station and seek donated pillows or make some with the class. They should be large, colorful, and comfortable. Fill the tub with the pillows and establish a schedule for "swimming in math."

The students should be told that once in the tub they will be totally immersed in mathematics. They may think only of the mathematics they are reading, learning, or doing once they are inside this hideaway. The "magical waters" of the Math Tub will help them to learn, and you can chart their progress across an "ocean of objectives" that can be attached to the insides and outsides of this innovative instructional area.

Classrooms should provide: (a) screened areas for students who are easily distracted, (b) open stations for children who prefer to be in the center of activity, and (c) informal sections for youngsters who prefer an informal design. (Photograph courtesy Center for the Study of Learning and Teaching Styles, St. John's University, New York.)

Reading Houses   Salvage old lumber, bolts, nails, sandpaper, packing cases, and other materials that will allow you to design a reading tree house right in your classroom. Involve the custodians, local fire marshal, skillful or willing parents, and anyone else who can assist. Design it first, and carefully measure where it will go. Construct steady and safe ladders, platforms, and spaces for three or four children. Elementary school youngsters will love to read or study quietly away from the rest of the class.

Office Buildings   Large sheets of cardboard or the sides of discarded delivery boxes can be used to construct separate compartments or "offices" for individual students. Those students who need to be alone to study or concentrate can crawl or climb into these spaces and screen out the rest of the class or even their neighbors in adjacent offices. The cardboard offices may be built in layers (two stories or levels) or into a maze to separate students. The office building can be painted with windows or with solid-colored walls.

Understanding and Using Varied Instructional Areas

Once the room has been totally redesigned, rules should be established for the use of varied instructional areas. Those students who demonstrate that they can learn effectively together by using any three or four small-group techniques without supervision should begin to use instructional areas such as Learning Stations, Interest Centers, Game Tables, Magic Carpets, Media Corners, and Little Theaters. In this way, youngsters may continue to work independently or with partners at defined learning spaces while the teacher focuses attention on the ones who cannot achieve without adult direction. Each instructional area serves specific purposes and thus attracts students with different learning styles, interests, and goals at varying times.

Separating the learning environment into multi-instructional areas encourages students to consider where they will find it most appropriate to do their work; where they will find the resources through which they may achieve their objectives; and whether they prefer working alone, with a friend or two, in a small group of peers, or directly with the teacher.

The instructional areas that may be established have characteristics in common. These include:

Media Corners, Reading Centers, and Magic Carpet areas are but a few of the many instructional stations that may be created to respond to varied learning styles and academic interests. (Photographs courtesy of Madison Prep, New York City.)

1. Clearly stated objectives (see Chapter 8), usually with some choice permitted, such as, "Complete three (3) of the following five (5) objectives"
2. Small-group techniques with which the students are familiar, such as Circle of Knowledge, Team Learning, Brainstorming, Case Study, Group Analysis, Role Playing, or Simulations
3. Introductory, reinforcement, and evaluative activities related to the important objectives
4. Alternative activities on different levels of difficulty: Task Cards, activity cards, Learning Circles, and games
5. Self-correcting activities: Task Cards, activity cards, Learning Circles, and games
6. Multiple options so that the student is required to make some choices as he progresses
7. Multisensory resources
8. Opportunities for creative and imaginative projects
9. Attractive signs and decorations

This sixth-grade classroom boasts a Learning Tree House that even the most reluctant children desire to work in. (Photograph courtesy of the P.K. Yonge Laboratory School, Gainesville, Florida.)

10. A self-contained space to provide privacy and a feeling of personal involvement

Each area should be designed so that a given number of students may use it at one time. Depending on the size of the area, the number may vary from four to six. See Figure 3–15 for the placement and design of various instructional areas.

Decide whether you will use a table, desk, carpeting, or selected furniture inside the area. If shelves are available, materials may be placed on them for use. If shelves are not available, a table or some other surface may be necessary for the display and use of related task cards, books, activity sheets, packages, and other similar materials. Use attractive and lively colors to decorate the dividers, the inner walls, and the materials. Clear adhesive-backed paper is a useful covering, for it lasts a long time and prevents deterioration of much-used resources.

Identify the major theme or topic to which a first center will be devoted

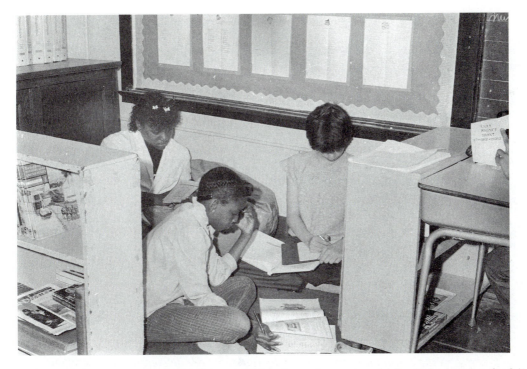

This classroom provides a small, carpeted informal area in which students who find it difficult to sit in wooden, steel, or plastic chairs may sit informally as long as they complete their work and do it well. *Amazingly, this privilege is rarely abused and often results in surprisingly improved test scores and behavior. (Photograph courtesy of Lafayette Academy, Cleveland, Ohio.)*

for the present. Develop clearly stated behavioral objectives that indicate to the students what they will need to learn about the current topic. Print some of the objectives on colored signs or banners and mount them on the inner walls. Have others duplicated for distribution to the youngsters working in this area. List the resources that are available for students for mastering the objectives you designed. Organize the resources for easy use through either shape or color codes, either to indicate various levels of difficulty or as suggestions for student selection based on ability.

Tape record the difficult parts of the books when it is necessary that students use specific pages in them. If you do not have the time to read all the paragraphs onto a tape, get a parent or older student to do so. As you teach group lessons, tape record whatever you say, the students' interruptions, your responses, their questions, and peer suggestions. Use these tapes as an auditory

Bookcases and the cardboard boxes in which appliances are delivered make excellent dividers to permit subdivision of the classroom and, ultimately, individual, small-group, and large-group spaces for varied instructional activities. (Photograph courtesy of Sacred Heart Academy, Hempstead, New York.)

resource for students who were absent, who need reinforcement, or who wish to relisten to the content.

Develop additional resources as you move more deeply into instructional area teaching, and have students develop others. There should be a number of multisensory materials available to provide appropriate learning aids that match the perceptual learning style strengths of each youngster.

Learning Stations

A learning station is an instructional area that houses multilevel resources related to a specific curriculum such as social studies, art, language arts, science, or mathematics. The station should have introductory resources for youngsters who are just beginning to learn about a special topic; reinforcement materials for youngsters who are experiencing some difficulty in mastering elements of the topic; advanced resources for very bright or very interested students;

and small-group techniques, such as Circle of Knowledge, Team Learning, Brainstorming, or Case Study, for youngsters who learn better when studying with one or two (or more) classmates.

Code the materials with color, shapes, or numbers to indicate to students those that are appropriate for their level of reading and comprehension ability. The station should be well organized, attractive, and nicely maintained so that youngsters can find what they need easily and with a minimum of frustration. Students should be cautioned to return resources to their correct place and category of difficulty when they no longer are using them.

A Learning Station may consist of a table and shelves with accumulated materials where students select items or activities and take them to their own desks (or another area); it may also include a table, a desk, files for materials, and a few chairs, cushions, or a carpeted corner or section for students who prefer an informal area in which to work.

The materials at several levels of the topic being focused on at the station should be interesting, varied, and self-corrective (to facilitate student independence), and might include books, magazines, Task Cards, cassettes, dittos, instructional packages, contracts, programmed sequences, workbooks, Learning Circles, tapes, filmstrips, films, photographs, cartridges, loops, Electroboards, study prints, assignments, slides, and games related to the selected topic. Directions for the use of resources should be attached to all items.

Access to the station should be open. Students should be able to visit, take items to another section of the larger room or area, or remain at the station to work or to discuss their activities with others. Regulations governing acceptable behavior in the area should be established so that students clearly understand exactly the ways in which they may function while at the station, including the sound level at which they may speak and work with others.

As students begin to use the instructional area, they will need to be taught how to:

- Locate, use, share, repair, and replace the available resources.
- Recognize materials that are appropriate to their individual reading and comprehension levels.
- Make selections from among approved alternatives.
- Evaluate their own and their peers' progress.
- Maintain accurate records of those objectives and activities that they have completed successfully.

These skills are essential for functioning in any program that requires students to become increasingly independent. It is at this point that students are most likely to learn the study skills that are necessary for their continued academic growth—they are actually using materials and must begin to depend on their own ability to assess their tasks correctly, locate appropriate resources and information, record what they need to remember, select ways of demon-

Writers' Tables provide a sense of journalistic identity for students who prefer to produce in a small group. A Shared Reading Area may include a rocking chair for kinesthetic youngsters who require movement while *concentrating. Bulletin boards, signs dropped from the ceiling, and attractively designed wall games and question-and-answer quizzes all stimulate thinking and surround the students with information directly related to what they are learning. (Photographs courtesy of the Northwest Elementary School, Amityville, New York.)*

strating accomplished skills and tasks, and evaluate their progress. Opportunities for creative experiences or performance demonstrations may be built into evaluation procedures. Use the first Learning Station as a beginning step toward establishing varied instructional areas. Motivated youngsters will move forward quickly, eager to become increasingly independent and to use varied materials with which they can function easily. The nonmotivated will progress more slowly, but they will begin to thrive as they become accustomed to imposed regulations and the selection of resources with which they can succeed.

Experiment, vary the resources and methods of providing access to them, and permit options so that students like working in (or out of) the area and feel comfortable without being under your direct supervision. Give the youngsters time to identify their own learning styles and to experiment with related materials. If it takes too long (more than two weeks), suggest methods and materials for them and supervise their beginning involvement. If one technique does not work, try another after a given amount of time; two weeks seems to be a fairly good guideline for experimenting with a selected strategy. Keep introducing and testing new resources until each youngster is achieving to your satisfaction. If you suspect that a learner needs longer adjustments periods,

proceed more slowly and extend some target dates. There is no foolproof formula to motivate every student, but your professional expertise will help you recognize what is working and what has failed.

Interest Centers

A second instructional area where students may congregate to learn is called an Interest Center. This section of the learning environment should house interdisciplinary resources concerned with a selected theme (topic, unit, study) such as energy, pollution, transportation, racial conflict, or dinosaurs. Here, items related to many curriculum areas may be found, but they would be focused on one central sphere of interest.

In addition to the media resource materials related to the topic (objects, books, magazines, pictures, films, filmstrips, slides, cassettes, tapes, loops, cartridges, study prints), students might find: (1) assignment sheets (machine copies or workbook-type pages); (2) small-group assignments (Circle of Knowledge, Team Learning, Brainstorming, Case Studies, Simulations, Role

Playing, or Group Analyses); and (3) games (crossword puzzles, fill-in-the-missing-letter assignments, Task Cards, and others) on which individuals or small groups might work. A program, contract, or instructional package on the topic could also be available.

Interest Centers serve many purposes: (1) they are available as another option for students—an alternative way of obtaining information and concepts about a given theme; (2) they provide students with a means of gathering facts and concepts independently; and (3) they build small-group activities into the learning process to provide social interaction and group achievement. Interest Centers, therefore, permit a teacher to begin to take advantage of individual learning styles by providing students with a choice of either working independently or with one or more other students. Although self-pacing is an important instructional goal, many youngsters prefer working with others; for them, isolated studying and learning may not be desirable. Indeed, even those students who seem to think best while working on independent units often need to interact with others in order to test ideas and to grow.

Game Tables

Educational games are used extensively in schools today. Their major contributions to the learning process include: (1) introduction of a topic or concept; (2) application of information or concepts; (3) increased motivation and stimulation; (4) provision of an alternative teaching method or device; (5) opportunities for either individual or small-group focus on information through alternative media-learning resources; (6) opportunities for independent concentration; (7) activities for small-group and interage shared experiences; (8) review or reinforcement of previously discussed or studied information; (9) remediation purposes; and (10) opportunities for relaxation as a break in the school day.

Games are available for all age levels from (preschool through adulthood), in all curriculum areas, and as interdisciplinary approaches to study. A repertoire of these instructional devices provides alternative resources, methods, and activities for students and increases their options for learning. At times you and the students may be able to invent new games or redesign existing ones to meet instructional goals or take advantage of individual learning styles.

Game tables should be available to students in different sections of the classroom for use at appropriate times. When students have completed assignments, need or decide to use the games as media learning resources or activities, or wish to relax for a while, they should be able to go quietly to the table and select whatever is appropriate to their task or abilities. Games should be catalogued according to their level of difficulty or their relationship to the curriculum. The student then will know which games may be chosen so that options can be exercised as decisions are made.

Little Theaters

Another area guaranteed to provide an exciting, dynamic learning atmosphere is called the Little Theater—an imaginative title for a creative and stimulating center. Here, in a section of the room that may be darkened or partitioned when necessary, students are free to become involved in a series of projects that require application of the information they have learned through the use of media resource alternatives. Students are permitted to make slides, filmstrips, films, negatives, photographs, scenery props, costumes, backdrops for productions, rolled-paper "movies," multimedia presentations, transparencies, books and scrapbooks, and many other educational project materials related to drama, creativity, and production.

These projects are, of course, appropriately related to the curriculum, contracts, programs, or instructional packages; they provide application, review, reinforcement, and synthesis of ideas for the students. Students may write dialogue, scenes, plays, and roles, or simply improvise, mime, or critically analyze what they see.

Media Corners or Centers

Most schools have limited equipment and must distribute their resources equitably among all classes in a given building. It is necessary, however, to provide each large group (twenty-five to thirty-five) of youngsters with enough hardware so that students may use the media equipment to obtain information, study concepts, and develop skills. At the same time, it is inefficient and unnecessary to carry heavy equipment from place to place.

Some school districts have established multimedia resource centers to house their computers, films, and filmstrips; carousel, opaque, and overhead projectors; and screens, cartridge viewers, duplicators, and other media equipment. In other schools this equipment is placed in various sections of the building, and students are permitted to leave their classrooms to use the media when appropriate.

Both methods of arranging media equipment have built-in drawbacks:

1. If students are to be free to use the equipment when it appears necessary or appropriate to them, they must also be free to leave their room (area) and go to the equipment in another section of the building. Since many students may need to leave their room at the same time, a constant flow of incoming and outgoing students will exist. Unless the administration feels comfortable about an informal attendance procedure, it may be extremely difficult to keep tabs on students' whereabouts. Of greater importance, the "right time" may slip by or be wasted traveling to the media or waiting in lines.

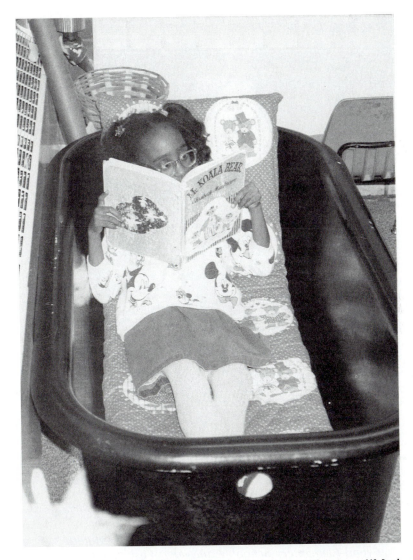

A painted old-fashioned bathtub can be converted into a "Math Tub" in which only mathematics can be studied, or into a secluded reading area for one single youngster who enjoys concentrating on difficult information privately. (Photo courtesy of Roland Andrews and the Brightwood Elementary School, Greensboro, North Carolina.)

Nothing may be better for an informal, learning-alone preferent than being housed in a tepee in a secluded part of the classroom. (Photograph courtesy of Angela Klavas and Sherwood Elementary School, Edmonds, Washington.)

2. The student leaves his teacher and classmates and goes to another area. His teacher can neither supervise nor assist him; his peers (unless they join him) do not share his learning experience.

In preference (or in addition) to either the totally centralized Multimedia Instructional Resource Center or the partially centralized Learning Center, teachers may establish a media corner in each room. This area can house one overhead projector, one or two single-viewer filmstrip machines, one or two computers, one super 8-mm cartridge viewer (optional), one sound projector (desirable but optional), three or four cassette tape recorders, and many blank tapes. Equipment may be exchanged among clusters of three or four classes joined together as "learning pods" or Media Instructional Areas (MIAs) when needed. The larger, more affluent media centers could be used as a library resource to provide special materials.

Students should be free to take software (filmstrips, films, tapes, slides) from either the Interest Center or the Learning Station to the Media Corner and use it there as a learning resource. The software should be replaced carefully when the student no longer needs it. Cadres of students should form team task forces to assume the responsibility for demonstrating how to use, care for, repair, replace, and organize the equipment and resources that complement the Media Center.

When one student begins to view materials, others are drawn into the procedure by interest, curiosity, or social awareness. Students should be permitted to join each other in viewing, discussing, studying, or analyzing the materials, provided each of the participants is receptive to the cooperative effort. In some cases, individuals require privacy and, perhaps, quiet while working with either instructional resources or media. Other youngsters are most productive while studying with a partner or with two or three classmates in a cooperating group with consistent verbal and/or physical interaction.

Alternative Room Designs

Some teachers who are just beginning are hesitant about creating a variety of instructional areas because they fear they will lose control. They often also are used to whole-class instruction that is essentially lecture-dominated, and they cannot understand how to teach without everyone learning the same material simultaneously.

If that is your concern, design an innovative area or two in the room and maintain the current environment. Permit those who need informal seating and mobility to experiment provided they: (1) obey your rules; (2) complete their assignment; (3) do not interfere with anyone else's learning; (4) pay attention whenever you *are* addressing the class; and (5) earn better test scores than they did previously. Should one or two individuals take advantage of your consideration for their learning style, take the privilege of sitting informally or using mobility judiciously away from them. Do *not* punish the students who are abiding by your regulations.

For small-group or large-group lessons, use an overhead projector to assist in teaching. Place the screen near the ceiling so that everyone can see whatever you write or illustrate. Using a projector with class lights off will increase attention *and* good behavior during a lecture or discussion.

Redesign as much as you can and continue to feel comfortable. Do it either in stages or all at once as prescribed earlier in this chapter. As long as *you* are comfortable with the steps, the interior decoration will go a long way toward helping children learn more quickly and retain longer than they have previously. Have the courage to experiment before you decide whether you can or cannot be successful with this type of environment. Be certain to ask the students how they feel in their new headquarters and watch their test scores as you permit a bit of option in the environment.

Gaining Parental Support

Now that you have redesigned your room to base your instructional program on individual learning styles, it is important to gain the support of your students' parents. Parents are interested in and often concerned about the concepts and strategies to which their children are being exposed, especially if they are new. Once the class has become adjusted to the redesigned room, invite parents in to visit and to discuss the rationale of the room or area redesign. Explain the advantages of capitalizing on each youngster's learning style and describe how the students participated in the developing arrangement. Once parents understand why the instructional environment has been altered, they usually are willing to support the effort until sufficient time has elapsed to yield both objective and subjective results, such as improvements in student responsiveness, teacher reactions, academic progress, and increased provision for individual differences and learning styles. Actually, the students themselves will presell the change with the enthusiasm they express at home about their new interior decoration.

If you are inclined to use media to win parental support for a learning styles–responsive environment, see the book, filmstrip, and accompanying audiotape specifically designed to give parents an understanding of learning style. Chapter 11 describes these materials, which are available from the Center for the Study of Learning and Teaching Styles, St. John's University, Jamaica, New York 11439.

As you read through subsequent chapters and experiment with having students make the tactual resources, Contract Activity Packages, Programmed Learning Sequences, and Multisensory Instructional Packages they can use for learning, remember that any or all of these may be placed into classroom instructional areas when appropriate. Also, having students *create* their own learning materials is one of the best ways we know of helping them master information and knowledge.

A Final Word on Redesigning Your Classroom

As you begin to (1) establish varied instructional areas; (2) collect cushions, bean bags, carpet squares, rugs, summer lawn furniture, a couch, a rocking or an easy chair; and (3) develop the courage to permit children to experiment with them, establish firm rules for working in the redesigned classroom.

- Only those students whose *Learning Style Inventory* printout confirms that an *informal* design is advantageous may use the informal areas, and no student's learning style may interfere with or distract anyone with a different style.
- Any student who abuses the privilege of working in his or her own style will forfeit that privilege.
- The grades of each student permitted to sit informally must be at least as good or better than he or she had prior to this experiment. Otherwise, it is not working, and there is no reason to continue.
- All assignments must be completed, but they may be done anywhere in the classroom as long as (1) these rules are maintained, (2) everyone can be seen by the teacher, and (3) children behave politely.

4

Global and Analytic Approaches to Teaching

Forward Can Be Backward for Many Students

Have you ever analyzed your own teaching style? Not through an observation form, your supervisor's evaluation, or even a peer conference but, rather, by focusing on how you *begin* a lesson? Most of us initially consider the content objectives, what was taught during the previous period, which items need reinforcement, and what might constitute a motivating opening. Sometimes the introduction is humorous, or interestingly related to a recent event, or it may seize students' attention because it reflects something that happened at the school or in their lives.

Even when we have planned well, however, some students do not respond to what we believe should be motivating, and others soon drift off into their own thoughts as the lesson sinks into a relatively dull, fact-by-fact development of a concept. Often the problem is that some of us are teaching in a way that is the reverse of the way in which many students learn.

Do you introduce new concepts with one fact after another until, gradually, your students begin to understand the idea? If you do, you are engaged in *analytic* teaching. This requires analytic processing, which means that a youngster's mind must be able to absorb many small pieces of information and then synthesize them into an overall understanding. That's the way many people learn, but it is not the way *most* people learn. In fact, the younger the children, the more likely they are to be *global* processors. At the secondary level, between 50 and 60 percent of all students tend to be global. An even higher percentage of those students who achieve slowly or of those having

This chapter is based on "Presenting Forwards Backwards: Teaching K–8" by R. Dunn and K. Dunn, 19 (2), pp. 71–73 (October 1988). Norwalk, CT: Early Years, Inc.

difficulty in school—as many as 85 percent—cannot learn successfully in an analytic mode.

As you are probably aware, analytic students are concerned with details, rules, procedures, and directions; they like specific, step-by-step instructions. Global students, on the other hand, are concerned with end results; they need overviews and the "big picture"; they like general guidelines, variety, alternatives, and different approaches.

Does the inability to remember facts mean that globals are less intelligent than analytics? Not at all. Several studies have verified that globals and analytics are equally able academically, but that each group achieves best when taught with instructional approaches that match its individual members' learning styles. Unfortunately, of the thousands of teachers we have tested, fully 65 percent are analytic. Thus, a serious mismatch between analytic teaching styles and global learning preferences occurs far too often, resulting in disaffected students with low scores, poor self-discipline, and damaged self-image.

But what about you? How do you begin a lesson? If you don't know, just listen to yourself as you introduce each new topic. Do you begin with one detail followed by another? If you do, you are teaching analytically. Or, instead, do you tell a story that gives your students the major focus of the lesson and then fill in the gaps with the pertinent details? That is a global approach. Neither approach is better than the other, but matching the instructional strategy to the appropriate student is crucial.

Many teachers, either intuitively or by design, use both global and analytic approaches when introducing lessons. If you do not, you would do well to examine the results in your classroom. Here is how you go about it: First, test your students to determine which are global and which are analytic. The *Learning Style Inventory* offers an easy way to tell which is which; see Chapter 2. Next, analyze your teaching style to see which approach you tend to use most often. Then examine the grades of the students who match your style and the grades of those who do not. You will find that the children who learn the same way you teach will achieve higher test scores than those who do not.

Guidelines for Teaching Global Students

If you are analytic and wish to teach your global students in ways that make it easier for them to understand and remember, try the following:

1. *Introducing material:* Begin the lesson with either a story, an anecdote, a humorous incident, or a joke that is directly related to the content you are teaching. If possible, relate the introduction to the students' experiences. If that is not feasible, relate the introduction to something that is realistic to them.
2. *Discovery through group learning:* Avoid telling the students too many facts directly; instead, get them to unravel the information by them-

selves. To do this, suggest that they divide into small groups—rather than work as individuals—unless specific students prefer to work toward solutions by themselves. Usually, global students find it less threatening and more fun to solve problems with others. For four easy-to-use small-group techniques that enable students to learn together in an organized, controlled way, see Chapter 5.

3. *Written and tactual involvement:* In addition to encouraging global students to think through, by themselves or in a small group, those details related to what they must learn (rather than telling them the answers), have them graph or map their new information and, if they can, illustrate it. Globals tend to draw meaning from pictures, photographs, symbols, and other visual representations; they respond less well to words and numbers. Thus, have them demonstrate their mastery of specific objectives by developing dioramas, graphs, charts, games, and so on. Since it helps for globals to dramatize what they are learning, you might also suggest creating pantomimes or plays and making puppets to demonstrate what they have learned. In addition, encourage students to develop their own teaching devices to share with classmates, so that others can learn through alternative strategies.

Guidelines for Teaching Analytic Students

If you are global and wish to reach your analytic students, try the following:

1. *Explanations and visual reinforcement:* Explain the procedures and approaches to be used in reaching specific objectives. Write key words on the chalkboard as you speak. (Analytics respond to words and numbers.) Answer questions about details directly, and use printed visuals on either an overhead projector, slides, or the chalkboard.

2. *Directions:* List all assignments, directions, test dates, and specific objectives on ditto sheets, and provide one for each student. If paper is in short supply, list the directions on a chart and have the students copy them.

3. *Learning through direct teaching or related resources:* Proceed step by step through the details that need to be assimilated to reach understandings or to acquire skills. Put key words on the chalkboard; distribute duplicated materials and fact sheets; underline important sections; check homework and notebooks daily. Teach students how to use the library independently and how to find and use reinforcing material directly related to the specific objectives of the sequence.

4. *Testing and feedback:* Test frequently; provide instant feedback on details in the sequence; respond to questions as soon as possible; itemize your expectations and requirements; if you give an assignment, check it; when you say you will test, do so.

Clues to Recognizing Analytic and Global Students:
What They Are Likely to Say to You

Analytics	Global
Does spelling count?	Why are we doing this?
Should I use a pen or a pencil?	Not now! I'll do it later!
Should I skip lines?	I need a break!
Will this be on the test?	Don't touch the piles on my desk.
When is this due?	Why does it really matter?
Can't I have some more time?	Let's start this project—and that one too!
What comes first? second?	Why can't I skip around in the book?
Why can't we do one thing at a time?	I'll come back to this later!
Please check my work before I submit it.	
What are you really looking for?	

Quicki Quiz: Global or Analytic?

In each of the following lesson-starters, Teacher 1 and Teacher 2 are introducing the same lesson. One teacher is using an analytic approach; the other, a global approach. Can you tell who's using what? Even more important: Do you recognize your own teaching style? The answers are at the bottom of the quiz, but no fair peeking until you've read all of the introductions.

IDIOMS (Grades 4–5)

(Adapted from a Programmed Learning Sequence developed by Eileen O'Keefe, American Martyrs School, New York.)

Teacher 1	Teacher 2
We have a young Russian immigrant staying at our house. He is trying to learn to speak English well enough to go to our school in September. He's doing very well, but is having trouble with some of our expressions. The	An idiom is a group of words which, when used together, has a very different meaning from each individual word in the group.
	Sometimes idioms can describe a funny picture in our minds. For in-

FIGURE 4–1 These examples of how the same content can be introduced analytically (step by step) or globally (through a short story, joke, or illustration) demonstrate the difference between the two approaches. When difficult instructional material is *introduced* through approaches that match an individual's processing style, mastery becomes easier and more enjoyable than when mismatched.

FIGURE 4–1 *Continued*

other night we were late for the movies. My husband had the car running, and I ran in and yelled, "Hurry up!" to Boris who was upstairs on the second floor. He came to the staircase and asked, "What do you mean 'Hurry up'? I am already up. I can go no higher!"

That night I made a list of expressions we use in English where certain words, when put together, mean something very different from the individual words.

I wrote: "blow your own horn," "nose to the grindstone," "shoulder to the wheel," and tried to figure out how to explain them to Boris. Can you name five others and explain them?

stance, the expression "on pins and needles" is an idiom. Can you imagine really sitting on sharp pins and needles? What do we really mean when we say, "John was on pins and needles as he waited to open his presents"? The expression "on pins and needles" does not mean that someone is actually sitting, standing, or lying on pins and needles. What it really means is that someone is nervous, anxious or uneasy.

Use the following idioms in sentences and describe what they mean: "blew her top," "raining cats and dogs," "threw in the towel," "time flies," "bone to pick." How do idioms help to make our language more colorful and interesting?

THE SCIENCE EXPERIMENT (Grades 5–6)

Teacher 1

Today we're going to boil equal amounts of water and seal the two quantities in Ehrlenmeyer flasks with corks. Then we'll cool one down to 40 degrees Fahrenheit and keep the other at 110 degrees. Now we'll place both into the refrigerator and see which one freezes first. Note that we've left room for expansion so that the flasks won't break.

From time to time you'll hear people say that hot water freezes first. Well, that happens for a number of reasons in an uncontrolled laboratory situation. First of all, we drive the air out of water when we heat it. Air acts as an insulator and helps to prevent cold water from freezing first.

Teacher 2

Mystery of Hot Water Freezing First: Last night we had a flood in our basement. One of the pipes burst. The plumber said it was our hot water pipe.

We know that water expands when it freezes, but shouldn't cold water freeze first? After all, the temperature of cold water is closer to freezing than hot water.

Design an experiment to demonstrate which freezes first—hot or cold water.

Under what circumstances will the hot water freeze first? Consider the exact laboratory conditions that must exist for the cold water to freeze first. *Clues to the Mystery:* Find books in

Continued

FIGURE 4-1 *Continued*

Secondly, there is a rapid loss of heat from the boiling or hot water once the source of heat is removed. This heat gradient, when plotted on a chart, is a sharp downward curve compared to the cold water.

Third, you must have equal volumes of water to be frozen, and last, you must prevent evaporation before the experiment begins.

the library which describe: air as an insulator; heat gradient; volume of cold and hot water in equal containers; evaporation of hot liquids.

Additional Activity: Visit or call a plant that makes ice cubes commercially. Ask them why their ice cubes are clear, whereas yours in the refrigerator are cloudy.

RELATED VOCABULARY WORDS (Grades 2–3)

Teacher 1

Every time I see signs that read, "The Circus is Coming to Town," I think of so many wonderful things! I think of clowns, wild animals in cages, dancing ballerinas on the backs of horses, tightrope walkers and small cars filled with many, many people. I also think of a midget, fat ladies and strong wrestlers. Why do you think circus signs remind me of all those things? (*Volunteers respond.*) That's right! Somehow those things seem to go together.

Let's see if other words go together, too. I'm going to write a word on the board and you call out all the words you can think of that seem to belong to my word. Let's try "baby." (*Volunteers respond.*)

Let's try it another way. I am going to divide you into groups of five. Then I will write many words on the board. Each group should decide which words go together and put them into columns of *related* words. If a word belongs in more than one column, it's all right. Let's see how many groups of related words each team can develop!

Teacher 2

Words have meanings of their very own, but they also mean something in relation to other words. Some words seem to go together. It isn't that they *have* to go together, but they seem to belong together even when you see them apart. For example, if I write the words "baby," "country," "cook," "mother," "clown," and "crib," on the board, which words do you think belong together? (*Volunteers respond.*) That's right, "baby," "mother" and "crib" go together. No, Bill, "baby," "country," "cook" and "clown" do not go together. What? "The baby in a foreign country sat in his crib and watched the clown on television while his mother cooked dinner"? Well, I guess that makes sense, but they don't all really go together. Why not? Because they don't.

Let's try another example. Every time I think of circus, I think of clowns, wild animals in cages, tightrope walkers, midgets, fat ladies, and strong wrestlers. Those words seem to go together. What, Bill? Strong wrestlers go with the Olympics and television? Yes, I guess they do.

FIGURE 4-1 *Continued*

Answers: *"Idioms,"* Teacher 1 (global), Teacher 2 (analytic); *"The Science Experiment,"* Teacher 1 (analytic), Teacher 2 (global); *"Related Vocabulary,"* Teacher 1 (global), Teacher 2 (analytic). [Note: These would be turned upside down.]

Try teaching globally at least part of the time. More than half your students will be motivated and interested in what happens next. Do not be surprised when analytics indicate displeasure with your global lessons. After all, for them global teaching is just as backwards as analytic teaching is for globals. Note the youngster who becomes impatient with your storytelling and asks, "Is this important? Is it going to be on a test?" Chances are, you have an extreme analytic on your hands, and you probably are going to have to teach that lesson both ways.

Well, why not? It certainly is not fair to teach to one style and not to the other. In addition, you will be successful with more students because you will be teaching forwards for *both* groups. And you are certain to find that when you teach globally to globals and analytically to analytics, the lesson moves more quickly than when one group is, in effect, being mis-taught.

Teaching to Both Groups Simultaneously

If you are willing to experiment once or twice to see the effects of teaching to each group correctly, try giving global students a Team Learning with creative assignments, inference questions, and factual material in that order at the beginning of a period while, simultaneously, you teach exactly the same information to analytics in reverse order. Succinctly instruct the analytics and then direct them to do the same Team Learning. Then bring the globals together and *elicit* the answers from them. Next, ask students to describe their reactions to this dual, matched instruction. Pay particular attention to the test results on the unit involved. Chances are good that most students will perform better after being *introduced* to the information through the correct processing style. They also should enjoy learning better than in nonmatched learning.

Effective Use of Computers: Assignments Based on Individual Learning Style

Once upon a time, a couple of decades ago, scientists were predicting the widespread use of computers to provide individualized instruction in schools across the nation. Indeed, within the past few years, zealous technology proponents have advocated a computer for each student in every classroom. That has not happened—partly because of the costs involved and partly—perhaps more so—because not everyone "takes" to computers. Why not? The mechanisms certainly provide explicit, to-the-point, step-by-step information in ways that any sequential mind should be able to absorb. However, the lack of computer literacy may be attributable to *exactly* that problem. Everyone does *not* process information sequentially—the style in which most software has been presented. Indeed, whether or not specific software responds to how an individual learns depends essentially on the differences in learning style that exist among students at every age and grade level (K–12).

The Problem with Most Computer Software: Global Versus Analytic Introductions to the Content

With few exceptions, most computer programs are designed for analytic (left) processors who think in a step-by-step sequential pattern—which is *the reverse of the way global processors think*. Globals learn in an overall holistic manner; instead of examining a plethora of facts, absorbing them, and extrapolating into either an understanding or conceptual framework, globals try to understand the idea or concept *first;* only then do they attend to the facts or details. Globals also learn from anecdotes, humor, and illustrations.

Analytics have few problems focusing on details. Conversely, globals need to understand *why* it is important that they memorize specific information *before* they subsequently are able to do so. Once they understand or are convinced that mastery is important, globals can do it, but the belief system must be in operation prior to the exertion of effort. Analytics, on the other hand, will memorize if they *need* to do so but are less concerned about why it is being required. Merely the fact that they must do so is sufficient to have many of them try to engage in the learning processes.

What does all this have to do with computers? It determines whether or not a particular student is likely to fare well with one software program rather than another. If teachers were aware of which students need global and which students need analytic packages, it would be intelligent to prescribe accordingly—or to demand that producers supply both kinds, which then could be prescribed on the basis of matches and avoided when perceived as mismatches. Is the match between students and globally or analytically formatted packages likely to affect achievement significantly? Let's examine some of the research.

Research Concerned with Global/Analytic Matching versus Mismatching

Nearly 1,100 developmental mathematics students in an urban technical college were required to master two analytic and two global lessons of equal difficulty—one matched to, and the other dissonant from, their learning style. Significantly higher mean test scores ($p < .0001$) were revealed in the matched treatments (Dunn, Bruno, Sklar, & Beaudry, 1990). Similar results were obtained in high school mathematics (Brennan, 1982), biology (Douglas, 1979), and nutrition (Tanenbaum, 1982); in junior high school social studies (Trautman, 1979); and in elementary school mathematics (Jarsonbeck, 1984).

Another Problem with Computer Use: Research on Perceptual Strengths

In well-designed, well-controlled research conducted during the past decade, individual perceptual strengths were identified, and each student experienced multiple treatments in both matched and mismatched conditions. (Carbo, 1980; Ingham, 1989; Jarsonbeck, 1984; Kroon, 1985; Martini, 1986; Urbschat, 1977; Weinberg, 1983; Wheeler, 1980, 1983). Please note that the *quality* of those studies earned national recognition three times. The findings across all those investigations evidenced that when students were *introduced* to new and difficult material through their primary perceptual strength (auditory, visual, or tactual), they achieved statistically higher test scores than when they were introduced through their secondary or tertiary channel. When they were *introduced* through their primary strength and then *reinforced* through their secondary or tertiary modality, they achieved even higher scores than when only initially taught through a primary strength—an additional $p < .05$! (Kroon, 1985; Wheeler, 1980).

Computer-literate advocates, however, assume that the computer is responsive to *everyone,* and Martini's data tend to support that belief. However, because of the findings concerned with the effects of sequencing instruction to respond to primary and supplementary modality strengths, would computer packages be *more* responsive—and thus more effective—if: (1) students' primary perceptual strengths were identified with the *Learning Style Inventory,* the instrument administered to diagnose the learning styles of the populations in most of the aforementioned studies, and then (2) the computer were used to introduce new and difficult material in the correct sequence to each youngster? If that were to be tested, auditory students would hear a lecture first and then use the computer package for reinforcement; visual students might begin by either reading a visual printed selection or working directly on the computer program, and then could be reinforced through either a tape or lecture—or by hands-on manipulatives if their second modality were the sense of touch. Strongly tactual students would begin with manipulatives such as task cards, Electroboards, Flip Chutes, or Pic-A-Holes (Carbo, Dunn, & Dunn, 1986; Dunn & Dunn, 1978), and then use the computer. *Would* that sequencing incorporated into the use of computer instruction make a significant difference in student achievement?

To Increase Computer Effectiveness

This section is intended to increase the effectiveness of computer use in schools. It highlights two main problems:

1. Most computer programs are written analytically. The research, however, is clear: Global students do not achieve well when instructed analytically. Thus, computer packages need to be rewritten to present the identical material both globally and analytically so that students with both learning styles find the instruction responsive.

2. Computer programs currently are visual and slightly tactual; when accompanied by verbal instructions, they are auditory as well. The research is clear on this point, too. Multisensory instruction is not sufficient for many students. What works is *introducing* difficult material through each student's strongest perceptual modality and then *reinforcing* through supplementary modalities. Thus, if we were to identify students' strengths and use computer packages in a responsive sequence, we would be likely to increase their effectiveness.

5

Designing Small-Group Instructional Techniques

Importance of Small-Group Techniques

Many students respond best to a learning situation that involves from two to five of their peers. Some of these youngsters may not be authority- or teacher-oriented for a variety of reasons. They may feel intimidated, anxious, or overly directed by adults or those in charge. Some may need the interaction of friends to stimulate them to learn; others are motivated by a team effort. Many relax when a group, rather than each of them individually, is responsible for a task, contract, or project. There also are students who gain persistence through group goals or who can deal more effectively with a short, specific portion of an assignment rather than with an entire task. Such youngsters often feel more responsibility to their peers than to either themselves or adults. For these reasons, or simple gregariousness, many youngsters' learning styles are best served if they often are permitted to work in groups.

First Concrete Step toward Individualization of Learning

Group work is a first step toward independence within the instructional setting, and working with others in school is early training toward that eventuality for most people in adult life.

Diagnose or observe the sociological elements of learning style for each of your students. Once you are convinced that a given youngster will learn best from and with peers, assign that student to a variety of small-group experiences.

Students who have been parent- or teacher-directed for most of their lives should first learn to make simple decisions and to assume the responsibility for completing simple tasks free of constant adult supervision. Use of selected techniques such as Circle of Knowledge, Team Learning, Brainstorming, Case Study, and Simulation provides a structure wherein learning occurs through cooperative small-group effort without the teacher serving as a constant guide or fountain of knowledge.

Small-group interactions also permit youngsters to solve problems in cooperation with other students so that they need not fear failure or embarrassment. Even if errors are made, sharing the responsibility with a group of peers sharply reduces the tension or trauma. Further, the small-group techniques help students to understand how other people reach decisions and work toward solutions. Finally, interaction with peers creates sounding boards on which to reflect ideas, build solutions, and suggest conclusions to the group and to the teacher.

Greater Learning through Sociological Preferences

Over the years, a number of researchers examined teams and groups as they strove toward achievement. Homans (1950) postulated that groups are separate entities and that results cannot be viewed simply as the sum total of its individual members. Argyris (1957), Lorge, Fox, Davitz, and Brenner (1958), Hankins (1973), and others in and out of education have demonstrated repeatedly that small teams often obtain better results than the individuals might have accomplished if working alone or with an adult. Poirier (1970) studied students as partners and reported increased learning, as did Bass (1965), who pointed to group recognition, respect, and affection, as well as fun, as motivating factors toward higher achievement.

According to Slavin (1983), the discrepant outcomes in cooperative learning research, where no clear small-group strategy produced better results than another, were due to intervening variables inherent in the research designs, settings, subject areas, and evaluation measures. Five years later, Slavin (1988) concluded that a fifth variable was concerned with whether individual or group accountability was required. However, the major intervening variable, which neither Slavin, the Johnsons (1987), nor their predecessors addressed, is the one of individual differences—which they neither identify nor analyze in their work.

Another deficiency of their studies is that they do not expose students to a variety of sociological experiences so that they then can determine whether, indeed, all children perform best in cooperative small groups. Their designs do not permit analysis of how well individuals achieve when permitted a variety of treatments and whether those same children *consistently* perform best in one condition or another. Another concern is that they do not address *initial* teaching to determine how effectively children can teach themselves, versus learning with peers, versus learning with adults, versus whether they learn best in the same way consistently when learning new and difficult information *for the first time through their learning style strengths.*

A Team Learning may be done completely alone by students who prefer concentrating on difficult material without either interruptions or interpretations from classmates. (Photograph courtesy of Northwest Elementary School, Amityville, New York.)

The Impact of Peer Interaction on Student Achievement

Research showed (Cholakis, 1986; DeBello, 1985; Dunn, Giannitti, Murray, Geisert, Rossi, & Quinn, 1990; Giannitti, 1988; Miles, 1987; Perrin, 1984) that when students' sociological preferences were identified and the youngsters then were exposed to multiple treatments both congruent and incongruent with their identified learning styles, each achieved significantly higher test scores in matched conditions and significantly lower test scores when mismatched. In the three studies where attitudes were included as a dependent variable, those also were significantly higher as an outcome of matched conditions. In the one investigation where an interaction effect did not occur (Cholakis, 1986),

Other students prefer working in a pair—but often not *as part of a group. (Photograph courtesy of Center for the Study of Learning and Teaching Styles, St. John's University, New York.)*

the population had been made up of students who had attended a parochial school for their entire education. The researcher suggested that the history of strong authority orientation of those youngsters may have skewed the results. However, those students learned equally well in both conditions.

Studies revealed that students learned more and liked learning better when they were taught through their identified learning styles. Those data were supported in secondary schools throughout the United States when site visitations, observations, interviews, and evaluation collection documented that students achieved more, behaved better, and enjoyed learning best when they were permitted to learn through their sociological preferences (Dunn & Griggs, 1988).

Since 1984 (Dunn, 1984), we have been experimenting with teaching students to teach themselves by capitalizing on their learning style strengths—of which sociological preference is only one variable. However, the first results are promising (Dunn, Deckinger, Withers, & Katzenstein, 1990; Knapp, 1991) and several additional studies currently are in progress.

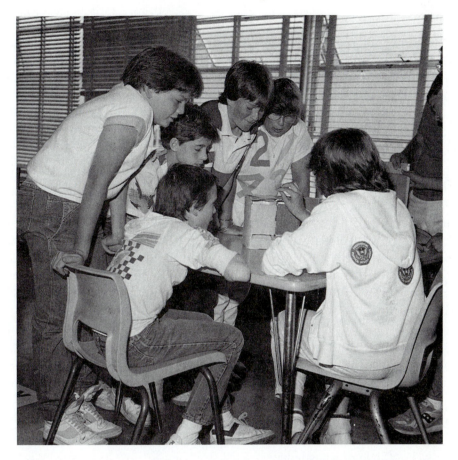

Some students prefer *working in a small group—particularly if they enjoy learning with the same type of instructional resources. (Photograph courtesy of Center for the Study of Learning and Teaching Styles, St. John's University, New York.)*

Learning Style Characteristics Responsive to Small-Group Techniques

Many learning style characteristics are responsive to small-group techniques which can be designed to accommodate multiple variations among students. They are especially appropriate for students who are peer-oriented, motivated, persistent, and responsible. They provide structure as well as auditory and visual experiences. Students who act as the recorder will gain additionally by writing (tactual) experiences.

Small-group techniques will accommodate the elements of light, temperature, design, time, intake, and mobility. Furthermore, motivation, persistence, and responsibility may be enhanced by the group process; members can exert positive peer pressure on those who are not strong in these areas.

Obviously, those who prefer to work alone or with adults and those who are creative and do not require structure are less likely to benefit from small-group techniques.

However, it is easy for teachers to post assignments with specific objectives and/or tasks and say to the class, "You may do this alone, in a pair, in a team of three, or with me. If you wish to work alone, sit wherever you will be comfortable in the room. If you wish to work in a pair, take a moment to decide where you want to work, but stay away from your classmates who need to be by themselves." After a momentary pause, students who wish to work in small groups may move together quietly and, after that, those who want to work directly with the instructor may move to a previously designated area in the room.

We strongly recommend however, that Team Learning and Circle of Knowledge—specific small-group strategies to teach and to reinforce difficult information—should become an integral part of the class repertoire *prior* to permitting sociological choices. These strategies enable students to work efficiently either alone or in a small group for long periods of time. Thus, they allow teachers sufficient time to teach the smaller group without interruption. These two easy-to-master instructional strategies are another good method for beginning to teach students through their individual learning styles.

Descriptions and Samples of Small-Group Techniques

Circle of Knowledge

The Circle of Knowledge technique is highly motivating and is an ideal technique for reinforcing skills in any subject area. It provides a framework for review in which everyone learns more or solidifies what he or she has already mastered.

This instructional approach permits students to:

- Review previously learned information in an interesting way.
- Focus thinking on one major concept at a time.
- Contribute to a group effort as part of a team.
- Serve as catalysts for additional responses.
- Develop ingenuity in helping team members to contribute.
- Be exposed to and learn information without becoming bored.

Procedures
Several small circles of four to five chairs (no desks) are positioned evenly about the room. One student in each group should volunteer or be drafted, ap-

These third-graders are busily engaged in a Circle of Knowledge on the floor while classmates are working equally diligently at their desks. (Photograph courtesy of Roosevelt Elementary School, Hutchinson, Kansas.)

pointed, or elected as the recorder; members also may take turns. Only the recorder writes, although everyone participates and concentrates on thinking of many possible answers. Each team member also checks for accuracy and incorrect answers or repetition.

A single question or problem is posed. Whether it is written and reproduced or printed on a chalkboard, it must have many possible answers. Examples include naming all fifty states, identifying the possible causes of war, citing the products of a country, or listing synonyms for the word *leader.*

Each Circle of Knowledge team will respond to the same question simultaneously (but quietly). A member in each group is designated as the first to begin, and the answers then are provided by one member at a time, clockwise or counterclockwise. No member may skip a turn, and no one may provide an answer until the person directly before him has delivered his; therefore, the answers stop while a member is thinking or groping for a possible response. No teammate may give an answer to another, but anyone in the group may draw, act out or pantomime hints to help the person remember an item, an answer, or a possible response. Only the recorder may write, and he or she jots down (in a phrase or two only) the suggestions (answers, responses, thoughts) that each participant *whispers* as the Circle of Knowledge continues.

At the end of a predetermined amount of time, the teacher calls a halt to the knowledge sharing, and all recorders must stop writing their group answers. The number of responses produced by each group is noted, but credit is not given for quantity.

The teacher divides the chalkboard or overhead transparency into columns and numbers them so that each represents one of the groups. In turn, a representative from each circle offers one of the answers suggested by that group. When an answer is provided, the teacher writes it in that group's column, and all the recorders in the room look at the list of answers developed by their group. If that answer is on the circle's list, the recorder crosses it off, thus gradually decreasing the length of the list until only the answers that have not yet been reported to the group and written on the board remain. This procedure continues until no circle has any remaining answers on its list. Recorders should add missing answers to the list and then cross them off immediately.

The answers given by each Circle of Knowledge can be awarded points that are then recorded on the board to produce competition among the teams. The teacher might decide that each correct response will earn one point (or 5 to 10 points) and that the circle achieving the most points will be the winner. Any time an answer is challenged by a rival circle, the teacher must decide whether it is right or wrong. If the answer is right and the challenger incorrect, the challenger's circle loses the number of points given for one correct answer. If the answer is incorrect and the challenger was right, the circle that sponsored the answer loses the potential points and the challenger's circle gains them.

The important thing to remember about Circles of Knowledge is that they may be used only to review something that already has been introduced and taught. Because the information required has been made available to the students previously, the time span permitted is usually a short one (two to five minutes).

Examples

- Name as many states in the United States as you can in 2 $\frac{1}{9}$ minutes.*
- Name all the United States presidents that you can remember in 1 $\frac{7}{9}$ minutes.
- List the ways that a desert child's life is different from yours (3 $\frac{11}{16}$ minutes).
- What are some of the ways that we can show people that we really like them (2 $\frac{9}{15}$ minutes)?
- List as many adverbs as you can (4 $\frac{3}{5}$ minutes).
- List as many products of [country] as you can recall in 4 $\frac{7}{9}$ minutes.

---

*Children tend to pay better attention when you add a strange fraction to the amount of time you permit for a Circle of Knowledge. Experiment with whole numbers versus odd fractions with your class and see which achieves the more directed concentration.

- Name all the songs that you can think of that have a girl's name in the title. (To avoid duplication, ask each circle to sing a line from the song it sponsors.)
- Make up as many examples as you can where two numbers added together equal 9.

  Model: _____ + _____ = 9
- Make up as many examples as you can where two numbers added together minus a third number equal 11.

  Model: _____ + _____ − _____ = 11
- How many examples can you create where two numbers, when added together and multiplied by a third number, equal 100?

  Model: _____ + _____ × _____ = 100
- Name as many nutritious foods as you can in $3\frac{2}{7}$ minutes
- Give as many synonyms as you can for the adjective *small* (or *large*).
- List as many equivalent fractions as you can in $1\frac{2}{9}$ minutes.

  Model: $\frac{4}{5}$ = _____ = _____ .
- List possible causes of war.
- List all the reasons that you can for people putting down other people.
- What are the things that you value most in life ($3\frac{1}{10}$ minutes)?
- Make up as many examples as you can where, when you use addition, subtraction, multiplication, and division (all four in one example), your answer equals 25.
- List as many rules as you can for writing a correct business letter ($5\frac{2}{13}$ minutes).

Team Learning

Team Learning is an excellent technique for introducing new material. All the advantages of peer interaction and support described earlier are apparent in this approach. Enthusiasm, motivation, good spirits, positive results, division of labor, responsibility, persistence, self-image, and group recognition of individual efforts usually result.

Procedures

Begin by writing original material or by copying sections of commercial publications to form short paragraphs containing new information to be learned. By developing Team Learning exercises of varied difficulty, you not only will be able to respond to different learning styles, you also will be able to establish groups to work on new material according to the ability level and rate of learning in each small team.

At the end of the printed reading (or diagrammatic) material, list a series of questions that should be answered by the group. Some of the questions should be related directly to the printed reading passages; others should be answered through inference and analysis by the group. In this way, students will develop two skills, and will be more likely to retain the new information. By finding answers in the assigned material through rereading, underlining, or discussion, the individuals in the group will learn how to seek and to obtain specific information. The more difficult inference questions will promote reasoning and group decision making. The last assignment in each Team Learning should require that the group *apply* the difficult information that is being taught by *applying* it creatively—for example, "Make a set of Task Cards showing each state and its capital."

When the printed materials are ready, you may assign students to groups of four to five. (Five should be the maximum for most small-group techniques.) As students demonstrate responsibility, you might permit some degree of self-selection of groups. Groups should be allowed to sit on the floor or at clustered tables according to their preferences. Other variations include a round circle of chairs, hassocks, or a couch and chairs in a conversational grouping. The learning style elements of design, mobility, time, intake, and so on should be considered as part of the team-learning assignment.

When comfortable, the group should elect, assign, or accept a volunteer to serve as recorder. It is the recorder (and only the recorder) who needs to write the group's responses to the questions. Short, succinct answers are important to keep the discussion and learning process moving. Some of the other students may elect to write the answers, too, but only because they believe they'll remember the material through note-taking.

Any member may help other participants on the same team, but all the effort must be concentrated within the group. One way to promote quiet and order if teams are in competition with a specific Team Learning exercise is to tell the class that other teams are free to use answers that are overheard from other groups working on the same exercise.

After one or two Team Learning experiences, groups of students will develop team relationships and begin to question and analyze the material with enthusiasm and animated but productive conversation. You will need to walk around and assist with the process the first time or two, but you will discover newfound freedom to work with individuals or other groups very soon after the students gain initial experience with this teaching strategy.

Time limits may be imposed or left open, depending on the learning style and need for structure of the members of each group. An alternative to strict time limits would be to assign some Team Learning prescriptions to a group as homework or as free-time activity.

For the purposes of comparison, participation, and reinforcement, the recorders of teams working on the same assignment should be asked to share with the entire group those responses to the material that were developed and approved by their membership. This is done by numbering each group and then asking Team 1 for a response to a question, asking Team 2 for a second one, and so on, in rotation.

Write each recorder's responses on the chalkboard or overhead projector, and instruct students to cross an answer off their lists if it duplicates theirs; thus, they will be left with only answers that have not yet been called out. Other team members should respond on the second or third round. The recorders should pass their lists to the students who will be answering next. Eventually, you and the class will proceed through all the questions, permitting most of the team members to participate. In this way, errors and misinformation are not likely to be retained. Moreover, all questions will be answered, and everyone will have had a chance to participate actively.

As with the Circles of Knowledge, you and your class may elect to use a team competition approach, with points based on the correct number of answers given by each team. Competition among teams is usually friendly and stimulating; often different teams win. Furthermore, the competition does not pit one individual against another, where loss of self-image is a serious risk.

Examples
Team Learning presents new material in a fashion that responds to such important learning style elements as structure, design, time, mobility, intake, learning with peers, motivation, persistence, responsibility, and visual and auditory perceptual strengths. (Kinesthetic and tactual resources could be added to Team Learning exercises for those who require them.) Sample Team Learnings are shown in Figure 5–1.

FIGURE 5–1   Sample Format for Team Learning

Elementary

Team Learning
Team Members:

1. _____
2. _____
3. _____
4. _____

   Recorder: _____

The History of Measurement*

Primitive people measured things by using parts of their own bodies—hands, feet, arms, legs, fingers. One of the most common ancient units of length was the cubit—the length of a forearm from the bend of the elbow to the tip of the outstretched middle finger. The length of a person's foot, the width of the palm, the length of a finger, the width of a thumb—these were all early units of measure.

Continued

*This Team Learning, "The History of Measurement," was designed by Laurie Borok, graduate student, St. John's University, New York, for her Contract Activity Package, "How Tall Are You in Metric Terms: Who's Counting?"

FIGURE 5–1 *Continued*

1. What are some of the different parts of the body used to measure things?

   List at least three (3).

   a. _____

   b. _____

   c. _____

   d. _____

   e. _____

2. How long was a cubit?

   _____

3. Which word tells you that measuring goes back a long way?

   _____

4. Do you think that using a person's own body is a good way to measure things? Why?

   _____

5. Early rulers used their own body measurements as the royal standards. Write an official document decreeing how to measure based on *your* arm and leg lengths. (May be written by individual or group.)

   _____

   _____

   _____

   _____

   _____

6. Have at least three (3) classmates follow your decree and measure one object agreed on by all of you.

   _____

   _____

7. Why is it important to know the history of measurement?

   _____

   _____

   _____

   _____

FIGURE 5-1   *Continued*

Upper Elementary

Team Learning
Team Members:

1. _____

2. _____

3. _____

4. _____

5. _____

6. _____

   Recorder: _____

Learning about the Eye*

Read the following:

> *Light is reflected from an object. It passes through the cornea, a clear covering that protects your eye. Then it passes through some liquid called "aqueous humor" and then through the pupil—the "window of your eye." (The pupil looks like a black dot in the middle of your eye.) A muscle opens the pupil when there is not much light and makes the opening smaller if there is a lot of light. The muscle is called the "iris." The iris is the colored part of your eye. Behind the pupil is the lens, which is something like the lens in a camera. The lens turns the picture upside down and projects it onto the retina, which is like a screen on the rear wall of your eyeball. Millions of nerve endings in the retina send messages through your optic nerves to your brain. Your brain turns the picture right side up again.*
>
> *Your eye has three protectors outside the eyeball. Shading your eyes are the eyelids, which protect them from lights that are too bright and from strong gases such as ammonia. You close your eyelids when you sleep, and you close them automatically when you blink. Blinking spreads tear fluid over the corneas and cleans them as windshield wipers clean the glass in an automobile. The eyelids and the eyelashes also protect your eyes from flying insects and bits of dirt. The eyelids close automatically when an object, such as a ball, comes toward your eyes. The eyebrows above the eyes are protectors, too. They act as cushions against blows from above and keep perspiration from dropping into your eyes.*

*This Team Learning, "Learning about the Eye," was designed by Irene K. Flatley, Rosedale, New York, for her Contract Activity Package, "Learning about our Eyes: Here's Looking at You!"

Continued

FIGURE 5–1 *Continued*

Assignment:

1. What are some parts of the eye mentioned in this writing?

   a. _____

   b. _____

   c. _____

   d. _____

   e. _____

   f. _____

Can you name at least four (4) more?

_____

_____

_____

_____

2. What are the functions of at least seven (7) parts of the eye?

   a. _____

   b. _____

   c. _____

   d. _____

   e. _____

   f. _____

   g. _____

3. Name the three protectors of the eye.

   a. _____

   b. _____

   c. _____

4. How does each of the protectors do its work?

   a. _____

   b. _____

   c. _____

FIGURE 5-1 *Continued*

5. Explain in your own words how the eye sees.

_____

_____

_____

_____

_____

_____

6. Think of what a camera looks like and think about its parts. Are there any similarities or differences between a camera and the eye? If so, list them.

_____

_____

_____

_____

_____

7. If you were unable to see, how would you find out what some things look like?

_____

_____

_____

_____

8. Write a short poem explaining how the eye works.

_____

_____

_____

_____

Brainstorming

Brainstorming is an exciting group participation designed to develop multiple answers to a single question, alternative solutions to problems, and creative responses. It is an associative process that encourages students to call out—one of the few times this is permitted in our schools. Thus, it responds to personal motivation and does not suppress natural spontaneity.

In addition to increasing motivation, the technique of brainstorming offers many practical advantages. Brainstorming is:

- *Stimulating:* It offers a unique, freewheeling, exciting, and rapid-fire method that builds enthusiasm in nearly all participants.
- *Positive:* Quiet and shy students usually become active participants because they are not put down; their contributions are masked by the group process. Conversely, those who usually dominate endless discussions are structured into offering succinct suggestions.
- *Focused:* Diversions and distractions are eliminated. Stories and speeches irrelevant to the question or otherwise not pertinent are eliminated.
- *Spontaneous and creative:* Students serve as a sounding board that generates new ideas. Creativity is released during the momentum of the process.
- *Efficient and productive:* Dozens of suggestions, facts, ideas, or creative solutions are generated in a matter of minutes. Additional steps or plans of an activity can be brainstormed, as well as more specific answers for general responses (subset brainstorming).
- *Involving and image-building:* Self-image is enhanced for students who see their ideas listed. Group pride and cohesiveness increase, too, as the members begin to feel a part of the unit that created the lists.
- *Ongoing and problem-solving:* The results are recorded and may be modified and used in new situations.

Procedures

The brainstorming leader also acts as recorder. His or her functions include recording all responses, asking for clarification or repetition, synthesizing large phrases into short key ideas, and keeping the group focused on each single topic. The leader should not comment, editorialize, or contribute; his or her effort should be concentrated on producing an effective and productive session.

Setting

From five to ten students should form a fairly tight semicircle of chairs facing the leader. (Larger groups can be effective at times.) Behind the leader is a wall containing three to five large sheets of lecture pad paper on newsprint double-folded to prevent strike-through marks on the wall (see Figure 5–2).

FIGURE 5–2 For optimum results, a brainstorming session consists of a tight semicircle of five to ten participants. (Illustration courtesy of Professor Edward Manetta, Chairman, Fine Arts Department, St. John's University, New York.)

These sheets, approximately twenty to twenty-four inches wide and thirty to thirty-six inches high, should be attached to the wall with masking tape and placed a few inches apart at a comfortable height for recording. The leader should use a broad-tipped felt marker for instant visability by the entire group. A timekeeper should be appointed for the two- or three-minute brainstorming segments, but he or she may participate. It is useful to have additional sheets available and an overhead projector to permit groups to analyze, plan, or do subset brainstorming for specific aspects of general answers.

Rules for Participants

1. Concentrate on the topic—"storm your brain."
2. Fill the silence—call out what pops into your head.
3. Wait for an opening—don't step on someone's lines.
4. Record the thoughts in short form.
5. Record *everything*—no matter how far out.
6. Repeat your contribution until it is recorded.
7. Be positive—no put-downs, body language, or editorial comment.
8. Stay in focus—no digressions.
9. Use short time spans—one to three minutes.
10. Analyze later—add, subtract, plan, implement.
11. Brainstorm from general to specific subsets.

Examples
Elementary
- Call out all the synonyms you can think of for *leader.*

- Instead of using a cliche such as "Quiet as a _____," (mouse is usually given) let's brainstorm: "As quiet as a _____ _____ing."

You will soon have delighted groups calling out as quiet as a "snow-flake falling," an "eyelid closing," a "mosquito landing," or a "mother worrying." You might do this for all of the usual cliches found in compositions, and praise those who use creative substitutions.

Upper Elementary
- List the desirable characteristics of good leaders.
- Provide synonyms for an entire sentence, one word at a time:

	(adjective)	(noun)	(verb)			(noun)
The	large	boy	ran	to	the	hill.

Take one minute (60 seconds) for each word. Then consider the limit-less number of combinations to find the funniest sentence, most precise description, most creative arrangement, and so forth.
- List all the solutions you can think of to car pollution.
- Call out as many ways as possible to prevent poverty.

Case Study

A Case Study stimulates and helps to develop analytical skills. Four to five students can spend considerable time discussing and interpreting short, relevant stories that teach them something you believe they ought to learn. Case Studies provide:

- A strategy for developing material within the student's frame of reference. The characters, situations, and events can, if constructed properly, strike responsive and understanding chords.
- An approach that can be stimulating and meaningful if student identification is fostered and debate is structured to understand different points of view on recognized problems and situations.
- Safe, nonthreatening situations for students who can enter the analysis without direct personal effect.
- Training and development in problem solving, analytical skills, arriving at conclusions, and planning for new directions in learning situations and in real life.

Guidelines for the Development of Case Studies

Format   Case Studies may be written as very short stories, audio- or video-taped dramatizations, films, psychodramas, news events, or historical happenings—real or fictional. The use of chronological sequence aids students in following the flow of events and in analyzing key issues. Flash backs and other complex approaches should be avoided except for the most advanced students.

Focus   The case should focus on a single event, incident, or situation. Ability to analyze is aided by a high degree of concentration on the factors that precipitated the event, the attitudes prevailing during a given incident, or the sharply defined points of view of those dealing with a problem.

Relevance   Reality or "potential credibility" related to the frame of reference of the students is critical to the success of this small-group technique. The participants involved in analyzing the case must be able to recognize, understand, or even identify with the people in the situation because what they do or say seems authentic or possible. The style of writing should attempt to capture the flavor of familiar places, people, and their actions at a level that is at, or slightly above, the levels of understanding of the participants.

Increasing Motivation   After initial training in the analysis of Case Studies, involve students in the actual writing and acting out of roles in subsequent cases. Both relevance and motivation will increase as students become involved and begin to feel a sense of ownership of their new creation or variation of an older case.

Procedures

Elect, seek volunteers, or appoint a leader and a recorder from among the four to five participants. Have the group read the case at the beginning of the session. As the students become more familiar with this approach, you may wish to assign the materials as prior reading exercises to increase the amount of time devoted to group discussion.

The leader should not dominate the session but should keep the group on target for the allotted time. The recorder should participate and also concentrate on capturing the essence of the group's responses to various analytical questions. He or she must periodically verify all notes with the group to obtain consensus.

Key questions for the Case Study or short story must be developed in advance, although others may be suggested by the group as they delve deeply into the problem or situation. Questions may begin with factual checkpoints but then should move quickly into possible reasons, alternative motives, and analysis of the subtleties and complexities of human experiences and interactions as well as values, standards, and other abstractions. Finally, students should be asked to reach conclusions and to apply developing insights to new situations.

Analyzing Case Studies should build student powers of interpretation, synthesis, description, observation, perception, abstraction, comparison, judgement, conclusion, determination, and prediction.

Examples

Sample Case Study: Elementary School—Values

Purpose: Understanding some of the factors that cause others to behave the way they do, even when they want to be different.

The New Student

Ellen arrived with her family from out of state in the beginning of November. She felt out of place and uncomfortable. It had been difficult to make friends in her former school, and here it seemed impossible. She felt left out and behind in her work here in the sixth grade, even though she was told that she had been an excellent student when she was younger. Everyone seemed to belong to an in-group.

Ellen was quiet at first, but then began to try to work her way into one of the groups. She walked into a circle of girls before class started and said: "You know, the way girls dress in this school is really way out of it. No one here is really cool. At my last school all the girls wore French jeans. Here, you're still wearing ordinary slacks. Why, no one here has even started to wear overalls, and we dropped them last year."

One of the girls stared at Ellen and said to the other, "Let's go into the classroom. The hall's getting polluted." They all left, leaving Ellen behind. She became embarrassed and fought to control developing tears as she ran down the hall.

Analysis questions:

- What is the key problem in this Case Study?
- Who is "right"—Ellen or the girls?
- What would you do immediately to help Ellen?
- What would you say to Ellen? To the group of girls?
- Pretend you are one of the other girls. What would you say about Ellen?
- What are three things you could do to help Ellen become part of the class and feel welcome?

(Scores of cases like this one and their analyses can be developed about a variety of situations dealing with values, attitudes, interactions, or preferences.)

Sample Case Study: Upper Elementary School—Living History

Purpose: Understanding emotions and attitudes, coping with a difficult situation, developing alternative solutions.

The Unwanted Visitor

At the time of the Boston Massacre, British soldiers were feared, despised, and unwanted by many colonists who still considered themselves loyal British subjects under the rule of King George III. Nevertheless, the crude, red-uniformed soldiers were housed in homes in Boston where they ate the food, used the bedrooms, and sometimes engaged in mistreatment of the local citizens. Their red uniforms earned for them the derogatory term "lobster back."

For their part, the British soldiers were not pleased to be far from home among hostile "barbarians." Some youngsters, perhaps of your age, undoubtedly found those red-coated lobster backs inviting targets for snowballs in the winter. This type of harassment, added to the irritable confrontations on the streets and commons of Boston, may very well have led to an accidental, or at least unnecessary, firing by the troops on the unarmed citizens of Boston.

Analysis questions:

- If you had lived in Boston during the American Revolution, how would you have felt about British soldiers living in your home? Why?
- Why was "lobster back" a derogatory term? Why was this term used instead of another one, such as "red flannel-head"?
- How would you feel if you were one of the British soldiers?
- What would you have done to ease the tension in town to prevent the massacre and needless loss of life?
- Have there been similar situations in history since the Revolutionary War?

A Final Word on Small-Group Techniques

These four small-group techniques and others you use or devise are essential to building independence and for responding to those youngsters whose learning style clearly indicates a need to work with peers.

- *Circle of Knowledge* reviews and reinforces previously learned material.
- *Team Learning* introduces new material and uses both factual and inferential questions, plus creative applications.
- *Brainstorming* releases creative energy and aids in planning and solving problems.

- *Case Study* develops analytical skills and builds empathy and under-standing of people as they work together to solve problems or cope with crises.

There are variations and other small-group techniques such as Simula-tions, Role Playing, Group Analysis, Task Forces, and Research Committees.

Each technique should focus on a specific objective—learning new mate-rial, developing higher order thinking skills, and so forth. Select or develop those that will respond to varied learning styles, and your instructional role will eventually take less effort and will be far more rewarding for you and for your individual students.

6

Designing Tactual and Kinesthetic Resources to Respond to Individual Learning Styles

The Importance of Recognizing Tactual and Kinesthetic Learners

Young children learn by touching, feeling, moving, and experiencing. Indeed, we have to protect them from being injured by sharp objects, electricity, hot water, and other items, which they eagerly grasp, squeeze or put into their mouths. During the school years, however, educators often ignore these tactual and kinesthetic preferences. Instead, classroom instruction focuses on auditory and visual teaching strategies.

Restak (1979) and others have indicated that many students do not become strongly visual before third grade, that auditory acuity first develops in many students after the sixth grade, and that boys often are neither strongly visual nor auditory even during high school. Therefore, since most children are tactual and kinesthetic learners, such resources should be developed and used, particularly for those who are experiencing difficulty learning through lectures, direct verbal instruction, "chalk talks" and textbook assignments. Instruction should be introduced through an individual's strongest perceptual strength and reinforced in the weaker modalities sequentially, (Carbo, 1980; Dunn, 1990a; Kroon, 1985; Ingham, 1989; Martini, 1986; Weinberg, 1983; Wheeler, 1980, 1983). Further, since many students are enthusiastic about designing and building tactual/kinesthetic games and materials, they easily can teach themselves through this procedure. Thus, the easy-to-follow directions in this chapter can be used to help elementary school youngsters achieve instructional independence.

When children who need either informal seating or a great deal of mobility use tactual or kinesthetic materials in sections of the classroom where they feel comfortable, their concentration, memory, and behavior improve. (Photograph courtesy of the Northwest Elementary School, Amityville, New York.)

Students who do well in school tend to be the ones who learn either by listening in class or by reading. Because of this, most of us believe that the brighter students are auditory and/or visual learners. In reality, however, we usually teach by telling (auditory) and by assigning readings (visual) or by explaining and writing on a chalkboard (auditory and visual). Therefore, youngsters who are able to absorb through these two senses are, of course, the ones who retain what they have been taught and, thus, respond well on our tests, which also are usually auditory (teacher dictates) or visual (written or printed).

Our own research during the past two decades verifies that many students who do not do well in school are tactual or kinesthetic learners (Dunn, 1990c); their strongest perceptual strengths are neither auditory nor visual. These boys and girls tend to acquire and retain information or skills when they either are involved in handling manipulative materials or are participating in concrete "real-life" activities. Because so little of what happens instructionally in most classes responds to the tactual and kinesthetic senses, these students are, in a very real sense, handicapped. What's more, once they begin to fall behind scholastically, they lose confidence in themselves and either feel defeated and withdraw (physically or emotionally) or begin to resent school because of repeated failure.

Most young children appear to be essentially tactual or kinesthetic learners. As they grow older, some youngsters begin to combine their tactual inclinations with visual preferences; for these, the resources suggested in this chapter will be helpful. Eventually, some youngsters develop auditory strengths and are able to function easily in a traditional class where much of the instruction is through discussion or lecture; this group, however, does not represent the majority.

Although we have found some parallels between age and perceptual strengths among students, upper elementary school children continue to be unable to learn well by either listening in class or by reading. Sensory strengths appear to be so individualized that it is vital to test each student and then to recommend resources that complement their strengths rather than their weaknesses. When you recognize that selected students are not learning either through their readings or from class discussions or lectures, experiment with several of the following resources to provide tactual or kinesthetic instruction that should prove to be helpful.

Learning Style Characteristics Responsive to Tactual and Kinesthetic Resources

Because tactual and kinesthetic materials tend to be gamelike, they usually are naturally motivating, particularly for young children. Where they are perceived as being babyish, however, they can cause embarrassment and turn off many youngsters. It is important that the students to whom these resources are assigned are positive about them and are therefore willing to follow directions for their use, care, and replacement. If they enjoy learning in this way, they will become persistent and will continue using the materials until they have achieved the goals or objectives that have been outlined for them. All the materials are self-corrective, so that should youngsters experience difficulty while using them, they are able to manipulate them to find the correct answers. Nevertheless, the motivation for using these materials is necessary if the students are to be responsible for them—for the parts or sections of each set need to be kept intact, returned to holders or boxes, and generally maintained in good condition. However, as we have observed previously, apathetic children may become highly motivated because of their interest in and enjoyment with Learning Circles, Task Cards, Electroboards, and games.

Other than the directions for using the resources, little structure is pro-

Tactual materials may be used alone, in pairs, or in a small group. They also may be used at either a table or desk and on the floor—for students so inclined. (Photographs courtesy of the P. K. Yonge Laboratory School, Gainesville, Florida.)

vided through these materials; students using them may, therefore, need some structure—but not too much. Beyond the need for motivation, persistence, responsibility, and structure, these resources respond to students who have visual-tactual, tactual-kinesthetic, or visual-kinesthetic inclinations and who do not learn easily either by listening or by reading.

Learning Style Characteristics to Which Tactual and Kinesthetic Resources Can Be Accommodated

Because these resources may be used in a classroom, in a library, in a corridor, or in an instructional resource center as well as at home, they can accommodate each student's environmental and physical preferences. Because they may be used independently, in pairs, with a small group, or with an adult, they also respond to each student's sociological needs.

Teacher-oriented students may use tactual resources under the instructor's supervision. However, because they are self-corrective, the voice on an accompanying tape provides sufficient direction and orientation. Note the Learning Circle with answers on clothespins, a pencil game, a Flip Chute, and earphones through which directions for use are provided. (Photograph courtesy of Longwood College Reading Clinic, Virginia.)

Step-by-Step Guide to Designing Tactual Resources

Developing tactual resources is easy. Once you have designed one or two samples, older students and parents can duplicate and create additional samples for you. Although many of these materials are available in primary and elementary schools, they often are used indiscriminately rather than with those youngsters whose perceptual inclinations would complement them, and they usually are commercially produced and do not respond directly to either the topics that you teach or the objectives on which you focus. After you have made a few samples for experimentation and observed the progress that certain students make through their use, you will become committed to their availability as an instructional resource for your classroom. Another advantage is that they save labor by being adaptable to different levels, questions, and even subject areas—for example, a Learning Circle with interchangeable parts.

Designing Learning Circles

A Learning Circle is an interesting way for children to review many worthwhile skills. For example, you can teach the formation or recognition of new words, mathematics concepts, historical data, and almost any kind of skill development through them. Why not try making one or two Learning Circles to see whether your slow achievers respond favorably to them? If they do, let them help you create more. You will find that auditory or visual achievers will enjoy them also—even though they do not need them.

Let us assume that you have been teaching students to add. Begin with a Learning Circle that provides them with opportunities to practice completing different number fact problems. You will need the following items:

Materials

- Two pieces of colored oaktag, heavy construction paper, or poster board
- One wire coat hanger (optional)
- Black thin-line felt pens, colored felt tip pens
- Eight clip-on clothespins (the colored plastic type are pretty and do not break easily)
- Masking tape or strong glue
- Clear or lightly colored transparent adhesive-backed paper
- Old magazines that may be cut up to either color-code or picture-code the mathematics examples and their answers (optional)

Directions

Figure 6–1 illustrates the steps for making the Learning Circle, as follows:

1. Cut two circles, 18 inches in diameter, for each Learning Circle.
2. Divide each circle into eight sectors.

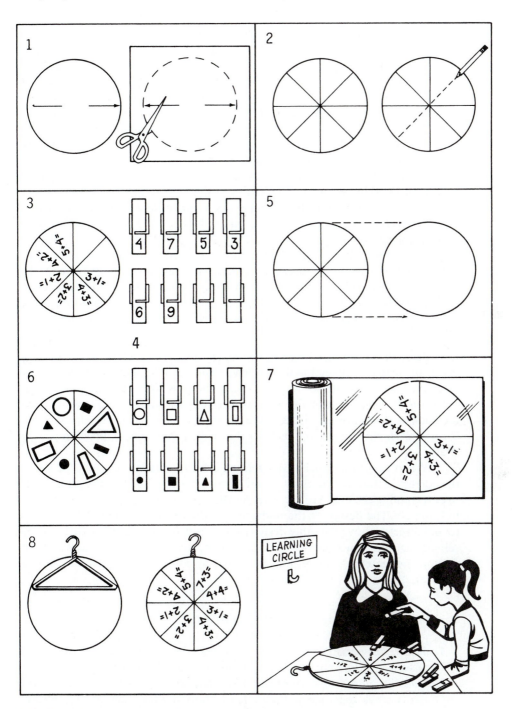

FIGURE 6–1   Constructing a Learning Circle.

3. In each of the eight sections, print (using a black felt pen) an addition problem that is simple enough to compute by the students for whom it is intended.

4. Print the answer to one of the math problems on the tip end (rather than the squeeze end) of a clothespin. Follow suit for each of the seven remaining problems and clothespins.

5. Turn the second circle so that its eight sections become its back. Place the front of the second circle against the back of the first circle (spoon-in-spoon fashion or blank sides together).

6. Either color-code or picture-code each correct answer to match its problem. Do this by placing an identically shaped and colored symbol underneath the clothespin that matches the problem and inside the section of the second circle (bottom one) that will be passed directly beneath the problem.

7. Cover both circles with clear adhesive-backed paper or laminate.

8. Glue the two circles together with a wire hanger securely fastened between them. The Learning Circle will remain in excellent condition despite extensive use, and it may be stored easily by hanging on a doorknob or a hook (see Figure 6–1). You may, of course, omit the wire hanger.

Store the Learning Circle in a convenient place in the classroom—preferably in or near an instructional area where the students may use this resource when they are free to do so. Remove the clothespins from their storage niche—either on the lower half of the wire hanger or in an oaktag pocket attached to the back of the Learning Circle. Have the student mix the clothespins and then try to match the answer on each to the related question or problem on the chart.

When the clothespins have been matched to what the student believes is the correct section of the chart, show him or her how to turn the entire chart over (revealing the back) to see whether the color-coded or picture coded symbols match. The design of the underside of the clothespin should be identical to and directly above the same design on the back of the second circle to permit self-correction. When the two symbols match, the answer is correct; when they do not, the matching answer may be found by comparing the paired colors or pictures.

Variations on the Design of Learning Circles

1. *Velcro answers:* Paste Velcro strips near the top of each sector. Attach answers to the matched Velcro strip instead of to clothespins.

2. *Question-and-answer booklets:* Use circles of two layers of clean contact paper stuck together and a circle of blank oaktag. Sew or glue pockets that exactly match the question sectors on the front and the answer sectors on the back. Thus, this "blank" Learning Circle may be used for

different sets of questions or problems, with appropriate answers cut to fit into the blank pockets.

You now have a Learning Circle with exchangeable construction paper problems, so that the same resource can be used for several different sets of problems. For example, one day you can insert math problems, another day you can insert language problems, and so on. The pockets on the back of the Learning Circle can be used to hold alternative sets of problems so that either you or your students may use different materials as they are needed.

Designing Learning Strips

A similar tactual resource is the Learning Strip, an elongated version of the Learning Circle (see Figure 6-2). It can be made by dividing a long piece of oaktag, construction paper, or poster board into eight or ten sections and printing a different number (or problem) in each box. Tape the wire hanger to the top of the back of the board. Place different numbers (within the student's range of addition facts) on each of the clothespins.

If the students for whom you are designing these resources are learning to recognize numbers, a simple match will do. If they are practicing the addition of numbers, then on the back of each section neatly print the number combinations that complement the addition of all the numbers on each clothespin that may be added to the number on the front. For example, if the number 3 is placed in the first section on the front of the Learning Strip, and if the number 1,2,3,4,5,6,7, or 8 each appears on a different clothespin, then on the back of the section of the learning strip that has number 3 on top, print the following:

$$3 + 1 = 4 \qquad 3 + 5 = 8$$
$$3 + 2 = 5 \qquad 3 + 6 = 9$$
$$3 + 3 = 6 \qquad 3 + 7 = 10$$
$$3 + 4 = 7 \qquad 3 + 8 = 11$$

Follow suit for each of the strips, providing the correct answer by printing all the correct number combinations added to the number on the front of the chart. In this case, you would not need to color- or picture-code.

Learning Circles or Strips are excellent resources for either introducing or reinforcing an endless number of facts or skills that your students may be required to learn. For example:

1. In each of the sections of the front of the resource, place the letters *an, and, at, ear, en, end, in,* and *on.* (Any word roots may be substituted.) Place a different letter on the top of each clothespin. By placing one clothespin at a time in front of each of the sections on the circle, your students may be

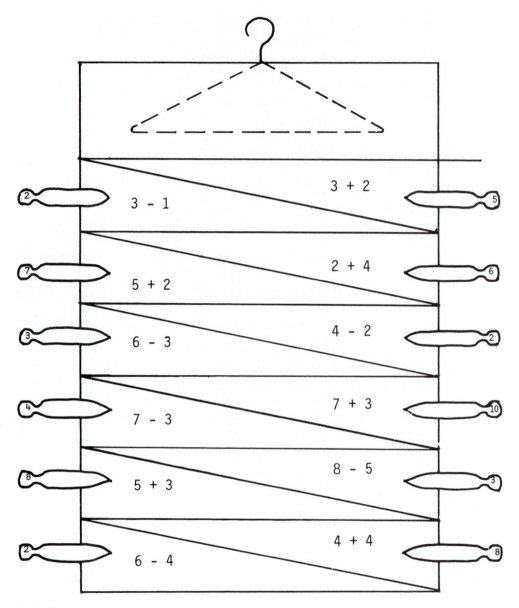

FIGURE 6-2 A Learning Strip.

able to form new words and read them. If they are just beginning to read well, they may need you to work with them to be certain that the words they form are correct. When they are able, perhaps toward the end of the year, write all the possible words that may be made by adding a single letter or group of letters to the basic letters on the chart. Do this on 3 × 5 inch index cards, which you can store in a pocket on the back of the chart.

2. Print the names of each of eight different geometric shapes on the chart and paste pictures of the shapes onto the clothespins. Your students will learn to recognize, spell, and write the names before most of their grade-level peers.

3. Print new vocabulary on the chart and paste pictures of the words onto the clothespins. By matching the pictures to the words, students will become familiar with the formation and letter combinations and will begin to read them—first on the chart and then in a text.

By using tactual, self-instructional, and self-corrective materials, your students will gradually become increasingly independent. By using Learning Circles or Learning Strips, you will be introducing them, without direct assistance from others, to the facts and skills they need to know. This activity will facilitate their academic achievement in later years when they will be expected to learn on their own.

Teaching Reading and Spelling through a Variety of Tactual Resources

As described in the review of the elements of learning style in Chapter 1, youngsters learn through different senses determined by their individual perceptual preferences or strengths. When teaching your tactually inclined students important skills such as language concepts, word recognition, reading, spelling, or writing, use more than one sense to help them to internalize what they learn.

When we teach by telling (either personally or on tape), we are appealing to a child's *auditory* (or listening) ability. When we teach by showing, we concentrate on the *visual* (or seeing) sense. When we teach through touching methods, we appeal to the *tactual* sense. Finally, when we teach by doing (providing real experiences, such as teaching inches and feet by building a wagon), we are emphasizing a *kinesthetic* (whole-body involvement) approach.

Materials that facilitate a tactual approach include clay; sandpaper; fabrics of varied consistency such as felt, velvet, or buckram (you can cut up old clothing that will no longer be worn); sand; water; fingerpaints; or uncooked macaroni. For example, if you wished to help your students to learn to spell a very difficult word, you might use any or all of the following activities, depending on their preferences and how long it would take for them to master the word.

1. Say the word. Explain its meaning. Give them an example of how it might be used in a sentence. Ask them to say the word and to use it in a sentence. When each student can do that, spell the word for them.

2. Print the word in black on a white sheet of paper, then print it in white on a black piece of paper. Repeat the spelling and point to each of the letters as you say it. Ask the students to look at the spelling and try to memorize the letters in correct sequence. Ask them to try to spell the word without looking at it.

3. Ask the youngsters to write the word by copying the letters that you wrote. If they can copy the letters accurately, ask them to spell the word again without looking. When they are correct, praise them. If they are not correct, show them the word written by you and point out their errors.

4. Empty the contents of a small bag of sand into an aluminum pan. Encourage your students to trace the letters of the word in the sand. Permit them to look at the printed word as they "write" the letters. Then see if they can write the letters without looking at the word. If they can, ask them to spell the word without looking and without writing.

5. Ask each youngster to dip one finger into a plastic cup of water and to write the word on the chalkboard without looking. Then have the student stare at the word as it evaporates.

6. Cut the small letters of the alphabet out of heavy sandpaper. Make duplicates of letters that are used often. Place all the letters into an empty shoe box and ask your students to find the letters in the spelling word without looking (strictly by feeling each of the letters and discarding those that are not in the word). When they have found all the letters, ask them to place them into the correct sequence so that the word is spelled correctly.

7. Cut the small letters of the alphabet out of old fabric. Place them into an unused shoe box. Follow the procedure suggested for using sandpaper letters.

8. Press different colored strips of clay into a pan. Ask your youngsters to write the word in the clay with a toothpick.

9. Keep a jar of uncooked macaroni available for spelling. If you have "alphabet macaroni," ask each student to find each of the letters in the word and to glue them onto a cardboard. They will then have a three-dimensional spelling list. If you have the more common forms of macaroni, print the word in large letters on an eight-and-a-half- by eleven-inch sheet of writing paper or shirt cardboard, and let them paste the food bits into the letters so that they, too, form the word.

10. They can also trace the word in salt, colored or white sugar, or with fingerpaints.

11. Students love to trace letters and words in Jell-o or chocolate pudding with their fingers (or a small spoon) and then fill the resulting changes with milk. The reward for carving the right answer is permission to eat the dessert or lick their fingers.

All these activities will not be necessary at one time, nor will all your students require so many tactual experiences. The variety was suggested to provide you with alternatives so that you approach teaching through varied—and thus interesting—techniques for youngsters who profit from more than an auditory-visual method. When your students learn to read or spell a word merely by hearing it, seeing it, writing it once or twice, or concentrating on or memorizing its letters, you need not introduce the tactual materials described here. But if learning does not occur through various reading approaches such as phonics or word recognition, offer them a choice of these activities and continue experimenting with the options until their task has been mastered. Unless your students indicate special preferences, use different activities for different words so that they do not become bored. As indicated in the research, use materials that teach students through their perceptual strengths from the strongest to the weakest—in sequence.

These suggestions may be used to teach numbers, letters, mathematical computations, geometric shapes, and other items in addition to reading and spelling words.

Understanding Task Cards

Task Cards are easy-to-make, multisensory resources that respond to a youngster's need to see and to touch simultaneously. Often designed in sets or groups, each series teaches related concepts or facts. This resource tends to be effective with students who cannot remember easily by listening or by reading. They are used both to introduce new material and to reinforce something the student has been exposed to but did not learn.

The most effective Task Cards are those that are self-corrective. These (1) permit students to recognize whether they understand and can remember the material, (2) allow no one other than the youngster using the cards to see errors made—thus preserving the student's dignity and self-image, (3) enable students who do make mistakes in their responses to find the correct answers, and (4) free the teacher to work with other students.

Task Cards can be made self-corrective through any one of several methods: color coding, picture coding, shape coding, or the provision of answers. Task cards for young children are usually simple and easy to manipulate. They may be used by individuals, pairs, or a small group. They permit self-pacing. Students may continue to use them until they feel secure in their knowledge of the topic; they can be reused as a means of reinforcement if specific information has been forgotten. They are gamelike in character and often win and sustain youngsters' attention. They appeal to young people who cannot learn through other available resources, and, therefore, they are important for those whom they do teach.

Students who select or are assigned Task Cards may work with them at their desks, in an instructional area such as a Learning Station or Interest Center, in the library, on carpeting, or anywhere they prefer in either the school or home environment.

Designing Task Cards

Task Cards are effective resources for tactual students at all levels. Begin by listing exactly what you want your students to learn about a specific topic, concept, or skill. Then translate your list into either questions and answers concerning what they should learn or samples of the answers—some true and others false. For example, if you were concerned about teaching idioms at the upper elementary level, you would list some of the more popular ones and what they mean in straightforward language—"time flies"—time passes very quickly; "on pins and needles"—nervous, uneasy, or anxious.

Materials

- Colored oaktag or cardboard
- Black felt pens
- Colored thin-line felt pens (optional) for illustrating text

Directions

1. Cut the colored oaktag or cardboard into three- by twelve-inch rectangles.

2. On the left side of each of the rectangles, in large, easy-to-read letters, print one of the idiomatic phrases on your list. On the right side of the rectangle print the corresponding derivation of the word. Be certain to leave space between the idiom and its meaning. Illustrate the idiom.

3. Either laminate or cover each rectangle with clear contact paper.

4. Cut each rectangle into two parts by using a different linear separation for each (to code them according to shape). For examples see Figure 6–3.

5. Package the set in an attractive box and place a title on top that describes the Task Cards inside. For the set we just discussed, appropriate titles might include:

STRANGE PHRASES WE USE EVERY DAY: 30 IDIOMS THAT COLOR OUR LANGUAGE

Additional Idioms:

raining cats and dogs	raining very hard
hurry up	hurry
Achilles' heel	vulnerable spot
ace in the hole	hidden strength
acid test	true measurement
all the traffic will bear	highest charge possible
ax to grind	hidden motive
back to the salt mines	back to work
get one's back up	ready to fight
make the fur fly	a fight
in the bag	accomplished
bail out	leave a risky situation

FIGURE 6–3   Sample Task Cards on Idioms.

on the bandwagon	attraction to something new
barking up the wrong tree	wrong issue, reason, or approach
on the beam	on target
beating around the bush	not getting to the point
big shot	important person
for the birds	not worthwhile
bite the bullet	face up to a difficult situation
blood money	price paid to a hired killer
once in a blue moon	hardly ever
blue bloods	aristocrats, wealthy people

by the boards	letting go
bone to pick	argument on an issue
brass ring	prize
break the ice	initiate conversation
bring home the bacon	earnings
bury the hatchet	make peace with someone
cool one's heels	wait a long time
crocodile tears	false crying

Source: These Task Cards on idioms were designed by Eileen O'Keefe, teacher, American Martyrs School, Bayside, New York.

Research and creative assignments would include: finding the original meanings and how the current definitions evolved; creating new, inventive idioms; using idioms in an original poem; illustrating idioms; compiling a dictionary of idioms; surveying usage of idioms; listing idioms under categories; and so on. Adding drawings and color increases interest.

One teacher, interested in getting her students to understand the concept of analogies, worked backward. She folded a large yellow envelope, and on the back flap she printed:

WHAT IS AN ANALOGY?

Below the title she also printed:

> *An analogy expresses a likeness between things that are otherwise unlike each other.*

Then she thought of several analogies and printed one on each of half a dozen cards. She cut each card into two sections and shape-coded them in the process. The end product was interesting way to teach (or reinforce the concept of analogies (see Figure 6-4).

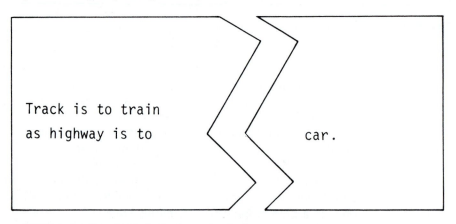

FIGURE 6-4   Sample Task Cards on Analogies.

FIGURE 6–4 *Continued*

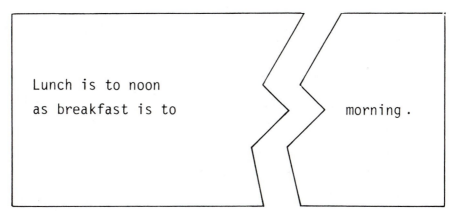

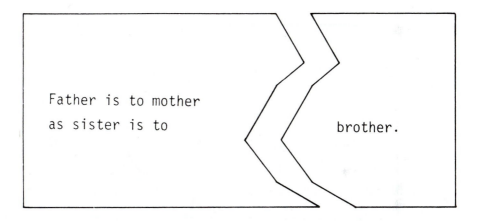

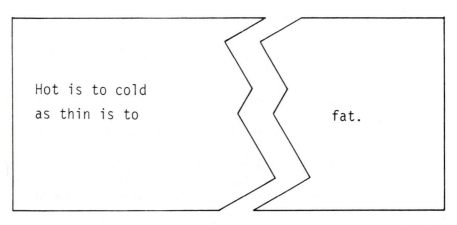

Continued

FIGURE 6-4 *Continued*

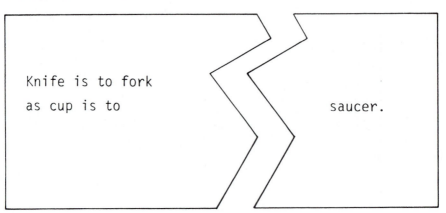

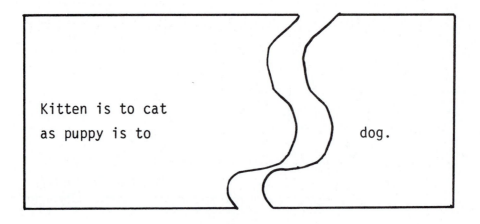

When designing Task Cards for young children, you might consider number facts and their answers as making up one set, word blends and possible letter combinations to form new words as another task, initial letters that can be combined with "letter families" to form new words as another alternative, and so on.

For older and more advanced students, you might consider:

1. Outlining the shape of each of the original states; adding their official state nicknames, their capital cities, and the rank order in which they became a state; then having the youngsters piece the facts together (see Figure 6-5).
2. Identifying famous buildings through illustrations (see Figure 6-6).

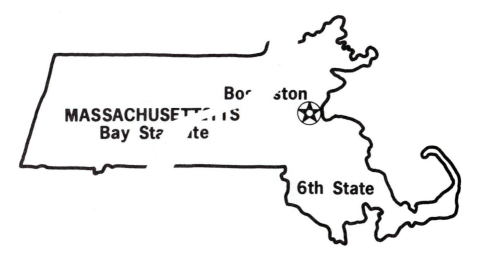

FIGURE 6–5 Sample Task Cards on States.
Source: This Task Card on states was designed by Dr. Jeanne Pizzo for a unit on the United States.

Flip Chutes are one of the best ways to help tactual youngsters remember factual information such as multiplication tables, spelling words, or new vocabulary. Questions are inserted at the top, and their answers flip out from the bottom! (Photograph courtesy of the Northwest Elementary School, Amityville, New York.)

The Supreme Court Building

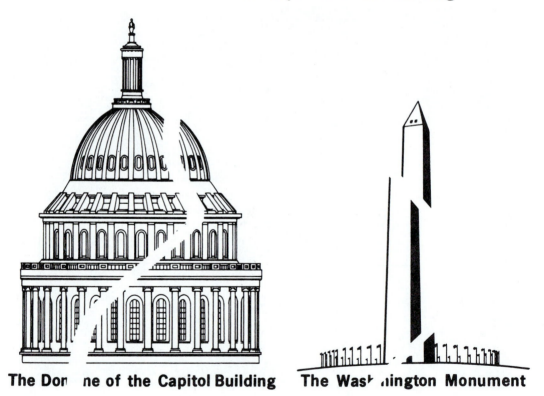

The Dome of the Capitol Building   **The Washington Monument**

FIGURE 6–6 Sample Task Cards on Famous Buildings and Monuments in Washington, D.C., designed by Dr. Jeanne Pizzo.

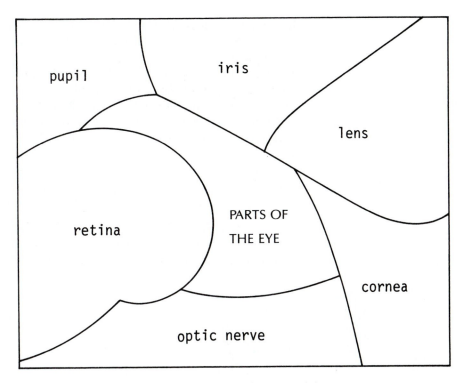

FIGURE 6–7   Sample Task Card Puzzle on the Parts of the Eye.

3. Place the name of a state, the person who founded it, and the year in which it was founded all on one Task Card that is divided into three sections; then have students piece together an entire set—perhaps entitled "Who Founded What and When?"
4. Complete a puzzle that combines the parts of the eye into a single Task Card (see Figure 6–7).

There is no limit to the intricacy and complexity that task cards may reach when subdivided into many parts. They are an effective introductory and reinforcement device for tactually and visually inclined students and often are successful in motivating students toward achievement after many previous methods have failed.

Designing Flip Chutes

Everything that can be taught through either a Learning Circle or a set of Task Cards also can be taught using a Flip Chute. We suggest alternating the resources to maintain the interest and enthusiasm of students who need variety; for those who prefer to use the same materials repeatedly, this single device will be a strong reinforcement.

Flip Chutes are attractive half-gallon orange juice or milk containers decorated to reflect the subject matter being studied. Small question and answer cards are designed to be inserted into the upper face of the container. As each card descends on an inner slide, it flips over and emerges through a lower opening with the correct answer face up.

Directions

1. Pull open the top of a half-gallon milk or juice container.
2. Cut the side folds of the top portion down to the top of the container.

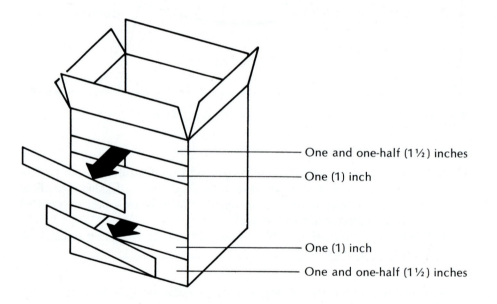

One and one-half (1½) inches

One (1) inch

One (1) inch

One and one-half (1½) inches

3. On the front edge, measure down both (a) 1½ inches and (b) 2½ inches. Draw lines across the container. Remove that space.
4. Mark up from the bottom (a) 1½ inches and (b) 2½ inches. Draw lines across the container. Remove that space.
5. Cut one 5 × 8 index card to measure 6½ inches by 3½ inches.
6. Cut a second index card to measure 7½ inches by 3½ inches.
7. Fold down ½ inch at *both* ends of the smaller strip. Fold down ½ inch at *one* end of the longer strip.

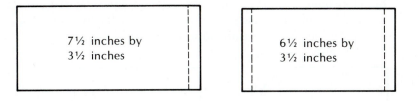

7½ inches by
3½ inches

6½ inches by
3½ inches

8. Insert the smaller strip into the bottom opening with the folded edge resting on the upper portion of the bottom opening. Attach it with masking tape.
9. Bring the upper part of the smaller strip out through the upper opening, with the folded part going down over the center section of the carton. Attach it with masking tape.

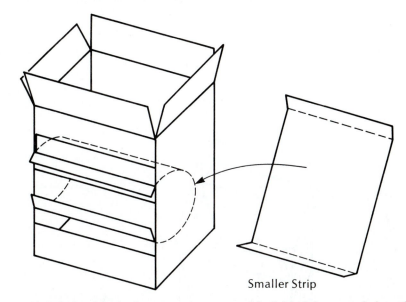

Step 8

Step 9

Smaller Strip

10. Work with the longer strip, one end is folded down and the other end is unfolded. Insert the unfolded end of the longer strip into the bottom opening of the container from the outside. Be certain that the strip goes up along the back of the container. Push it into the container until the folded part rests on the bottom part of the container. Attach it with masking tape.
11. Attach the upper edge of the longer strip to the back of the container creating a slide. Secure it with masking tape about ⅝" from the top of the carton.
12. Fold down the top flaps of the container and tape them in place, forming a rectangular box.

13. Use small, 2 × 2½ inch index cards to write the question on one side and the answer upside down on the flip side. Notch each question side at the top right to insure appropriate positioning when the student uses the cards.

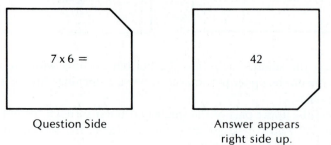

Question Side

Answer appears
right side up.

(Flip Chute directions were developed by Dr. Barbara Gardiner.)

Side View of Container

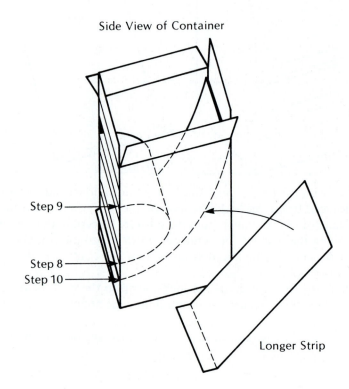

Step 9

Step 8

Step 10

Longer Strip

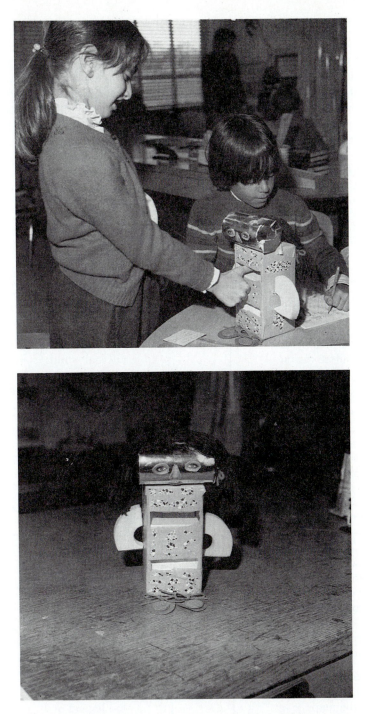

Flip Chutes can be made and decorated by children to reflect their current unit of study or a favorite character they enjoy. (Photographs courtesy of P.S. #220, Queens, New York.)

If you want to make the Flip Chute reflect a particular theme or area of study, add a rounded section at the top to represent a head, arms, or other "special effects." Paint, color, or cover with colored contact paper or vinyl wall covering and add lettering describing this particular Flip Chute's purpose. When completed, an everyday sample should look similar to the one in the photographs on page 161.

Sample Flip Chute Card Sets
The following tactual/kinesthetic samples in this chapter relate to their respective Contract Activity Packages in Chapter 4.

Breaking the Map Code

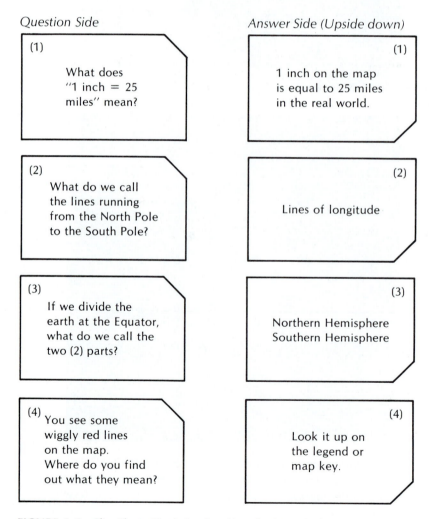

FIGURE 6–8   Flip Chute Cards for Breaking the Map Code.

FIGURE 6–8 *Continued*

Question Side   *Answer Side (Upside down)*

(5)
Which symbol do
you look at to
find directions
on a map?

(5)

The compass rose

(6)
If we divide the
earth along the
main longitude,
what do we call the
two (2) parts?

(6)

Western Hemisphere
Eastern Hemisphere

(7)
What do we use
in helping us
estimate distances
from place to
place on the map?

(7)

The map scale

(8)

Why is the globe
always round like
a ball?

(8)

The Earth is a sphere,
and the globe is a
model of the Earth.

(9)

What do we call the
lines that run around
the globe in circles?

(9)

Lines of
latitude

(10)

In a map grid, what
do we use key letters
and key numbers for?

(10)

We use them to <u>name</u>
the squares.

Continued

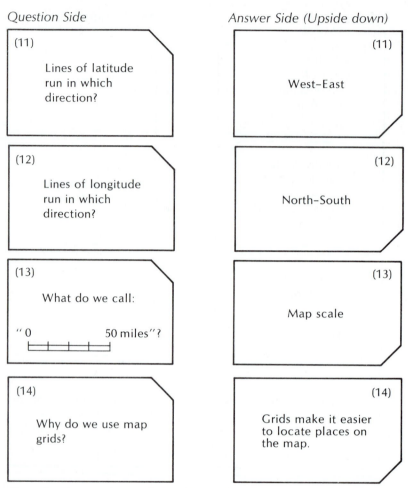

Question Side

Answer Side (Upside down)

(11) Lines of latitude run in which direction?

(11) West–East

(12) Lines of longitude run in which direction?

(12) North–South

(13) What do we call:
"0   50 miles"?

(13) Map scale

(14) Why do we use map grids?

(14) Grids make it easier to locate places on the map.

(These Flip Chute Cards were designed by Bohilde Iglesias.)

Magnetism: The Power of Attraction

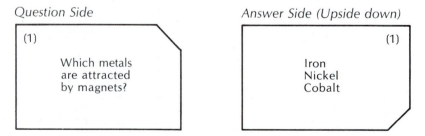

Question Side

Answer Side (Upside down)

(1) Which metals are attracted by magnets?

(1) Iron
Nickel
Cobalt

FIGURE 6–9 Flip Chute Cards for Magnetism.

FIGURE 6–9 *Continued*

Question Side   Answer Side (Upside down)

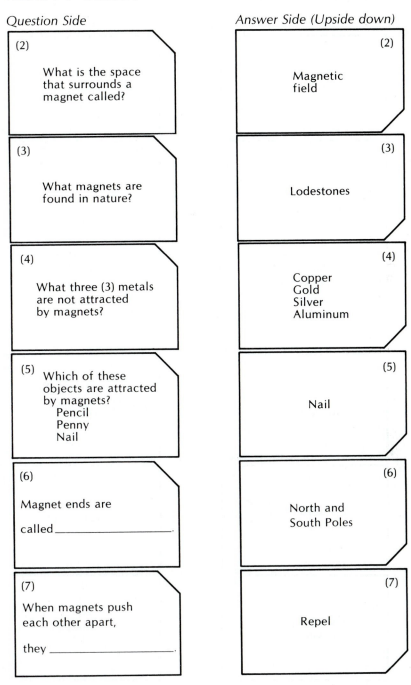

(2)

What is the space that surrounds a magnet called?

(2)

Magnetic field

(3)

What magnets are found in nature?

(3)

Lodestones

(4)

What three (3) metals are not attracted by magnets?

(4)

Copper
Gold
Silver
Aluminum

(5) Which of these objects are attracted by magnets?
    Pencil
    Penny
    Nail

(5)

Nail

(6)

Magnet ends are

called _____.

(6)

North and South Poles

(7)

When magnets push each other apart,

they _____.

(7)

Repel

Continued

FIGURE 6–9 *Continued*

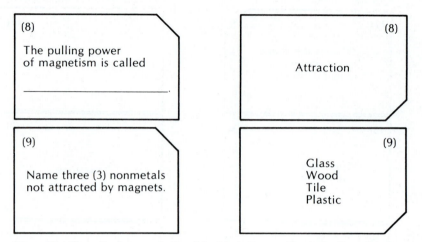

(These Flip Chute Cards were designed by Maria Turano Giresi, Teacher, The Growing Tree, Ridgefield, Connecticut.)

Welcome to New England

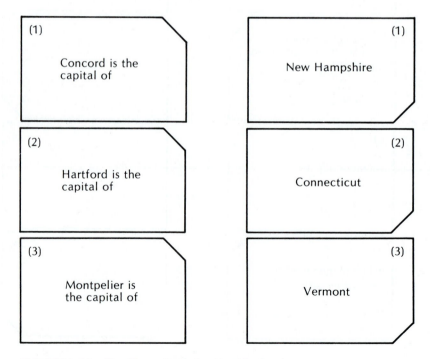

FIGURE 6–10 Flip Chute Cards for New England.

FIGURE 6–10 *Continued*

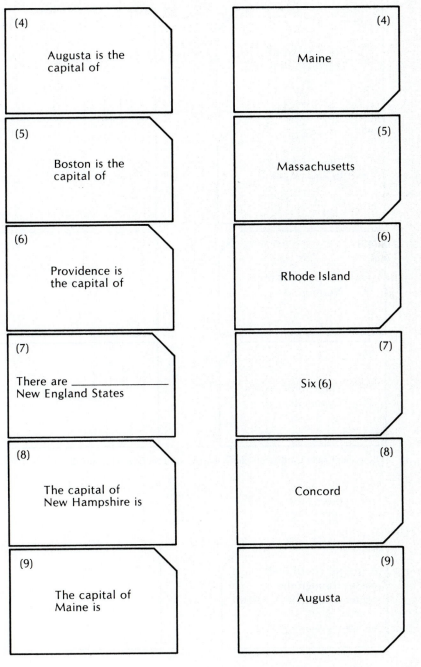

(4) Augusta is the capital of	(4) Maine
(5) Boston is the capital of	(5) Massachusetts
(6) Providence is the capital of	(6) Rhode Island
(7) There are _____ New England States	(7) Six (6)
(8) The capital of New Hampshire is	(8) Concord
(9) The capital of Maine is	(9) Augusta

Continued

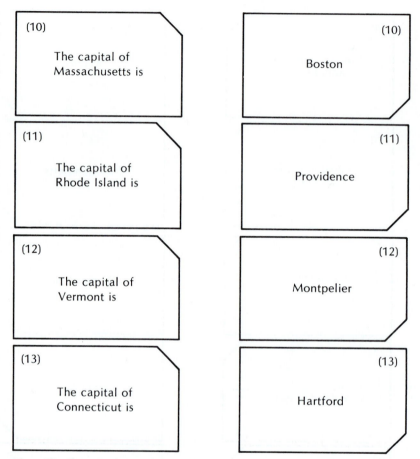

(These Flip Chute Cards were designed by Nora McGee, Howard Beach, New York).

Circumference of a Circle

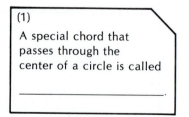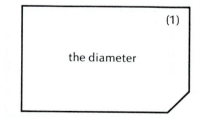

FIGURE 6–11   Flip Chute Cards for Circumference.

FIGURE 6–11 *Continued*

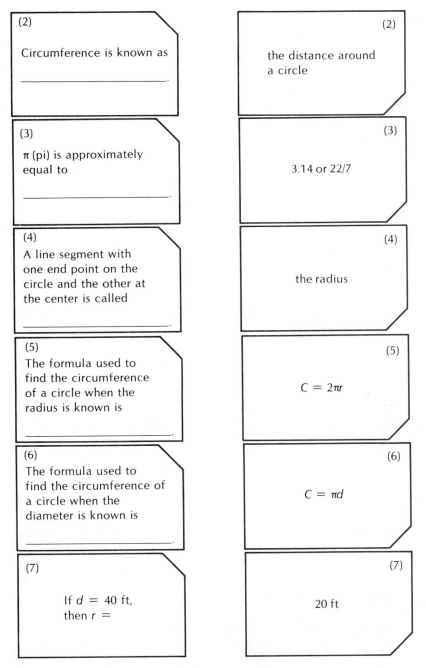

(2)

Circumference is known as

_____.

(2)

the distance around
a circle

(3)

π (pi) is approximately
equal to

_____.

(3)

3.14 or 22/7

(4)

A line segment with
one end point on the
circle and the other at
the center is called

_____.

(4)

the radius

(5)

The formula used to
find the circumference
of a circle when the
radius is known is

_____.

(5)

$C = 2\pi r$

(6)

The formula used to
find the circumference of
a circle when the
diameter is known is

_____.

(6)

$C = \pi d$

(7)

If $d = 40$ ft,
then $r =$

(7)

20 ft

Continued

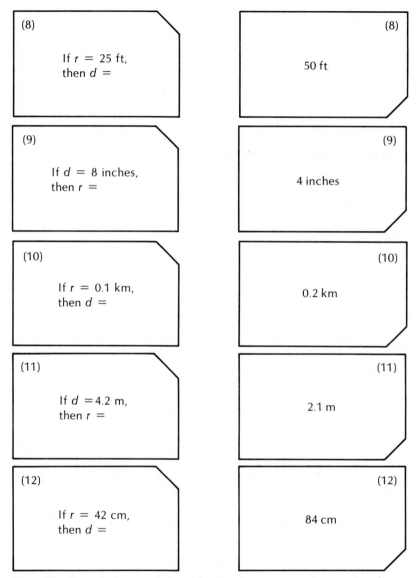

(8)	(8)
If $r = 25$ ft, then $d =$	50 ft

(9)	(9)
If $d = 8$ inches, then $r =$	4 inches

(10)	(10)
If $r = 0.1$ km, then $d =$	0.2 km

(11)	(11)
If $d = 4.2$ m, then $r =$	2.1 m

(12)	(12)
If $r = 42$ cm, then $d =$	84 cm

(These Flip Chute Cards were designed by Daniel J. Purrus, graduate student, St. John's University, New York).

Designing Pic-A-Holes

Pic-A-Holes are more of an introductory than a reinforcement type of re-source. A Pic-A-Hole offers choices from among three options; should a youngster's first or even second choice be incorrect, the self-corrective feature of the device ensures eventual success in a private, nonthreatening environ-ment.

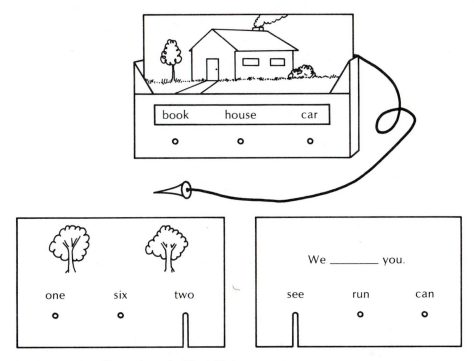

FIGURE 6–12 Illustration of a Pic-A-Hole.
(Created by Dr. Barbara Gardiner, New York City.)

The Pic-A-Hole (Figure 6–12) is similar to a series of cards with printed questions. Students consider answers and look at three possible options at the bottom. Using a tied-on golf tee, they place the point directly below the option they believe to be correct and then attempt to lift the question card. If the answer selected is correct, the card lifts easily and can be removed; if it is incorrect, the card will not budge.

Directions

1. Cut a colorful piece of cardboard or poster board 24⅜ inches by 6½ inches.
2. Following the guide below, measure and mark the cardboard (on the wrong side) to the dimensions given. Use a ballpoint pen and score the lines heavily.

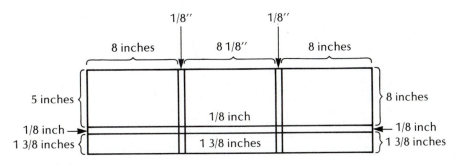

171

3. Remove the 1 ⅜ inch bracketed areas at right and left. Use a ruler and a razor or exacto knife to get a straight edge. The piece of poster board then should look like the following illustration.

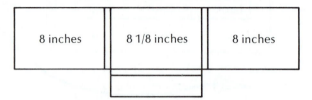

4. Working on the wrong side of the center section only, follow the measurement guide given below.

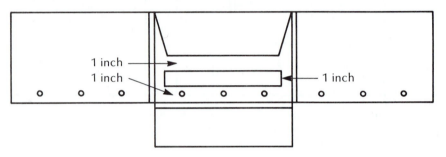

5. Remove the shaded areas with a ruler and razor or exacto knife.
6. Fold on all the drawn lines using a ruler as a guide to obtain sharp, straight fold lines.
7. Punch three holes as shown in the diagram.
8. Place an index card under the center section. Trace the openings onto the card. Remove the same areas from the index card. This will serve as a guide for placement of questions and answers, which can be written on 5 × 8 inch index cards in appropriate places. Punch holes.
9. Using 5 × 8 inch index cards, mark holes and punch them out. Use the guide for the placement of information.
10. Fold over the first side under the center section; then fold up the bottom flap; now fold over the last side. Paste or staple them together, being certain that the bottom flap is in between.

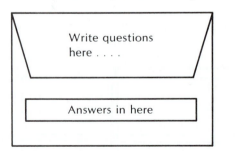

(Pic-A-Hole directions were developed by Dr. Barbara Gardiner.)

Samples
Figures 6–13 and 6–14 show examples of Pic-A-Holes.

Breaking the Map Code

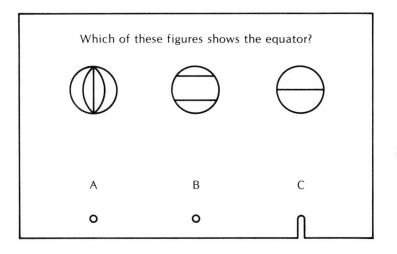

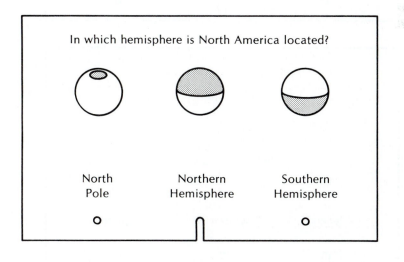

Continued

FIGURE 6–13   Pic-A-Hole for Breaking the Map Code.

FIGURE 6-13 *Continued*

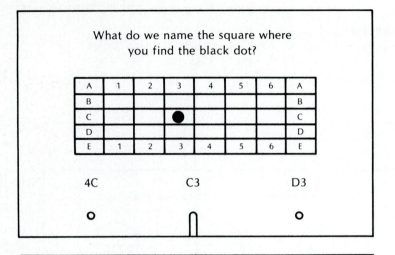

What do we name the square where
you find the black dot?

	1	2	3	4	5	6	
A							A
B							B
C			●				C
D							D
E	1	2	3	4	5	6	E

4C   C3   D3

○   ∩   ○

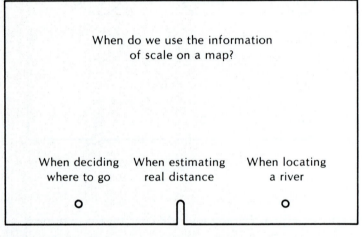

When do we use the information
of scale on a map?

When deciding   When estimating   When locating
where to go   real distance   a river

○   ∩   ○

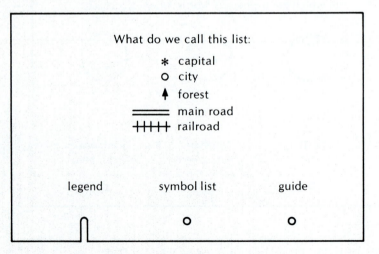

What do we call this list:

     ∗ capital
     ○ city
     ♠ forest
    ═══ main road
  ++++ railroad

legend   symbol list   guide

∩   ○   ○

FIGURE 6-13 *Continued*

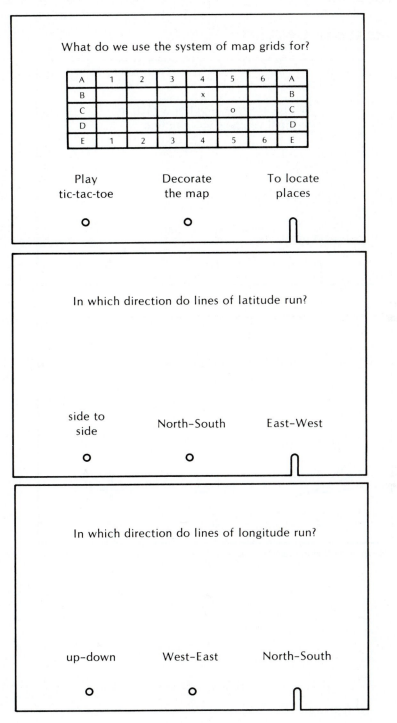

What do we use the system of map grids for?

A	1	2	3	4	5	6	A
B				x			B
C					o		C
D							D
E	1	2	3	4	5	6	E

Play
tic-tac-toe

○

Decorate
the map

○

To locate
places

In which direction do lines of latitude run?

side to
side

○

North–South

○

East–West

In which direction do lines of longitude run?

up–down

○

West–East

○

North–South

Continued

FIGURE 6–13 *Continued*

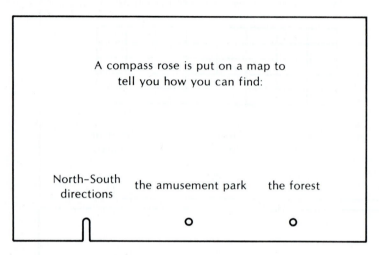

A compass rose is put on a map to
tell you how you can find:

North–South   the amusement park   the forest
directions

○   ○

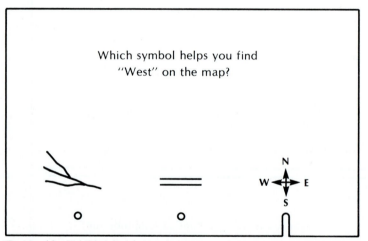

Which symbol helps you find
"West" on the map?

○   ○

○

(Designed by Bohilde Iglesias, Teacher, New York City.)

Magnetism: The Power of Attraction

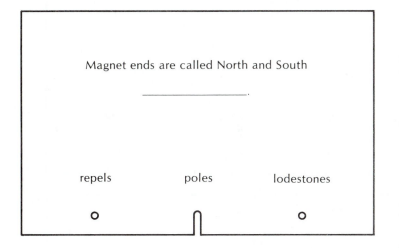

Magnet ends are called North and South

_____.

repels   poles   lodestones

Iron, nickel, and cobalt are examples of metals

that are _____ by magnets.

attracted   repelled   poles

FIGURE 6–14   Pic-A-Hole for Magnetism.

FIGURE 6–14 *Continued*

A magnetic field is the space

_____ a magnet.

inside   around   below

○   ∏   ○

When a magnet uses "pushing power," we say it

_____.

attracts   magnetism   repels

○   ○   ∏

Magnets that are found in nature are called:

lodestones   magnetic fields   staffs

∏   ○   ○

FIGURE 6–14 *Continued*

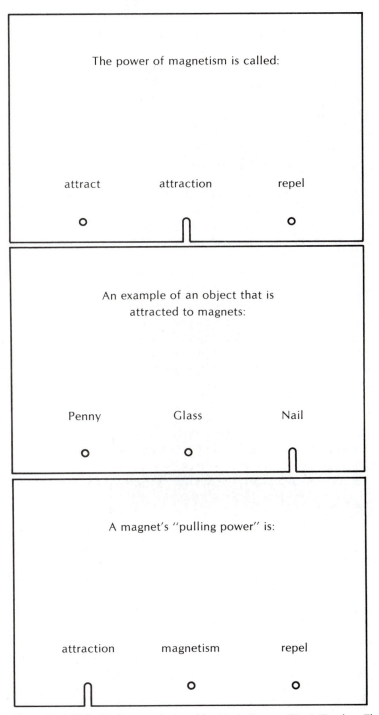

The power of magnetism is called:

attract   attraction   repel

An example of an object that is
attracted to magnets:

Penny   Glass   Nail

A magnet's "pulling power" is:

attraction   magnetism   repel

(These Pic-A-Hole Cards were designed by Maria Turano Giresi, Teacher, The Growing Tree, Ridgefield, Connecticut.)

Designing Electroboards

Although most youngsters pay rapt attention to what they are trying to deci-
pher when the tactile component is added, Electroboards may be the single
resource that consistently holds their attention. They appear to be less tactual
than Learning Circles, where clothespin answers must be sought, handled, and
attached to their matching questions; they require less handling than Task
Cards, which merely need to be shuffled, examined, and then placed side by
side with their correct half. Indeed, Electroboards certainly require no more
tactile involvement than do Flip Chutes, where an answer, once selected, is
placed into the upper slot and caught as it emerges from the bottom opening.
The Pic-A-Hole, if anything, is more tactual, for students must choose the
correct answer and then insert the golf tee into the correct hole, attempt to
pull out the card, place it onto a nearby surface, and then reach for the cards
and tee again.

Electroboards, however, have a bulb that lights up whenever the chosen
answer is correct, and—as with a slot machine or a computer—that facet appears to mesmerize children because the lighted bulb provides immediate visual feedback of the student's success. These resources take longer to make,
but once completed will be worth every moment devoted to them.

Generally speaking, questions are listed on one side of the resource while
answers are listed on the opposite side, but out of order, so that they do not
match correctly. Students hold a two-part continuity or battery tester in their
hands. They attach one prong to the questions they are trying to answer and,
after reading the list of possible answers on the opposite side of the board,
touch what they believe is the correct answer with the second prong. If they
are correct, the bulb lights up; in some instances a bell rings, but the sound
can be disconcerting to some students.

Electroboards and any other tactual resources are particularly delightful
when their outer shapes are in harmony with the subject matter they are trying
to teach. For example, the Electroboard for magnetism could be designed in
the shape of a magnet.

Directions
Creatively vary the outer dimension of each Electroboard so that it reflects
the theme or unit being studied and is easy for the children to locate without
assistance. For example, they will learn that when looking for an Electroboard
dealing with a unit on transportation, its outline will very likely be in the shape
of a car, a train, or a plane. Thus, when they are focusing on a specific theme,
all the tactual resources for that theme should have the same shape. A unit on
the New England states might all be in the shape of a map of the northeastern
section of the United States; a unit on community workers might have a Learning Circle, a set of Task Cards, a Flip Chute, a Pic-A-Hole, and an Electroboard, all in the shape of a firefighter's or police officer's hat.

Electroboards may be used anywhere in the environment. This child enjoys using one at her desk. (Photograph courtesy of the P. K. Yonge Laboratory School, Gainesville, Florida.)

1. Begin with two pieces of poster board or oaktag cut into exactly the same size and shape (12 × 10 inches to 24 × 10 inches).

2. On a piece of paper, list the questions that you want the Electroboard to ask; then list their answers. Count the number of questions and divide the left side of the Electroboard into evenly sectioned spaces so that all the questions fit on the left side.

3. Use a paper hole puncher to make one hole on the left side of the Electroboard for each question you developed. Then punch corresponding holes on the same horizontal level, but on the right side of the answer space (½ inch in and 1 to 2 inches apart).

4. Print the questions and answers separately in large, black capital letters either directly onto the oaktag or poster board or, to be sure of neat, attractive lines, onto double-lined strips (2 × 8 inches) of opaque white correction tape. This tape can be obtained in most large stationery stores. When you are satisfied with the printing of the questions and their corresponding answers, peel the correction tape from its base. Carefully place each question next to one of the prepunched holes on the left side of the developing

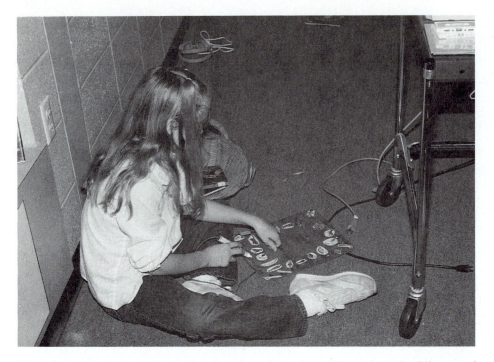

This elementary youngster prefers learning through an Electroboard while seated informally on the floor. Observe such students when their answer correctly matches the question. Watch their eyes light up when the bulb turns on! (Photograph courtesy of St. John's University's Center for the Study of Learning and Teaching Styles, New York.)

Electroboard's face and each answer next to one of the prepunched holes on the right side. Be certain that each question and answer is placed on a horizontal plane with the other and that even spaces remain in between. It is important to randomize the answers so that no answer is on the same horizontal level as its matched question.

5. Turn the oaktag or poster board face down, and on its back create circuits made with aluminum foil strips and masking tape. One at a time, place quarter-inch-wide strips of aluminum foil in lines "connecting" a question with the correct answer and punched holes. Cover each foil strip with three-quarter-inch- to one-inch-wide masking tape, being certain to press both the foil and the masking tape cover so that they (a) completely cover the punched holes and (b) remain permanently fixed. An easy way to be certain that the foil is covered involves laying the appropriate length of masking tape on a desk or table sticky side up, and then placing the foil on the tape.

6. Note the positions of each question-and-answer set so that you can prepare a self-corrective guide in case one is necessary for substitute teachers or aides. Write the name and number of the Electroboard (assuming you have several) at the top of the code. Place the answer key in a secure place where access is available when necessary.

7. Using a continuity tester, which can be purchased in any auto supply or hardware store, check every circuit as it is being constructed to be certain that each is working correctly. Do this by touching each question with one prong of the continuity tester and its related answer with the other prong. If the circuits are put together correctly, the tester's bulb will light. (Remember to use fresh batteries as required in the tester.) Experiment with touching several questions and incorrect answers (one at a time) to be certain that the bulb does not light inappropriately. Remove sharp points if any exist on the tester!

8. Next tape the second, identically shaped and sized piece of oaktag or poster board to the back of the first piece on which you have been doing all this tactile work; the second piece will conceal the circuits so that your students do not know which questions are paired with which answers. Tape the entire perimeter of both cards together, or as Bruno and Jessie suggest (1983, p. 3), "connect the cards using double-faced tape."

Electroboard Variations

Efficiency in developing multiple Electroboards may be achieved by creating blank circuit boards with room for question-and-answer cards to be placed in the middle and attached by using one of the following: (see Figure 6–15):

1. Velcro
2. Plastic binder spines
3. Pocket made of oaktag

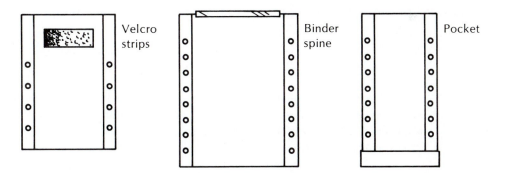

FIGURE 6–15 Three ways of designing blank Electroboards are shown here. Questions and answers can be placed between the aluminum foil contact points to provide different information for different units without constructing totally new Electroboards. Velcro strips, plastic binder spines or holders, and oak tag pockets all can be used to hold posters with questions on one side and out-of-order, mixed-up questions on the other.

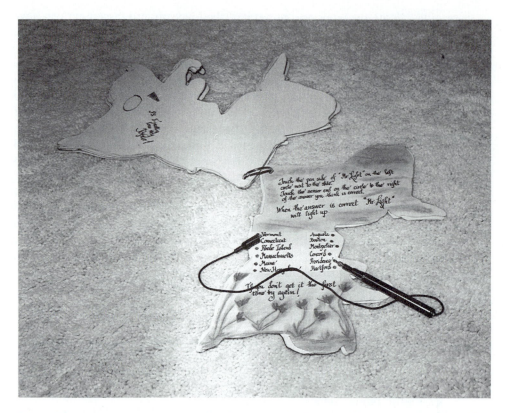

These Electroboards are part of Multisensory Instructional Packages on Traveling Through New England and Magnetism, respectively. Notice how the illustrations and shapes attract the eye and invite usage. (Photographs courtesy of Center for the Study of Learning and Teaching Styles, St. John's University, New York.)

Further, additional circuit patterns are presented by turning the Electroboard upside down, turning it over (where the holes have been punched through and show on both sides), or using both sides as well as the top and bottom (Figure 6–16).

Examples of Electroboards

Figures 6–17 and 6–18 are examples of Electroboards. Laminate or use clear contact paper on all boards after questions and answers are completed but before holes are punched. Insert a paper fastener into each hole for permanence.

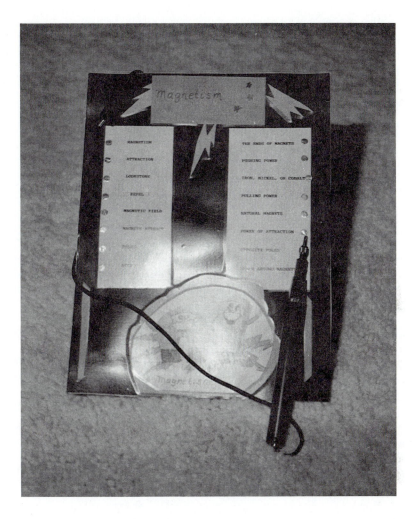

Tactual-Visual Games

Any games that students play by both seeing and moving them with their hands are, in a sense, tactual-visual; they are not always as tactual as are task cards, but they often facilitate learning for youngsters who require some tactual involvement with the learning materials.

"The Mystery Animal" (see Figure 6-19) is one such device and is easy to duplicate at any level. In fact, given an example to study and the following directions, many upper elementary students can make new samples for you.

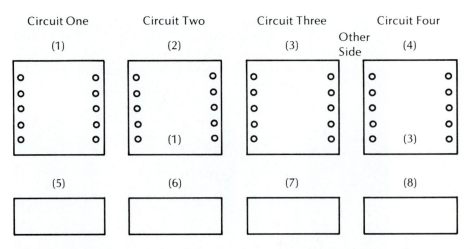

FIGURE 6-16   Circuits can be changed to limit memorization of patterns by turning circui
boards upside-down (circuits one and two), using the other side (circuits three and four), a
turning them sideways (circuits five and six, and circuits seven and eight).

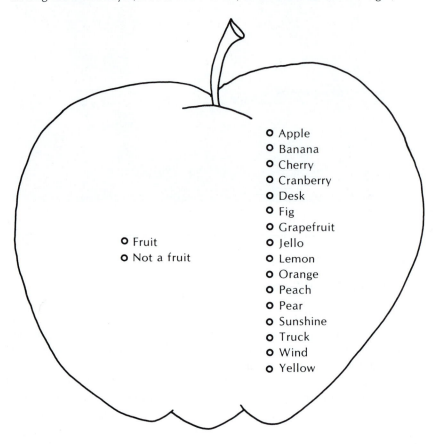

FIGURE 6-17   Samples of a Fruit Electroboard.

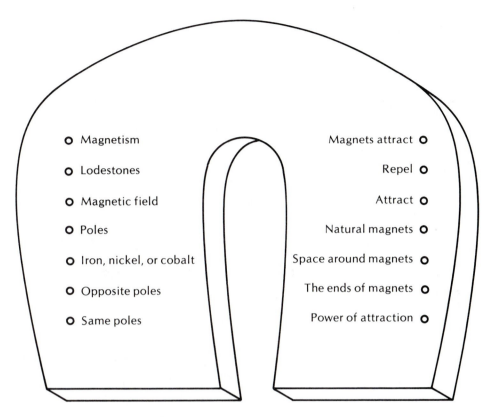

O Magnetism   Magnets attract O

O Lodestones   Repel O

O Magnetic field   Attract O

O Poles   Natural magnets O

O Iron, nickel, or cobalt   Space around magnets O

O Opposite poles   The ends of magnets O

O Same poles   Power of attraction O

FIGURE 6-18   Sample of Magnetism Electroboard.

Materials

- A photograph or illustration of something connected with the theme that your students are studying
- A piece of colored construction paper the same size as the illustration you select. Light colors are preferable.
- Colored felt pens
- Clear contact paper to cover the front and back of the illustration
- A glue stick

Directions

1. Back the illustration by gluing the construction paper to it.
2. On the construction side, print questions all over the paper at varying angles. Turn each question upside down, and beneath it print the answer to it. (Separate each question-and-answer pair with enough space.)
3. With clear contact paper cover both the illustration side and the construction paper side of the game.

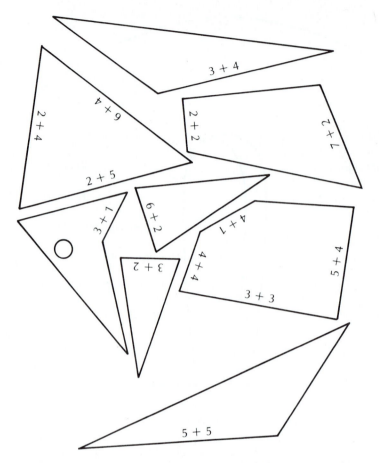

FIGURE 6–19 Mystery Animal Math Puzzle. Place an attractive, colored illustration of an animal onto an 8 × 10 inch poster board or heavy construction paper. Turn the entire item over and develop math examples in which two pairs of different numbers each add up to the same total. Place those two pairs of numbers at adjoining contact points, and then laminate the entire resource on both sides. Neatly cut the rectangle into shapes so that, when students compute which pairs add up to the same total and place them next to each other, the animal illustration will be formed. If you advise the youngsters to piece the matching sections together in the cover of an 8 × 10 inch gift box. When the puzzle has been completed it can be turned over carefully and the Mystery Animal will be revealed!

Once shown how to design tactual/visual games, manipulatively talented elementary children can create these educational resources for themselves and classmates with similar strengths. (Photographs courtesy of Center for the Study of Learning and Teaching Styles, St. John's University, New York.)

4. Cut the illustration into several pieces—each question separated from its answer. (Test it first using a paper sample.)
5. Cover a box or an envelope with construction paper and use it to store the question and answer pieces. Label it to explain the contents and directions for use. If the box cover is large enough, suggest that the students piece together the question and answer sections inside the top of the box. When the written puzzle has been completed, it can be flipped upside down, and the original illustration should be intact.
6. Cover the box or envelope with contact paper to protect it.

Example: The Mystery Animal

Cut out the pieces. Put them together by matching the numbers that add up to the same totals. If you piece them together correctly, you will see a mystery animal.

Step-by-Step Guide to Designing Kinesthetic Activities

Some youngsters can learn only be doing; for them, real-life experiences are the most effective way of absorbing and retaining knowledge. It is easy to teach students to convert pints to quarts and quarts to gallons through baking and cooking, or to teach them inches and feet by helping them to build a scooter or antique doll house, but it is not simple to teach all the skills and information that must be achieved through reality-oriented activities. To begin with, such activities are time-consuming; second, many activities require supervision; finally, we are not used to teaching that way and to do so requires an endless source of creative suggestions. There is, however, a new kind of kinesthetic (whole-body) game that you can design for classroom use, and ever-continuing learning by your slower charges.

Designing Body-Action Games

Many teachers save old things and then use them creatively to instruct their students. Now is the time to locate all the large plastic tablecloths, shower curtains, carpet and furniture coverings, and sails that may be hidden away in basements, attics, garages, and wherever else too-good-to-throw-away things are placed. Old sheets and bath towels may also be pressed into service, but they are not as durable as plastic, and when they are washed the printed matter on them often fades and occasionally disappears altogether. If you are not a collector of old valuables, you may need to either solicit cast-off materials from others or purchase a large sheet of plastic from your neighborhood bargain store.

Materials

- One large sheet of plastic, approximately 4 × 5, 5 × 5, or 5 × 6 feet, or another material within that size range
- Smaller pieces of multicolored plastic that can be cut into decorations and illustrations and then glued or sewn onto the larger sheet
- Black thin-line permanent ink pens
- Black and brightly colored permanent ink felt pens
- Glue that will make plastic adhere to plastic
- Assorted discarded items that, depending on your imagination and creativity, you use as part of the game you design
- Pad and pencil for sketching ideas

Directions

1. Identify the information or skills that you want your students to learn.

2. Consider ways in which you can either introduce that information or reinforce it through a body action game in which selected students can hop or jump or merely move from one part of the large sheet to another as they are exposed to the major (or finer) points of the topic.

3. Sketch a design on a sheet of paper to work it out before you begin cutting, pasting, or sewing.

4. When you are satisfied with your conceptualization of the game, plan a layout of the various sections on the plastic sheet that you will use; consider the placement of articles, and list the additional items that you can use, noting the ways in which you can use them.

5. In pencil, lightly sketch on the large sheet where you will paste each item, the dimensions that you must plan for, and where you will place key directions.

6. Cut the smaller plastic pieces into appropriate shapes or figures and glue them onto the larger sheet.

7. With a felt pen that will not wash off, trace over those penciled lines that you wish to keep.

8. Develop a set of questions and answers or tasks that students may complete as they use the body action game. Then either develop an answer card so that students may correct themselves or color-code or picture-code the questions and answers so that the game is self-corrective.

9. If you teach either very young children or poor readers, develop a tape that will tell them how to play the game, what the game will teach them, and how they can recognize that they have learned whatever it is the game is designed to teach.

Kinesthetic children literally learn best "on the move." Large floor games, footsteps (which they walk over as they memorize), and movement directions promote learning for these children, who do not concentrate when sitting still. Large, oversized Pic-A-Holes or task cards often provide the mobility that helps these children remember what they experience. (Photographs courtesy of Center for the Study of Learning and Teaching Styles, St. John's University, New York.)

10. If your students are capable of reading and following printed directions, print or type a set of directions for them and attach it to the sheet (perhaps in a pocket that you cut out and glue or sew onto its underside).

Examples

For an instructional package on "Perimeters," several activities were designed that taught students to find the perimeter of a series of different shapes. A body action game was created for an introductory activity.

Directions

1. To play this game, you must find the perimeter of each shape as you come to it. Travel along the path according to the direction on the an-

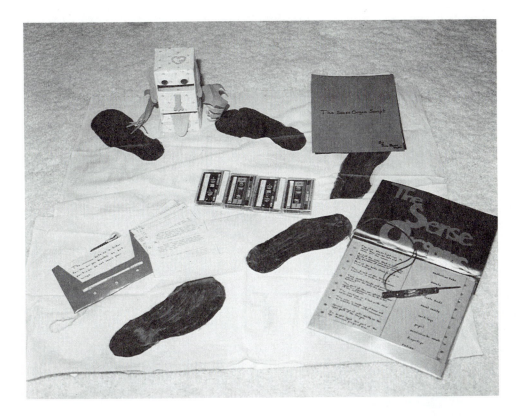

swer side of each card. Begin by finding the perimeter of the first shape that is part of the path.

2. Look at Answer Card 1 in the pocket on the underside of the game. If your answer is correct, hop on one foot to the next shape. If you are not correct, take "baby steps" to the next shape.

3. You now should be standing on the yellow shape. It has five sides. Three of its sides measure 12 inches each, and two of its sides are 10 inches each. What is the perimeter of the yellow shape?

The directions guided students through a series of varied geometric shapes, permitting them to check their answers and, if they had computed incorrectly, to learn why they were wrong. When the body game was completed, a duplicated sheet attached to the larger package tested them on their ability to determine the perimeter of a variety of shapes. The teacher then checked their final assessment responses.

For a social studies unit on "The Battle of Manila Bay: May 1, 1898," a body action game was designed that duplicated the geographical maps of the South China Sea, the Philippines, and Manila Bay. Students were asked to reenact the first and second battles in sequence using toy ships and other replicas.

For a unit on westward expansion, a map of the entire United States, including many geographical representations and divisions representing the acquisition of territory, was recreated on an 8 × 10 foot plastic sheet. Students

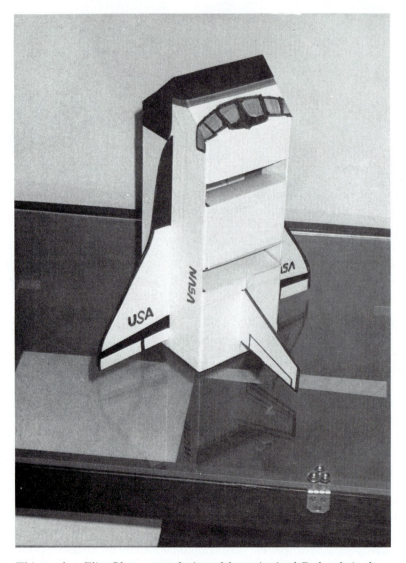

This rocket Flip Chute was designed by principal Roland Andrews and students at the Brightwood Elementary School in Greensboro, North Carolina. (Photograph courtesy of Angela Klavas.)

were directed to play a game in which they identified which territories were added and when, what their contribution to the country ultimately was, and the value of those contributions to present-day students.

A Final Word on Kinesthetic Resources

Try them! Kinesthetic games can be invented weekly by you and your students. One teacher decided to use her students' energy by creating "relay math" using Velcro darts and a board that included many multiplication questions the first day, division questions the second day, and so forth. Students lined up in teams of four while other students kept score. Each student raced to the target board ready to answer after hitting a specific question. Boards can be designed with items like "6 × 7"; "12 − 3"; "find the verb"; "use the correct punctuation mark."

One sixth-grade class built pinball machines with nails, rubber bands, marbles, a clothespin, and discarded wood. Each semicircle of nails was labeled with a point score pile. If the question was answered correctly, the student added points to his score and could "shoot" again.

Granted, extensive time and effort is needed to develop such body action games. But if you find that students who rarely achieved before they were exposed to this method suddenly begin to learn and to enjoy learning, won't you agree that the outcomes are well worth the input? Besides, the sheets can be used over and over again for different sets of facts and skills by merely changing the direction and the cards that are given to the students.

A Final Word on Tactual Resources

When you have measured and cut the patterns for your first Pic-A-Hole, Flip Chute, Electroboard, and set of Task Cards, *before* you put the sections together to complete each resource, trace the outlines and make several copies. Those copies then can be used as *patterns* which your students trace and merely fold together to create their own personal tactual resources. Once the children have made a Flip Chute or Pic-A-Hole, they need only change the cards for each new unit you teach. Creating their own tactual resources and learning how to use them is the first concrete step toward teaching youngsters to teach themselves.

Chapter 10 includes many more suggestions for helping children to become self-directed learners. If you are global, you may wish to skim through that section of Chapter 10 now. However, if you are analytic, take one step at a time and read Chapter 7 next!

7

Designing Programmed Learning Sequences (PLSs) to Respond to Individual Learning Styles

Using Programmed Learning Sequences for Selected Students

A second basic method for individualizing instruction is to program material so that it may be learned in small, simple steps without the direct supervision of an adult. Like any other method, programmed instruction enhances only selected learning style characteristics and therefore should not be prescribed for all students.

Commercial programs are designed around preselected concepts and skills, called *objectives* that must be mastered by each student. Objectives range from the simple to the complex and are sequenced so that, after taking a pretest, students are assigned only those that they have not achieved before being exposed to the program. Each youngster is then introduced to the programmed materials at the point where the remaining objectives are either partially repetitive or introductory. All students proceed through the identical sequence but may pace themselves and use the program when and where they prefer to study. Programmed instruction is individualized only in terms of diagnosis, prescription, level, and, when used flexibly, selected aspects of learning style.

Programs that have been commercially produced have had only limited effectiveness because they are visual—similar to short workbooks—and therefore appeal to students who read fairly well and who can retain information by seeing. The firms that produce such programs maintain that cassettes and filmstrips occasionally supplement their resources. When multimedia materials are available, they should be used to facilitate the program's effectiveness

197

for those youngsters who are auditory while serving as reinforcement for those who are visual.

In actual practice, students are each given a program for which they are responsible and, as the various objectives and their related tests are completed, gradual progress is made toward completing the material. Unless learners need and seek assistance, they may be virtually isolated for long periods of instructional time. It is also possible for them to engage in hours of study without benefiting from either adult or peer interaction. There are youngsters who prefer to work alone, but the Poirier methods instituted at the University of California verified that for many students, retention was increased after peer discussions of what was being learned. A teacher who chooses to use programmed materials for students who are peer-oriented may overcome the isolation factor, however, by incorporating selected small-group techniques into the programs—such as Team Learning, Circle of Knowledge, Group Analysis, Case Study, Simulation, and Brainstorming.

Learning Style Characteristics Responsive to Programmed Learning Sequences

Because programmed materials are used independently (alone or with one classmate), it is important that those students to whom this resource is assigned are motivated to learn the contents of the package. They should also be persistent, suggesting that they normally would continue using the materials until the program has been completed. Should they experience difficulty, they either will review the previous frames and continue to try to progress or they will seek assistance from appropriate persons. Programmed instruction also requires responsibility from students; should they daydream or neglect to work toward completion of the materials, they will be wasting valuable instructional time.

By organizing everything that should be learned so that only one item at a time is presented, the sequenced materials in each program provide a great deal of structure. A student cannot proceed until what must be achieved at each stage has been fully understood, as demonstrated through a short quiz at the end of each frame or page. Youngsters who prefer to be directed and told exactly what to do will feel at ease with programmed packages, while creative students may find them boring and, thus, irritating.

Programmed learning is ideally suited to youngsters who *prefer to work either alone or with a friend*. It is also a perfect match for students who learn best by seeing and for those who need to read and, perhaps, reread materials before they can be absorbed. It also is effective for tactual students who are motivated.

Teachers who believe that selected students are not motivated, persistent, or responsible, but who recognize that they are slow achievers, visual or tactual learners, and in need of structure, should experiment with programmed instruction. Because this strategy presents concepts and skills simply, gradually, and repeatedly, and may be used alone—without causing either the embarrassment or the pressure that emerges when one has difficulty achieving among one's peers—many youngsters often *become* motivated, persistent, or responsible when using a program. When the "right" method is matched correctly with the "right" student, increased academic achievement and improved attitudes toward learning are likely to result.

Learning Style Characteristics to Which Programmed Learning Sequences (PLSs) Can Be Accommodated

Because a program may be used in a classroom, in a library, in a corridor, or in an instructional resource center as well as at home, it can accommodate each student's environmental and physical preferences. For example, the package can be taken to a silent area if quiet is desired, or it may be used in the midst of classroom activity when the learner can block out sound. It can be moved to either a warm section of a room—near a radiator, perhaps, or to a cool area. It can be studied at a desk or on a carpet, either in a well-lit area or away from the bright sunshine. A student may snack or not as he or she works, may use the package at any time of day that is convenient, and may take a break or two if mobility is necessary. Since the program is visual, it will utilize the perceptual strengths of students who learn best by reading or seeing. For auditory youngsters, a teacher should add a tape that repeats orally what the text teaches visually. When students are either tactual or kinesthetic learners, the teacher should add instructional resources like Pic-A-Hole games to introduce or reinforce the program's objectives through those senses. For students who learn slowly or with difficulty, it is wise to supplement a visual programmed sequence with three other types of perceptual resources—auditory, tactual, and kinesthetic. When appropriate, a PLS may be completed by pairs or a team of students. When a student is tactually strong, *introduce* difficult information through tactual resources and *reinforce* through a PLS!

Case Studies Describing Students Whose Learning Styles Are Complemented by Programmed Learning Sequences

1. Only the sound of his own name was able to break through into his thoughts. As Mrs. Diamond's voice repeated the question, Kerry sat up in his seat. He had been so engrossed in contemplating the effects of the civil rights movement—an item on which the teacher had been focusing ten minutes earlier—that his imagination had carried him from the advent of slavery in the United States to the psychological implications of being a despised minority in a majority culture.

Mrs. Diamond's voice was sympathetic. "Do you know the answer?" Kerry sat up quickly in embarrassment.

"I'm sorry," he answered. "I was thinking about something else."

"What?" she asked. He merely shrugged. He was reluctant to reveal that he was mentally involved with an item that had been discussed a while before—one only tangentially related to what the class was studying.

"Please keep up with us," the teacher urged, and slowly shook her head in exasperation.

Students who are motivated to learn but who need more time to consider items or to concentrate than is usually permitted by group instruction may learn more effectively through programmed instruction.

2. Mark could not work out the fifth example. He pulled his text out from the desk and fingered through its pages until he found the chapter that explained how to convert fractions. He read the section related to that process and still was not certain of how to apply the rule. He leaned over toward a classmate and asked for assistance. When the directions for solving the problem were clear to him, he turned back to the papers on his desk and continued working.

Students who are persistent—who continue working toward the completion of an assignment and find ways to do so—usually respond well to programmed instruction.

3. Barbara's elbow was on her desk, her forehead rested on the fingers of her clenched hand, and her eyes had just closed tightly. She was trying to reconstruct the page she had read, which described the elements of a short story. Suddenly she recalled the page and was able to "see" the listing of elements. She relaxed, picked up her pen, and began to answer the text questions.

Students who are visual or tactual learners—who remember more by reading and seeing or touching than they do by listening—usually respond well to programmed instruction.

4. Tim was having a great time with the kids on his committee. As members tried to find the information for their assignment, he collected their pens, pencils, and notes and hid them inside his desk. When the boys reconvened to decide on how they would present their report, Tim alternated between wandering around the room and tipping his chair to see how far back it could go without falling. When the teacher cautioned him to settle down and work with the group, he picked up a pencil and began to organize the presentation.

Students who do not work well in groups may work better alone knowing that they, personally, are responsible for completing an assignment. Such youngsters may respond well to either programs, contracts, or instructional packages.

5. Claire was at her teacher's side again. "Mr. Dawes, am I doing this right?" she asked.

"You asked the same question five minutes ago!" the teacher responded.

"I know," Claire answered, "but I want to be sure!"

Students who require structure—who need to know exactly what to do and how to do it—usually respond well to programmed instruction.

Programmed Learning: Controversy and Criticisms

At one time or another, all instructional methods have been criticized. Few people recognize that no one strategy is effective for everyone and that few methods will ensure academic achievement for a majority of learners. The controversy surrounding programmed instruction has had many dimensions, but it is important to recognize that in no published research studies concerning this strategy have students' learning styles been identified prior to their assignment to programmed materials. Therefore, in all the investigations, achievement results were analyzed with no reference to whether this method could be an effective way of learning for the individual students involved in the studies.

Ideally, students should be analyzed to determine their learning styles. Those whose data indicate that they could function well with programmed learning—those who are motivated, persistent, responsible, and in need of structure, and who prefer learning alone or in a pair and are visually or tactually oriented—should be assigned a programmed package. For those students, academic achievement should be excellent. It is fallacious to assign programmed materials indiscriminately and then to compare the results of that experiment, for the youngsters whose learning style cannot be complemented by programming cannot learn well through that method.

It is this major deficiency that diminishes the findings of researchers who in the past conducted investigations into the effects of programmed materials. For example, Roderick and Anderson (1968) found that achievement levels of undergraduates who used a programmed psychology unit were no different from the scores achieved by students who used a written summary presented in conventional textbook form. These researchers noted, too, that it took four times longer to complete the program than to read the summaries, but they ignored the importance of the program strategy that required that, in addition to reading the material, the students had to consider each item and respond to questions concerning it, and could not advance without complete mastery of each previous phase. Obviously such a procedure takes longer, but numerous studies verify that it also helps students to internalize the information and to increase retention.

To his credit, Kress (1966) appears to have recognized that, normally, students who prefer to learn by themselves will do well with programmed materials. As early as 1966, he cautioned that learners who lacked the necessary independent study skills to work with programs under individual, self-paced conditions should not be permitted to do so. Gotkin's (1963) observations of boredom among youngsters who worked on programs in isolation for prolonged periods of time may also have been related to the concept that some students prefer to learn alone, while others, in contrast, prefer to study with peers. Had the learning styles of the students in these studies been tested, the data might have revealed that those who preferred to work alone were not bored, whereas those who preferred either paired or grouped learning or, possibly, adult instruction, could not be successful with this type of method unless it were revised to permit such options.

In addition, students who are neither motivated nor persistent will find it difficult to acquire the focusing strategy required of those who learn successfully through programming. Indeed, researchers contend that under certain circumstances stereotyped and repetitious use of prompted frames can impair the effectiveness of the materials themselves. This research suggests that students often begin to respond on the basis of the prompt alone and do not actually pay attention to the content. Finally, programmed learning should be recognized as a strategy that appeals to visual learners, and that those who require auditory, tactual, or kinesthetic techniques will benefit from a program only after these supplements have been added. (See Chapter 6 for directions on developing such materials.)

Basic Principles of Programmed Learning Sequences

Programmed instruction is designed on the basis of several important principles that tend to facilitate academic achievement for students with selected learning style elements. All programs tend to follow a similar pattern, which includes each of the following characteristics:

1. *Only one item is presented at a time.* A single concept or skill that should be mastered is introduced through a simple written statement. After reading the material, the learner is required to answer a question or two to demonstrate that what has been introduced on that frame (page, section) has been understood. This procedure prevents the lesson from advancing faster than the student, and it does not permit the student to fall behind. The youngster may learn as quickly as he or she is capable of comprehending the material, or as slowly and with as much repetition as may be needed. No one may continue into a subsequent frame or phase of the program until each previous one has been mastered.

Presenting one item at a time if effective for the analytic youngster who wants to learn (is motivated), who will continue trying (is persistent), and who wants to do what is required (is responsible). For students in need of structure, being exposed to one item at a time breaks the content into small phases and the process into short steps that can be mastered gradually. Understandably, this process is not effective for the student who needs to be exposed to a gestalt of the information—who, rather than piecing a totality together bit by bit, prefers to develop an overall view of the end product. It is also inappropriate for those who cannot continue to work with the same set of materials for any continuing amount of time and who need diversity and variety. In addition, it appears to be a method that does not attract and hold creative students who want to add their own knowledge and special talents to what is being learned before they have accomplished the entire task.

2. *The student is required to be an active, rather than a passive, learner.* Unlike large-group instruction, where a student may merely sit and appear to be listening, programming requires that a response be made to questions related to each introduced item. Youngsters cannot progress through the program without responding, and only accurate answers permit continuation of this learning process.

3. *The student is immediately informed of the correctness of each response.* As soon as a youngster has read the frame, he or she is required to answer a question based on the material that has just been read. The moment that the student's response has been recorded, the youngster may turn to a section in the program where the correct answer is stated. The student, therefore, is immediately made aware of the accuracy or inaccuracy of the response. This technique of "immediate reinforcement" is a highly effective teaching strategy with most learners.

4. *The student may not continue into the next phase of a program until each previous phase has been understood and mastered.* When the program reveals that a student's response to the questions related to each frame are correct, the student is directed to continue into the next section (frame, page, or phase). When students' responses are not correct, they are directed either to restudy the previously read frames or to turn to another section of the program that will explain the material that has not been understood in a different way. Because each phase of the program must be mastered before students are permitted to continue into the next phase, learners do not move ahead aimlessly while grasping only parts of a concept or topic. Their base of knowledge is solid before they are exposed to either new ideas or related ones.

5. *The student is exposed to material that gradually progresses from the easy to the more difficult.* Frames are written so that the first few in a series introduce what should be learned in an uncomplicated, direct manner. Gradually, as the student's correct answers demonstrate his or her increasing understanding of what is being taught, more difficult aspects of the topic are introduced. Through this technique, students are made to feel both comfortable and successful with the beginning phases of each program and their confidence in their own ability to achieve is bolstered. Youngsters who find themselves achieving are likely to continue in the learning process.

6. *As the student proceeds in the program, fewer hints and crutches are provided.* Programming uses a system of "fading," or gradually withdrawing easy questions or hints (repeated expressions, illustrations, color coding, and similar crutches) so that the student's developing knowledge is tested precisely. This technique enables the teacher to accurately assess the youngster's progress and mastery of the material.

Step-by-Step Guide to Designing a Programmed Learning Sequence

Developing a program is not difficult, but it does require that you organize the topic that will be taught into a logical, easy-to-follow sequence. Begin with step 1 and gradually move through each of the remaining steps until you have completed your first program. Each consecutive program will become easier and easier to design. By their questions and responses, students will provide direct feedback on how to revise and improve your initial efforts. Subsequent programs will require fewer revisions.

Step 1   Begin by identifying a topic, concept, or skill that you want to teach. A good choice would be something that most youngsters in your classes need to learn. Since all students are not capable of learning at the same time, in the same way, and at the same speed, a program is one way of permitting individuals to self-pace themselves with materials whenever they are ready to achieve. Thus, some youngsters may use this program early in the semester, while others will use it later. Some will use it to learn before the remainder of the class is exposed to a new idea, and others will use it to reinforce an idea that you have already taught—but which they did not master.

Step 2   Write the name of the topic, concept, or skill that you have decided to teach as a heading at the top of a blank sheet of paper. Add a subtitle that is humorous or related to a real-life experience to appeal to global learners. Plan to design the covers in a shape that represents the topics to appeal to the tactual children. If you can include some humor, it, too, will appeal to the more global students.

Examples

- Electricity: A Shocking Experience
- Math IV: Divide and Conquer
- Graphing: Get the Point
- The Mind and the Brain: Or—Getting Your Head Together!

Step 3   Translate the heading that you have written at the top of the sheet into an introductory sentence that explains to the youngsters using the program exactly what they should be able to do after they have mastered what the materials are designed to teach.

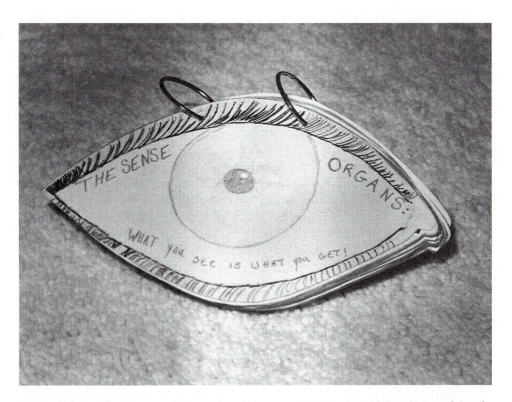

If possible, a Programmed Learning Sequence (PLS) should be designed in the shape of the subject matter it is trying to teach. It also should have both a straight analytic title and a humorous global subtitle. Thus, this PLS on ''The Sense Organs: What You See Is What You Get!'' was created in the shape of a human eye. (Photograph courtesy of Center for the Study of Learning and Teaching Styles, St. John's University, New York.)

Examples

- By the time you finish this program, you should be able to recognize *adjectives* and identify the *nouns* that each of the adjectives modifies.
- When you have completed this program, you should be able to explain at least five (5) ways in which your life is *different* from a desert child's life and at least five (5) ways in which your lives are *similar*.
- This program will teach you to recognize at least five (5) geometric shapes and to spell each of their names correctly. You also will be able to draw each of the different shapes.
- I am so pleased that you are going to work with this program, because it will teach you how to:

    1. Punctuate a sentence correctly.
    2. Write a series of correctly punctuated sentences to form a paragraph.

Step 4   List all the prerequisites for using the program effectively.

Examples

- Before you use this program, you should be familiar with the meanings of each of the following words: *desert, nomad, oasis, arid, mirage.*
- Be certain that you begin using this program either on or near a large table so that you will have ample room to use these materials and the tape recorder at the same time.

Since you may recognize that certain knowledges or skills are, indeed, prerequisite after you have moved beyond step 4, leave space on your paper so that you may insert additions as they come to mind.

Step 5   Create a global story, fantasy, cartoon, or humorous beginning that relates to the topic. Place this global opening just before the information and question frames begin. (See sample programs for global openings.)

Step 6   Decide which of the two basic types of programming you will use.

Type 1: Linear Programming
This type of programming presents material in a highly structured sequence. Each part of the sequence is called a *frame*, and each frame builds upon the one immediately preceding it. Each frame ends with an item that requires an answer—in either a completion or a multiple-choice format. Prior to the introduction of each subsequent frame, the answer to the previous frame is supplied. Program efficiency increases when the correct answer is accompanied by an explanation. Additional comprehension is developed when the incorrect answers also are accompanied by explanations (See Figure 7–1).

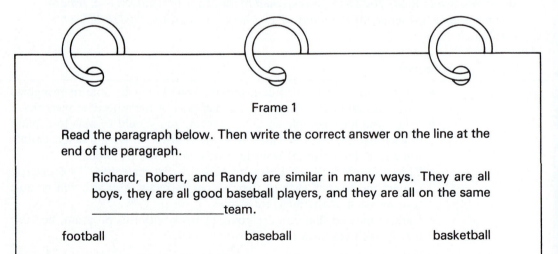

Frame 1

Read the paragraph below. Then write the correct answer on the line at the end of the paragraph.

Richard, Robert, and Randy are similar in many ways. They are all boys, they are all good baseball players, and they are all on the same _____team.

football   baseball   basketball

FIGURE 7–1   This example of linear programming builds reading comprehension step by step through the provision of correct answers on the back of each frame accompanied by explanations.

Back of Frame 1

Answer: baseball

> The paragraph tells us that the three boys are good *baseball* players. It does not tell us whether or not they play football or basketball.

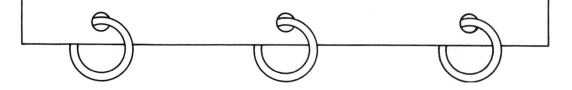

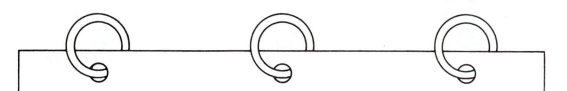

Frame 2

Write the correct answer on the line at the end of the paragraph.

> Richard, Robert, and Randy are all fourteen. They enjoy many sports. In addition to baseball, they each play_____.

cooking   dancing   basketball

Back of Frame 2

Answer: basketball

> Boys can cook or dance, but we do not say that anyone can "play cooking" or "play dancing." Also, the paragraph stated that they enjoy sports, and basketball is a sport; cooking and dancing are not.

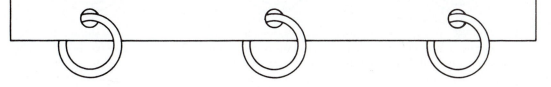

Type 2: Intrinsic Programming

Intrinsic programming also presents material in a highly structured sequence, but the major difference between linear and intrinsic types is that the intrinsic programming recognizes that some youngsters can move through learning experiences faster than others can, and it permits those who score correct answers to skip over some of the reinforcement frames.

When students may bypass frames that teach the same aspect of a subject, the system is called *branching*. Branching, in effect, permits a faster rate of self-pacing.

When a student answers a question incorrectly, he must continue from one frame to the next, to the next, and so on until every frame in the entire program has been completed. When a student studies several introductory frames and then answers the questions correctly, he may branch over additional reinforcement frames if the program is an intrinsic one (See Figure 7–2).

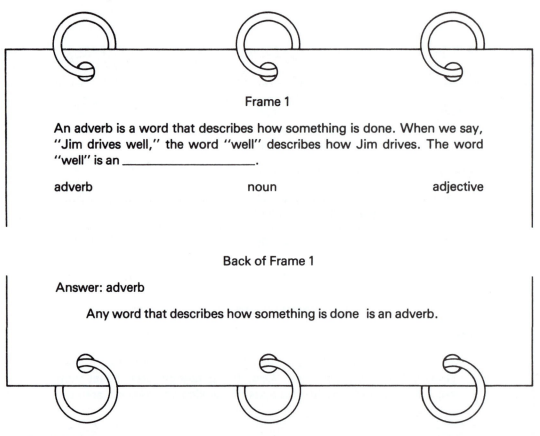

Frame 1

An adverb is a word that describes how something is done. When we say, "Jim drives well," the word "well" describes how Jim drives. The word "well" is an _____.

adverb   **noun**   **adjective**

Back of Frame 1

Answer: adverb

Any word that describes how something is done is an adverb.

FIGURE 7-2 Intrinsic programming permits *branching,* a term that indicates a student may bypass one or more frames when a correct answer is given. This example outlines how branching is included within a structured sequence on adverbs.

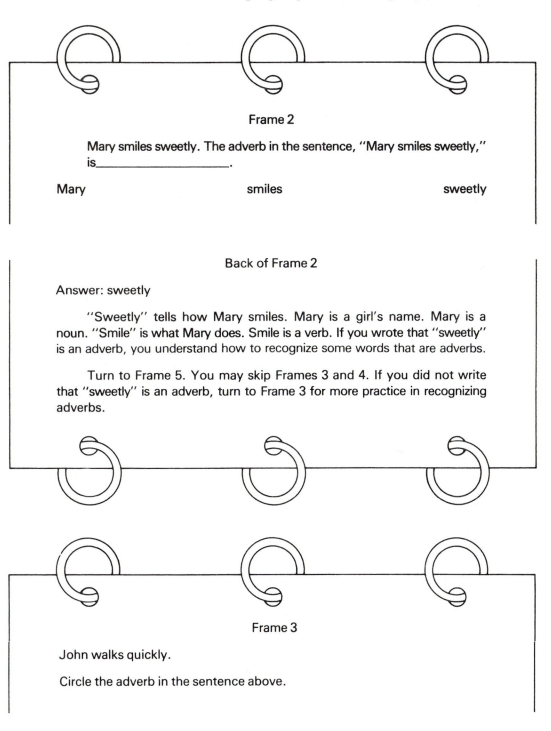

Frame 2

Mary smiles sweetly. The adverb in the sentence, "Mary smiles sweetly," is_____.

Mary   smiles   sweetly

Back of Frame 2

Answer: sweetly

"Sweetly" tells how Mary smiles. Mary is a girl's name. Mary is a noun. "Smile" is what Mary does. Smile is a verb. If you wrote that "sweetly" is an adverb, you understand how to recognize some words that are adverbs.

Turn to Frame 5. You may skip Frames 3 and 4. If you did not write that "sweetly" is an adverb, turn to Frame 3 for more practice in recognizing adverbs.

Frame 3

John walks quickly.

Circle the adverb in the sentence above.

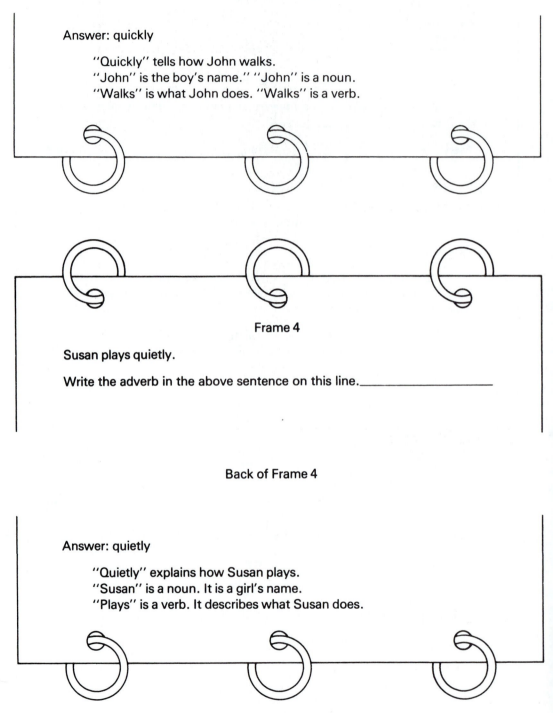

Back of Frame 3

Answer: quickly

"Quickly" tells how John walks.
"John" is the boy's name." "John" is a noun.
"Walks" is what John does. "Walks" is a verb.

Frame 4

Susan plays quietly.

Write the adverb in the above sentence on this line._____

Back of Frame 4

Answer: quietly

"Quietly" explains how Susan plays.
"Susan" is a noun. It is a girl's name.
"Plays" is a verb. It describes what Susan does.

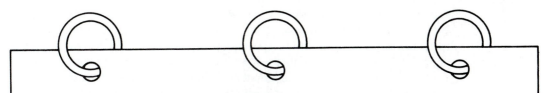

Frame 5

Circle the two adverbs in the next sentence.

The boys were playing quietly and nicely.

Back of Frame 5

Answers: quietly and nicely

"The" is an article.
"Boys" is a noun.
"Were" and "playing" are verbs. They tell what the boys were doing.
"And" is a conjunction.

If you had both answers correct, turn to Frame 8. If you did not have both "quietly" and "nicely" correct, turn to Frame 6.

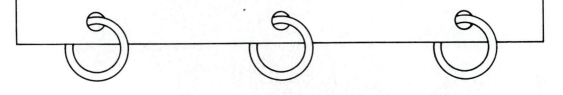

Step 7   Outline how you plan to teach the topic. Use short, simple sentences, if possible. Most people have two different vocabularies: One is used for speaking, the other for writing. When you begin to outline your program, make believe that you are speaking to the student who will have the most trouble learning this material. Use simple words and sentences. Then write exactly the words that you use when you act out the way you would teach this material if you were actually talking to that youngster. In other words, use your speaking vocabulary rather than your professional writing vocabulary to develop the program.

Step 8 Divide the sentences in your outline into frames. Frames are small sections of the topic that teach part of the idea, skill, or information. After listing the sentences that teach, ask a question that relates to the material. The student's answer will demonstrate his or her growing understanding of the subject. Think small! Most people who begin to write programs try to cover too much in a frame. Keep it a simple, small part of the total knowledge represented by your instructional objectives. In some cases you may wish to start with a simple generalization and move to specific examples and applications.

Pose fairly easy-to-answer questions in the first two or three frames to:

- Build a student's self-confidence;
- Demonstrate to the student that he or she can learn independently through the program; and
- Provide the student with a couple of successful experiences by using the process of programmed learning (Figure 7–3).

Step 9 Using a 5 × 8 inch index card to represent each frame, develop a sequence that teaches a subject and, simultaneously, tests the student's growing knowledge of it.

Step 10 Refine each index card frame.

1. Review the sequence to be certain that it is logical and does not teach too much on each frame.

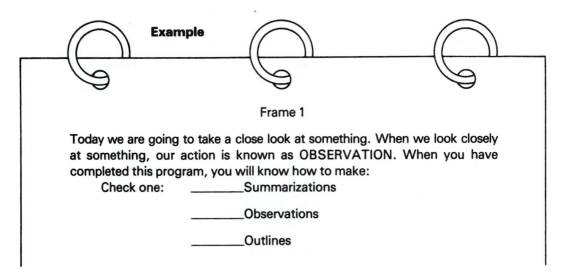

Example

Frame 1

Today we are going to take a close look at something. When we look closely at something, our action is known as OBSERVATION. When you have completed this program, you will know how to make:

Check one: _____Summarizations

_____Observations

_____Outlines

FIGURE 7–3 Initial frames in a sequence should be simple and concise. Think ''small''! This example on vocabulary building is an easy-to-answer frame early in the program.

2. Check the spelling, grammar, and punctuation of each frame.
3. Examine the vocabulary to be certain that it is understandable by the lowest achievement youngsters who may use the program. Avoid colloquialisms that are acceptable in conversation but are less than professional in written form. Remember to use good oral language as opposed to good written language.
4. Reread the entire series to be certain that each frame leads to the next one, and so on.

Step 11 *When you are satisfied with the content, sequence, and questions on the frames, add colorful illustrations to clarify the main point on each index card.* It you do not wish to draw, use magazine cutouts or gift wrapping paper to graphically supplement the most important sections of the text.

Step 12 *Read the written material on each frame onto a cassette so that poor readers may use the program by listening to the frames being read to them as they simultaneously read along.* (See Chapter 6 for directions on making a tape.)

Step 13 *Ask three or four of your students to try the program, one at a time.* Observe each youngster using the material and try to identify whether any errors, omissions, or areas of difficulty exist. Correct anything that requires improvement.

Step 14 *If necessary, revise the program on the basis of your observations of student usage.*

Step 15 *Laminate each of the index cards that make up the program or cover them with clear Contact paper.* Student use will cause the index cards to deteriorate unless they are protected by a covering. Laminated programs have lasted for years and can be cleaned with warm water and soap. They can be written on with grease pencils or water-soluble felt pens and then erased for use by another youngster.

Step 16 (optional) *Add a tactual activity in game form for reinforcement of the most important information in the program* (see Chapter 6). The program, as designed through step 14, will respond only to youngsters who learn through either their visual or auditory senses. If you can add tactual reinforcement through materials such as Task Cards, Learning Circles, or an Electroboard, you will be providing youngsters who need to learn through their sense of touch with a method appropriate for them. You thus will be adding to the effectiveness of the program and increasing the number of students who can learn successfully through it.

Step 17 *Ask additional students to use the program.*

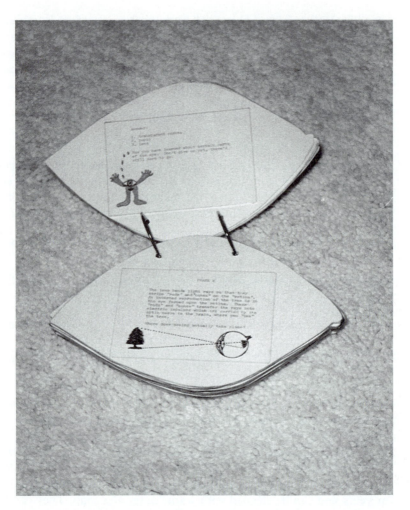

This PLS teaches about the human eye. Its frames contain many illustrations and supplementary tactual activities. (Photographs courtesy of Center for the Study of Learning and Teaching Styles, St. John's University, New York.)

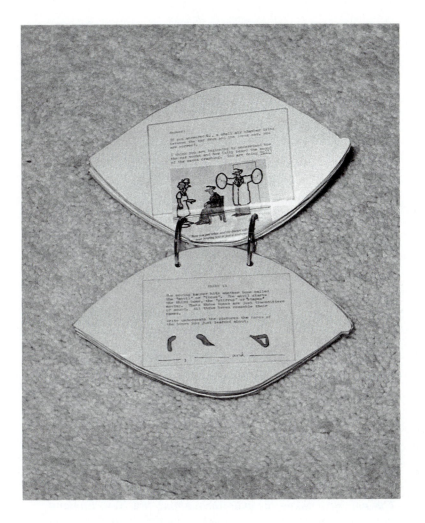

This PLS, "Travels with Popie," designed by Norann McGee, describes a summer spent by a young boy with his grandfather. The narrative takes the pair throughout the New England states and, simultaneously, explains the developing relationship between the older man and the lonesome boy whose parents had recently been divorced. (Photograph courtesy of Center for the Study of Learning and Teaching Styles, St. John's University, New York.)

Step 18 *When you are satisfied that all the "bugs" have been eliminated, add a front and back cover.* Place the title of the program on the front cover, and, if possible, shape and illustrate the cover to represent the subject matter. Bind the covers to the index card frames. You may use notebook rings, colored yarn, or any other substance that will permit easy turning of the index cards. Be certain that the answers to each frame, which appear on the back of the frame, are easily readable and are not upside down. When the program has been completed, make it available to students whose learning styles are complemented by this resource.

Step 19 *Design a record-keeping form so that you know which students are using and have used the program and how much of it they have completed successfully* (see Figure 7–4).

Language Arts Programs Completed

Student	Adjec-tives	Test Score	Ad-verbs	Test Score	Pro-nouns	Test Score	Recommended Prescriptions
Adams, William	3/17	87	3/25	88	3/29	90	Continue programs.
Altman, Susan	3/9	94	3/10	93	3/15	98	Continue programs; try a contract.
Baron, Mary	3/15	82	3/21	80	3/10	85	Supplement adverbs program with games.
Brice, Amy	3/9	89	3/20	81	3/23	86	Supplement adverbs program with games.
Caldor, John	3/10	76	3/15	75	3/20	75	Try instructional packages.
Friedman, Joan	3/10	96	3/12	98	3/17	100	Continue programs; alternate with small groups; try a contract or two.

FIGURE 7–4 Record-keeping Form for Programmed Learning.

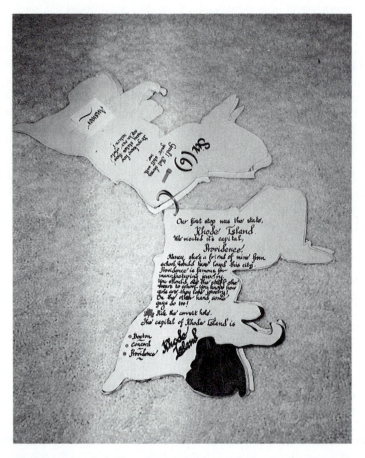

*As the story of the boy's and his grandfather's trip through-
out New England unfolds, mini-Electroboards and Pic-a-
Holes are provided to reinforce the information on the states
and their capitals. A Flip Chute in the shape of an old-fashioned New England barn is available as part of the total Multisensory Instructional Package (MIP) to reinforce the information presented in the PLS text. (Photograph courtesy of
Center for the Study of Learning and Teaching Styles, St.
John's University, New York.)*

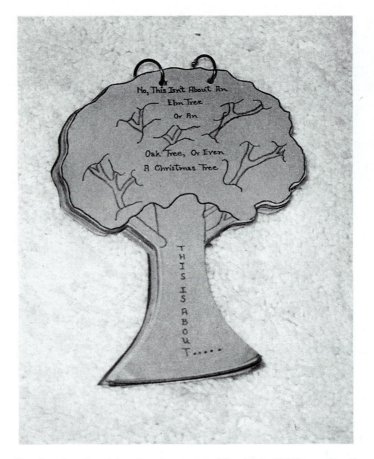

Teasing in the title also is acceptable. This PLS on family trees begins with, "No, This Isn't an Elm Tree, or an Oak Tree, or Even a Christmas Tree; This Is about . . . —and then the humor! (Photograph courtesy of Center for the Study of Learning and Teaching Styles, St. John's University, New York.)

Sample Programs

Following are several samples of programs developed by teachers and used successfully at different levels with children whose learning styles matched the approach intrinsic to programmed learning.

FIGURE 7–5   Programmed Learning Sequence: Geography—Break the Map Code.

BREAK THE MAP CODE: YOU DON'T HAVE TO BE A SQUARE TO DO IT*

This Programmed Learning Sequence on "Break the Map Code" was designed by Bodhilde Iglesias, a graduate student at St. John's University, New York, and a New York City elementary school teacher.

The PLS "Breaking the Map Code: You Don't Have to Be Square to Do It" uses a favorite character, "Navigator Nitwit," to introduce, teach, and reinforce the skills necessary for understanding how to read a map. The character appeals to many children, and the shape of the PLS is inviting to visual/tactual youngsters. (Photographs courtesy of Center for the Study of Learning and Teaching Styles, St. John's University, New York.)

PROGRAMMED LEARNING SEQUENCE:
GEOGRAPHY—BREAK THE MAP CODE

Frame 1

Remember E.T.? He had so much trouble when he landed on Earth. If he had learned how to use earthly maps, his visit here might have been more fun. Sometimes you Earthlings also have trouble getting places. You need to know how to read a map.

My name is Nitwit. I have no trouble going anywhere because I can read maps. I am a Navigator. A navigator tells how to get from one place to another. My co-travelers call me NAVIGATOR NITWIT.

Turn to the next frame and you will find a little rap poem about my favorite thing.

Frame 2

A map is really like
A picture of a place,
You need to know directions
Or you'll be in a daze!

It's not a big secret
What all the codes mean,
You just have to look them up
On the Key or Legend screen!

These are some words you'll need to know:
North, South, East, and West.
They tell in which direction to go,
The Compass Rose tells you best!

Latitude, Longitude—oh, how confusing!
When we are finished—you'll find it amusing.
Equator is also an imaginary line,
Like Axis is the Earth's Spine.

Frame 3

HOW TO USE THE PROGRAM

Read the statement on each frame and answer the question on the bottom of the frame. Then, check your answer on the back of the frame.

Some frames have a test on them. If you answer those incorrectly, follow the instructions given to you on the back of the frame.

Use the grease pencil provided. When you are finished, please wipe off all your answers.

Back of Frame 3

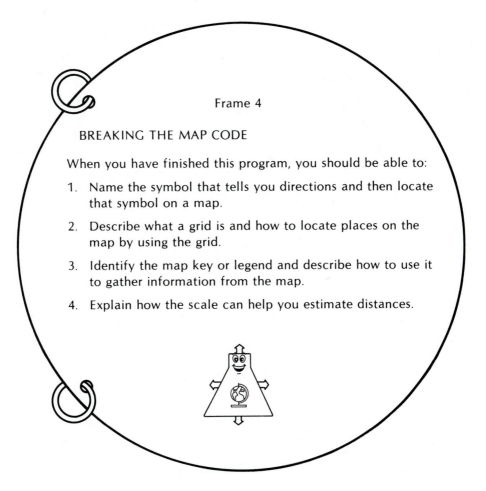

Frame 4

BREAKING THE MAP CODE

When you have finished this program, you should be able to:

1. Name the symbol that tells you directions and then locate that symbol on a map.

2. Describe what a grid is and how to locate places on the map by using the grid.

3. Identify the map key or legend and describe how to use it to gather information from the map.

4. Explain how the scale can help you estimate distances.

Frame 5

Before you can do
anything with a map, you must know directions.
The main directions are <u>north, south, east,</u> and <u>west</u>.

One of the symbols on a map is the <u>compass rose</u>.
The compass rose points out the directions for you.

Sometimes it looks like this:

Sometimes it looks like this:

The symbol that shows directions on the map is called

_____.

Back of Frame 5

If you answered <u>compass rose</u>,
you are correct.

Frame 6

We use the compass rose to find
directions on the map. To make it easy for us,
most maps are made so that the compass rose points
<u>north</u> at the top of the map and <u>south</u> at the bottom.

N
↑
┼
↓
S

On most maps you will find _____ at the

top, and _____ at the bottom.

Back of Frame 6

If you filled in <u>north</u> and <u>south</u>, you are correct.

From now on, we do not say "<u>up</u>" and "<u>down</u>"
when we speak of directions; instead, we say
"north" and "south."

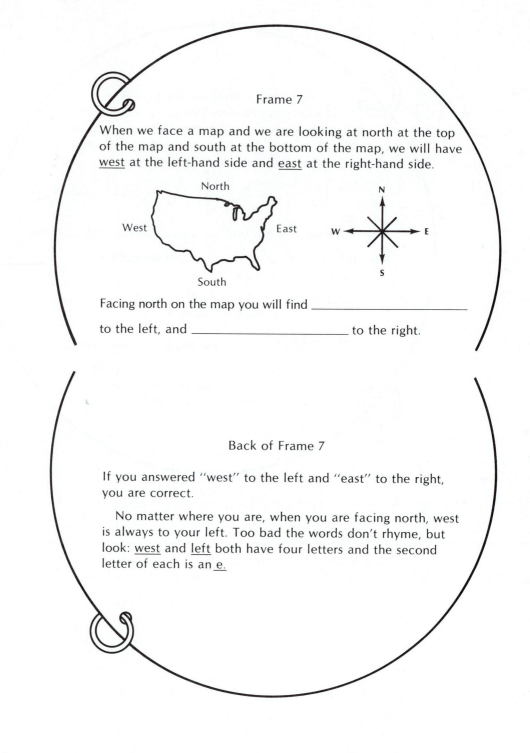

Frame 7

When we face a map and we are looking at north at the top of the map and south at the bottom of the map, we will have <u>west</u> at the left-hand side and <u>east</u> at the right-hand side.

North

West   East

South

N

W   E

S

Facing north on the map you will find _____

to the left, and _____ to the right.

Back of Frame 7

If you answered "west" to the left and "east" to the right, you are correct.

No matter where you are, when you are facing north, west is always to your left. Too bad the words don't rhyme, but look: <u>west</u> and <u>left</u> both have four letters and the second letter of each is an <u>e.</u>

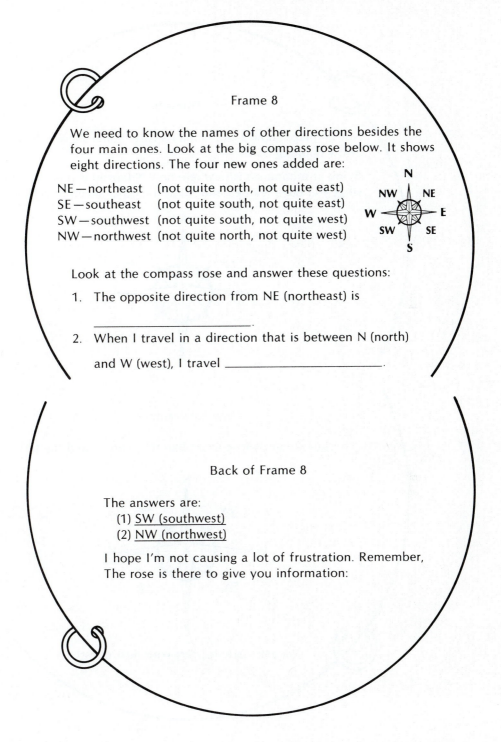

Frame 8

We need to know the names of other directions besides the four main ones. Look at the big compass rose below. It shows eight directions. The four new ones added are:

NE—northeast   (not quite north, not quite east)
SE—southeast   (not quite south, not quite east)
SW—southwest (not quite south, not quite west)
NW—northwest (not quite north, not quite west)

Look at the compass rose and answer these questions:

1. The opposite direction from NE (northeast) is

_____.

2. When I travel in a direction that is between N (north)

and W (west), I travel _____.

Back of Frame 8

The answers are:
   (1) <u>SW (southwest)</u>
   (2) <u>NW (northwest)</u>

I hope I'm not causing a lot of frustration. Remember, The rose is there to give you information:

Frame 9

Not all maps show a full compass rose. Some show only an arrow pointing north.

Below is a compass rose where only N (north) is filled in. Use what you have learned and fill in the other seven directions.

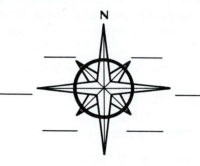

Back of Frame 9

If your compass rose looks like this, you passed the test.

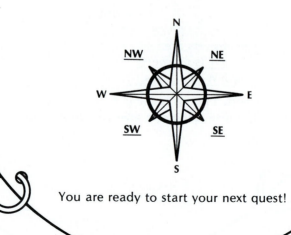

You are ready to start your next quest!

Frame 10

Map makers draw lines on maps to make it easier to find places. One set of lines runs north and south. These lines are called lines of <u>longitude.</u>

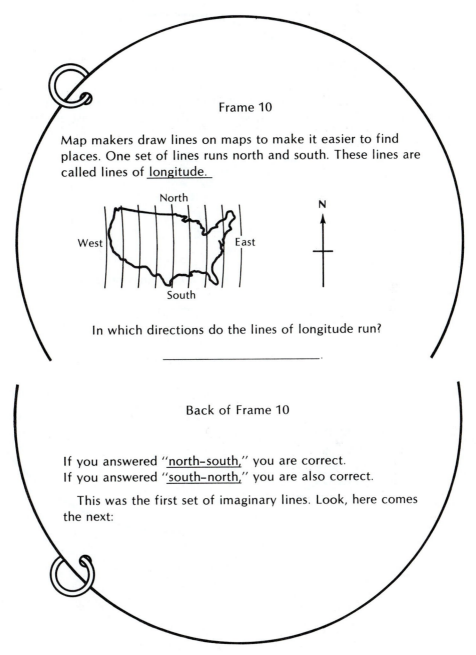

In which directions do the lines of longitude run?

_____.

Back of Frame 10

If you answered "<u>north–south,</u>" you are correct.
If you answered "<u>south–north,</u>" you are also correct.

This was the first set of imaginary lines. Look, here comes the next:

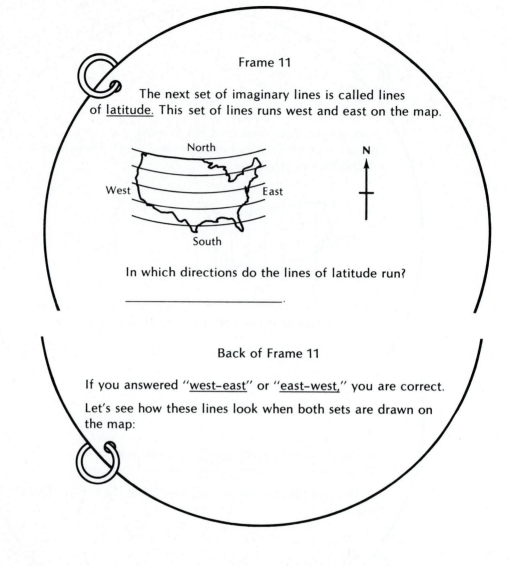

Frame 11

The next set of imaginary lines is called lines of <u>latitude.</u> This set of lines runs west and east on the map.

In which directions do the lines of latitude run?

_____.

Back of Frame 11

If you answered "<u>west–east</u>" or "<u>east–west,</u>" you are correct.

Let's see how these lines look when both sets are drawn on the map:

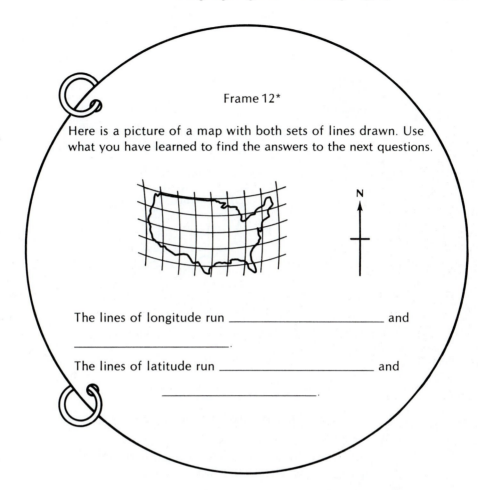

Frame 12*

Here is a picture of a map with both sets of lines drawn. Use what you have learned to find the answers to the next questions.

The lines of longitude run _____ and

_____.

The lines of latitude run _____ and

_____.

*Sample complete frame without back.

Frame 13

The lines of latitude and longitude make a grid on the map. Map makers use a grid system to make it easier for us to find places.

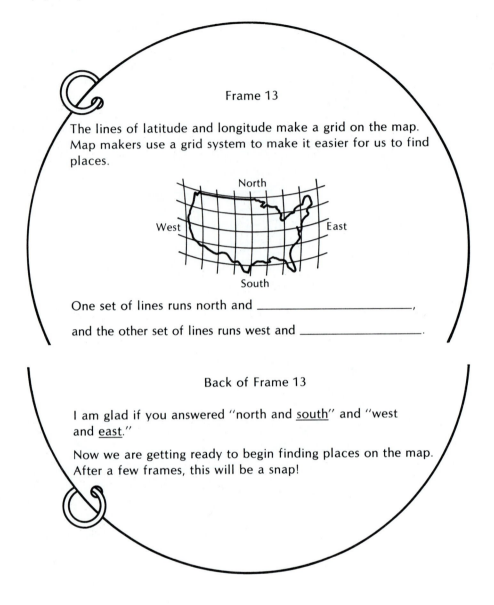

One set of lines runs north and _____,

and the other set of lines runs west and _____.

Back of Frame 13

I am glad if you answered "north and <u>south</u>" and "west and <u>east</u>."

Now we are getting ready to begin finding places on the map. After a few frames, this will be a snap!

Frame 14

The lines running west–east, make rows on the map.
Map makers label the rows with <u>key letters:</u> A, B, C, . . .
Check this map labeled with key letters:

On the map above, what do we call the letters A, B, C, D, E?
Mark your choice with an X.

( ) the alphabet

( ) key letters

( ) row letters

Back of Frame 14

If you marked <u>key letters,</u> you were correct.

We have started to break the code.
From now on, I hope you stay in the mode!

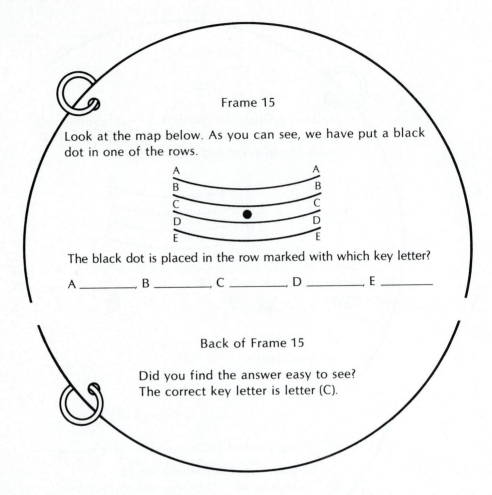

Frame 15

Look at the map below. As you can see, we have put a black dot in one of the rows.

The black dot is placed in the row marked with which key letter?

A _____, B _____, C _____, D _____, E _____

Back of Frame 15

Did you find the answer easy to see?
The correct key letter is letter (C).

Frame 16

Map makers label the rows made by north–south lines in the same way, except they use <u>key numbers:</u> 1, 2, 3, . . .

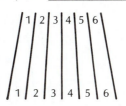

On the map above, what do we call 1, 2, 3, 4, 5, 6? Mark your choice with an X.

    (   ) number line

    (   ) row numbers

    (   ) key numbers

Back of Frame 16

If you marked <u>key numbers,</u> you chose correctly.

What did you say? This is all the same? You will find it easy on the next frame!

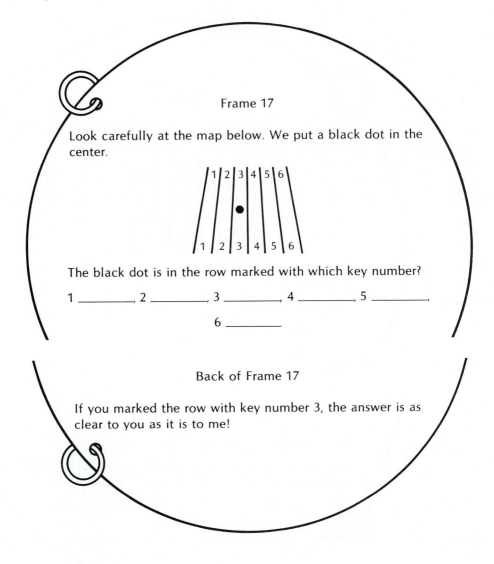

Frame 17

Look carefully at the map below. We put a black dot in the center.

The black dot is in the row marked with which key number?

1 _____, 2 _____, 3 _____, 4 _____, 5 _____,

6 _____

Back of Frame 17

If you marked the row with key number 3, the answer is as clear to you as it is to me!

Frame 18

On a map, the west–east lines and north–south lines make a
grid. We use the grid to make it easier to find places. With
the grid, we can make the area on the map smaller. When
navigators speak, we point to the smaller squares with names
such as B3, C5, D1, etc. Did you notice that we write key letter
first? Let's look at this map:

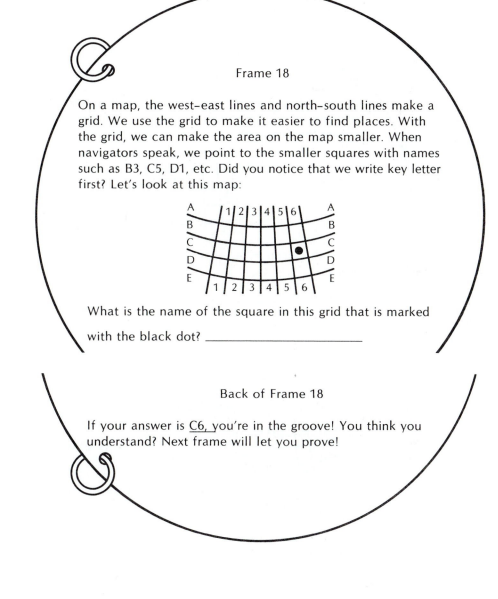

What is the name of the square in this grid that is marked

with the black dot? _____

Back of Frame 18

If your answer is <u>C6,</u> you're in the groove! You think you
understand? Next frame will let you prove!

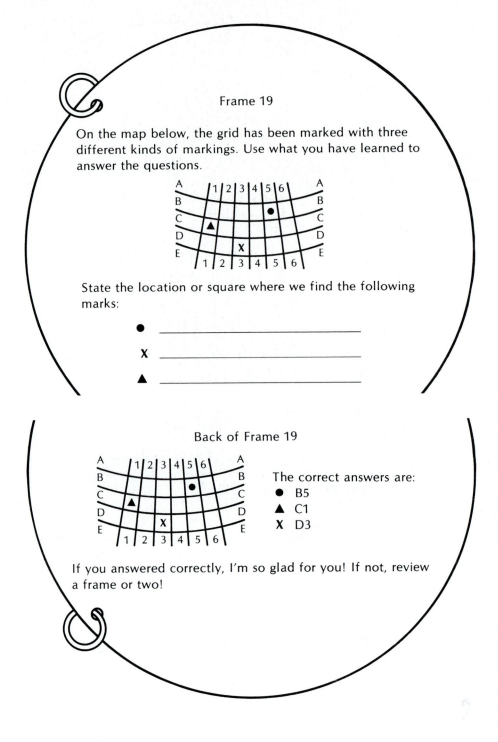

Frame 19

On the map below, the grid has been marked with three different kinds of markings. Use what you have learned to answer the questions.

State the location or square where we find the following marks:

● _____

X _____

▲ _____

Back of Frame 19

The correct answers are:
● B5
▲ C1
X D3

If you answered correctly, I'm so glad for you! If not, review a frame or two!

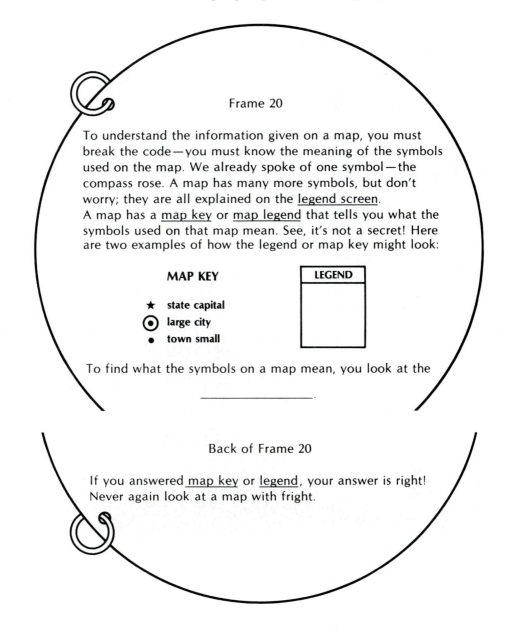

Frame 20

To understand the information given on a map, you must break the code—you must know the meaning of the symbols used on the map. We already spoke of one symbol—the compass rose. A map has many more symbols, but don't worry; they are all explained on the legend screen.
A map has a map key or map legend that tells you what the symbols used on that map mean. See, it's not a secret! Here are two examples of how the legend or map key might look:

MAP KEY

★   **state capital**
◉   **large city**
•   **town small**

LEGEND

To find what the symbols on a map mean, you look at the

_____.

Back of Frame 20

If you answered map key or legend, your answer is right!
Never again look at a map with fright.

Frame 21

The legend or map key will be different depending on what information we are supposed to gather from the map. Therefore, a map that shows the ski areas of Vermont will have different symbols from a map of Australia showing state borders and its major cities.

Compare the map keys:

Explanation of Symbols

State Parks (with camping facilities)	✈ Airports	═══ Free Limited–Access Highways
	■ Points of Interest	═══ Toll Limited–Access Highways
State Parks (without camping facilities)	▲▼ Service Areas	═══ Other Four-Lane Divided Highways
	⊐ Rest Areas	─── Principal Highways
Waysides, Roadside Parks	S.P. State Parks	─── Other Through Highways
	S.F. State Forests	─── Other Roads
▲ Campsites	S.R. State Reserves	─── Unpaved Roads
		╌╌╌ Scenic Routes

Two symbols are the same for these two different maps.

What are those symbols? _____ and

_____

Back of Frame 21

The two symbols are:

<u>state boundaries</u> or <u>state border</u>
and
<u>other cities</u> or <u>towns, cities</u>

If you knew the answer, you are great! Remember: The <u>key</u> to the <u>code</u> is in the <u>legend</u>!

Frame 22

A map can show a whole city, state, or continent. But the <u>sizes</u> and <u>distances</u> are much smaller than they really are on Earth. How can you tell the real distances between places on a map? Use the <u>map scale</u>!

A scale shows how distances on a map compare with the real distances on Earth. When you have a model car, it is made to show how a real car looks, only smaller.

Here is one way a scale may be shown: 1 inch = 400 miles. That means that 1 inch on the map equals 400 miles on Earth. Sometimes maps use a <u>bar scale</u> like this.

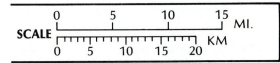

A bar scale looks like a ruler; sections on the scale stand for real distances on Earth. If the distance from your house to school is 5 miles, the road on the map would cover a space as big as the space 0–5 on the map scale.

To measure the real distances from one place to another on the map, we use the _____.

Back of Frame 22

If you answered <u>scale</u> or <u>map scale</u>, that's true. Soon you'll become one of my crew!

Frame 23*

Map scales are the reason two maps of the same place might look different. Remember, maps are like a picture of a place; some pictures are taken from far away, and others are close-ups. Compare the two maps below. They are both of Texas. Look at the scale [**Note**: Two maps are shown with different scales]:

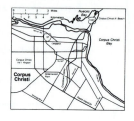

MAP A
On this map the scale is:
1 inch = 300 miles

MAP B
On this map the scale is:
1 inch = 60 miles

To change the map of a place into a close-up, map makers

change the _____.

Back of Frame 23

If you answered <u>scale,</u> you answered correctly.

The scale is what makes the close-up map look different from another map.

*Teacher: Add appropriate maps based on your local area.

Frame 24

The scale is most important when you want to find how far it is from one place to another on the real Earth.

Let's say that you live in a town called Oak Grove. Your best friend moves to another town called Custer. You have a map that has these two towns marked off.

The map scale reads: <u>1 inch equals 20 miles</u>
You can estimate the distance between your house in Oak Grove and your best friend's house in Custer by using a ruler.

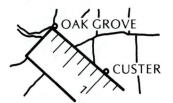

By using your ruler and comparing distance with the map scale, you will find how far apart Oak Grove and Custer are.

How many miles apart are they? _____

Back of Frame 24

You estimated correctly if your answer is <u>20 miles</u>.

It will not take your Mom long to drive you there for a visit! Go to the next frame to learn a different way of estimating.

Frame 25

Here we have a map of Alaska. It has a compass rose, a legend, and a scale. This time, what we are interested in is the scale, so I have pointed it out to you with a red box.

Let's say we want to fly from <u>Point Hope</u> to <u>Nome</u>. (I put an arrow there to make it easy for you to find.)

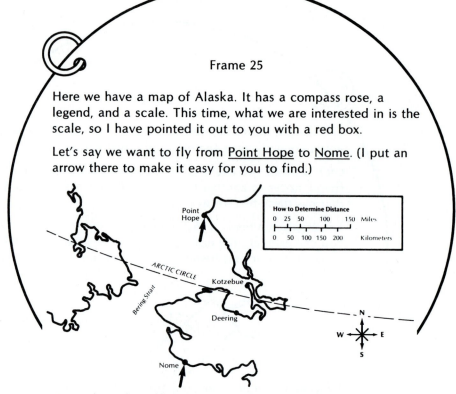

Now, place the edge of a piece of paper on the map so it touches the two points on the map. (On this map find Point Hope and Nome.) Then, put <u>marks</u> on <u>the paper</u> at each point. Finally, place the marked paper along the scale. Estimate the distance between the two towns. Which answer is correct? Circle your choice.

(a) 200 miles   (b) more than 200 miles   (c) 300 miles

Back of Frame 25

If you circled (b), I agree with you.

It's a pretty long distance to look so short on the map. While the plane's in the air, just take a nap!

Frame 26

Let's stop here,
     This has all been the same—
I'm growing tired,
     Let's try a game.

The game's like this:
     You have to match—
A word with a statement—
     You knew there was a catch!

Open this envelope. Take out the map Task Cards. Match the
card pairs:

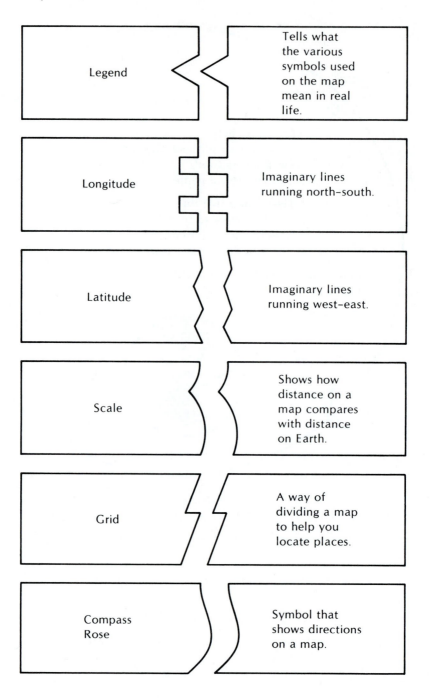

Legend — Tells what the various symbols used on the map mean in real life.

Longitude — Imaginary lines running north-south.

Latitude — Imaginary lines running west-east.

Scale — Shows how distance on a map compares with distance on Earth.

Grid — A way of dividing a map to help you locate places.

Compass Rose — Symbol that shows directions on a map.

Frame 27

A globe is a model of Earth; that's why it's round! I would like to tell you a few things to make you understand more about the globe.
Do you remember the north–south lines we called longitude?

On a globe, the lines of longitude are drawn from the North Pole to the South Pole.

Describe how the lines of longitude are drawn on a globe.

Back of Frame 27

The correct answer is:

Lines of <u>longitude</u> are drawn from the North Pole to the South Pole.

Looking at that little globe, do you see why some people say the North Pole is at the top of the world? Of course, <u>we</u> don't; we say that the North Pole is <u>north</u> of us.

Frame 28

The main line of longitude is drawn through a city in England called Greenwich. If we follow that longitude to the South Pole, and back to the North Pole on the other side of the globe, and then cut the globe following those two lines of longitude, we have sort of sliced the Earth in half. Each half is called a <u>hemisphere</u> (which means "half a sphere"). Here is a picture of the globe cut in half:

When we cut the globe in half (make-believe, of course), we get two halves, each called a _____.

Back of Frame 28

If you answered <u>hemisphere,</u> your answer is correct.

On the next frame you will find that each hemisphere has a more specific name.

Frame 29

As we divided the globe along the main longitude, we ended up with one part of the Earth in the <u>Western Hemisphere</u> and one part in the <u>Eastern Hemisphere.</u> North and South America are in the Western Hemisphere, and most of the rest of the world's continents are in the Eastern Hemisphere.

Western   Eastern
Hemisphere   Hemisphere

In which hemisphere do you find North America?

_____

Back of Frame 29

If you said <u>Western Hemisphere,</u> your answer is correct.

This is where you live and grow.
This is where to school you go.
And map skills are just one of the things you need to know!

Frame 30

Let me remind you about the lines of latitude. On a map, the lines of latitude run west–east. On a globe, the lines of latitude run around the globe, making circles.

N

S

Describe how the lines of latitude are drawn on a globe.

Back of Frame 30

The correct answer is:
    Lines of <u>latitude</u> are drawn in circles in the directions of <u>west–east</u>.

If you drew circles on your ball, you would see the circles getting smaller and smaller toward each pole.

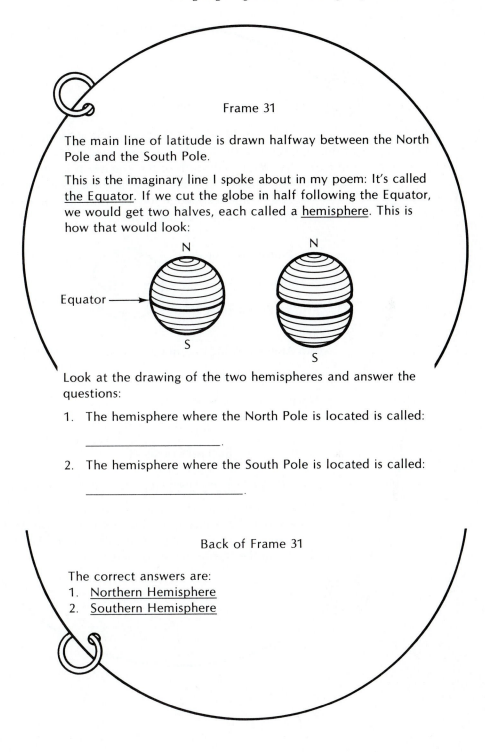

Frame 31

The main line of latitude is drawn halfway between the North Pole and the South Pole.

This is the imaginary line I spoke about in my poem: It's called the Equator. If we cut the globe in half following the Equator, we would get two halves, each called a hemisphere. This is how that would look:

Equator →

Look at the drawing of the two hemispheres and answer the questions:

1. The hemisphere where the North Pole is located is called:

    _____ .

2. The hemisphere where the South Pole is located is called:

    _____ .

Back of Frame 31

The correct answers are:
1. Northern Hemisphere
2. Southern Hemisphere

Frame 32

Now we know that the part of the Earth that is located north of the equator is in the Northern Hemisphere, and the part of the Earth that is located south of the equator is in the Southern Hemisphere. Below is a drawing of the globe showing North and South America. See if you can find the answer to the question at the bottom of the frame.

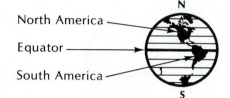

North America is located in the: [Circle your answer]

Southern Hemisphere

Northern Hemisphere

Back of Frame 32

If you circled <u>Northern Hemisphere,</u> your answer is correct.

Yes, I know there could have been another correct answer, but then we should have sliced the globe differently. Depending on how you slice it, North America is located in the Western Hemisphere and the Northern Hemisphere.

Map Electroboard: Test Yourself

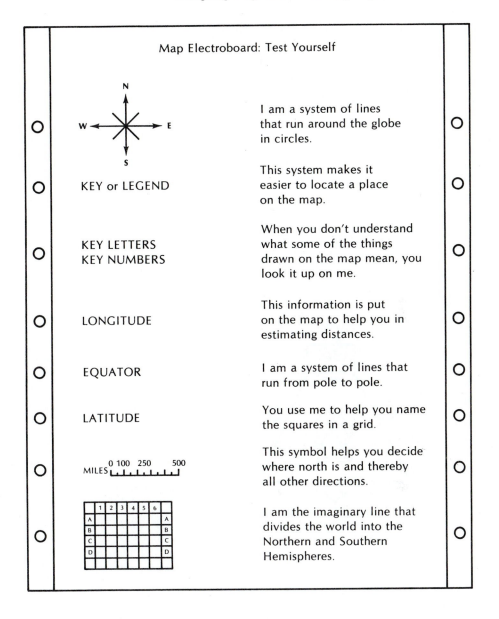

KEY or LEGEND

KEY LETTERS
KEY NUMBERS

LONGITUDE

EQUATOR

LATITUDE

MILES 0 100 250   500

I am a system of lines
that run around the globe
in circles.

This system makes it
easier to locate a place
on the map.

When you don't understand
what some of the things
drawn on the map mean, you
look it up on me.

This information is put
on the map to help you in
estimating distances.

I am a system of lines that
run from pole to pole.

You use me to help you name
the squares in a grid.

This symbol helps you decide
where north is and thereby
all other directions.

I am the imaginary line that
divides the world into the
Northern and Southern
Hemispheres.

What you have learned is a useful tip
So pick up a map for each future trip.
Should you venture to an amusement park
A map will show the way so you won't be "in the dark!"
To break the code: <u>You</u> are the key!
And remember, please, you learned it with me!

Happy Navigating!

I knew you could do it!

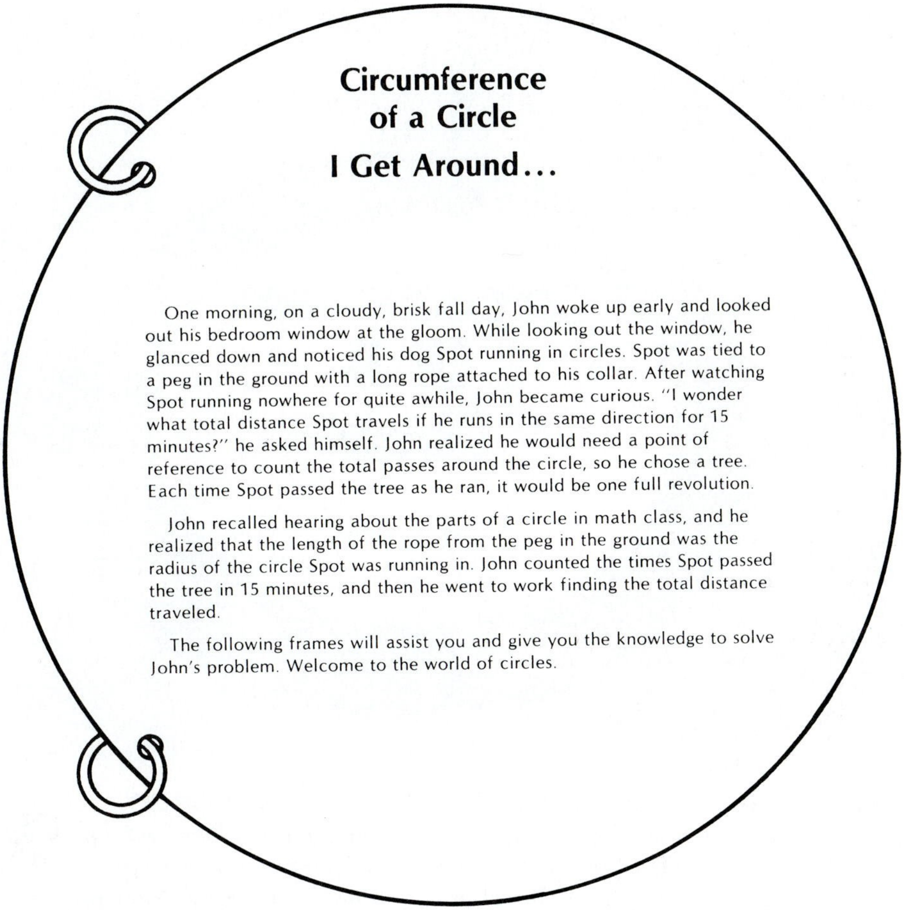

**Circumference
of a Circle

I Get Around…**

One morning, on a cloudy, brisk fall day, John woke up early and looked out his bedroom window at the gloom. While looking out the window, he glanced down and noticed his dog Spot running in circles. Spot was tied to a peg in the ground with a long rope attached to his collar. After watching Spot running nowhere for quite awhile, John became curious. "I wonder what total distance Spot travels if he runs in the same direction for 15 minutes?" he asked himself. John realized he would need a point of reference to count the total passes around the circle, so he chose a tree. Each time Spot passed the tree as he ran, it would be one full revolution.

John recalled hearing about the parts of a circle in math class, and he realized that the length of the rope from the peg in the ground was the radius of the circle Spot was running in. John counted the times Spot passed the tree in 15 minutes, and then he went to work finding the total distance traveled.

The following frames will assist you and give you the knowledge to solve John's problem. Welcome to the world of circles.

FIGURE 7–6   Programmed Learning Sequence: Mathematics—Circumference of a Circle.

This Programmed Learning Sequence on "Circumference of a Circle: I Get Around" was designed by Daniel J. Purus, teacher, Ridgewood Intermediate School #93, Queens, New York City.

The PLS "The Circumference of a Circle (or) I Get Around!" is circular and includes multiple Task Cards, illustrations, a mini-Pic-A-Hole, and a mini-Electroboard to reinforce the information taught. (Photographs courtesy of Center for the Study of Learning and Teaching Styles, St. John's University, New York.)

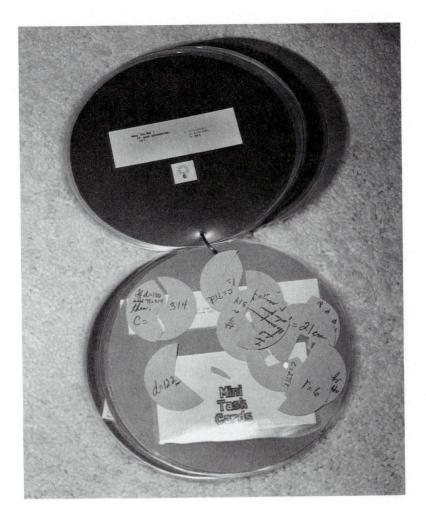

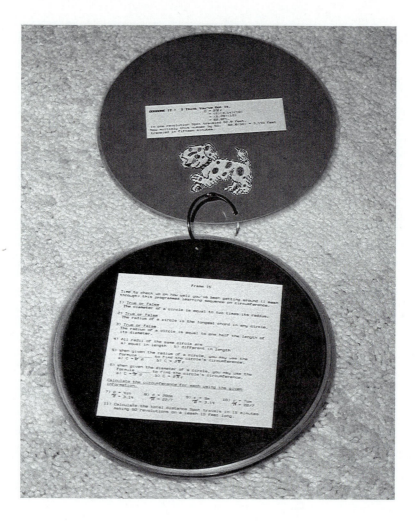

Frame 1
Vocabulary

Radius: A line segment with one endpoint at the center of the
  circle and the other endpoint on the circle.

Chord: A line segment with two (2) endpoints on the circle.

Diameter: A special chord that passes through the center of
  the circle. It is the longest chord in any circle.

Circumference: The distance around a circle.

π (pi): The circumference of any circle divided by its diameter.
  Pi is known as an irrational number (a nonrepeating,
  nonterminating decimal number). It is approximately equal to
  3.1428571. We will use 22/7 or 3.14 to simplify our calculations.

Back of Frame 1

Objectives:

You will be able to:

- Find the diameter of a circle, given the radius

- Find the radius of a circle, given the diameter

- Use the formula $C = \pi d$ and $C = 2\pi r$ to find the circumference
  of a circle

Frame 2

All radii (plural of radius) of the same circle are equal in length. Line segment OA, line segment OB, and line segment OC are all radii of circle O.

Write in the best answer:

All radii of the same circle are _____ in length.

different   sometimes equal   equal

Back of Frame 2

I Hope You Knew...

All radii of the same circle are *equal* in length.

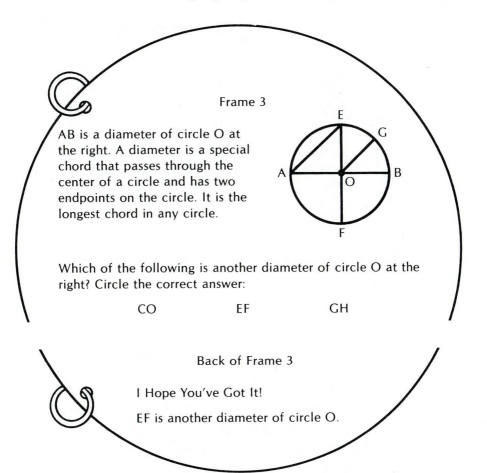

Frame 3

AB is a diameter of circle O at the right. A diameter is a special chord that passes through the center of a circle and has two endpoints on the circle. It is the longest chord in any circle.

Which of the following is another diameter of circle O at the right? Circle the correct answer:

CO   EF   GH

Back of Frame 3

I Hope You've Got It!

EF is another diameter of circle O.

Frame 4

The diameter of a circle is equal to two times its radius. We can say also $d = 2(r)$. Remember, ( ) represents multiplication. If the radius of a circle is 4 cm, then its diameter equals two times 4 cm, or 8 cm. Or we can express it as

$$d = 2(r)$$
$$= 2(4)$$
$$= 8 \text{ cm}$$

Find the diameter of a circle whose radius is 7 mm. Underline the correct answer.

14 mm   7 mm   8 mm

Back of Frame 4

If your answer was:

14 mm, two times the length of the radius 7 mm,

then it was **TREEmendous!**

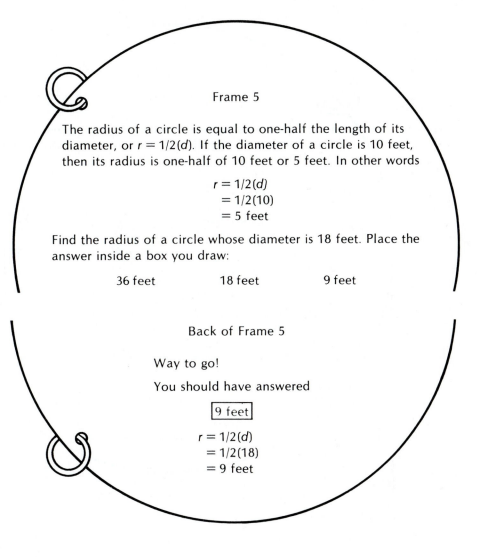

Frame 5

The radius of a circle is equal to one-half the length of its diameter, or $r = 1/2(d)$. If the diameter of a circle is 10 feet, then its radius is one-half of 10 feet or 5 feet. In other words

$$r = 1/2(d)$$
$$= 1/2(10)$$
$$= 5 \text{ feet}$$

Find the radius of a circle whose diameter is 18 feet. Place the answer inside a box you draw:

36 feet   18 feet   9 feet

Back of Frame 5

Way to go!

You should have answered

9 feet

$$r = 1/2(d)$$
$$= 1/2(18)$$
$$= 9 \text{ feet}$$

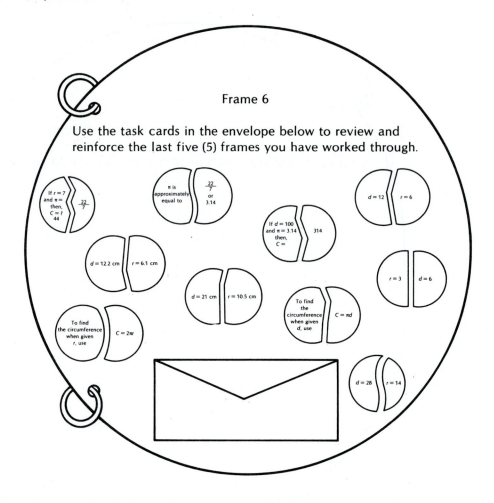

Frame 6

Use the task cards in the envelope below to review and reinforce the last five (5) frames you have worked through.

Frame 7

To find the circumference of a circle (distance around a circle) when given the diameter, we mulitply the diameter of the circle by pi.

Writing it as a formula, we get $C = \pi d$.

Finding the circumference of a circle involves mulitplying pi

by _____ of the circle.

the radius   the diameter   the chord

Back of Frame 7

You seem to be BARKING up the right tree!!

the diameter

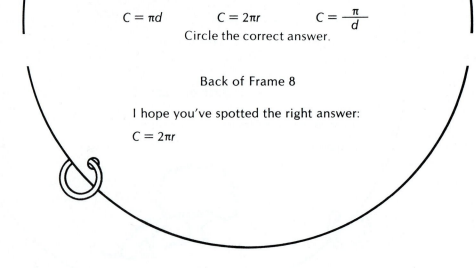

Frame 8

The circumference of a circle may also be found by using a different formula when *only* the *radius* is given. The formula is $C = 2\pi r$, which means two times pi times the radius.

To find the circumference when given only the radius of the circle, we use the formula:

$$C = \pi d \qquad\qquad C = 2\pi r \qquad\qquad C = \frac{\pi}{d}$$

Circle the correct answer.

Back of Frame 8

I hope you've spotted the right answer:

$$C = 2\pi r$$

Frame 9

Enjoy this Word Search!!

Getting Around

```
C Q P Y S Q X O J R E T N E C X L M
S M C I R C U M F E R E N C E I N E
E J H E A K S K T S I L R P I O F D
Y U O K D I A M E T E R C R V D A Y
A V R X I Q V R H A U A R C R A A Z
J Q D D U W C K D N R D D E I C X R
Z I M K S R M C F G F I Y N E R Y H
R U A T C I R C L E P I O T H E H O
E O R D R W A E E N N O F E P N T M
Q J C H O R D O E T N U T R T A E Z
F U M Q N V I T I R C D A F E T X Y
S O M C L X I V L R C E N T E R S Z
E P R A D I U S I G R E G V F L L R
O S A E P G H U Y A D V E F T I T I
T T D I A M E T E R J U N A N T J N
T M I D D F X V C C E N T E R E F S
Y M I U Q A A M X X Y W Z I F Y P Y
A I F P C J Y M G V E V G M V N F Y
```

There are 10 words here. Can you find them?
Here are the words to look for:

ARC	CENTER
CHORD	CIRCLE
CIRCUMFERENCE	DIAMETER
PI	RADII
RADIUS	TANGENT

Back of Frame 9

Getting Around

```
· · · · · · · · · · · · · · · · · · ·
· · C I R C U M F E R E N C E · · · ·
· · H · A · · · · · · · · · · · · · ·
· · O · D I A M E T E R · · · · · · ·
· · R · I · · · · A · A R C · · · · ·
· · D · U · · · · N · D · E · · · · ·
· · · · S · · · · G · I · N · · · · ·
· · · A · C I R C L E P I · T · · · ·
· · R · · A · · · N · · E · · · · · ·
· · C H O R D · · T · · T R · · · · ·
· · · · · · I · · · · · · A · · · · ·
· · · · · · I · · · · · C E N T E R · ·
· · R A D I U S · · · · · G · · · · ·
· · A · · · · · A · · E · · · · · · ·
· · D I A M E T E R · · N · · · · · ·
· · I · · · · · · · C E N T E R · · ·
· · I · · · · · · · · · · · · · · · ·
· · · · · · · · · · · · · · · · · · ·
```

271

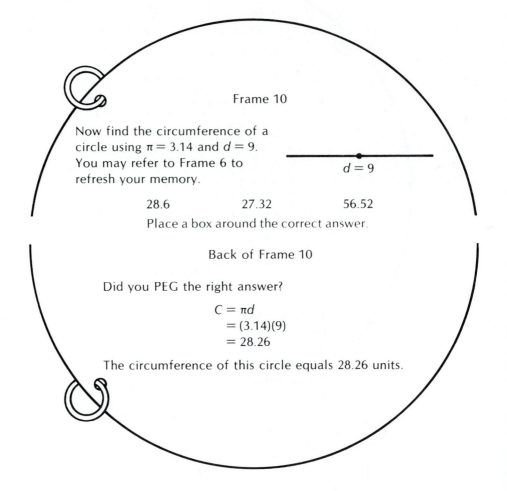

Frame 10

Now find the circumference of a
circle using $\pi = 3.14$ and $d = 9$.
You may refer to Frame 6 to
refresh your memory.

$d = 9$

28.6   27.32   56.52

Place a box around the correct answer.

Back of Frame 10

Did you PEG the right answer?

$$C = \pi d$$
$$= (3.14)(9)$$
$$= 28.26$$

The circumference of this circle equals 28.26 units.

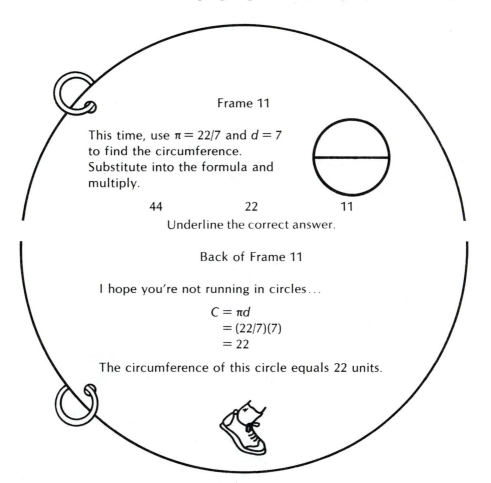

Frame 11

This time, use $\pi = 22/7$ and $d = 7$
to find the circumference.
Substitute into the formula and
multiply.

44   22   11

Underline the correct answer.

Back of Frame 11

I hope you're not running in circles...

$$C = \pi d$$
$$= (22/7)(7)$$
$$= 22$$

The circumference of this circle equals 22 units.

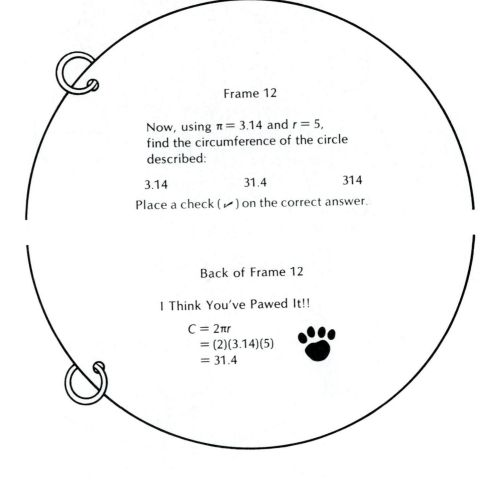

Frame 12

Now, using $\pi = 3.14$ and $r = 5$,
find the circumference of the circle
described:

3.14   31.4   314

Place a check (✓) on the correct answer.

Back of Frame 12

I Think You've Pawed It!!

$$C = 2\pi r$$
$$= (2)(3.14)(5)$$
$$= 31.4$$

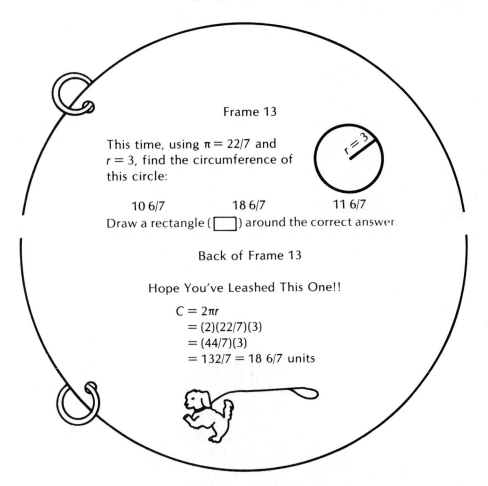

Frame 13

This time, using $\pi = 22/7$ and $r = 3$, find the circumference of this circle:

10 6/7   18 6/7   11 6/7

Draw a rectangle (☐) around the correct answer.

Back of Frame 13

Hope You've Leashed This One!!

$C = 2\pi r$
$\quad = (2)(22/7)(3)$
$\quad = (44/7)(3)$
$\quad = 132/7 = 18\ 6/7$ units

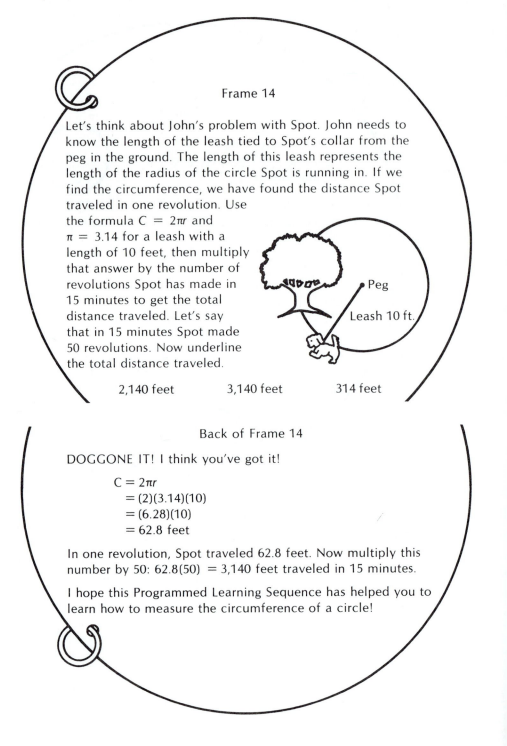

Frame 14

Let's think about John's problem with Spot. John needs to know the length of the leash tied to Spot's collar from the peg in the ground. The length of this leash represents the length of the radius of the circle Spot is running in. If we find the circumference, we have found the distance Spot traveled in one revolution. Use the formula $C = 2\pi r$ and $\pi = 3.14$ for a leash with a length of 10 feet, then multiply that answer by the number of revolutions Spot has made in 15 minutes to get the total distance traveled. Let's say that in 15 minutes Spot made 50 revolutions. Now underline the total distance traveled.

Peg

Leash 10 ft.

2,140 feet   3,140 feet   314 feet

Back of Frame 14

DOGGONE IT! I think you've got it!

$$C = 2\pi r$$
$$= (2)(3.14)(10)$$
$$= (6.28)(10)$$
$$= 62.8 \text{ feet}$$

In one revolution, Spot traveled 62.8 feet. Now multiply this number by 50: $62.8(50) = 3,140$ feet traveled in 15 minutes.

I hope this Programmed Learning Sequence has helped you to learn how to measure the circumference of a circle!

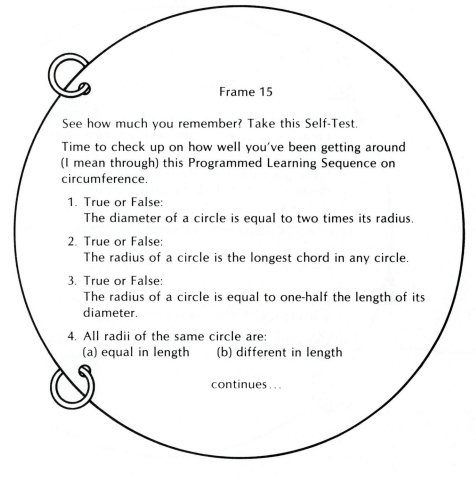

Frame 15

See how much you remember? Take this Self-Test.

Time to check up on how well you've been getting around (I mean through) this Programmed Learning Sequence on circumference.

1. True or False:
   The diameter of a circle is equal to two times its radius.

2. True or False:
   The radius of a circle is the longest chord in any circle.

3. True or False:
   The radius of a circle is equal to one-half the length of its diameter.

4. All radii of the same circle are:
   (a) equal in length   (b) different in length

continues...

Back of Frame 15

5. When given the radius of a circle, you may use the formula _____ to find the circle's circumference.
   (a) $C = \pi d$ (b) $C = 2\pi r$

6. When given the diameter of a circle, you may use the formula _____ to find the circle's circumference.
   (a) $C = \pi d$ (b) $C = 2\pi r$

Calculate the circumference for each using the given information.

7. $d = 4$ inches   8. $d = 28$ cm
   $\pi = 3.14$ $\pi = 22/7$

9. $r = 9$ m   10. $r = 7$ cm
   $\pi = 3.14$ $\pi = 22/7$

11. Calculate the total distance Spot travels in 15 minutes making 50 revolutions on a leash 15 feet long.

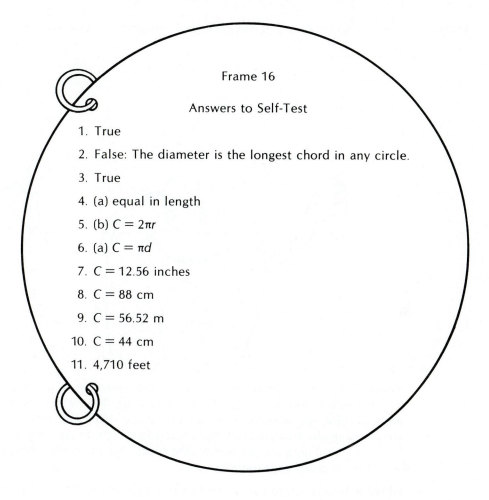

Frame 16

Answers to Self-Test

1. True

2. False: The diameter is the longest chord in any circle.

3. True

4. (a) equal in length

5. (b) $C = 2\pi r$

6. (a) $C = \pi d$

7. $C = 12.56$ inches

8. $C = 88$ cm

9. $C = 56.52$ m

10. $C = 44$ cm

11. 4,710 feet

FIGURE 7-7   Programmed Learning Sequence: Science—Magnetism: The Power of Attraction

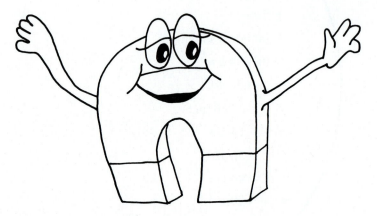

IMAGINE what it would be like if you had one very special magical power. This magical power is called MAGNETISM. With this special power of MAGNETISM you would only have to raise your hand and certain things would magically float through the air and land right in your hand. Imagine how you could amaze your friends, the tricks you could play, how easy it would be to clean your room!

IMAGINE how much fun you could have if only you had the magical power of MAGNETISM!!!

This Programmed Learning Sequence on magnetism was designed by Maria Geresi, teacher, The Growing Tree, Ridgefield, Connecticut.

The PLS "Magnetism: The Power of Attraction" has a magnet on the cover. That magnet character moves throughout the text, teaches as it jokes, and makes puns about things related to magnets. Tactual reinforcements are provided within the PLS's pockets to make the presentation interesting and fun, and to respond to the tactual strengths of youngsters learning with this approach. (Photographs courtesy of Center for the Study of Learning and Teaching Styles, St. John's University, New York.)

Pronunciation card:

magnetism **mag** ni tizm
lodestone **lod** ston
magnetic mag **net** ik
attraction a **trak** shn
nickel **nik** l
cobalt **ko** bolt
repel ri **pel**

I am so glad that you are going to work with this program because it will teach you to:

Identify and describe an object that attracts iron, nickel, or cobalt.

Describe the space around an object that attracts iron, nickel, or cobalt.

Compare the results of bringing like and unlike ends together.

Frame 1

Long ago shepherds carried wooden staffs with iron tips. Sometimes the iron tips seemed to stick to the ground, and sometimes pieces of stone stuck to the iron tips of their staffs.

Pieces of _____ sometimes stuck to the

_____ tips of shepherd's staffs.

Back of Frame 1

Answers:

Pieces of <u>stones</u> sometimes stuck to the <u>iron</u> tips of shepherd's staffs.

Shepherds had no use for these marvelous STONES that stuck to the IRON tips of their staffs.

Frame 2

These marvelous stones were called lodestones. <u>Lodestones</u> make strange things happen. They can pick up pins, paper clips, and nails.

_____ can pick up pins, paper clips, and nails.

Write the correct answer in the space.

Back of Frame 2

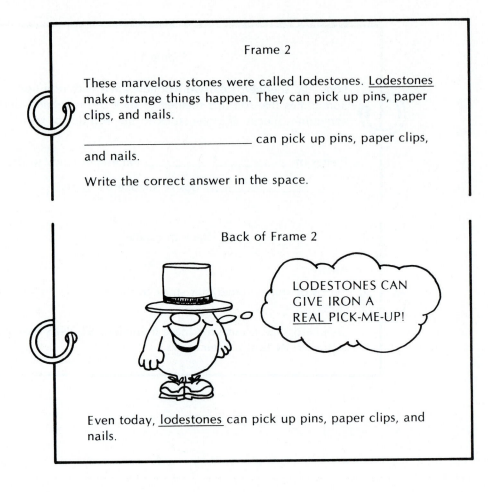

LODESTONES CAN GIVE IRON A <u>REAL</u> PICK-ME-UP!

Even today, <u>lodestones</u> can pick up pins, paper clips, and nails.

Frame 3

I hope you thought of me! Hi! My name is <u>Magnet.</u> I have the same pulling power as a lodestone. I can make a nail jump into the air and stick to me like glue.

A lodestone acts just like a:

paperclip   magnet   can opener

Circle the best answer.

Back of Frame 3

A <u>magnet </u>has pick-up power just like a lodestone.

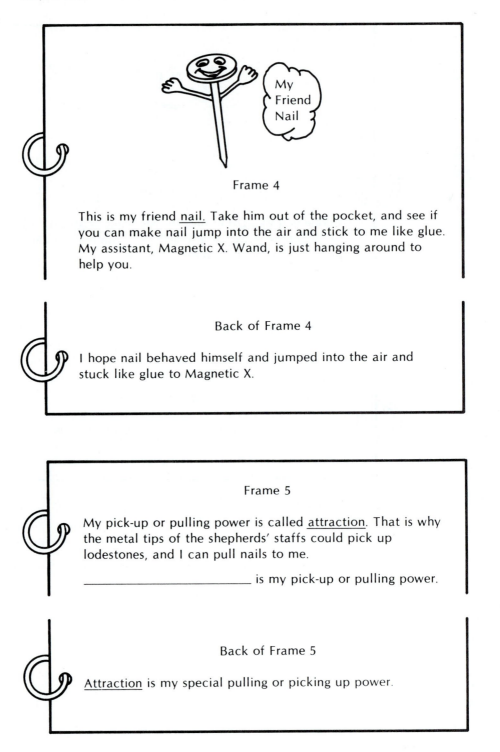

My
Friend
Nail

Frame 4

This is my friend <u>nail.</u> Take him out of the pocket, and see if you can make nail jump into the air and stick to me like glue. My assistant, Magnetic X. Wand, is just hanging around to help you.

Back of Frame 4

I hope nail behaved himself and jumped into the air and stuck like glue to Magnetic X.

Frame 5

My pick-up or pulling power is called <u>attraction</u>. That is why the metal tips of the shepherds' staffs could pick up lodestones, and I can pull nails to me.

_____ is my pick-up or pulling power.

Back of Frame 5

<u>Attraction</u> is my special pulling or picking up power.

Mr. Iron Circle   Mrs. Rubber Circle

Plastic Circle   Nickel Button Circle
(daughter)   (son)

Frame 6

These are my neighbors, the Circle family. Use my assistant
Magnetic X. Wand to see which members fall under my
magical power of attraction. Draw a circle around them.

Back of Frame 6

Mr. Iron Circle and their son Nickel Button Circle are my
friends.

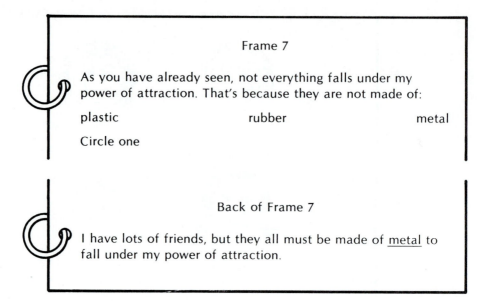

Frame 7

As you have already seen, not everything falls under my power of attraction. That's because they are not made of:

plastic   rubber   metal

Circle one

Back of Frame 7

I have lots of friends, but they all must be made of <u>metal</u> to fall under my power of attraction.

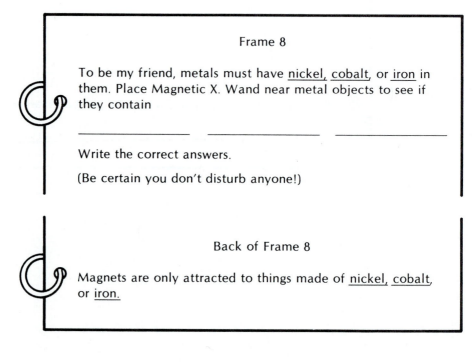

Frame 8

To be my friend, metals must have <u>nickel</u>, <u>cobalt</u>, or <u>iron</u> in them. Place Magnetic X. Wand near metal objects to see if they contain

_____   _____   _____

Write the correct answers.

(Be certain you don't disturb anyone!)

Back of Frame 8

Magnets are only attracted to things made of <u>nickel</u>, <u>cobalt</u>, or <u>iron.</u>

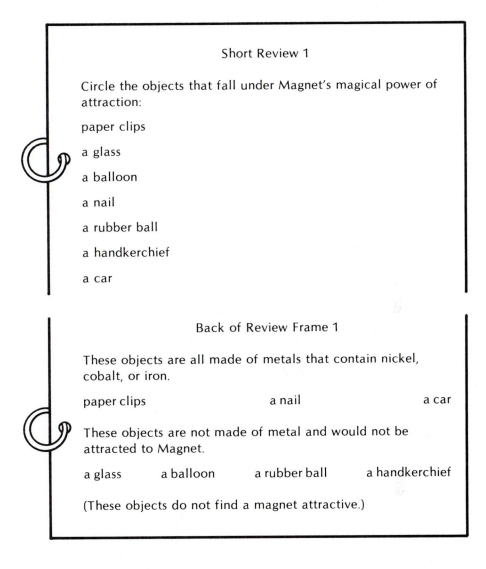

Short Review 1

Circle the objects that fall under Magnet's magical power of attraction:

paper clips

a glass

a balloon

a nail

a rubber ball

a handkerchief

a car

Back of Review Frame 1

These objects are all made of metals that contain nickel, cobalt, or iron.

paper clips   a nail   a car

These objects are not made of metal and would not be attracted to Magnet.

a glass   a balloon   a rubber ball   a handkerchief

(These objects do not find a magnet attractive.)

Frame 9

<u>Magnetism</u> is a very special part of my power of attraction. <u>Magnetism</u> means that some of my attracting power can pass through metal objects to other metal objects.

Circle one:

Attraction   Magnetism

means that my magical power to attract can pass through to other metals.

Back of Frame 9

<u>Magnetism</u> is my magical power of passing attraction along to my other metal friends.

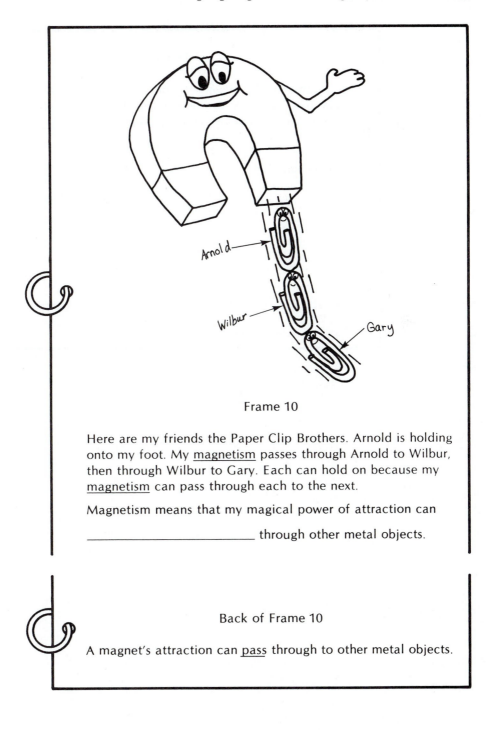

Frame 10

Here are my friends the Paper Clip Brothers. Arnold is holding onto my foot. My <u>magnetism</u> passes through Arnold to Wilbur, then through Wilbur to Gary. Each can hold on because my <u>magnetism</u> can pass through each to the next.

Magnetism means that my magical power of attraction can

_____ through other metal objects.

Back of Frame 10

A magnet's attraction can <u>pass</u> through to other metal objects.

Frame 11

You can't see my <u>magnetism</u>, but you can see what it does. Take the Paper Clip Brothers out of the envelope and experiment to discover my magical power of <u>magnetism</u>.

Circle:

Magnetism:

can be seen   cannot be seen

Back of Frame 11

We say that magnetism is invisible, because it cannot be seen.

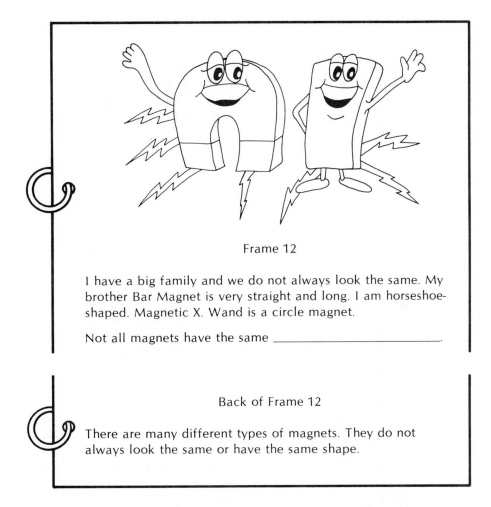

Frame 12

I have a big family and we do not always look the same. My brother Bar Magnet is very straight and long. I am horseshoe-shaped. Magnetic X. Wand is a circle magnet.

Not all magnets have the same _____.

Back of Frame 12

There are many different types of magnets. They do not always look the same or have the same shape.

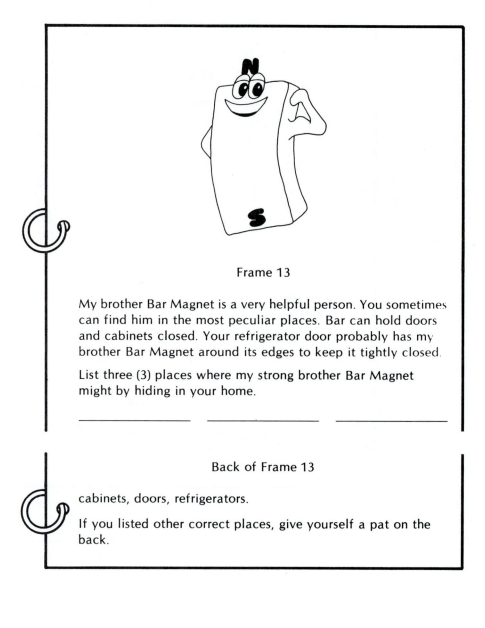

Frame 13

My brother Bar Magnet is a very helpful person. You sometimes can find him in the most peculiar places. Bar can hold doors and cabinets closed. Your refrigerator door probably has my brother Bar Magnet around its edges to keep it tightly closed.

List three (3) places where my strong brother Bar Magnet might by hiding in your home.

_____   _____   _____

Back of Frame 13

cabinets, doors, refrigerators.

If you listed other correct places, give yourself a pat on the back.

Frame 14

Around my magnet family and me are special places where our attraction or "pulling power" works best. These places are called our _poles._ They are found at each end.

Magnets have "pulling power" ends called

_____.

Write the correct answers in their correct spaces in the sentence.

Back of Frame 14

A magnet's "pulling power" ends are called _poles_. There are two...one at each end.

Frame 15

No matter what their shape is, all magnets of my magnet family call their poles either _north pole_ or _south pole_.

Our poles are called the _____ pole and

the _____ pole.

Back of Frame 15

A magnet's poles are called the _north pole_ and the _south pole._

Frame 16

Our poles are attracted to each other, but in a very special way. My north pole is always attracted to a south pole. My south pole is always attracted to a north pole.

A north pole is attracted to a _____ pole.

A south pole is always attracted to a _____ pole.

Back of Frame 16

That's right. Opposite poles always attract. North poles always attract south poles. South poles always attract north poles.

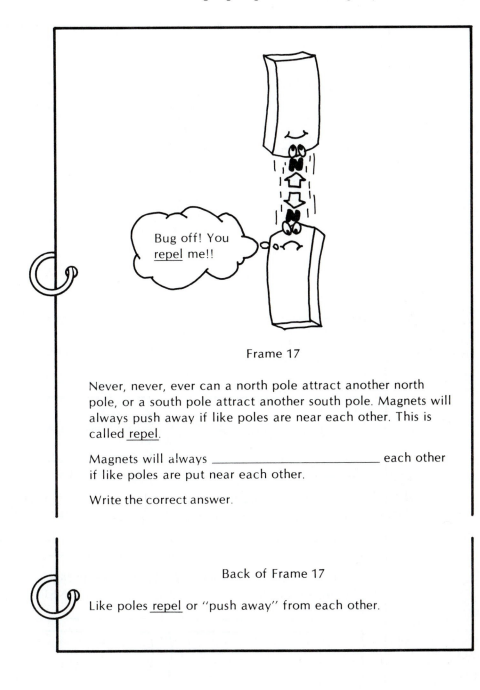

Frame 17

Never, never, ever can a north pole attract another north pole, or a south pole attract another south pole. Magnets will always push away if like poles are near each other. This is called _repel_.

Magnets will always _____ each other if like poles are put near each other.

Write the correct answer.

Back of Frame 17

Like poles _repel_ or "push away" from each other.

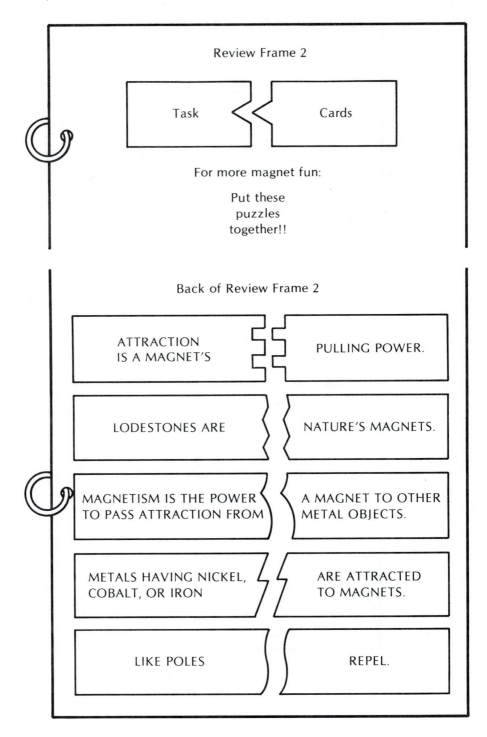

Review Frame 2

Task Cards

For more magnet fun:

Put these
puzzles
together!!

Back of Review Frame 2

| ATTRACTION IS A MAGNET'S | PULLING POWER. |

| LODESTONES ARE | NATURE'S MAGNETS. |

| MAGNETISM IS THE POWER TO PASS ATTRACTION FROM | A MAGNET TO OTHER METAL OBJECTS. |

| METALS HAVING NICKEL, COBALT, OR IRON | ARE ATTRACTED TO MAGNETS. |

| LIKE POLES | REPEL. |

Review Frame 3

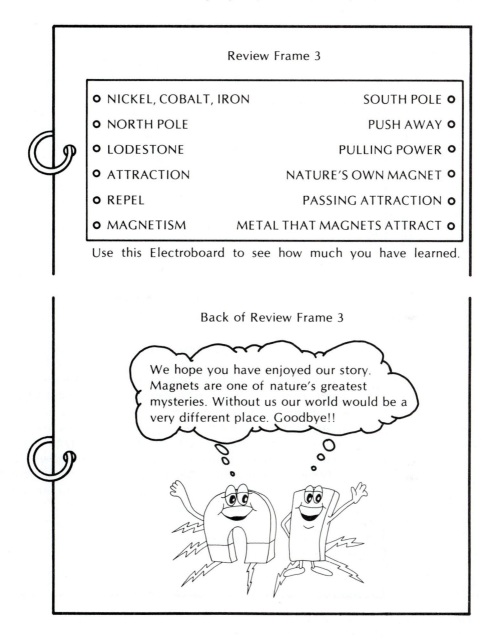

o NICKEL, COBALT, IRON   SOUTH POLE o

o NORTH POLE   PUSH AWAY o

o LODESTONE   PULLING POWER o

o ATTRACTION   NATURE'S OWN MAGNET o

o REPEL   PASSING ATTRACTION o

o MAGNETISM   METAL THAT MAGNETS ATTRACT o

Use this Electroboard to see how much you have learned.

Back of Review Frame 3

We hope you have enjoyed our story. Magnets are one of nature's greatest mysteries. Without us our world would be a very different place. Goodbye!!

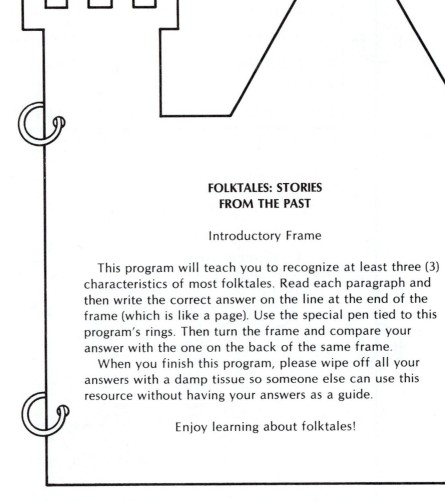

FOLKTALES: STORIES
FROM THE PAST

Introductory Frame

This program will teach you to recognize at least three (3)
characteristics of most folktales. Read each paragraph and
then write the correct answer on the line at the end of the
frame (which is like a page). Use the special pen tied to this
program's rings. Then turn the frame and compare your
answer with the one on the back of the same frame.
When you finish this program, please wipe off all your
answers with a damp tissue so someone else can use this
resource without having your answers as a guide.

Enjoy learning about folktales!

FIGURE 7-8   This Programmed Learning Sequence, "Folktales: Stories from the Past," was designed by teachers Jeannette Bauer and Mary Dawber, New York.

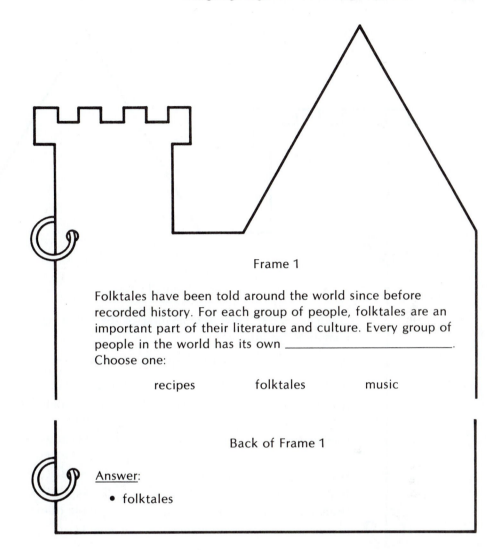

Frame 1

Folktales have been told around the world since before recorded history. For each group of people, folktales are an important part of their literature and culture. Every group of people in the world has its own _____.
Choose one:

recipes   folktales   music

Back of Frame 1

Answer:
- folktales

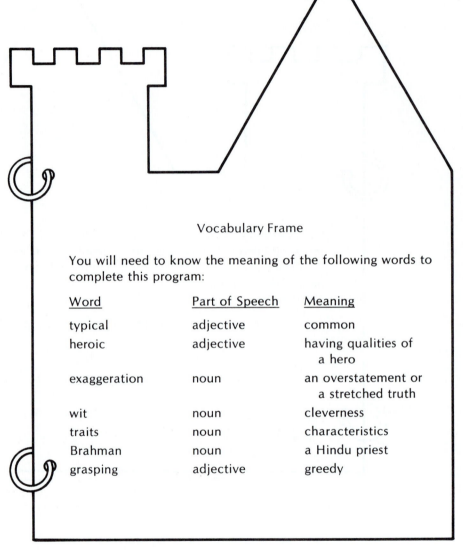

Vocabulary Frame

You will need to know the meaning of the following words to complete this program:

Word	Part of Speech	Meaning
typical	adjective	common
heroic	adjective	having qualities of a hero
exaggeration	noun	an overstatement or a stretched truth
wit	noun	cleverness
traits	noun	characteristics
Brahman	noun	a Hindu priest
grasping	adjective	greedy

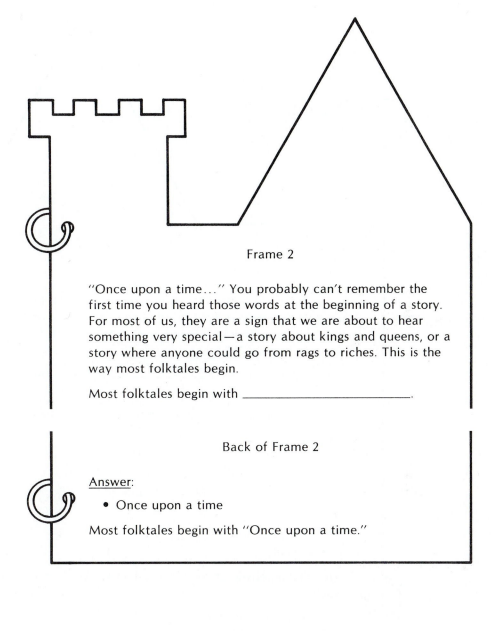

Frame 2

"Once upon a time..." You probably can't remember the first time you heard those words at the beginning of a story. For most of us, they are a sign that we are about to hear something very special—a story about kings and queens, or a story where anyone could go from rags to riches. This is the way most folktales begin.

Most folktales begin with _____.

Back of Frame 2

<u>Answer</u>:

• Once upon a time

Most folktales begin with "Once upon a time."

Frame 3

Most folktales describe what happened long ago, as "Once upon a time" suggests. Other phrases, such as "There was once," "Once there lived," and "Long, long ago," often are used by the author as opening lines. Those are all typical ways to begin a folktale.

Most folktales have _____ opening lines.

typical   uncommon   symbolic

Choose one:

Back of Frame 3

Answer:

• typical

One characteristic of folktales is their typical opening lines, such as:

• Once upon a time
• Long, long ago
• There once was a...
         or
• Once there lived a...

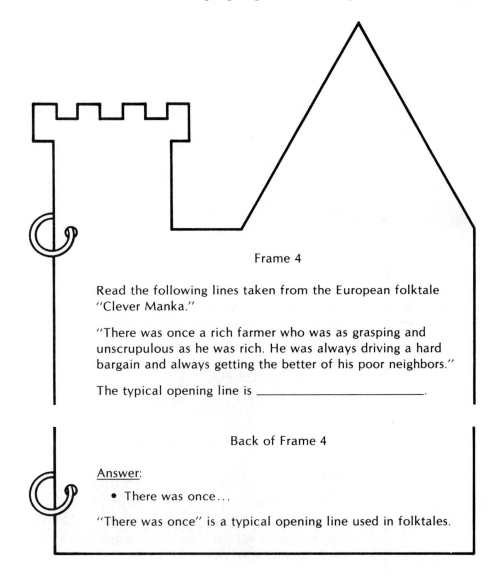

Frame 4

Read the following lines taken from the European folktale "Clever Manka."

"There was once a rich farmer who was as grasping and unscrupulous as he was rich. He was always driving a hard bargain and always getting the better of his poor neighbors."

The typical opening line is _____.

Back of Frame 4

Answer:

* There was once...

"There was once" is a typical opening line used in folktales.

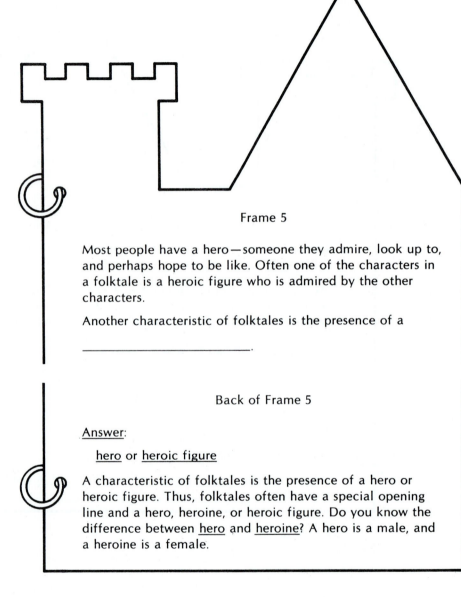

Frame 5

Most people have a hero—someone they admire, look up to, and perhaps hope to be like. Often one of the characters in a folktale is a heroic figure who is admired by the other characters.

Another characteristic of folktales is the presence of a

_____.

Back of Frame 5

<u>Answer</u>:

<u>hero</u> or <u>heroic figure</u>

A characteristic of folktales is the presence of a hero or heroic figure. Thus, folktales often have a special opening line and a hero, heroine, or heroic figure. Do you know the difference between <u>hero</u> and <u>heroine</u>? A hero is a male, and a heroine is a female.

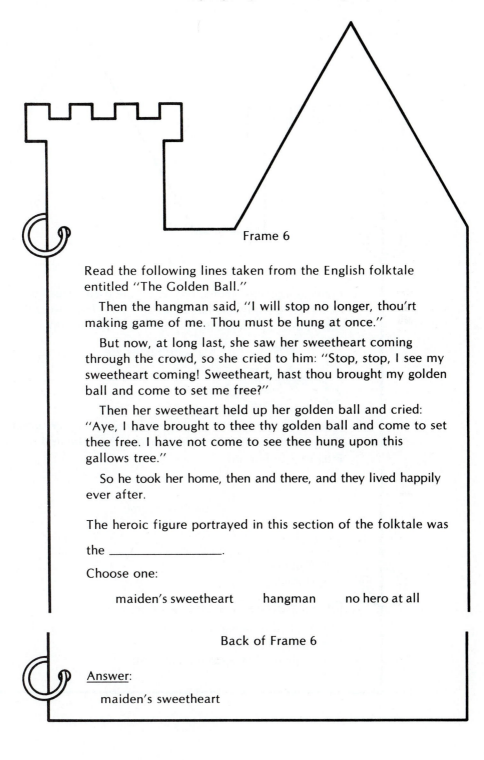

Frame 6

Read the following lines taken from the English folktale entitled "The Golden Ball."

Then the hangman said, "I will stop no longer, thou'rt making game of me. Thou must be hung at once."

But now, at long last, she saw her sweetheart coming through the crowd, so she cried to him: "Stop, stop, I see my sweetheart coming! Sweetheart, hast thou brought my golden ball and come to set me free?"

Then her sweetheart held up her golden ball and cried: "Aye, I have brought to thee thy golden ball and come to set thee free. I have not come to see thee hung upon this gallows tree."

So he took her home, then and there, and they lived happily ever after.

The heroic figure portrayed in this section of the folktale was

the _____.

Choose one:

maiden's sweetheart   hangman   no hero at all

Back of Frame 6

<u>Answer:</u>

maiden's sweetheart

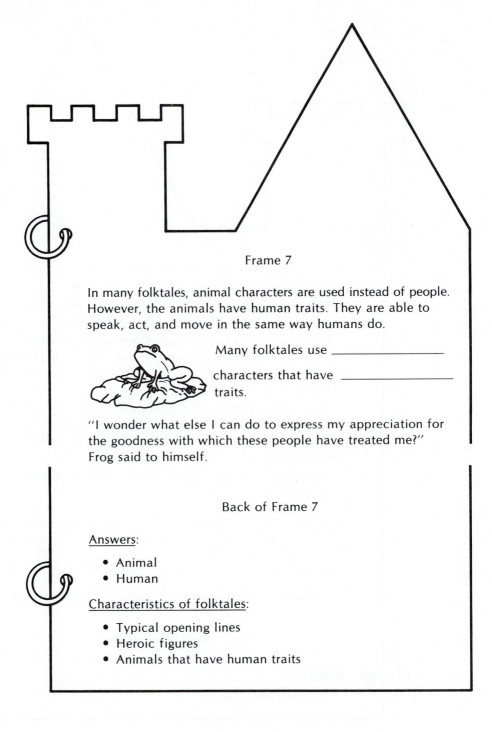

Frame 7

In many folktales, animal characters are used instead of people. However, the animals have human traits. They are able to speak, act, and move in the same way humans do.

Many folktales use ＿＿＿＿＿＿＿

characters that have ＿＿＿＿＿＿＿

traits.

"I wonder what else I can do to express my appreciation for the goodness with which these people have treated me?" Frog said to himself.

Back of Frame 7

Answers:

- Animal
- Human

Characteristics of folktales:

- Typical opening lines
- Heroic figures
- Animals that have human traits

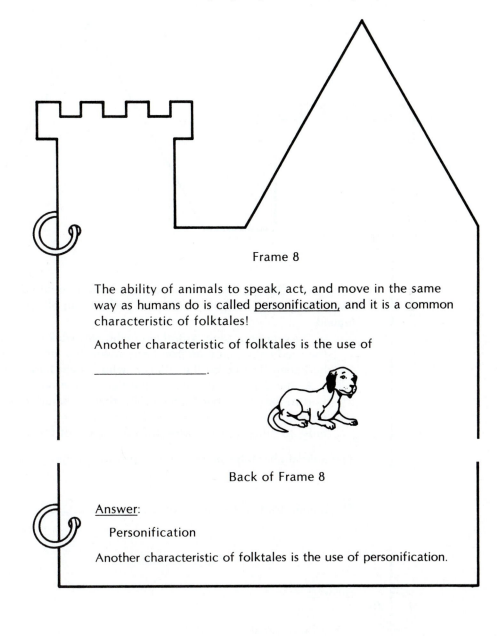

Frame 8

The ability of animals to speak, act, and move in the same way as humans do is called <u>personification,</u> and it is a common characteristic of folktales!

Another characteristic of folktales is the use of

_____.

Back of Frame 8

<u>Answer:</u>

   Personification

Another characteristic of folktales is the use of personification.

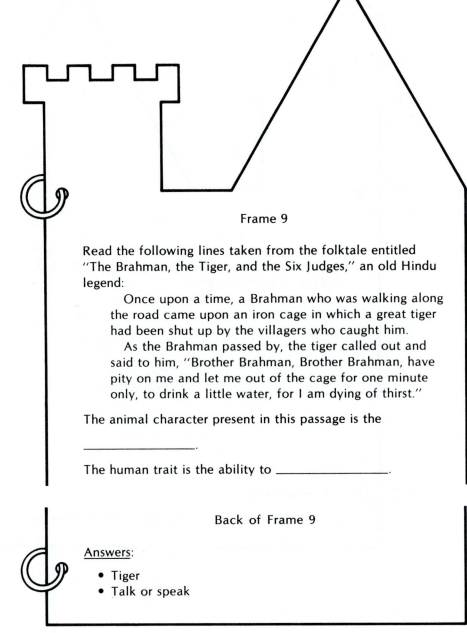

Frame 9

Read the following lines taken from the folktale entitled "The Brahman, the Tiger, and the Six Judges," an old Hindu legend:

> Once upon a time, a Brahman who was walking along the road came upon an iron cage in which a great tiger had been shut up by the villagers who caught him.
>
> As the Brahman passed by, the tiger called out and said to him, "Brother Brahman, Brother Brahman, have pity on me and let me out of the cage for one minute only, to drink a little water, for I am dying of thirst."

The animal character present in this passage is the

_____.

The human trait is the ability to _____.

Back of Frame 9

<u>Answers</u>:

- Tiger
- Talk or speak

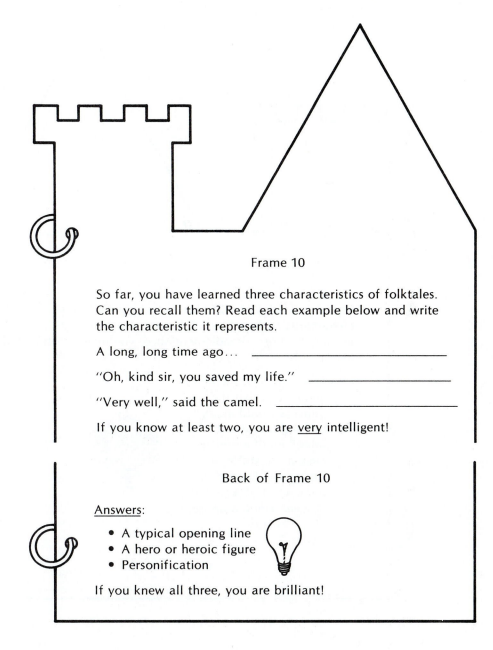

Frame 10

So far, you have learned three characteristics of folktales. Can you recall them? Read each example below and write the characteristic it represents.

A long, long time ago... _____

"Oh, kind sir, you saved my life." _____

"Very well," said the camel. _____

If you know at least two, you are <u>very</u> intelligent!

Back of Frame 10

<u>Answers</u>:

- A typical opening line
- A hero or heroic figure
- Personification

If you knew all three, you are brilliant!

Frame 11

Remember that not all folktales will have all these characteristics, but they will have a few. If an author doesn't use any of those already mentioned, you may find something like this...

Then one day, the king announced that the princess would marry the one who would bring him three things. First, a glassful of all the waters. Second, a bouquet of all kinds of flowers. Third, a basket of ay, ay nuts.

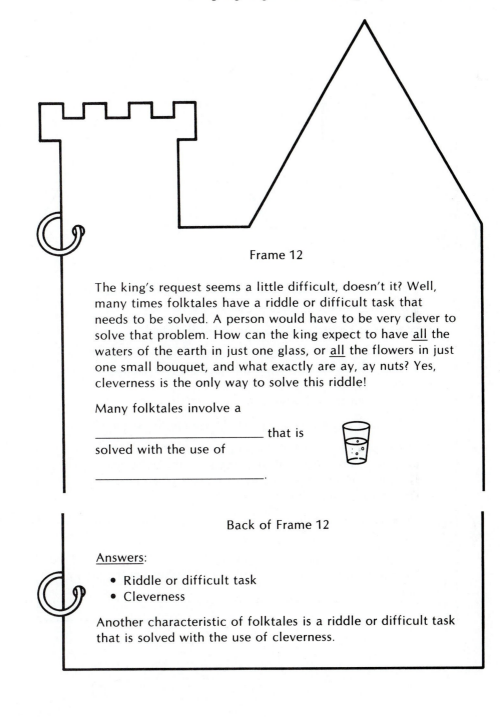

Frame 12

The king's request seems a little difficult, doesn't it? Well, many times folktales have a riddle or difficult task that needs to be solved. A person would have to be very clever to solve that problem. How can the king expect to have <u>all</u> the waters of the earth in just one glass, or <u>all</u> the flowers in just one small bouquet, and what exactly are ay, ay nuts? Yes, cleverness is the only way to solve this riddle!

Many folktales involve a

_____ that is

solved with the use of

_____.

Back of Frame 12

<u>Answers</u>:

- Riddle or difficult task
- Cleverness

Another characteristic of folktales is a riddle or difficult task that is solved with the use of cleverness.

Frame 13

The shepherd was very clever indeed in solving the king's riddle. Read on to find out just how clever he was...

"Give me the first one," commanded the king.

"Here is a glass of all waters," said the shepherd. "It contains all the waters—waters from the rain, the mountains, the hills, the valleys, the brooks, the springs, and the rivers, for it comes from the sea where all the waters flow."

"Well said," cried the king. "Now give me the second."

The shepherd presented the king a bouquet of all the flowers. "Here, your majesty, indeed, is the most beautiful bouquet I could find. It contains flowers of all kinds, put together by the bees in this honeycomb."

"Good indeed!" merrily shouted the king. "Now for the last one."

"Your majesty," said the shepherd, "The last thing you will have to pick out yourself. Here in this basket are the ay, ay nuts."

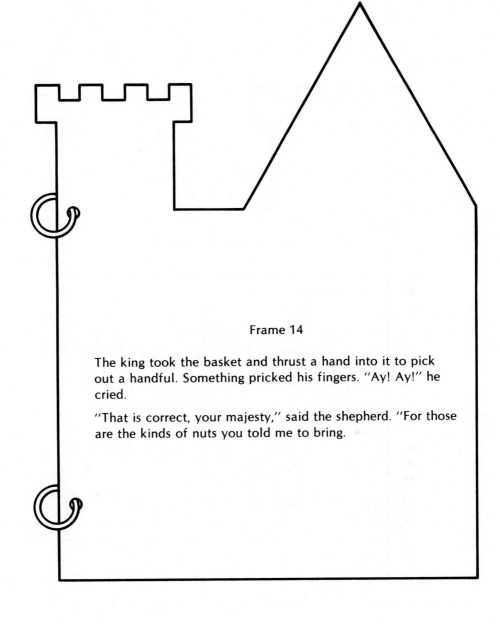

Frame 14

The king took the basket and thrust a hand into it to pick out a handful. Something pricked his fingers. "Ay! Ay!" he cried.

"That is correct, your majesty," said the shepherd. "For those are the kinds of nuts you told me to bring.

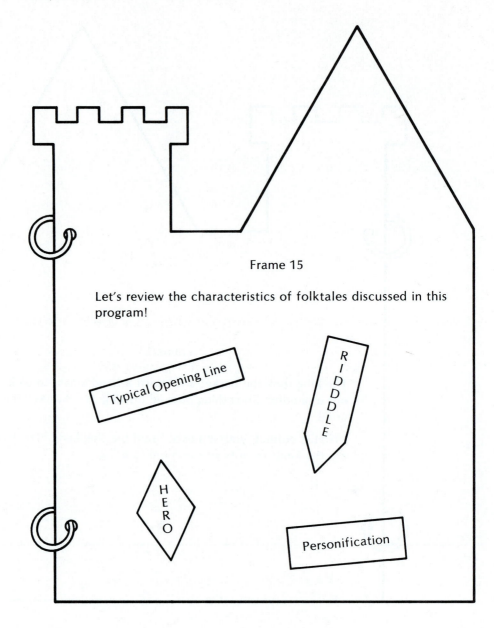

Frame 15

Let's review the characteristics of folktales discussed in this program!

Typical Opening Line

RIDDDLE

HERO

Personification

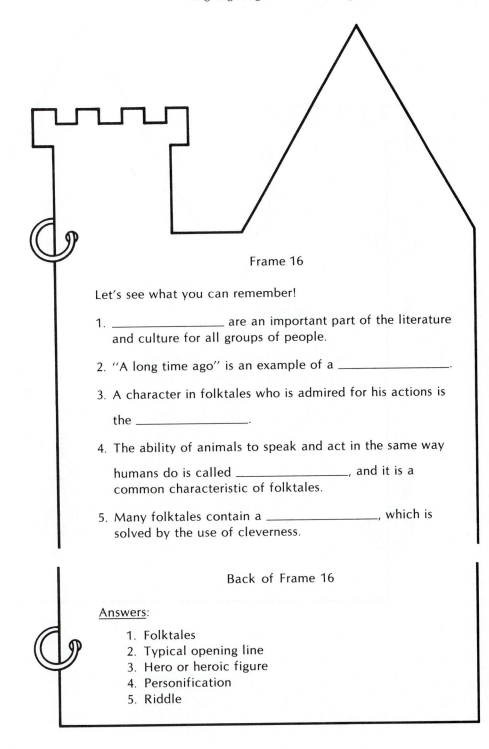

Frame 16

Let's see what you can remember!

1. _____ are an important part of the literature and culture for all groups of people.

2. "A long time ago" is an example of a _____.

3. A character in folktales who is admired for his actions is

   the _____.

4. The ability of animals to speak and act in the same way

   humans do is called _____, and it is a
   common characteristic of folktales.

5. Many folktales contain a _____, which is
   solved by the use of cleverness.

Back of Frame 16

Answers:
1. Folktales
2. Typical opening line
3. Hero or heroic figure
4. Personification
5. Riddle

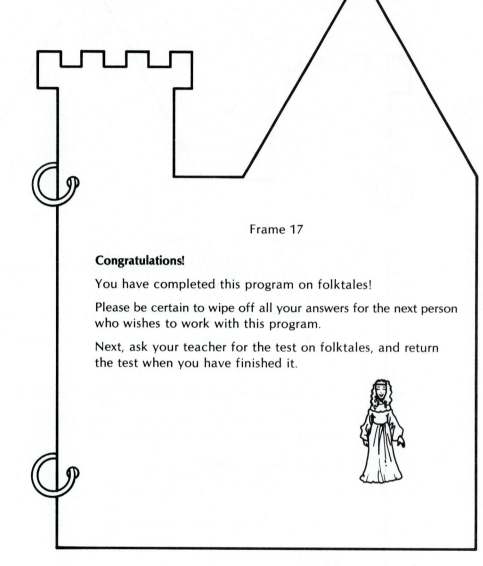

Frame 17

Congratulations!

You have completed this program on folktales!

Please be certain to wipe off all your answers for the next person who wishes to work with this program.

Next, ask your teacher for the test on folktales, and return the test when you have finished it.

Elementary school children can be taught to follow the directions in Chapter 10 for developing Programmed Learning Sequences. Many youngsters are computer-literate and can apply the identical principles for creating a PLS to designing software that responds to global learners. Tactual supplements then can be available for reinforcement. (Photograph courtesy of Center for the Study of Learning and Teaching Styles, St. John's University, New York.)

This Programmed Learning Sequence on "Photosynthesis: It Lights Up Your Life"
carries the leaf shape throughout the resource and uses direct book text for the basic
information.

A Final Word on Programmed Learning Sequences

Programmed Learning Sequences (PLSs) permit children who require structure to achieve at their own pace and learn more, more rapidly than when they are required to participate in whole-class instruction which is relatively ineffective for them. PLSs respond well to students' visual and tactual strengths, and an accompanying tape permits auditory youngsters and those who do not read well to use this approach efficiently. PLSs maintain childrens' interests through their global stories, varied tactual games, immediate feedback, small amounts of instruction on each of the frames, and humorous responses on the back of some. Chapter 10 describes how to help children program their textbooks to create their own PLS- and increase their retention even more than by using teacher-developed materials.

8

Designing Contract Activity Packages (CAPs) to Respond to Individual Learning Styles

Why Contract Activity Packages Are Effective

Contract Activity Packages (CAPs) are one of the three basic methods of individualizing instruction. The other two, Programmed Learning Sequences (PLSs) and Multisensory Instructional Packages (MIPs), are described in Chapters 7 and 9. Sample CAPs, PLSs, and MIPs all have been designed to teach the same objectives. Thus, three diverse strategies are available to respond to three different basic learning style patterns and different ability and performance levels. Generally, CAPs are appropriate for average or above-average, gifted, and/or nonconforming (LSI scores of 40 or below on Responsibility) students, (Dunn, 1989b). In addition to responding to specific learning style differences among learners, Contract Activity Packages are more effective than a large-group lecture or question-and-answer discussion for the following reasons:

Permit Self-Pacing

When we stand before a group of students and explain what we are trying to teach, youngsters can absorb the content only as quickly as we are able to relate it. Given different resources through which to learn, many youngsters could achieve more rapidly than some of their classmates. Others, of course, find that the flow of our words is too rapid for them to understand fully. We teachers cover in each lesson what we believe the majority of students in that group are capable of assimilating, but we proceed with the full knowledge that some are capable of learning much more than they are being exposed to in a given time, whereas others are capable of learning only a fragment of what we are highlighting. We understand that the lecture method is effective for only a percentage of students, but for the most part we have not replaced it with better techniques.

If we teach too much too quickly, we are bound to lose the less able student. If we keep a pace that is slow enough so that the less able student may keep abreast, we unwittingly irritate or bore the brighter youngster. If we try to vary the pace to provide interest, both groups may miss important information during the presentation.

In contrast to a group lecture, Contract Activity Packages permit individual pacing so that students may learn as quickly or as slowly as they are able to master the material. In addition, youngsters are neither embarrassed because others grasp the content more quickly than they do, nor bored because they must wait for classmates to catch up with them before the class is introduced to the next knowledge or skill area. Each learner works independently but may, by choice, team up with classmates who can pace themselves similarly.

Provide Varied Academic Levels

Whenever we address an entire class, instruction is, of necessity, geared to the academic level of the largest number of children present. We all know, however, that in every group some can absorb information in its simplest form, whereas others first become interested when the concepts become complex and challenging. Auditory students can hear something once and retain it, whereas others require extensive reinforcement before they are capable of either understanding or remembering. Those who learn easily in class are likely to be bored by the detailed repetition that certain classmates require; those who learn slowly may become frustrated by their inability to acquire the knowledge that their counterparts do with ease. In contrast to a group lecture, Contract Activity Packages can be designed so that students can function on their current academic level but master concepts or facts through resources that clarify the content because of their style responsiveness. This may be accomplished in four ways:

1. Resource Alternatives teach the required objectives at different reading levels.
2. Activity Alternatives require application of the content.
3. Reporting Alternatives cause review of the content with peer discussion and, if necessary, correction.
4. Small-group techniques provide another instructional strategy through peer learning.

Foster Independence

When we speak to a large group, students are dependent on us for their intellectual growth and stimulation. Further, each youngster is required to learn the same thing at the same time to the same extent and in the same way. Since learners differ from one another in ability, achievement, interests, and learning styles, their dependence on us as a primary source seriously limits the academic progress of some. Finally, despite our skills and sensitivities as teachers, it is important to recognize that some students learn better through a multimedia approach, computer programs, simulations, projects, or tactual/kinesthetic resources than they do from an articulate, knowledgeable adult, and that the large-group lecture does not enable them to learn easily. Since nature endowed each person with unique sensory strengths and limitations, many students are able to learn more and learn it better by beginning with visual, tactual, or kinesthetic resources rather than through an auditory approach— which is what a lecture or discussion is.

Through the use of Contract Activity Packages, youngsters become personally responsible for learning what is required. They are given specific objectives and a choice of media resources through which they may learn. Although they are told exactly what they must master, they are given no indication of which resources contain the necessary answers. Because of their exposure to a variety of materials in their search for the explicit information in their objectives, students obtain a great deal of ancillary knowledge. Often the required concepts are included in several resources, thus providing multisensory repetition.

Moreover, since the students may select the resources they use (from a list of approved ones), the self-selection factor improves their motivation, reduces their nonconformity inclinations, and permits them to work in ways in which they feel most comfortable. Self-pacing permits them to learn as quickly as they can, but well enough to retain what they have studied. As they become accustomed to exercising freedom of choice and assuming responsibility, they become increasingly independent of their teacher and learn to use resources to their advantage. They begin to recognize that they can learn easily and well by themselves, and gradually they develop sufficient confidence to move into new studies and design their own resources. They eventually take pride in their ability to teach themselves, and ultimately they use the teacher as a guide and facilitator rather than as a fountain of knowledge from which to absorb information.

Teachers who believe that the greatest gifts they can give to their students are a love of learning and the tools to teach themselves easily will enjoy the effects of contracting. Those who teach for the self-gratification of having students serve as an admiring audience for their performances will find it more difficult to encourage independent learning and to adapt instructional strategies to their students' learning styles. Nevertheless, for optimal learning to occur, those teachers will need to identify the students who require an authority figure, those who learn by listening, those who are able to learn at the time of day when they are scheduled for classes, those who can remain seated passively for the length of each class or subject period, and those who are so motivated that they will learn merely because the teacher suggests or projects that it is important to do so.

Reduce Frustration and Anxiety

If education is important, as the compulsory education laws imply, then everyone should become educated. If everyone should be educated, everyone should be encouraged to learn as well and as quickly as is possible—for that person. Since the majority of youngsters are neither gifted nor extremely bright, imagine how discouraged they must feel every day of the week when they realize that they must use all their resources to live up to the teacher's expectations while a few of their classmates exert little effort and invariably appear to know all the answers.

Although some successfully hide their anxiety, many verbalize that they don't like school, while others drop out even as they occupy their seats in the classroom. Despite the fact that both national and state commissions have recommended the development of alternative programs that respond to "the great diversity of students and needs . . . within the schools" (Rise Report, 1975), innovative or different approaches to learning often are suspect and are expected to continually produce higher academic achievement and more positive student attitudes than are evidenced in traditional educational settings.

Contract Activity Packages reduce student anxiety and frustration without requiring extensive changes in class organization. They can be used in a self-contained classroom at any level and with many students. Youngsters are permitted to learn in ways that they find most amenable—by themselves, with a peer or two, in a small group, with the teacher, through resources of their choice, at their seats, on the floor, and so on.

When students are permitted to learn through this method, it is important that rules be established to indicate clearly those behaviors that are acceptable and to insist that these regulations be adhered to firmly. It is also important that students be trusted to proceed seriously and to accomplish their objectives. Youngsters who do not work effectively on their CAPs should be cautioned and advised that they will not be permitted to continue learning in this way unless they achieve a certain minimum grade on each examination related to their studies. Research has demonstrated that, in many cases, teachers are unable to identify the special learning styles of youngsters. Instead, they teach all students in the ways the teachers feel most comfortable. When learning style strengths are complemented, however, student motivation and achievement increases significantly (see Appendix A). Moreover, independence is enhanced when students are allowed to take CAPs to the library, study areas, or their homes to pursue them at the right time of day, in quiet or with music, with food or not, and so forth.

Capitalize on Individual Student Interests

All students must learn to read, to write, to express themselves well, and to compute. Beyond these *musts,* however, there is no curriculum that every student everywhere should, of necessity, master. There is no need for every youngster to know the annual rainfall in exotic places or to commit to memory foreign products, capital cities, rivers, and other such extraneous facts that make up the required curriculum for many classes. It is equally ludicrous for every student to be required to study algebra, a foreign language, industrial arts, music appreciation, or many of the subjects in a standard curriculum. We understand that the intent of extensive exposure to a variety of different studies is to expand the horizons and interests of students—but the opposite often occurs. When youngsters are forced to take specific subjects without choice, they often become recalcitrant and negative.

Perhaps schools might experiment with a series of cluster subjects, such as those that are found in most curricula, and offer their students a choice of any four out of seven, or five out of eight. It is true that some students might never be exposed to social studies, or literature, or the arts, but we suggest that most would learn in depth the areas that they do select to study. As Mager and McCann (1963) suggested, motivation increases with the amount of control we exercise over what, when, and how we learn.

If you believe it is necessary for all students to learn the conventional school curriculum, consider the topics we seldom if ever discuss in school that often touch their lives directly—divorce, pollution, racism, sex roles, poverty, the energy crisis, inflation. A Contract Activity Package can be used to introduce these and other topics of interest to those for whom they will have value. CAPs, therefore, will free you to direct your major energies toward, first, students who need direct interaction with you and, second, subjects that require mastery by all—reading, language, computational skills, and interpersonal values. Basic knowledge in other areas can easily be added to interdisciplinary themes through the use of additional CAPs and other teaching strategies.

Learning Style Characteristics Responsive to Contract Activity Packages

Contract Activity Packages are responsive to most learning style characteristics, for they may be used flexibly with some students and with a precise structure for others, as described in the following examples:

1. For students who need sound, an earplug may be used to isolate radio or recorded music for those who benefit from it. If discussion is important, an instructional area (such as a Learning Station or Interest Center) can be established in a section of the room and blocked off by perpendicular dividers to provide an inner sanctum for its occupants and to protect their classmates from being distracted by movement or talk. Rules for discussion need to be established so that no one outside the instructional area hears the words of anyone inside, but that is a management strategy that will be necessary whenever you begin to accommodate the classroom to individual learning styles. The youngster who requires silence can use another instructional area where no one may speak and where the adjacent dens or alcoves are used for essentially quiet activities.

2. When students are permitted to work on their CAPs anywhere in the classroom as long as they work quietly, do not interrupt others, and respect the rules that have been established, they will automatically adjust light, temperature, and design to their learning style characteristics.

3. The motivated, persistent, and responsible students should be given a series of objectives to complete, a list of the resources that they may use to obtain information, suggestions for how and where to get help should they experience difficulty, and an explanation of how they will be expected to demonstrate their achievement of the objectives. They then should be permitted to begin working and to continue—with occasional spot-checking—until their task has been completed. The unmotivated, the less persistent, and those who tend to be less responsible should be given only a few objectives, the listing of resources that may be used, and suggestions for obtaining assistance when they need it. These youngsters, however, require frequent supervision and constant encouragement and praise for their progress. You will need to circulate among them, ask questions, check on their understanding of what they are doing, and comment favorably when you observe their efforts. Were you to treat the motivated students in the same way, you would be interrupting their concentration and diverting them. But if you don't check on the unmotivated students when they have difficulty with an assignment, they will become frustrated, get involved in diversionary activities, or give up.

4. The CAP permits students to work either alone, with a friend or two, or as part of a team through the small-group activities that are included. Youngsters also may work directly with the teacher when difficult objectives require adult assistance.

5. The Resource Alternatives section of the CAP includes auditory, visual, and tactual or kinesthetic (T/K) resources (at different levels), thus permitting students to learn through their strongest perceptual strength and to reinforce what they've learned through the next strongest sense or senses. The CAP may be used anytime—during the early morning hours, after dinner—to match the individual learner's best time of day for concentrating and producing. Further, youngsters may snack on raw vegetables or other nutritious foods if they feel the need to, and they also may take short breaks for relaxation—

This motivated student with a suggested Resource Alternative of the Contract Activity Package he has been assigned. (Photograph courtesy of Sacred Heart Academy, Hempstead, New York.)

as long as they return to their objectives and continue working on them until they have been completed. You are encouraged to experiment with CAPs for students who have the potential for mastering objectives either alone or with a classmate or two. However, when a youngster using a CAP does not perform well on the final assessment for that topic, immediately transfer him or her to another instructional approach, such as a PLS, an MIP, or T/K resources. CAPs are *best* for motivated, auditory, or visual learners; they also are responsive to nonconformists.

Basic Principles of Contract Activity Packages

A Contract Activity Package is an individualized educational plan that facilitates learning because it includes each of the following elements:

1. *Simply stated objectives that itemize exactly what the student is required to learn:* Do you recall studying for a test in college and trying to determine the important items on which you might be tested? Teaching at all levels is often conducted in an atmosphere of mystery; we introduce many concepts, facts, and skills and then require students to intuit those items that, in our opinion, are worthy of commitment to memory and retention. This approach, though common, is not logical. If specific knowledge is worthwhile, we ought to indicate that to our students and then encourage them to learn those things so well that they retain them. Knowing what is expected is central to individual motivation.

Instead of continuing the pedagogical game of "I'll teach many things, and you try to guess which I'll include on the test!," we recognize that all students cannot learn everything that we teach—because of their individual abilities, experiences, interests, and learning style differences. We then diagnose each student to identify whether he or she is capable of learning many things sequentially (60 or above on Persistence) or just a few things in a series of short, multiple assignments (40 or below on Persistence), which can then be prescribed as a lesson, Contract Activity Package, Programmed Learning Sequence, or Multisensory Instructional Package. Motivated, persistent, responsible students may be given longer tasks to complete; their opposites should be given many, shorter fewer tasks. Brighter students may be assigned a number of things to master; slower achievers should be given several shorter prescriptions.

When we tell youngsters what they are expected to achieve, we have given them their objectives. When we also explain the ways in which they may demonstrate that they have mastered their objectives, we are giving them a statement that is called a *behavioral objective.* More information about how to write objectives for students is provided in the next section of this chapter.

When students are given simple statements that itemize those objectives for which they are responsible, they need not be concerned about *everything* but can focus on just the tasks that they must master. This freedom from unnecessary anxiety reduces stress and permits them to proceed to and learn required objectives and aspects of specific interest to them.

2. *Multisensory Alternative Resources that teach the information that the objectives indicate must be mastered:* Students are given a list of available resources that they may use to learn the information required by their objectives. The resources should be multisensory: visual materials such as books, films, filmstrips, study prints, computer programs, or transparencies; auditory materials such as Task Cards, Learning Circles, and games; and interesting kinesthetic materials such as body games or extremely large tactual devices. The resources are *suggested* sources of information, but the students are free either to use them or to identify other instructional materials through which they may learn. If students use resources that have not been listed in the teacher-designed Contract Activity Package, they must identify them by direct reference when demonstrating the knowledge they have gained. Because youngsters are free to select the materials through which they will learn, the choices are called *Resource Alternatives.* It is important, of course, to help students recognize their perceptual strengths so that they use Resource Alternatives that respond to their strongest sense to introduce information, and materials that respond to their next strongest senses to reinforce what they have learned.

3. *A series of activities through which the information that has been mastered is used in a creative way:* When we first became involved in individualizing instruction in 1967, we used Learning Activity Packages (LAPs) that included behavioral objectives, special and assigned readings, resources through which to learn (which were called "activities"), and a posttest by which to assess the student's progress. We found that students were able to examine their objectives, use the resources, acquire the necessary information, and pass the test at the end of the LAP. Three months later, however, the average retention rate was approximately 58 percent.

When experimenting with alternatives to LAPs, we found that if we added two procedures to the existing system, we could increase students' ability to remember information that had been learned by approximately 20 percent. The first was a series of activities in which students were required to use the information they had learned in a creative way. On the basis of Mager and McCann's studies completed in 1963, we gave students a choice from among approved alternatives of the activities they would complete. This section of the CAP is thus called *Activity Alternatives.* Activity Alternatives may be labeled A (auditory), V (visual), T (tactual), or K (kinesthetic). They provide multisensory options that match perceptual strength and learning style.

4. *A series of alternative ways in which creative instructional resources developed by one student may be shared with one or more—but no more than six to eight—classmates:* The second procedure that tends to increase retention for peer-oriented students is called *Reporting Alternatives.* We found that when students engage in a creative activity, they often want to share it with their peers. The sharing serves as either an introduction or a reinforcement of the material to the person who is being shown the activity, but it also provides the person who created it with reinforcement and a sense of accomplishment. This sharing—or reporting—increases retention of what has been learned and, in addition, serves as a self-fulfilling experience for some. Teaching others often promotes learning for the "student" teacher.

5. *At least three small-group techniques:* Individualization does not imply that children must work or learn in isolation. Rather, it suggests that each student's learning style be identified and that each learner be permitted to achieve in ways that complement his or her style. Since many students prefer to work in small groups or in a pair (Poirier, 1970), and since others evidence this preference when their requirements become difficult, at least three small-group techniques (of the teacher's choice) are added to each Contract Activity Package so that sections of the CAP that are difficult may be attacked (and conquered) by a few students working together. A Team Learning to teach each difficult objective should *always* be included among or in addition to the three small-group techniques.

Although the small-group requirements are not mandated for every youngster, they do serve as an aid for students who find it difficult to complete intricate tasks or to learn difficult concepts by themselves.

6. *A pretest, a self-test, and a posttest:* Each Contract Activity Package has a single test attached to it. This test may be used to assess the student's knowledge of the information required by the CAP's behavioral objectives before the CAP is assigned, so that students who have already mastered those concepts and skills need not be burdened with the same subject matter again. To avoid loss of motivation, the pretest should be eliminated in all cases where the teacher knows scores will be very low.

This pretest assessment also may be used as a self-assessment by the student to identify how much of the information required by the behavioral objectives he or she has already mastered and how much remains to be learned even after he or she has ostensibly completed the CAP. Self-assessment builds ownership of the contract and its objectives. Self-testing reduces stress and promotes self-confidence.

Finally, we may use the same assessment to test the student after resources have been used, the Activity Alternatives have been completed and shared with selected classmates, the three small-group techniques have been done, the self-test has been taken, and the behavioral objectives have been mastered. If you wish, you may develop three separate assessment devices, but since the test questions are directly related to the individual behavioral objectives, it is just as valuable to use the identical test for all three situations. This approach establishes a pattern of revealing what is expected, removes the mystery, and builds motivation. Should you become concerned about rote memorization of answers, you can change the order of the questions on the final CAP test. Your students' confidence and interest will be retained.

Step-by-Step Guide to Designing a Contract Activity Package

The first Contract Activity Package that you design takes time because you must adopt several new techniques with which you may be relatively unfamiliar. The second CAP is not difficult to write at all, and by the time you embark on your third, you'll be helping colleagues and administrators by explaining the process and the reasons for each stage. Many elementary students are capable of designing their own CAPs after they have worked successfully with three or four. Initially, you may want to provide the objectives and permit them to design the remaining parts. Eventually they will be able to create complete CAPs—whether alone or with a friend or two (see Chapter 10).

Step 1. *Begin by identifying a topic, concept, or skill that you want to teach.* Write the name of the topic, concept, or skill that you have decided to teach as a title at the top of a blank sheet of paper. There are two kinds of CAPs. The first, a curriculum CAP, covers a topic that you would like to teach to all or most of the students in your class. The second, an individual CAP, is designed for a topic in which only one or a few students might be interested. Because we are assuming that this is your first effort at CAP development, we suggest that you identify a topic that would be appropriate for most of your students. When you have completed this first CAP, you will have the skills to write as many as you wish—some for individuals, others for small groups, and the majority for use with an entire class at different times during the semester. The Center for the Study of Learning and Teaching Styles at St. John's University's provides excellent sample CAPs at almost cost to practitioners who prefer to follow perfected ones as a guide.

Curriculum contracts, once they are colored and laminated, will remain useful for years. Sharing copied CAPs and building a library of varied topics will provide an expanding resource for schools and districts. Gifted students, parents, aides, and education majors at local colleges can assist in the effort to stock a central "bank" of effective and valuable CAPs. All CAPs may be duplicated for multiple use by teachers in the appropriate subject classrooms.

Step 2. *Develop a humorous or clever global subtitle.*

Examples

"Life in the Universe: Give Me Some Space"
"Electricity: The Shocking Truth"
"Graphics: Get the Point?"
"DNA: The Double Helix Is Not a Roller Coaster Ride"

Step 3. *List the things about this topic that you believe are so important that every student in your class should learn them.* Then list the things about this topic that are important, but that slow achievers need not necessarily learn. Finally, consider the things about this topic that might appeal to special students—for example, the musician, the artist, the traveler, the carpenter, the cook, and so on. List these as special interest items.

Examine your developing list of objectives. Be certain that the most important ones to be learned are placed first. These should be followed by items that are also of consequence but that everyone need not necessarily master.

Finally, add the items that you believe might be of interest to students with special talents or interests. Objectives concerning sports, dance, drama, music, or the culinary arts often increase interest when related to subject matter content.

All the most important items will become the required learning for your students. Many of the secondary list of important items will be required, but students should be given some choices among these items. Thus, the way in which you assign the number, of required objectives will help you personalize the CAP according to individual achievement and/or interest levels.

When the CAP is completed and ready for use, assign the first group of required objectives to all. Remember that motivation is increased by options—so if you can permit students some choice, even among the first objectives, you will observe nonconformists beginning to evidence interest in the assignment. For example, you might say that the class must master "any seven of the following nine objectives." Some teachers suggest: "Complete the first three and any additional five of your choice." Another alternative would be, "Do any three in the first group, numbers 1 to 3 in the second group, and any two in the third group." In short order, many gifted students will complete the most difficult questions, design two or three objectives of their own, or create an entire CAP!

Step 4. *Translate the important items into behavioral objectives.* When students are given a list of items that should be learned, these items are called *objectives,* and they become the students' short-term instructional goals. Because acquired information can be demonstrated in many ways, it is important that youngsters be given an idea of how they will be expected to demonstrate what they have mastered. Recognizing individual differences, we acknowledge that people are capable of evidencing knowledge through different skills and talents. We therefore give students:

1. A general indication of how they may verify mastery of their instructional objectives and
2. Specific alternatives to increase their motivation, diffuse their nonconformity inclinations, and capitalize on their strengths.

Many years ago, Mager (1962) suggested that a behavioral objective should include the following:

1. An identification and name of the overall behavioral act
2. The conditions under which the behavior was to occur
3. The criterion of acceptable performance

After years of working with objectives, we are convinced that when all three items are included, the objectives become too long and complicated for most students to comprehend; are not individualized, and therefore do not respond to learning style, interest, ability levels, or talents; and are not used as efficiently or as humanistically as is possible.

Therefore, we suggest that behavioral objectives—which list the behaviors that may be used to demonstrate mastery of specific learning goals—be written in the following generalized way, and that specific behaviors that may be used to demonstrate acquired knowledge or skills be *optional* through a series of Activity Alternatives. Further, the action prescribed at the beginning of the behavioral objectives should be direct and explicit—for example, list, divide, collect, identify, predict. (See Figure 8-1 for subject applications and 8-2 for general applications of appropriate samples.)

Example

Identify five major causes of World War II.

This objective clearly indicates what must be learned, but it does not restrict learners to explaining in a specific way. Because the causes of World War II can be described in many different ways, we give the students a choice of how they will show that they know the answer by listing a series of Activity Alternatives directly below the behavioral objective and permitting each individual to decide which of the activities he or she prefers.

Step 5. *Design at least three or four Activity Alternatives for each behavioral objective (or for a group of related objectives) so that students may choose how they demonstrate that they have learned what the objectives require of them.* In effect, the Activity Alternatives permit students to determine the conditions under which they will perform or will demonstrate their mastery. See Figure 8-3 for samples of perceptually related Activity Alternatives that can be incorporated into a CAP.

Example

Behavioral Objective   Identify five (5) major causes of World War II.

1. With a group of your classmates, dramatize (role-play) at least five (5) major causes of World War II

2. On a cassette, list at least five (5) major causes of World War II.

3. Write a story about at least five (5) different things that happened to cause World War II.

4. Draw a map of Europe just before World War II. Use symbols, drawings, photographs, or artwork to portray five (5) causes of World War II.

Step 6. *Create a Reporting Alternative for each of the Activity Alternatives that you have designed.* As indicated before, the Activity Alternative gives students a choice of how they will apply the information they have

FIGURE 8–1   Sample Subject Applications

Arts and Crafts
assemble
blend
brush
build
carve
color
construct
crush
cut
dab
dot
draw
drill
finish
fit
fix
fold
form
frame
grind
hammer
handle
heat
illustrate
make
melt
mend
mix
mold
nail
paint
paste
pat
position
pour
press
process
roll
rub
sand
saw
sculpt
sew
shake
sharpen
sketch
smooth
stamp
stick
stir
trace
trim
varnish
wipe
wrap

Drama
act
clasp
correct
cross
direct
display
emit
enter
exit
express
leave
move
pantomime
pass
perform
proceed
respond
show
start
turn

Language
abbreviate
accent
alphabetize
argue
articulate
capitalize
edit
hyphenate
indent
outline
print
pronounce
punctuate
read
recite
speak
spell
state
summarize
syllabicate
translate
type
verbalize
write

Mathematics
add
bisect
calculate
check
compound
compute
count
derive
divide
estimate
extrapolate
extract
graph
group
integrate
interpolate
measure
multiply
number
plot
prove
reduce
solve
square
subtract
tabulate
tally
verify

Music
blow
bow
clap
compose
conduct
finger
harmonize
hum
mute
play
pluck
practice
sing
strum
tap
whistle

Physical Education
arch
bat
bend
carry
catch
chase
climb
coach
coordinate
critique
float
grip
hit
hop
jump
kick
knock
lift
march
perform
pitch
run
score
skate
ski
somersault
stand
stretch
strike
swim
swing
throw
toss

Science
calibrate
compound
connect
convert
decrease
demonstrate
dissect
graft
grow
increase
insert
lengthen
light
limit
manipulate
nurture
operate
plant
prepare
reduce
remove
replace
report
reset
set
specify
straighten
time
transfer
weight

Behavior
accept
agree
aid
allow
answer
buy
communicate
compliment
contribute
cooperate
disagree
discuss
excuse
forgive
greet
guide
help
inform
interact
invite
join
laugh
lend
meet
offer
participate
permit
praise
react
relate
serve
share
smile
supply
talk
thank
volunteer
vote

FIGURE 8-2 Sample General Applications

Simple Tasks
attend
choose
collect
complete
copy
count
define
describe
designate
detect
differentiate
discriminate
distinguish
distribute
duplicate
find
identify
imitate
indicate
isolate
label
list
mark
match
name
note
omit
order
place
point
provide
recall
repeat
select
state
tally
tell
underline

Study Skills
arrange
attempt
categorize
chart
cite

circle
classify
compile
consider
diagram
document
find
follow
formulate
gather
include
itemize
locate
map
organize
quote
record
relate
reproduce
return
search
signify
sort
suggest
support
underline
volunteer

Understanding
conclude
estimate
explain
fill in
justify
rephrase
represent
restate
transform
translate

Analysis Skills
analyze
appraise
combine
compare
conclude

contrast
criticize
deduce
defend
evaluate
explain
formulate
generate
induce
infer
paraphrase
plan
present
save
shorten
structure
substitute
switch

Knowledge
collect
complete
copy
count
define
duplicate
find
identify
imitate
list
label
mark
match
name
note
omit
order
place
point
recall
repeat
select
state
tally
tell
underline

Synthesis Skills
alter
change
design
develop
discover
expand
extend
generalize
modify
paraphrase
predict
propose
question
rearrange
recombine
reconstruct
regroup
rename
reorganize
reorder
rephrase
restate
restructure
retell
rewrite
signify
simplify
synthesize
systematize

Evaluation
argue
assess
judge
predict
validate

Application
construct
demonstrate
draw
illustrate
indicate
isolate
make
record

FIGURE 8–3 Sample Perceptually Related Activity Alternatives

Auditory

Develop a(n):
lecture
oral report
court trial
panel discussion
debate
tape recording
song
poem
mini-operetta
musical performance
skit
puppet show
verbal game
travel lecture
taped scenario, poem, or story
play
videotape
television program
radio show
verbal fairy tale
down-through-the-ages folklore
retold ''most exciting'' ending
quiz show
choral song answering questions like
   the most interesting, most humorous,
   most unlikely ending possible . . .
comic routine
10:00 news report to the nation

Kinesthetic

conduct a survey
design a questionnaire
create a Multisensory Instructional Package
simulate
create a game
build a machine
create an invention
develop a product
campaign for a belief
perform
dramatize
demonstrate through ballet
videotape
photograph
interview
advertise
apply for . . .
put on a puppet show
interpret _____

design a floor maze/game
role-play
act out what *you* would have done

Visual (Pictorial)

Develop a(n):
diagram
map
graph
chart
photograph
illustration
display
cartoon
collage
mural
flip book
historical time line
collection of relics
coloring book
poster
slide show
television show
filmstrip
movie
book jacket
costume
picture game

Tactual

Design a(n):
model
puzzle
Programmed Learning Sequence
scrapbook
sculpture
poster
display
stitchery
cartoon
Flip Chute cards
Set of task cards
collage
stage setting
Pic-a-Hole
character paper dolls
three-dimensional map
artistic display
coloring book
mobile
job description

FIGURE 8–3 *Continued*

diorama
collection
sand table representation
tapestry
jewelry of the time
life-size replica
woven/sewn items
chart
directions for . . .
highlight the most . . .
review
illustrate
pictorial
computer program
Contract Activity Package
pantomime
graph
list new information
crossword puzzle
journal
edited story
newspaper
letter to a friend
written review
symbol-story

Visual (Words)
Develop a(n):
book of poems
poem
diary
lyric
original story
tall tale
written report
book review
biography
editorial
comparison between/among
collection of articles
crossword puzzle
advertisement
imaginary letter
magazine article
newspaper article
letter to a legislator
test/quiz
scramble word game
campaign report
advertisement

learned so that it is reinforced. Once an activity has been completed, most students enjoy sharing their product with others. Sharing an Activity Achievement with classmates or friends provides additional reinforcement for the person who developed it. In addition, it serves as either an introduction of new material or a repetition of previously studied material for the students who serve as the listeners, viewers, players, or participants. Furthermore, the sharing may be another way of demonstrating acquired knowledge or skill.

Example

Behavioral Objective   State at least one (1) important date and event in the life of any eight (8) of the following people and explain how each person impacted on World War II.

1. Hitler	2. Mussolini
3. Franklin D. Roosevelt	4. Churchill
5. Chamberlain	6. Quisling
7. Hirohito	8. Patton
9. Montgomery	10. Eisenhower
11. Lenin	12. Stalin

If you can complete this for ten (10) of the above people, you have excellent potential for becoming a historian!

Activity Alternatives	Reporting Alternatives
1. Make a time line listing the dates and events in the lives of the eight (8) or ten (10) people that you choose. Through illustrations, show the role each played in World War II.	1. Mount the time line in our room and answer any questions your classmates may ask about it.
2. Draw and then dress paper dolls as they would have been dressed had they been the people listed above. Then talk for the dolls and describe at least one important date and event in their lives and how each person impacted on World War II.	2. Give a two-minute talk to three or four people telling them about the characters you drew and how each impacted on World War II.
3. Write a poem or produce a record that describes how each person impacted on World War II.	3. Mount your poem or record that tells at least one important thing about these people.
4. Write an original story, play, or radio or television script that describes a date and event in the life of each of the people about whom you chose to learn. Explain the parts each played in World War II.	4. Read the story or play, on a radio or television show. Rehearse the script with classmates and ask a few students to observe it and then comment in writing. Add their comments to your CAP folder.
5. If you can think of an activity that you would prefer to the ones listed above, write it on a piece of paper and show it to your teacher for possible approval.	5. If your original activity is approved, develop a Reporting Alternative that complements (matches) it.

What follows is a list of Activity and Reporting Alternatives that may be used to develop options for all students. You will want to identify those activities that would be motivating for your students, adapt and rewrite them so that they are appropriate for the specific Contract Activity Package objectives that you are designing, and use them as part of the choices you permit.

They may also be used as homework assignments to add interest to and provide application for required items. The application through development of an original creation using the student's perceptual strengths contributes substantially to retention of difficult information.

Examples

Activity Alternatives

1. Make a miniature stage setting with pipe-cleaner figures to describe the most important information you learned about your topic.
2. Make a poster "advertising" the most interesting information you have learned.

3. Design costumes for people or characters you have learned about.

4. Prepare a travel lecture related to your topic.

5. Draw a series of pictures on a long sheet of paper fastened to two rollers. Write a script for it.
6. Describe in writing or on tape an interesting person or character that you learned about.
7. Write or tell a different ending to one of the events you read about.

8. Pantomime some information you found very interesting.

Reporting Alternatives

1. Display the stage setting and figures and give a two-minute talk explaining what they represent and why you selected them.
2. Display the poster and give a two-minute talk explaining why you found the information interesting.
3. Describe to a group of classmates how you determined what the costumes should be, how you made them, and the people who would have worn them.
4. Give the lecture before a small group of classmates. You also may tape record it for others who are working on the same topic.
5. Show your movie to one or more small groups of classmates.

6. Ask a few classmates to tell you what they think of the person you portrayed.
7. After sharing your thoughts with a classmate or two, ask them to think of other ways the event could have ended.
8. Let a few classmates try to guess what you are pantomiming.

9. Construct puppets and use them in a presentation that explains an interesting part of the information you learned. Have a friend photograph your presentation.

9. Display the pictures and the puppets. Do the presentation.

10. Make a map or chart representing information you have gathered.

10. Display the map or chart and answer questions about it.

11. Broadcast a book review of the topic, as if you were a critic. Tape record the review.

11. Permit others to listen to your tape and tell you if they would like to read the book.

12. Make a clay, soap, or wooden model to illustrate a phase of the information you learned.

12. Display the model and answer questions about it.

13. Construct a diorama to illustrate an important piece of information.

13. Display the diorama and answer questions as an artist might.

14. Dress paper dolls as people or characters in your topic.

14. Give a two-minute talk about the doll characters.

15. Make a mural to illustrate the information you consider interesting.

15. Display the mural and answer questions that arise.

16. Build a sand table setting to represent a part of your topic.

16. Explain the setting to other students. Ask them to evaluate your effort in a few short sentences.

17. Rewrite an important piece of information, simplifying the vocabulary.

17. Develop a project about the information with two (2) classmates.

18. Make a time line, listing important dates and events in sequence.

18. Display the time line and be prepared to answer questions.

19. Write a song including information you learned.

19. Sing the song in person or on tape for a small group of students.

20. Make up a crossword puzzle on this topic.

20. Let other students try to complete it. Check and return their answers to them.

21. Make up a game using information from your topic.

21. Play the game with other members of your class.

22. Direct and participate in a play or choral speaking about your topic.

22. Present the dramatic or choral creation to a small group of classmates.

23. Write a script on this topic for a radio or television program. Produce and participate in this program.
24. Develop commentaries for a silent movie, filmstrip, or slide show on your topic. Use your own photographs or slides, if possible.
25. With others, plan a debate or panel discussion on challenging aspects of your topic.
26. Write a news story, an editorial, a special column, or an advertisement for the school or class newspaper explaining your views concerning any one aspect of your topic.
27. Write an imaginary letter from one character to another. Tell about something that might have happened had they both lived at the time and place of your topic.
28. Make up tall tales about characters in the topic.
29. Keep a make-believe diary about your memorable experiences as you lived through the period concerned with your topic.

30. Try to find the original manuscripts, old page proofs, first editions of books, book jackets, taped interviews with authors or other interesting persons in the community, autographs of authors, or any other

---

23. Present the program for a group of classmates.

24. Present the program for a group of classmates.

25. Hold the debate and participate in it.

26. Mail your writing to the paper. Ask three students to write "letters to the editor" praising or chastising you as a reporter.

27. Display the letter.

28. Permit others to react to them.
29. Read a portion of your diary to some of your classmates. See whether they can identify the period concerned with the topic. Add the diary to the Resource Alternatives available forother people who are studying the topic.

30. Take a group trip concerned with your topic. Share the most interesting information you found with those who accompany you.

documentation related to your topic. If the material cannot be brought to school, organize a small group trip to visit the place where you found the items.

31. Document some original research you've found on your topic using bibliographies, footnotes, and quotations.

31. Submit the research to your teacher.

32. Search the library card index and/or bring photographs and a description of new materials concerned with your topic to class.

32. Add the information to the Resource Alternative for your topic.

33. Develop a computer software program for this objective.

33. Show two friends how to use the software.

34. Broadcast a program to another country giving your point of view about this topic.

34. Have four (4) students receive the broadcast and relate your conclusions.

Step 7. *List all the resources you can locate that students may use to gain the information required by their behavioral objectives.* Try to find multisensory resources if they are available. Categorize the materials separately—for example, books, transparencies, tapes, records, magazines, and games. If you have them, include Programmed Learning Sequences, Multisensory Instructional Packages, Pic-A-Holes, Flip Chutes, Electroboards, Task Cards, or Learning Circles. Use these broad divisions as titles; underline each title and, below it, list the names of the resources that are available. Students may use additional materials if they wish, but they should either show these materials to you or refer to them in their work. Because students may select which resources they will use, these materials are called Resource Alternatives. For examples, see the Resource Alternatives included in the sample CAPs in this chapter.

If available, include materials at different reading levels to bracket the range of abilities in the class using the CAPs. For example, a CAP on the solar system may present information at the third- through sixth-grade levels for a heterogeneous fifth-grade class in health.

Step 8. *Add at least three small-group techniques to the developing Contract Activity Package.* Always include a Team Learning. Identify the most difficult objectives in your CAP. Develop a Team Learning to introduce those objectives that require in-depth knowledge, insight, or extensive explanation. Design a Circle of Knowledge to reinforce what you taught through Team Learning. Use any of the remaining strategies, such as Brainstorming, Group Analysis, or Case Study, to help peer-oriented youngsters gain information. Circles of Knowledge are simple to create; try a few. Team Learnings require more time but are well worth the effort, for they will enhance retention for many of your students and, simultaneously, free you to work directly with those who are authority-oriented and need your supervision and guidance. For examples, see the samples of small-group techniques included in Chapter 5 and in the CAPs in this chapter.

Step 9. *Develop a test that is directly related to each of the behavioral objectives in your CAP.* An assessment instrument or examination that is directly related to stated objectives is called a *criterion-referenced test.* Questions for such a test are formed by either restating the objective or phrasing it in a different way.

For example, if the behavioral objective was "List at least five (5) major causes of World War II," then the question on the examination should also be "List at least five (5) major causes of World War II."

You may, of course, be creative in the way you test your students. The test may include maps, puzzles, games, diagrams, drawings, and photos for those who learn best in those ways.

The test may be used at three different times: (1) as a pretest to assess whether the student knows a major portion of the topic and does not need to pursue all objectives in the CAP, (2) as a self-test to determine readiness for the final assessment, and (3) as the teacher's final evaluation of knowledge gained. Knowing what is expected improves attitudes toward learning and increases motivation. The order in which the questions are given on the pre-, self-, and posttests may be changed if the teacher suspects that individual students are memorizing answers without truly internalizing the knowledge. If that happens, those are the wrong students for a CAP! If you are global and visual, see Figure 8–4 for a graphic overview of a Contract Activity Package against which you can check your initial efforts.

Step 10. *Design an illustrated cover for the Contract Activity Package.* (See the sample CAPs that follow.)

Step 11. *Develop an informational top sheet.* On the page directly after the illustrated cover, provide information that you believe is important. Some items that may be included are as follows:

- The name of the Contract Activity Package
- The student's name
- The student's class
- The objectives that have been assigned to or selected by that student
- The date by which the CAP should be completed

Contract Activity Package

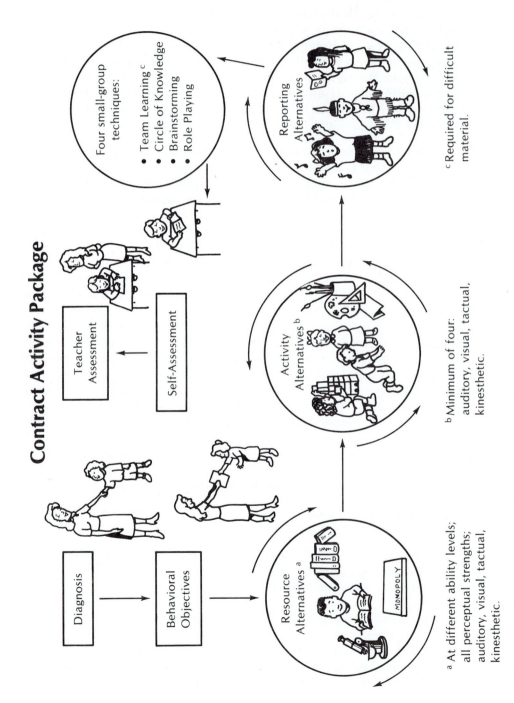

FIGURE 8–4 Contract Activity Package

a At different ability levels; all perceptual strengths; auditory, visual, tactual, kinesthetic.

b Minimum of four: auditory, visual, tactual, kinesthetic.

c Required for difficult material.

- The dates by which selected parts of the CAP should be completed (for students in need of structure)
- A place for a pretest grade
- A place for a self-test grade
- A place for a final test grade
- The names of the classmates that may have worked on this CAP as a team
- Directions for working on or completing the CAP

Step 12. *Reread each of the parts of the Contract Activity Package.* Make certain that they are clearly stated, well organized, in correct order, and grammatically written. Check your spelling and punctuation.

Step 13. *Add illustrations to the pages to make the CAP attractive and motivating.*

Step 14. *Duplicate the number of copies you will need.*

Step 15. *Design a record-keeping form so that you know which students are using and have used the Contract Activity Package and how much of it they have completed successfully* (see Figure 8–5.)

Step 16. *Try a CAP with those students who can work well with any two or three small-group techniques.* Be prepared to guide and assist the students through their first experiences with a CAP. Establish a system whereby they can obtain assistance if they need your help. Placing an "I Need You" column on the chalkboard or on a chart and having youngsters sign up for help when they are stymied is usually effective. Direct them to place their names beneath the title and to return to their places until you are free to come to them. They should not interrupt you but, rather, should busy themselves on other objectives or tasks—or get help from a classmate—until you can get to them.

Suggestions for Perfecting a Contract Activity Package

1. Although it is not incorrect to state repeatedly, "You will be able to . . . ," it does become repetitious and often provokes humor. It is suggested, therefore, that at the top of the page you write:

Behavioral Objectives

Example

By the time you have finished this contract, you will be able to complete each of the following objectives:

1. List at least five (5) major causes of World War II.
2. State at least one important action taken by eight (8) important historical figures during the period just before and during World War II.

OBJECTIVES	DATE COMPLETED	ACTIVITIES COMPLETED	GROUP TECHNIQUES COMPLETED
1.			
2.			
3.			
4.			
5.			
6.			
7.			
8.			
9.			
10.			
11.			
12.			
13.			
14.			
15.			
16.			

NAME: _____   CONTRACT: _____

OBJECTIVES TO BE COMPLETED _____

FIGURE 8–5 This form provides an overview of a student's progress and is used with the contract system where students select their objectives from a list of enumerated options.

Any time that you use a number in the objectives, spell out the number; then, in parentheses, write the numeral. This technique is used to accentuate the number for youngsters who may overlook specific details.

Example

List at least three (3) tools that archeologists use in their work.

Use complete and grammatically correct sentences. Do not capitalize words that should not be capitalized. Contracts should be excellent examples of good usage, spelling, and grammar for students. If you wish to emphasize a word that may be new to the student's vocabulary, underline the word.

Use the phrase *at least* before any number of required responses to motivate selected students to achieve more than is required.

Example

> *List at least five (5) events leading up to World War II. Can you think of a sixth (6th)?*

Be certain that the objective does not become an activity. The objectives state what the student should learn. The activity enables the youngster to demonstrate that he or she has learned it by using the information while making a creative, original product.

Example

> Objective: *Describe the events that directly led to the outbreak of World War II.*

Activity Alternatives

> *1. Draw a mural showing the events that led directly to the outbreak of World War II.*
>
> *or*
>
> *2. Write a poem describing the events that led to the outbreak of World War II.*

For each small-group technique, begin at the top of a new page. Name the technique and then number from one (1) through four (4) and place lines on which the students' names may be written. Add another line for the recorder's name.

Example
TEAM LEARNING

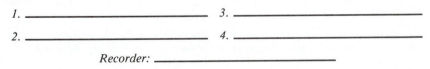

In the Reporting Alternatives, never ask a youngster to report to the entire class. Have an activity shared with one, two, or a few classmates, or with the teacher. It is difficult for a student to hold the entire class's attention; and if one student is given the opportunity, it should be offered to all. Instead, have the students report to a small group. If the activity is outstanding, ask the

This page from a Contract Activity Package on New England itemizes the objectives across the top, the Activity Alternatives that demonstrate students mastery on the left, the Reporting Alternatives through which youngsters share the creative activities they have made at the right, and a colorful illustration representing the kind of home that exists in that geographical location. (Photograph courtesy of Mrs. Norann McGee, Center for the Study of Learning and Teaching Styles, St. John's University, New York.)

student to share it with a second small group. You may either assign students or ask for volunteers to listen to the report.

The title of each of the major parts of the CAP should be underlined—for example, *Behavioral Objectives* or *Activity Alternatives.*

Sample Contract Activity Packages

Following are several samples of elementary school (grades 3–6) Contract Activity Packages developed by teachers and used successfully at different levels with students whose learning styles matched the approach of this method.

If this is your students' first experience with CAPs, assign only a few objectives to introduce them to the process. Give them a few opportunities to begin to feel secure with this method before deciding whether it is effective for each individual. If it stimulates and provokes their thinking and knowledge, continue using it. If you find that selected students do not respond well to it (even if they are permitted to work with just one or two classmates), set aside the CAP system for those youngsters and introduce either Programmed Learning Sequences or Multisensory Instructional Packages to them. The last of these methods is potent for students who require multisensory resources and structure, are self-oriented (rather than peer-oriented or teacher-oriented), and learn essentially through tactual or kinesthetic means.

The Contract Activity Package is most effective with youngsters who are motivated and either auditory or visual, or are nonconforming. You will note that it is an especially well organized system, although it does permit flexible learning arrangements and options for students.

Independent Contract

Individual CAPs also may be designed by gifted, bright, and/or creative students in the patterns described in this chapter. Those students could pursue a specific interest unrelated to the required curriculum. They need only think through and respond to the following curriculum questions.

1. What is a particular interest of mine that I would like to investigate?
2. What important things do I want to learn?
3. Which resource should I use?
4. How can I use what I need to learn in a creative, original way that I can eventually share with others?
5. If I rewrite the objectives (what I need to learn), how can I translate them into a self-assessment? See Chapter 10 for specifics concerning the development of student-designed CAPs.

Read the following Contract Activity Packages and perhaps try them with motivated or nonconforming students in your class. Then develop one based on your curriculum. Use the following guidelines for correcting a CAP so that you know you have a product with which your students are likely to succeed.

Guidelines for Correcting a CAP

1. Do you have both an analytic and a global title?
2. Are the objectives clearly stated, requiring absolutely no further explanation?
3. Do the objectives begin each page at the top?

This Contract Activity Package, "The Sense Organs: Can You Make Sense of Them?" uses simple illustrations to describe and explain individual sensitivities. Inside the CAP, the objectives are written across the top of each page followed by matched (paired) Activity and Reporting Alternatives and humorous captions that accent the concept of touching, smelling, seeing, hearing, and so forth. (Photographs courtesy of Center for the Study of Learning and Teaching Styles, St. John's University, New York.)

4. Where multiple responses are required, do you say, "Describe *at least* _____ . . ." so that motivated students may respond to more than the minimum number required?

5. When you use numbers, are they written *both* ways (in word and symbol form)?

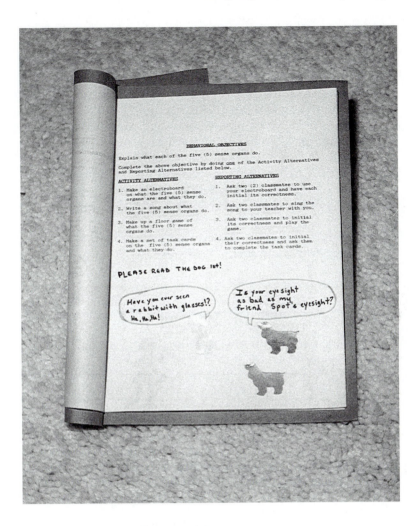

6. Does each objective have related Activity and Reporting Alternatives?
7. Are the Activity Alternatives multisensory?
8. Does each Reporting Alternative ally itself *directly* with its Activity Alternative?
9. Do the Activity Alternatives require that the student *make* something creative?
10. Is only one Activity and Reporting Alternative required for each objective?
11. Does the CAP have a listing of multisensory Resource Alternatives?
12. Is there a Team Learning for each difficult objective?
13. Does the Team Learning *teach* something and then ask three different types of questions concerned with what was taught (factual, higher level cognitive, and creative)?

14. Does the CAP have one or more Circles of Knowledge?
15. Is there a *third* small-group technique, such as Case Study or Brainstorming?
16. Is the assessment directly related to the objectives?
17. Are there pictures, illustrations, or graphs directly related to the CAP content throughout the CAP?
18. Is the printing or typing well done and easy to read?
19. Are there any spelling or grammatical errors in the CAP?
20. Does each objective begin with a verb?
21. Does the CAP provide some choices for the student?
22. Is the CAP attractive and easy to use?
23. Is each of the objectives in the related PLS included in the CAP?

Suggest that students check each other's original CAP, complete the following form below, and submit it to you.

The CAP I have examined is: _____

created by _____

The following items need to be corrected: _____

_____

Name: _____

Date: _____

Contract Activity Package on Breaking the Map Code: You Don't Have to Be Square to Do It!

This Contract Activity Package was created by Bodhild Iglesias, a graduate student at St. John's University and a New York City elementary school teacher.

Breaking the Map Code: Behavioral Objectives

By the time you have finished this contract, you will be able to:

1. Explain the purpose of the COMPASS ROSE and demonstrate how to use it.
2. Describe at least four (4) differences between GLOBES and flat MAPS.
3. Given a globe and map, describe the lines of LATITUDE and LONGITUDE and locate the following places: (a) North Pole, (b) South Pole, (c) Equator, (d) Arctic Circle, (e) Antarctic Circle.
4. Explain what SYMBOLS are and how to use map KEYS and LEGENDS.
5. Use a map SCALE to estimate the distances between places on the map.
6. Name three (3) different types of maps and explain the kind of information they give.

You must do objectives one (1) through five (5). To learn more about maps, try number six (6) by doing the group analysis.

You have one (1) week to complete the Contract.

Name: _____

Objectives completed: _____

Date started: _____

Date finished: _____

Final test score: _____

Objective 1

Explain the purpose of the COMPASS ROSE and demonstrate how to use it.
There are four (4) Activity Alternatives with corresponding Reporting Alternatives. You must do at least one (1) pair of the alternatives.

Activity Alternatives	*Reporting Alternatives*
1. Make a compass rose of your own. On a tape, explain the compass rose and its purpose.	1. Ask three (3) friends to listen to the tape and to tape their own comments.

2. Draw a map of your neighborhood. Give directions to your house using the eight directions on the compass rose. Make two (2) copies of your map.

3. Use a map from our collection and write seven (7) or more questions using any of the compass rose directions.
4. Make a game illustrating different compass roses. Use them to find your way to the finish line.

2. Ask two (2) friends to trace with a marker how they would walk to your house, using your map and directions. Ask them to write a one- (1-) sentence comment on your map.
3. Choose three (3) classmates to answer the questions. Display the map, questions, and answer key.
4. Display your game and explain to a friend how the compass roses are the same and how they are different. Play the compass rose game with three other students.

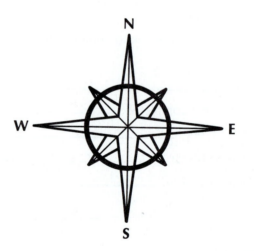

Objective 2
Describe at least four (4) differences between GLOBES and flat MAPS.

There are four (4) Activity Alternatives with corresponding Reporting Alternatives. You must do at least one (1) pair of the alternatives.

Activity Alternatives

1. Look at a globe and a flat map. List the land masses

Reporting Alternatives

1. Play the tape for four (4) classmates. Ask them to

which appear to be different on the flat map. Find out why there is a difference. Make a three- (3-) minute tape of what you have found.

check what you have found by looking at the globe and the map. Ask them to comment on your findings.

2. Make a list of at least two (2) reasons for using flat maps, and two (2) reasons for using globes. (You may use each reason only once.)

2. Read your list to two (2) students. Ask them to correct it and add information. Display the list with its additions.

3. Use an old ball and split it in half. Try to flatten it. (You may also use a cleaned-out grapefruit half.) Write a story for the school newspaper about what happened to your hemisphere. Be sure to explain how this is similar to what happens to land masses on a flat map.

3. Submit your story to the editor of the school newspaper and encourage others to try to flatten a hemisphere while learning about globe and map differences.

4. Write a poem about maps and globes that describes four (4) differences between them.

4. Read the poem to three (3) friends and display it.

Objective 3

Given a globe and a map, describe the lines of LATITUDE and LONGITUDE and locate the following places: (1) North Pole, (b) South Pole, (c) Equator, (d) Arctic Circle, (e) Antarctic Circle.

There are four (4) Activity Alternatives with corresponding Reporting Alternatives. You must do at least one (1) pair of the alternatives.

Activity Alternatives

1. Using the globe as a guide, draw a circle (or use a round balloon) and label places (a) through (e).

Reporting Alternatives

1. Show your drawing (or balloon) to three (3) classmates and ask them to label their own drawings (or balloons) using the globe as a guide. Compare the results. Make corrections as needed.

2. Write a letter to a friend and describe the lines of latitude and longitude. Point out places (a) through (e).

2. Give your friend the letter and ask him or her to use it as a guide to locate lines and places on the globe. Ask your friend to respond orally or in a letter with comments about your descriptions.

3. Make a short tape recording and describe the lines of latitude and longitude. Include directions on how to locate places (a) through (e).

3. Give the tape to one (1) classmate and ask him or her to use it as a guide to locate places (a) through (e) on the globe. Ask him or her to record any comments about the experience. Add the tape to our Social Studies Resources.

4. Use tracing paper to trace the outlines of land masses on a world map. With two (2) different-colored markers, draw the lines of latitude and longitude and label places (a) through (e).

4. Mount your tracing paper on poster board and display it. Have two (2) students find places (a) through (e), identifying the lines of latitude and longitude.

Objective 4
Explain what SYMBOLS are and how to use map KEYS and LEGENDS.

There are four (4) Activity Alternatives with corresponding Reporting Alternatives. You must do at least one (1) pair of the alternatives.

Activity Alternatives

1. Select four (4) maps from our collection and make a large legend of your own, using as many different kinds of symbols as you can find.

2. Make a list of symbols that you find are the same on many different maps. Write a short paragraph describing these symbols.

3. Cut out pictures that may be used for symbols and paste them on a simple map that you make.

Reporting Alternatives

1. Display your legend and explain to one (1) classmate how the symbols are used to give information.

2. Show this list to three (3) friends and discuss why you think it might be a good idea to memorize the symbols or debate why you should not.

3. Display your map with a reaction sheet attached. Ask three (3) classmates to write their reaction to these symbols.

4. Using the blank side of index cards, make a card game using map symbols. Write directions for your game.

4. Ask four (4) classmates to read the directions and play the game. Add your game to our game collection. (Make corrections to improve the game if necessary.)

Objective 5

Use a map SCALE to estimate the distances between places on the map.

There are four (4) Activity Alternatives with corresponding Reporting Alternatives. You must do at least one (1) pair of the alternatives.

Activity Alternatives

1. Collect maps showing the same area but in different scales. (Use as many maps as you can, but collect at least two sets). Label the sets 1a, 1b; 2a, 2b; and so on. Place them in a folder labeled MAP SCALES.

2. Gather some toy cars; find out if these are made to scale. Measure at least three (3) parts of the toy cars. Compare those parts to the same parts on a real car.

3. Make a floor plan of your bedroom using the following scale: 1 inch equals 1 foot. Include scale drawings of three (3) pieces of furniture. (*Hint:* It is easy if you use graph paper with four squares to the inch.)

4. Choose a map and make a photocopy of it. Use a red pen to mark two towns. On tape, explain how you will go about estimating the distance between these two towns. State the scale or underline it on the map. Write the estimated distance on a separate piece of paper.

Reporting Alternatives

1. Show your collection to two (2) friends and answer questions that they may have. Add your collection to the class Social Studies Resources.

2. Explain to two (2) students how using the scale on one (1) toy car is similar to using the map scale.

3. Show the floor plan to three (3) classmates. Display it. Have them measure a piece of furniture in their bedrooms and add them to your floor plan.

4. Give the tape and a copy of the map to three (3) classmates. Ask them to follow your taped directions and estimate the same distance. Compare your answers and make corrections if necessary.

Resource Alternatives

Books

1. Norman Carlisle, *The True Book of Maps.*
2. Samuel Epstein, *The First Book of Maps and Globes.*
3. David Greenhood, *Down to Earth Mapping for Everybody.*
4. James Madden, *The Wonderful World of Maps.*
5. J. E. Oliver, *What We Find When We Look at Maps.*
6. Barbara Rinkoff, *A Map Is a Picture.*
7. Beulah Tannenbaum, *Understanding Maps.*

Atlases

1. *Encyclopaedia Britannica World Atlas.*
2. *Hammond-Scholastic New World Atlas.*
3. *National Geographic Atlas of the World.*
4. *Rand McNally World Atlas.*

Other Resources
MIP: "Breaking the Map Code—(Resource Center)"
Filmstrips:
1. "Working with Maps"
2. "Maps Are Fun"
3. "Reading Maps"

Globes

Team Learning

Team Members:

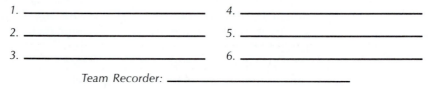

1. _____   *4.* _____

2. _____   *5.* _____

3. _____   *6.* _____

Team Recorder: _____

Read the following poem and answer the questions.

Maps
by Goldie Capers Smith

A map is a picture
Of where we are going.
The wiggly lines show us
Where rivers are flowing;
The red lines are highways
On which we will travel;
The black lines are byways
Topped sometimes with gravel.
The dots are the cities
Where gas stations are,
And each capital city
Is marked with a star.

1. What is a map? _____

2. The poem mentions five (5) symbols used on maps. What are they?

   a. _____

   b. _____

   c. _____

   d. _____

   e. _____

3. Besides what the poem tells us, can you think of anything else a map

   shows us? _____

4. Do you think it is important to have maps? Why? _____

   _____

5. Make a set of task cards or a matching game using the symbols in the
   poem.

6. Write a poem, song, or rap music verse on what you have learned about
   maps.

   _____

   _____

   _____

   _____

Small-Group Activities

Circle of Knowledge
Circle Members:

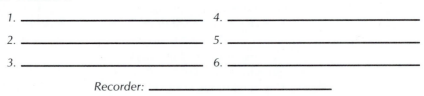

Recorder: _____

Name as many map symbols as you can in three (3) minutes.

Group Analysis
Group members:

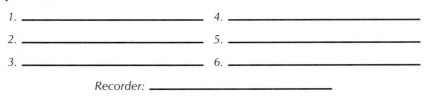

Recorder: _____

Below is a list of some kinds of maps available for your use. Find them in our class collection.

1. Political maps
2. Physical maps
3. Road maps or travel maps
4. Sightseeing maps
5. Weather maps
6. Historical maps

Objective
Tell what kind of map you would use to get the following information. Give one reason for each of your choices.

Information	Map Type	Reason for Choice
1. Total rainfall in the United States last year	_____	_____
2. Temperature ranges in Canada	_____	_____
3. Location of Mexico	_____	_____
4. What the people who lived before Columbus believed the world looked like	_____	_____
5. Places we pass on a train ride from New York to Chicago	_____	_____

6. Location and the varying heights of the Rocky Mountains

   _____   _____

7. Where to find a hamburger stand in an amusement park.

   _____   _____

Self-Assessment Test

1. All maps have a compass rose. Why? _____

2. A compass rose may look like this:

   Where is North? Where is West? Draw your own compass rose and mark it with _N_ and _W_.

3. What are lines of longitude? _____

4. What are lines of latitude? _____

5. What is a map key or legend? _____

6. Why do maps have legends? _____

7. How can you find out how far it is from one town on a map to another?

   _____

8. List four (4) differences between globes and flat maps.

   a. _____   c. _____

   b. _____   d. _____

9. What kind of information do we find on a road map? _____

   _____

10. What kind of information do we find on a political map? _____

    _____

Test-Page Map

Note to Teacher: Provide reproductions of a local street map, an area road map, your state map, a U.S. map, and a map of North America with questions based on your objectives for this Contract Activity Package.

Contract Activity Package on Circumference of a Circle:
I Get Around . . .

After objectives have been mastered through Resource Alternatives of the student's choice, but from among those listed by the teacher, *Activity Alternatives require* application *of the difficult material in a creative, original way, and matching Reporting Alternatives per-*mit youngsters to share *the wonderful things they make. (Photo-*graphs courtesy of Center for the Study of Learning and Teaching Styles, St. John's University, New York.)*

This Contract Activity Package was created by Daniel J. Purus, mathematics teacher, Ridgewood Intermediate School #93, Queens, New York.

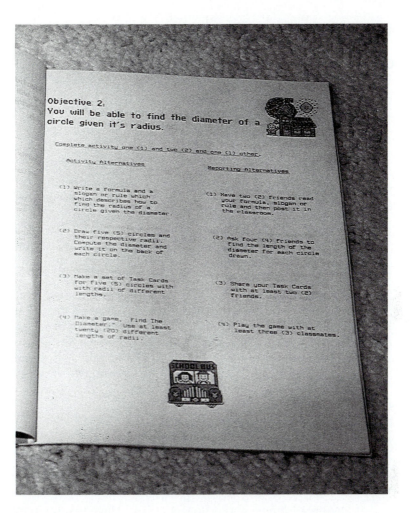

Name: _____

Class: _____

Objectives completed: _____

Date started: _____

Completion date: _____

Directions: Complete all six (6) of the objectives on the following pages. Begin with the pretest. If you have any questions, be sure to ask your teacher.

Pretest score: _____

Selftest score: _____

Final test score: _____

Behavioral Objectives

Objective 1
Define each of the following terms and label a circle using each:
    a. center   c. circle   e. circumference
    b. chord   d. diameter   f. pi   g. radius

Complete Activity One (1) and one other pair.

Activity Alternatives	*Reporting Alternatives*
1. Make a list of each word and its definition on looseleaf paper.	1. Show your list to two (2) friends and have them read it.
2. Make a mini-Electroboard using the terms listed above and including their definitions.	2. Have three (3) classmates use your mini-Electroboard.
3. Draw a circle using a compass and label all its parts.	3. Share your diagram with three (3) friends and then display it in the classroom.
4. Make a crossword puzzle using the above terms and their definitions.	4. Have a few copies made and have at least three (3) friends complete your puzzle.

Objective 2
Find the diameter of a circle given its radius.

Complete Activities One (1) and Two (2) and do one (1) other pair.
Note: Be sure to use different radii for every circle.

Activity Alternatives	*Reporting Alternatives*
1. Write a formula and a slogan or rule that describes how to find the diameter of a circle when given its radius. Check your formula by using it with five (5) circles that have different radii. Do not write in the diameters found.	1. Have two (2) friends use your formula, slogan, or rule to calculate the diameters of those five (5) circles that you used to check your formula. Post the results in the classroom.
2. Draw five (5) circles and their respective radii. Compute each diameter and write it on the back of the circle.	2. Ask four (4) friends to find the length of the diameter for each circle drawn.
3. Make a set of task cards for five (5) circles with radii of different lengths.	3. Share your task cards with at least two (2) friends.

4. Design a game, "Find the Diameter." Use at least twenty (20) different lengths for the radii.

4. Play the game with at least three (3) classmates.

Objective 3
Find the radius of a circle when given its diameter.

Complete Activity One (1) and one (1) other pair.

Activity Alternatives

1. Write a formula that demonstrates how to find a radius when only the diameter is given. Draw five (5) circles of various sizes and "talk" the problem-solving steps out loud.

2. Make a Pic-A-Hole with at least ten (10) cards and questions asking for the radius when given a diameter's length.

3. Draw and color ten (10) circles and label the different diameters. Write the length of each radius on the back of every card.

Reporting Alternatives

1. Have at least two (2) friends use the formula to find the radius for three (3) circles that are found in the classroom.

2. Show the Pic-A-Hole to your teacher and then share it with three (3) friends.

3. Ask at least two (2) friends to give you the length of the radius for each card you show them.

Objective 4
Decide if you should use the formula $C = \pi d$ or $C = 2\pi r$ to find the circumference based on the given information.

Complete Activity One (1) and one (1) other pair.

Activity Alternatives

1. Make an Electroboard with six (6) circles on the top. Let three (3) show the radius and three (3) the diameter. Write the two (2) formulas ($C = \pi d$ and $C = 2\pi r$) on the bottom and decide which one you would use to find the circumference of each circle.

Reporting Alternatives

1. Share your Electroboard with at least three (3) classmates. They must show which formula is to be used with each circle in order to find the circumference.

2. Make a set of task cards matching the correct formula with an example giving the radius or diameter.
3. Make a poster with the two (2) formulas and explain when to use each.

2. Have three (3) classmates use your Task Cards.

3. Show your poster to the teacher and one (1) friend; then display it in your classroom.

Objective 5

Given the diameter of a circle, you will be able to compute the circumference using $\pi = 3.14$ and $\pi = 22/7$

Complete Activity One (1) or Two (2) and Activity Three (3).

Activity Alternatives

1. Draw a circle on poster board with a diameter of 14 cm. Use $\pi = 3.14$ and calculate the circumference using the proper formula. Show all problem-solving steps on the poster.
2. Find the circumference of a circle with a diameter of 28 inches using $\pi = 3.14$ and then again using 22/7. Draw some conclusions about the similarities between the two solutions.
3. Measure the diameter of two (2) circular objects found in the classroom. Compute the circumference of each object using $\pi = 22/7$. Then make a sign for each object and display the information you discovered.
4. Design a set of Task Cards that display twelve (12) circles and their circumferences on one side and the correct $C = \pi d$ formulas on the other.

Reporting Alternatives

1. Explain your illustration and calculations to two (2) friends. Then post the illustration in the classroom.

2. Share your conclusions with three (3) classmates.

3. Share your findings with two (2) friends and have them help you post the signs.

4. Have two (2) students match the cards after computing the correct solutions.

Objective 6
Given the radius of a circle, you will be able to compute the circumference using $\pi = 3.14$ and $\pi = 22/7$.

Complete Activity One (1) or Two (2) and Activity Three (3).

Activity Alternatives

1. Find the circumference of a circle with a radius of 21 inches using $\pi = 3.14$, and then again using 22/7. Draw some conclusions about the similarities between the two solutions.
2. Draw a circle on poster board with a radius of 6 inches. Use $\pi = 3.14$ and calculate the circumference using the proper formula. Show all the problem-solving steps on the poster.
3. Measure the radius or calculate the diameter of two (2) circular objects in the classroom. Find the circumference of each object using $\pi = 22/7$. Then make a sign for each object and display the information you found.
4. Design a game using different-sized colored circles with their radii shown. The student correctly determining the most circumferences in five (5) minutes wins.

Reporting Alternatives

1. Share your conclusions with three (3) classmates.

2. Explain your illustration to two (2) friends and then post it in the classroom.

3. Share your findings with two (2) friends and have them help you post the signs.

4. Play the game with three (3) friends.

Resource Alternatives

Books

1. I. Dressler, *Integrated Mathematics: Course 1,* pp. 612–618.
2. Holt, Rinehart and Winston, *Holt Mathematics 8,* pp. 208, 209.
3. Scott, Foresman, *Invitation to Mathematics: 6,* pp. 290–293.

4. Scott, Foresman, *Invitation to Mathematics: 7,* pp. 281, 294, 295.

5. Scott, Foresman, *Invitation to Mathematics: 8,* pp. 224, 225, 240, 241.

6. E. Stein, *Second Course in Fundamentals of Mathematics,* pp. 375, 423–425.

Teacher-made Resources

1. Flip Chute
2. Electroboard
3. Pic-A-Hole
4. Task Cards

Games

1. Getting Around

Small-Group Activities

Team Learning
Team Members:

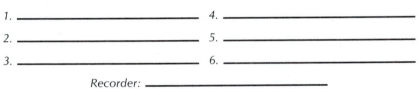

1. _____   *4.* _____

2. _____   *5.* _____

3. _____   *6.* _____

Recorder: _____

Read the following passage, follow the model problems, and then reach consensus with the other group members so that all the questions are answered. Where there is lack of agreement, those who disagree with the majority may write in their own answers.

Symbols:
     C = circumference d = diameter r = radius π (pi; pronounced "pie") = 3.14 or 22/7

To find the circumference of a circle (the distance around a circle), we use one of two formulas. One formula is $C = \pi d$, where π = 3.14 or 22/7 and d = the length of the diameter (the longest chord in any circle that passes through the center of the circle). We use the above formula, which represents multiplying the diameter by pi.

Model 1 $C = \pi d$
               $= (3.14)\,(5\text{cm})$
               $= 15.70$ cm or 15.7 cm
               Substitute in the given values and multiply.

We use the second formula, $C = 2\pi r$, when we are given the length of the radius (a line segment drawn from the center of the circle to a point on the circle) and the value for *p*.

Model 2 $C = 2\pi r$
               $= (2)\ (3.14)\ (7\ in.)$
               $= (6.28)\ (7\ in.)$
               $= 43.96\ in.$
            Substitute in the given values and multiply.

Team Assignment

1. Define:

(1) circumference _____

(b) diameter _____

(c) radius _____

2. Solve each of the two (2) above model problems using $\pi = 22/7$ instead of 3.14.

3. Explain why the solutions to the models are equivalent to but not equal

to the solutions you found in the above question. _____

_____

4. Cut out pictures or make a drawing of at least two (2) objects for which

the circumference may be found. _____

5. Write an original story or word problem where finding the circumfer-

ence is the solution to the problem. _____

Brainstorming
Team Members:

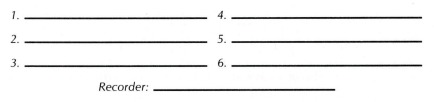

1. _____   *4.* _____

2. _____   *5.* _____

3. _____   *6.* _____

Recorder: _____

You will have three (3) minutes to think of and call out as many objects as possible that have a diameter or radius, implying that the circumference of each of these objects may be found.

Circle of Knowledge
Circle Members:

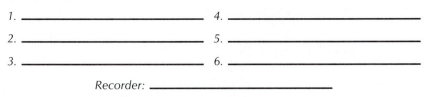

1. _____   4. _____

2. _____   5. _____

3. _____   6. _____

Recorder: _____

The problem: In ten (10) minutes, draw as many circles as you can, labeling both the diameter and radius for each.

Make up as many examples as you can of circles, giving the measurement of both their diameter and their radius.

Indicate: d = _____; r = _____

_____

_____

_____

_____

_____

_____

_____

_____

_____

_____

_____

_____

Self-Assessment Test: Circumference

Name: _____

1. True or False

   The diameter of a circle is equal to two times its radius. _____
2. True or False

   The radius of a circle is the longest chord in any circle. _____
3. True or False
   The radius of a circle is equal to one-half the length of its diameter.

_____

4. All radii of the same circle are _____.

   (a) equal in length (b) different in length

5. When given the radius of a circle, you may use the formula to find the

   circle's circumference. _____

   (a) $C = \pi d$ (b) $C = 2\pi r$

6. When given the diameter of a circle, you may use the formula _____

   to find the circle's circumference. _____

   (a) $C = \pi d$ (b) $C = 2\pi r$

Calculate the circumference for each using the given information.

7. $d = 4$ in. _____

   $\pi = 3.14$ _____

8. $d = 28$ cm _____

   $\pi = 22/7$ _____

9. $r = 9$ m _____

   $\pi = 3.14$ _____

10. $r = 7$ cm _____

   $\pi = 22/7$ _____

Contract Activity Package on Magnetism:
The Power of Attraction

This Contract Activity Package was designed by Maria Geresi, teacher, The Growing Tree, Ridgefield, Connecticut.

The cover and interior pages of the Contract Activity Package on "Magnetism: The Power of Attraction" includes colorful illustrations and catchy global subtitles and puns. (Photographs courtesy of Center for the Study of Learning and Teaching Styles, St. John's University, New York.)

Name: _____

Objectives completed: _____

Date received: _____

Date completed: _____

Final test score: _____

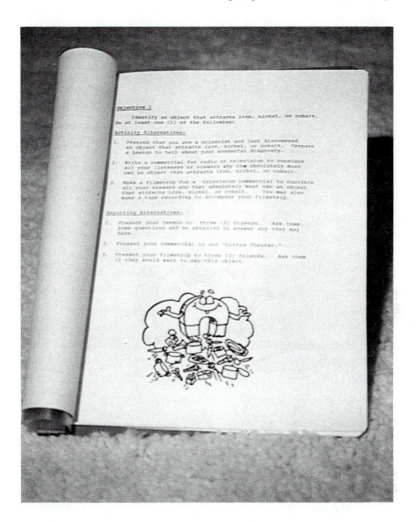

Few scientific phenomena appear more mysterious than magnetism. The way in which a magnet can move an object from some distance away looks magical. Why do magnets cause objects to behave the way they do? We are able to put magnetism to work in many machines. Without magnetism we would have no television, no tapes, no cassette players, no telephones, and no computers!

By doing the activities in this contract, you will discover for yourself how magnets behave. Among the experiments are some which show odd and unexpected things that magnets can do.

Take care of your magnets. Dropping them will cause them to lose their magnetism.

Behavioral Objectives

Complete objectives _____ through _____ and any other _____.
Also complete the young scientists' lab sheets. You may color all the
illustrations!

Objective 1
Identify an objective that attracts iron, nickel, or cobalt. Do at least one (1) of
the following pairs:

Activity Alternatives

1. Pretend that you are a scientist and have just discovered an object that attracts iron, nickel, or cobalt. Prepare a speech or tape recording.
2. Write a commercial for radio or television to convince all your listeners or viewers of why they absolutely must own an object that attracts iron, nickel, or cobalt.
3. Make a film strip for a television commercial to convince all your viewers of why they absolutely must own an object that attracts iron,

Reporting Alternatives

1. Present your speech or recording to three (3) friends. Ask them some questions and be prepared to answer any they may have.
2. Present your commercial in our Little Theater.

3. Present your filmstrip to three (3) friends. Ask them why they would want to own this object.

nickel, or cobalt. You may
also make a tape recording to
accompany your filmstrip.

Objective 2
Describe an object that attracts iron, nickel, or cobalt. Choose at least one (1)
of the following pairs:

Activity Alternatives	*Reporting Alternatives*
1. Make a mural of an object that attracts iron, nickel, or cobalt.	1. Mount your magnificent mural on the bulletin board. Show it to four (4) classmates.
2. Write a short paragraph about how an object that attracts iron, nickel, or cobalt looks.	2. Tape record your story and play it for two (2) friends.
3. Make up a silly or serious poem describing an object that attracts iron, nickel, or cobalt.	3. Recite your poem to three (3) friends.
4. Make a clay, wood, cardboard, or aluminum foil model of an object that attracts iron, nickel, or cobalt.	4. Display your model and answer the questions of two (2) students as a scientist might.

Objective 3
Describe the space around an object that attracts iron, nickel, or cobalt. Select
at least one (1) of the following pairs:

Activity Alternatives	*Reporting Alternatives*
1. Plan a demonstration to show the space around an object that attracts iron, nickel, or cobalt by using iron filings that have been placed in a sealed box with a plastic lid.	1. Show your demonstration to three (3) of your classmates. Answer any questions they might have.
2. Organize a group to pantomime the space around a magnet.	2. Let a small group of three (3) to five (5) children try to guess what you are pantomiming.
3. Pretend you are this object. Write a story about the space around you.	3. Share your story with three (3) friends. Be ready to answer any questions they might have.

4. Make a transparency illustrating the space around an object that attracts iron, nickel, or cobalt.

4. Show your transparency to a small group of friends and explain the space around an object that attracts iron, nickel, or cobalt.

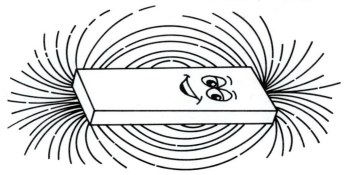

Objective 4

Compare the results of bringing unlike poles together. Choose at least one (1) of the following pairs:

Activity Alternatives

1. Pretend you are a scientist. Prepare a poster to explain how unlike poles attract.
2. Write a short newspaper article explaining how unlike poles attract.

3. Make a miniature stage setting with clay magnet models to describe how unlike poles attract.
4. Organize a pantomime with a friend to demonstrate how unlike poles attract.

Reporting Alternatives

1. Display your poster and explain to three (3) students how unlike poles attract.
2. Type your news article on a computer. Print three (3) copies and ask your friends to "Read all about it."
3. Display your stage setting in our display center and explain to three (3) friends why unlike poles attract.
4. Act out your pantomime for three (3) other friends. Help them guess what you are showing.

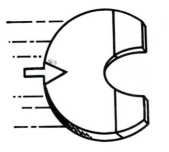
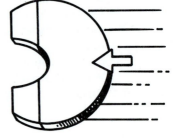

Objective 5

Compare the results of bringing like poles together. Choose at least one (1) of the following pairs:

Activity Alternatives

1. Make a cartoon comic strip to explain the results of bringing like poles together.
2. Prepare a tape scenario of yourself as a scientist explaining what happens when like poles are brought together.
3. Prepare a demonstration to explain what happens when you bring like poles together.
4. Write a funny or serious short story about what happens when you bring like poles together. You may also illustrate your story.

Reporting Alternatives

1. Display your comic strip in our display area. Show it to six (6) students.
2. Play the tape for two (2) friends. Be prepared to answer any of their questions.

3. Give your demonstration in our Little Theater for two (2) friends.
4. Share your story with two (2) friends and add it to our library.

Resource Alternatives

Books

1. David Adler, *Magnets.*
2. Irving Adler, *Magnets.*
3. Neil Ardley, *Magnetism: Experiments.*
4. Frances L. Behnke, *Magnetism*
5. Helen Challand, *Magnetism: Experiments.*
6. Ed Chatherall, *Magnets.*
7. Rocco Feravolo, *Magnetism: Experiments.*
8. Owen S. Lieberg, *Magnetism.*
9. Laurence Santrey, *Magnetism.*
10. Ed Victor, *Magnets.*
11. Kathryn Whyman, *Magnetism.*
12. Raymond Yates, *Magnetism.*

Films

1. *The Magnet*

Filmstrips

1. *The Wonderful World of Magnetism*
2. *Magic Magnets*

Games

1. Magnet Fun
2. The Red Magnet Box

Teacher-Made Resources

1. Young Scientist's Lab Sheets
2. Task Cards
3. Electroboard
4. Flip Chute
5. Pic-A-Hole
6. Learning Circle
7. Body Game

Charts, pictures, and transparencies, as well as books and sources within school and public libraries, may be used.

Small-Group Activities: Young Scientist's Lab Sheet 1

Team Learning
Team Members:

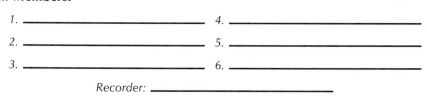

1. _____   4. _____
2. _____   5. _____
3. _____   6. _____

Recorder: _____

Magnets have strange power. They attract things made of iron, nickel, or cobalt. They seem to work like magic.

Hold a magnet near, but not touching, a pin. The pin jumps to the magnet and clings to it. Even when you lift the magnet, the pin hangs on. Try a nail. The same thing happens. We say the magnet attracts the pin and nail.

To learn how a magnet works, test it with different objects. Hold it close to a plastic button on your coat. Nothing happens. Hold it over a piece of paper. The paper won't move. See if you can pick up a penny and a quarter. The coins will stay on the table.

Now try the magnet with a metal paper clip. Watch the clip jump! Slide your magnet very slowly across the table toward the paper clip. Notice how far the clip jumps. A strong magnet will pull a paper clip from more than an inch away.

You can experiment with dozens of different items. Find two cardboard boxes and label them WILL ATTRACT and WILL NOT ATTRACT. Now start testing paper clips, keys, pencils, scissors, screws, aluminum foil, glass, and anything else you find. Everything that sticks to the magnet goes into the WILL ATTRACT box. Everything else goes into the WILL NOT ATTRACT box.

Take a careful look at all the objects that went into the WILL ATTRACT box. You will see that each of them is made of iron, nickel, or cobalt. Magnets always attract items made of metals containing iron, nickel, or cobalt. They won't attract copper, lead, gold, silver, aluminum, brass, zinc, or most other metals. They won't attract glass or wood or plastics.

1. Magnets attract metals made of:

    a. _____

    b. _____

    c. _____

2. Which word tells you the magnet pulls the pin to it?

    _____

3. Do you think a magnet could be a good detective to help you discover objects made of iron, nickel, or cobalt? Why?

    _____

    _____

4. List at least six (6) objects magnets can attract.

    _____

    _____

    _____

5. List at least six (6) objects magnets do not attract.

    _____

    _____

    _____

6. Tell why some objects are attracted to magnets while others are not.

    _____

    _____

    _____

7. Make a picture showing why it is important to know how magnets work.

_____

_____

_____

_____

Young Scientist's Lab Sheet 2

BE A MAGNET DETECTIVE!

You can be a detective, and your magnet will help you. A magnet can tell you what things really are! You already know that a magnet won't pull anything made of copper. Take out the paper clip that looks like copper and watch it jump to the magnet. This is because the paper clip isn't really copper. It is iron colored like copper. A magnet attracts iron. Try your magnet on the house key that is the color of iron. House keys are usually made of soft metals. Does the key stick? No, it does not. Keys are usually made of metals that do not contain iron, nickel, or cobalt.

Use your magnet to uncover five (5) objects that either appear as if they should be attracted to your magnet and are not, or appear as if they should not be attracted and are. Be sure to explain why this happens. If you can find more than five (5), you are a REAL MAGNET DETECTIVE! The first one is already started for you.

1. _Object:_ Classroom door hinge

Prediction: Attracted/Not Attracted _____

Observation: _____

Reason: _____

2. _Object:_ _____

Prediction: Attracted/Not Attracted: _____

Observation: _____

Reason: _____

3. _Object:_ _____

Prediction: Attracted/Not Attracted _____

Observation: _____

Reason: _____

4. *Object:* _____

Prediction: Attracted/Not Attracted: _____

Observation: _____

Reason: _____

5. *Object:* _____

Prediction: Attracted/Not Attracted: _____

Observation: _____

Reason: _____

6. *Object:* _____

Prediction: Attracted/Not Attracted: _____

Observation: _____

Reason: _____

USE THE BACK OF YOUR PAPER FOR ADDITIONAL SPACE IF NEEDED.

Young Scientist's Lab Sheet 3

Circle of Knowledge
Circle Members:

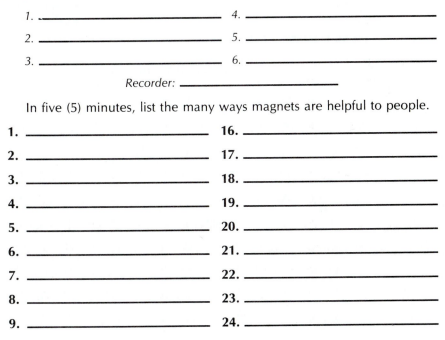

1. _____   *4.* _____

2. _____   *5.* _____

3. _____   *6.* _____

Recorder: _____

In five (5) minutes, list the many ways magnets are helpful to people.

1. _____   **16.** _____

2. _____   **17.** _____

3. _____   **18.** _____

4. _____   **19.** _____

5. _____   **20.** _____

6. _____   **21.** _____

7. _____   **22.** _____

8. _____   **23.** _____

9. _____   **24.** _____

10. _____	25. _____
11. _____	26. _____
12. _____	27. _____
13. _____	28. _____
14. _____	29. _____
15. _____	30. _____

Young Scientist's Lab Sheet 4

Experiment: Temporary Magnets

A piece of iron or steel can be made to act as a magnet for a short time. Then it loses its magnetism. It is called a *temporary magnet.*

   An iron nail can be used to make a temporary magnet. Take a permanent magnet and stroke the nail in one direction. Do this 50 to 100 times. The pull of the permanent magnet will slowly line up the atoms (tiny particles of matter in the nail). It becomes magnetized. Test this temporary magnet by picking up one paper clip. Take a second paper clip and touch it to the first one. Be careful that it does not touch the magnet. Is the first paper clip also

magnetized? _____ How long does the nail hang onto

the clips? _____ That is the reason the nail is called a temporary magnet.

Young Scientist's Lab Sheet 5

Magnetism Word Search

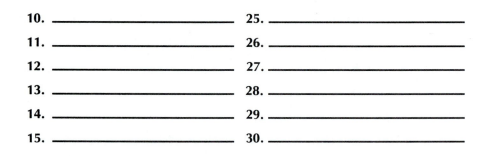

```
E  B  R  M  A  G  N  E  T  I  C  F  I  E  L  D  H
M  L  E  A  T  T  R  A  C  T  I  O  N  L  O  U  O
A  T  P  R  T  F  H  J  K  U  L  I  K  I  D  I  R
G  E  E  D  R  M  A  G  N  E  T  I  S  M  E  Y  S
N  S  L  W  A  G  J  Y  K  U  K  S  N  F  S  E  E
E  D  S  E  C  E  H  J  K  Y  H  E  T  G  T  E  S
T  E  D  C  T  X  S  W  E  F  G  L  R  T  O  T  H
T  E  M  P  O  R  A  R  Y  D  E  O  D  B  N  B  O
D  E  F  A  P  U  L  L  N  I  G  P  O  W  E  R  E
U  K  M  A  G  N  E  T  I  C  D  F  E  R  S  A  A
```

You're a real magnet detective if you can find all twelve (12) words!

ATTRACT	MAGNET	POLES
ATTRACTION	MAGNETIC	PULLING POWER
HORSESHOE	MAGNETIC FIELD	REPEL
LODESTONE	MAGNETISM	TEMPORARY

Self-Assessment Test

1. Draw and illustrate a magnet.

_____

_____

_____

2. Describe at least two (2) magnet shapes.

_____

_____

_____

3. What does *attraction* mean?

_____

_____

_____

4. What three (3) metals must an object contain to attract a magnet?

_____

_____

_____

5. List at least five (5) objects a magnet can attract.

_____   _____

_____   _____

_____   _____

_____   _____

6. Explain the space around a magnet. Be sure to include what this space is called.

_____

_____

_____

7. Describe and explain what happens when *like* poles move together.

_____

_____

_____

8. Describe and explain what happens when *unlike* poles move together.

_____

_____

_____

9. *Matching:* Write the letter of the word that goes best with each phrase.

a. magnetism   _____ 1. Space around a magnet

b. attraction   _____ 2. Magnet found in nature

c. repel   _____ 3. Pulling power

d. lodestone   _____ 4. Pushing power

e. magnetic force   _____ 5. Passing attraction

10. List five (5) uses for magnets.

_____   _____

_____   _____

_____

Make up a poem using all the things you learned about magnets.

Contract Activity Package on Folktales

This Contract Activity Package on "Folktales" was designed by Jeannette Bauer, teacher, Middle Village, New York, and Mary Dawber, teacher, Astoria, New York.

Name: _____ Class: _____

Objectives completed: _____

Date started: _____

Date completed: _____

Final test grade: _____

Procedure

Select and read three (3) folktales from the following list. You may use texts provided by the school, or bring your own from home or from the local library.

"The Grasshopper and the Coyote"	Zuñi folktale
"Don't Shake Hands with Everybody"	West African folktale
"Clever Manka"	European folktale
"Winning without Hands"	Japanese folktale
"The Shepherd and the Princess"	Pura Belpré tale
"The Brahman, the Tiger, and the Six Judges"	Old Hindu legend

Reminders: You may read as many folktales as you wish! There are many, many folktales, and they come from all over the world!

For each objective, be certain to name the folktale or folktales that you are reading.

"Once upon a time . . ." You probably can't remember the first time you heard these words at the beginning of a story. For most of us, they are a signal that we are about to hear something special. Perhaps they introduce a story set in a time when kings and queens reign in enchanted castles, or tell about a world where a tortoise can outrun a hare. Indeed, in folk stories anyone can go from rags to riches or turn from an ugly duckling into a handsome swan.

The range of folktales is deep and wide. Nursery rhymes, tall tales, and parables are all examples of folk wit and wisdom. Folktale characters may be of royal blood, ordinary people, or animals with human traits; they may even be historical figures whose deeds have become legends in the retelling. But whatever form folktales take, those entertaining stories teach customs and morals to each generation and help to explain beliefs.

Folktales have been told around the world since before recorded history. For all people, folktales are a vital part of their literature and culture. Every group of people in the world has its own traditional tales. All through time, people have gathered to hear the storyteller spin a web of enchantment with words.

Behavioral Objectives

By the time you have completed this contract, you will be able to do objectives 1 and 2 and one additional objective of your choice, to be selected from the remaining two.

Objective 1
In each of the folktales you have selected to read, you will be able to identify at least two (2) of the following characteristics:

      a. Typical opening line
      b. A heroic figure
      c. Animal characters that have human traits

Do at least one (1) of the following:

Activity Alternatives		*Reporting Alternatives*	
A	1. Pretend you are a story-teller. Begin spinning a folktale using two (2) of the three characteristics above.	1. Read your story to several of your classmates and teacher.	A
V	2. Find another folktale which demonstrates two (2) of the characteristics above. Make a chart depicting what you have found.	2. Mount your chart in your classroom.	V
A/V	3. Find and tape record a short folktale that demonstrates two (2) of the characteristics above.	3. Play the tape for a group of four (4) classmates. Have them identify the characteristics.	A

Objective 2
Many folktales involve situations where a character is required to solve a riddle or perform a difficult task. In order to do this, cleverness is used to outwit another character. Describe the use of cleverness in any of the folktales you have selected.
    Do at least one (1) of the following:

Activity Alternatives		*Reporting Alternatives*	
V/T	1. Write a newspaper feature story discussing	1. Share the article with a group of four (4) class-	A/V

the cleverness within the riddle and how it was solved.

mates. Have them decide whether you presented the situation accurately as a good reporter should.

A 2. Tape record the scene that demonstrates the use of cleverness. Be creative in the use of your voice.

2. Play the tape for a small group of classmates and your teacher.   A

V/T 3. Make a Word Search puzzle of all the clever words associated with the riddle.

3. Have three (3) classmates solve the puzzle.   V/T

Objective 3

In folktales, the author often supplies a moral to the story. It may be explicit (stated in the story) or implicit (suggested in the story). You will be able to describe the moral of a story and (optional) indicate whether it is explicit or implicit.

Do at least one (1) of the following:

Activity Alternatives

V 1. Choose three (3) folktales and decide what the moral lesson is for each one. Make a chart that includes: title, author, country from which the tale comes, and the moral. (Feeling ambitious? Add to your chart whether the moral is implicit or explicit.)

Reporting Alternatives

1. Share your chart with at least two (2) classmates. Have each initial it to verify that it is correct.   V/T

V/T 2. Write a folktale of your own that teaches a lesson.

2. Read your folktale to a group of four (4) classmates. Have them decide what the moral is.   A

V/T 3. Sketch a series of cartoons that illustrate a character learning a lesson. Caption each frame appropriately.

3. Display the cartoons for your classmates and teacher.   V/T

Objective 4

On the basis of the folktales you have read, decide how folktales make use of the exaggeration of characters. Consider the language used by the author.
Do at least one (1) of the following:

Activity Alternatives	*Reporting Alternatives*
V/T 1. Draw a portrait of two (2) characters in a folktale you have read as you visualize them from the exaggerated descriptive passages in the folktale. Attach a brief explanation of why you visualize the character in this way.	1. Display your portraits. V/T
V/T 2. Make a collage depicting the exaggerated qualities associated with the character in the folktale.	2. Display your collage. V/T
A/V 3. Tape a radio talk show that interviews an exaggerated character. Record the responses to your questions on the importance of the exaggerated character's role in the folktale.	3. Play your tape for a A/V group of four (4) classmates.

Resource Alternatives

Books

1. Edward S. Curtis, *The Girl Who Married a Ghost and Other Tales from the North American Indian.*
2. Paul Delarve, ed., *The Borzoi Book of French Folk Tales.*
3. Richard M. Dorson, *American Folklore.*
4. Virginia Haviland, *North American Legends.*
5. David C. Laubach, *Introduction to Folklore.*
6. Dmitri Nagishkin, *Folktales of the Amur.*
7. Jane Polley, ed., *American Folklore and Legend.*
8. Milton Rugoff, ed., *The Penguin Book of World Folktales.*
9. Irwin Shapiro, *Heroes in American Folklore.*

10. Frances Toor, *A Treasury of Mexican Folkways*
11. Bernard J. Weiss, Peter S. Rosenbaum, Ann M. Shaw, and Millicent J. Tolbert, *To See Ourselves.*

Films

1. *Folk Hero William Tell*
2. *The Aesop's Fables Series*

Records

1. *Ashanti Folktales of Ghana*
2. *European Folktales*
3. *Fables of India*
4. *Special Folkdances*

Teacher-Made Resources

1. Worksheets
2. Circle of Knowledge
3. Charts and pictures in the classroom as well as in books and sources within the school and district library.

Small-Group Activities

Team Learning
Team Members:

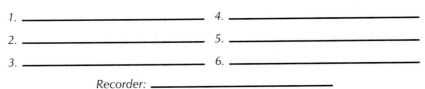

1. _____ 4. _____
2. _____ 5. _____
3. _____ 6. _____

Recorder: _____

> The Lion Makers
> Scholarship is less than sense:
> Therefore seek intelligence:
> Senseless scholars in their pride
> Made a lion; then they died.

In a certain town were four Brahmans who lived in friendship. Three of them had reached the far shore of all scholarship but lacked sense. The other found scholarship distasteful; he had nothing but sense.

One day they met for consultation. "What is the use of attainments," said they, "if one does not travel, win the favor of kings, and acquire money? Whatever we do, let us all travel."

But when they had gone a little way the eldest of them said, "One of us, the fourth, is a dullard, having nothing but sense. Now nobody gains the favorable attention of kings by simple sense without scholarship. Therefore we will not share our earnings with him. Let him turn back and go home."

Then the second said, "My intelligent friend, you lack scholarship. Please go home." But the third said, "No, no. This is no way to behave, for we have played together since we were little boys. Come along, my noble friend. You shall have a share of the money we earn."

With this agreement they continued on their journey, and in a forest they found the bones of a dead lion. Thereupon one of them said, "A good opportunity to test the ripeness of our scholarship. Here lies some kind of creature, dead. Let us bring it to life by means of the scholarship we have honestly won."

Then the first said, "I know how to assemble the skeleton." The second said, "I can supply skin, flesh, and blood." The third said, "I can give it life."

So the first assembled the skeleton, the second provided the skin, flesh, and blood. But while the third was intent on giving the breath of life, the man of sense advised against it, remarking, "This is a lion. If you bring him to life, he will kill every one of us."

"You simpleton" said the other. "It is not I who will reduce scholarship to a nullity."

"In that case," came the reply, "wait a moment, while I climb this convenient tree."

When this had been done the lion was brought to life, rose up, and killed all three. But the man of sense, after the lion had gone elsewhere, climbed down and went home.

And that is why I say:

"Scholarship is less than sense . . ."

—An Indian Folktale

Assignment

1. Why did the Brahmans decide to travel? _____

_____

_____

_____

2. What was the major difference among the four Brahmans?

_____

_____

_____

3. How was each of the Brahmans able to demonstrate his scholastic abilities?

_____

_____

_____

_____

_____

_____

_____

4. What is the moral lesson of this Indian folktale? Is it explicit or implicit?

_____

_____

_____

5. Do you think the Brahmans were justified in their treatment of the fourth member of their group? _____

_____

_____

_____

_____

6. Three of the Brahmans believed strongly in scholarship but lacked sense, while the fourth Brahman had no scholarship, only sense. Which of these situations is the better one? _____

_____

_____

_____

7. On the following page, write a short group poem explaining the events that would have occurred if the Brahmans had listened to the advice of the fourth member. Be sure to include the moral.

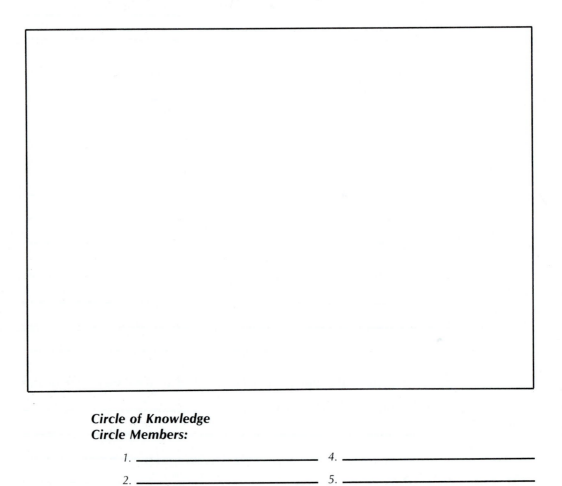

Circle of Knowledge
Circle Members:

1. _____ *4.* _____

2. _____ *5.* _____

3. _____ *6.* _____

Recorder: _____

In two (2) minutes, list the many countries from which folktales come:

Circle of Knowledge
Circle Members:

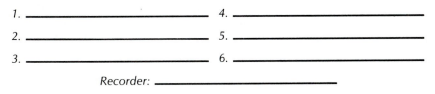

In two (2) minutes, list the many characteristics of folktales:

_____

_____

_____

_____

_____

_____

_____

Brainstorming
Group Members:

1. _____   4. _____

2. _____   5. _____

3. _____   6. _____

Recorder _____

One of the characteristics of folktales is the use of exaggeration of characters. In order to achieve this, the author is required to use fresh and different words to make the story more interesting.

The sentence below has many tired words; that is, they have been used so often they are worn out. Take one minute (60 seconds) for each word in italics, and with a group of classmates list as many synonyms as you can. Then consider the limitless number of combinations to find exciting, funny, and clever sentences! Who said vocabulary was boring?

The *man*	carefully *told* the	*folktale.*

Worksheet 1

Feeling creative? Write at least ten (10) new sentences using words from the list of synonyms you just have made.

1. _____

2. _____

3. _____

4. _____

5. _____

6. _____

7. _____

8. _____

9. _____

10. _____

Jumble

The letters of the words below are jumbled. Rearrange the letters to find their correct order.

L	C	V	E	E	R

G	E	X	G	A	R	A	I	O	E	N	T
		Ⓖ	Ⓖ					Ⓞ	Ⓝ		

With the letters that are circled, find the solution to the clue by arranging the letters in the proper order.

Clue
The time folktales refer to. . . .

Print your answer here:

| | | | | | | | |

Answer (below):

Answers

clever   moral   hero   exaggeration   riddle

Worksheet 3

Refer to the list of Resource Alternatives and choose a folktale that is related to your ethnic background. Following the reading of the tale, complete the chart below.

Title: _____

Origin of folktale: _____

　　　Answer: long ago

Author (If named): _____

Characters _____

_____

_____

Brief summary: _____

_____

_____

_____

_____

_____

Characteristics of folktales that are present: _____

_____

_____

_____

_____

Self-Assessment Test

1. For each of the characteristics listed below, identify a folktale that demonstrates the characteristic and briefly describe how it is done:

    a. Typical opening line: _____

    _____

    _____

    b. Heroic figure: _____

    _____

    _____

    _____

    c. Animals that have human traits _____

    _____

    _____

    _____

2. Describe how cleverness and wit are used in a folktale. Cite an example from a folktale you have read.

---

3. List at least three (3) moral lessons that were presented in the folktales you have read. Identify the tales.

You're terrific if you can name more!

---

4. For at least two (2) characters presented in the folktales you have read, describe how the author makes use of exaggeration. Why is this an effective tool in the writing of tales?

CONGRATULATIONS!!
YOU HAVE COMPLETED YOUR CONTRACT ACTIVITY PACKAGE
ON FOLKTALES.

Student's comments: _____

_____

_____

_____

_____

Teacher's comments: _____

_____

_____

_____

_____

Independent Contracts

Independent Contracts may be assigned to elementary level students on the basis of key questions:

1. What I want to learn
2. What I can use to learn
3. What I learned
4. How I feel about what I learned
5. What I would change if I were to start over

Analytic students who require structure and sequence can proceed through steps 1–5 in order. Global students may elect to skip around during their assignment, do two or more steps at the same time, or return to earlier questions during the learning process. Students in grades 2 and 3 (and sometimes 4) may enjoy completing the independent contract by filling in portions of the learning person (Figure 8–6), coloring sections to indicate closure, and taping the parts together as shown. Each learning person contract is signed by the student, checked by the teacher and becomes a bulletin board or hall display for other students to read or for open school night for parents. Older students may invent their own version of the drawing or simply follow the questions.

Begin this activity by sitting in a small circle (the teacher and four or five students) with youngsters holding an 8 x 10 ditto sheet of the legs portion of the learning person. This "foundation of learning" includes the title *What I Want to Learn* and motivates students because it involves them in generating a topic of direct interest. They will respond with topics such as dinosaurs, animals, money, fish, cars, TV games, and so forth. After entering these topics on the legs (Figure 8–7), each student should highlight the Number One topic of interest to him or her and then color the remainder with crayons or felt tip pens. This step provides a sense of closure and builds motivation and confidence. Progression to the next step becomes a natural internalized process for the individual learner.

Next distribute the ditto sheet of the hand (Figure 8–8) titled "What I Can Use to Learn." The hands are used to record titles of books, films, and other useful Resource Alternatives as well as to list appropriate pages, video recordings, pictures on file, and realia that are available. Once the student and teacher agree on what the student can use to learn, those items are highlighted and the rest colored with crayons or felt tip pens.

Information, processes, higher-order thinking skills, and other things learned are recorded in the head (Figure 8–9), where the brain is. The words "what I observed," "what I sense," "what I can tell others" may be changed to "what I saw," "what I heard," "what I did," and "what I know" (about the topic) as appropriate to the ability level and sophistication of the learner. Again, have the youngster use highlighters on the head when finished with that portion, taking care not to obliterate the information record.

The next section "How I Feel About What I Learned (Figure 8–10), gives the youngster numerous opportunities for participation, decision making, and creative, aesthetic, and emotional involvement. The students are instructed to evaluate in words and to contribute poems, drawings, short stories, and collages that reinforce what has been learned. This section is then highlighted and carefully colored, as were the others; students are to be reminded that what they have written is valuable and should be visible to other readers.

Finally, ask each student what he or she would change if starting over (Figure 8–11). If that concept appears too difficult for some learners, this "hand" could include more facts that were learned or creative projects to be shared. Modifications can be made on any portion as needed; the learning

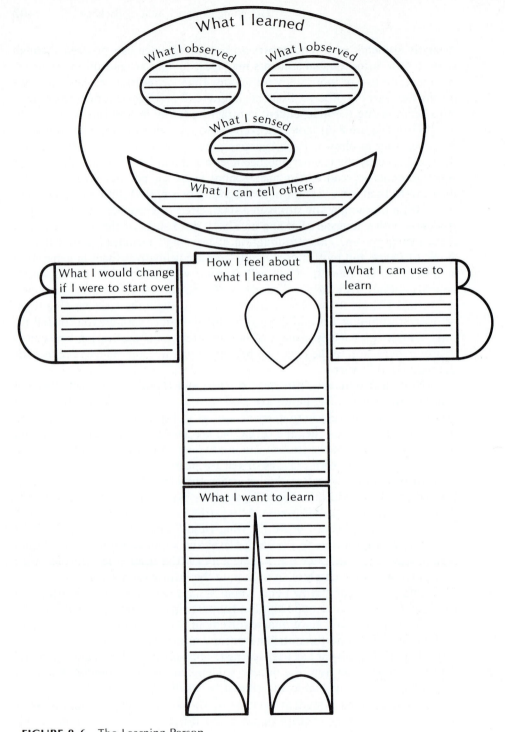

FIGURE 8–6 The Learning Person
Source: Devised by faculty members of the Westorchard School, Chappaqua, New York.

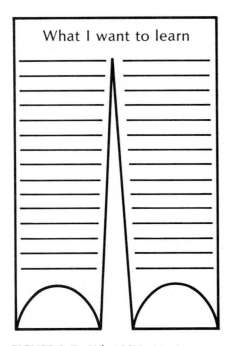

FIGURE 8–7   What I Want to Learn

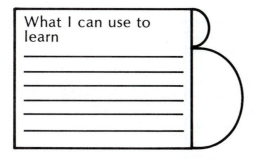

FIGURE 8–8   What I Can Use to Learn

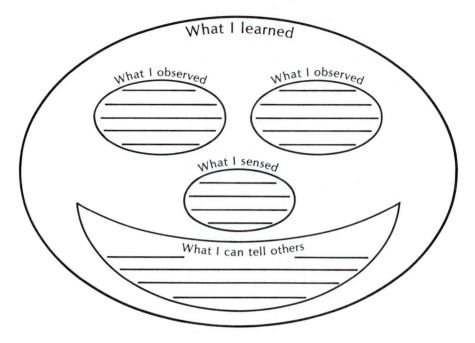

FIGURE 8-9 What I Learned

FIGURE 8-10 How I Feel about What I Learned

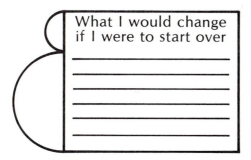

FIGURE 8–11   What I Would Change If I Were to Start Over

person remains an excellent strategy that promotes independence and learning how to learn.

A Final Word on Contract Activity Packages

Contract Activity Packages are not effective for everyone, but they will give motivated, able students the ability to move ahead at their own pace on the basis of their personal interests and unique learning styles. Contracts also are appropriate for nonconforming youngsters who require (1) an understanding of *why* they need to complete specific objectives in predesignated ways, (2) choices, and (3) collegiality rather than authoritarianism. *Begin* instruction for gifted, highly achieving, independent, and/or nonconforming students with this instructional method. When interest or motivation is evidenced by others, permit those youngsters to use a contract as well—but only *after* new and difficult material has been introduced through resources that better complement their styles.

9

Designing Multisensory Instructional Packages (MIPs) to Respond to Individual Learning Styles

Multisensory Instructional Packages (MIPs) are especially appealing to students who find it difficult to sit quietly for long periods of time or who cannot listen to a teacher without frequently interrupting or losing attention. Using a package, these youngsters can concentrate for the amount of time that suits them, take breathers whenever they wish, and then continue with their work. Instructional packages are not as effective for students who need continual direct interaction with either adults or peers; but very often they may be suitable for several learners at the beginning of a semester, for others a few weeks later, for others at midterm, and so on. They also may be designed so that one or two of the multisensory activities may be bypassed if less concentration on the topic is necessary.

Instructional packages are a boon to teachers who want to individualize instruction through direct appeal to personal learning styles but who cannot stretch themselves thin enough for a class full of children with a variety of needs and problems. Because students work independently (or with a friend) and the materials are self-corrective, the packages can meet the needs of learners on several academic levels—youngsters with learning disabilities who require special attention; slow learners who need more time to grasp new material; average youngsters, who prefer working on their own or for shorter or longer blocks of time; advanced students who are capable of progressing faster than their peers; and any interested student who wants to learn about a topic, concept, or skill at the moment that he or she desires, not when the teacher is able to get to the subject. The packages don't take up much classroom space and are particularly well suited to home study.

As an example of what is possible in a single classroom, one student might be working with a MIP on nouns while another, in a different section of the room, could be mastering the concept of fractions. As the first manipulates a noun game, the second completes a fraction puzzle. A third youngster may be hopping on a large plastic sheet that has been separated into sections and organized into a game that reviews parts of speech. The teacher moves among several small groups, pairs, and individuals while the instructional packages completely absorb the students using them.

Learning Style Characteristics Responsive to Multisensory Instructional Packages

Because of their multisensory activities, instructional packages are very motivating to slow learners, who usually require repetition and varied approaches through many senses before they are motivated to acquire and retain new knowledge and skills. The tape, written script, tactual, and kinesthetic mate-

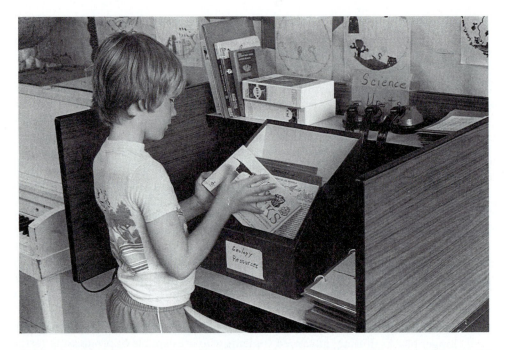

Students with either tactual/kinesthetic or no perceptual strengths, who enjoy multiple activities and find it difficult to sit still and listen, often perform extremely well with a Multisensory Instructional Package. (Photograph courtesy of P. K. Yonge Laboratory School, Gainesville, Florida.)

rials may be used over and over again until the youngster masters the objectives of the package.

Each instructional package focuses on a single objective or concept to be taught. This isolated goal is well suited to the recalcitrant learner who often finds it difficult to concentrate on more than one thing at a time. Conversely, unless the material in the package is extremely challenging, it is unlikely to interest high achievers, who quickly become bored by repetition.

Instructional packages are especially appropriate for those youngsters who require structure. The step-by-step procedures provide clear, sequenced directions that are repeated in a variety of ways until success is achieved.

Students who prefer working alone usually enjoy this multisensory method immensely. They can take the materials to an instructional area in the room, to the library, or even to their homes to work on intensively and without the distractions of the classroom and their peers.

Sound, in the form of your recorded voice, music, or other taped effects, can be provided or modulated through earphones or a cassette player.

All perceptual strengths are appealed to: By definition, instructional packages include visual, auditory, tactual, and kinesthetic activities. Even

Students who enjoy working with peers and/or find a particular topic or subject difficult, will learn most easily through a Multisensory Instructional Package. (Photograph courtesy of Brightwood Elementary School, Greensboro, North Carolina.)

when a student has only a single perceptual strength, he or she is likely to learn and to complete objectives because everything that is taught is introduced and reinforced through the four major learning senses.

Teachers should be aware of those youngsters who prefer instructional packages but who lack responsibility. Encouragement and piecemeal success on portions of the package should be promoted. Careful monitoring will aid those students in building responsibility. At times it may be necessary for the teacher or selected peers to work with those youngsters who respond well to instructional packages but who also require interaction with an authority figure or friends to stimulate learning.

Generally speaking, instructional packages are ideal for slowly achieving students who require structure and who can be sufficiently motivated by their multisensory activities to progress independently and successfully.

Learning Style Characteristics to Which Multisensory Instructional Packages Can Be Accommodated

Instructional packages can be taken to wherever the light, temperature, and design of the physical environment are exactly as the student wishes them to be. Because instructional packages are portable and may be worked on alone, the choice of where to use these resources belongs to the student, who may select the amount of light, the degree of temperature, and the kind of design in which he or she feels most comfortable.

Motivation is often developed or stimulated through these packages because of (1) the choice that students have in their selection or in the topic that will be studied, (2) the way the packages accommodate to the environmental and physical elements of learning style, (3) the control that youngsters exercise over the amount and pace of learning in which they engage at a given time, and (4) the academic progress that is virtually assured by the package's multisensory repetition.

Three other important aspects of learning style—intake, time of day, and mobility—are accommodated by instructional packages. It is easy to take advantage of intake while working independently on an instructional package. Raw vegetables, nuts, raisins, or other nutritious foods can be available in a bowl wherever the youngster is working, provided that rules have been established beforehand for access, eating, discarding, and the care of the premises.

Packages may be used at any time of the day or night without interfering with others and without interrupting other scheduled activities. Therefore, students can select the most appropriate and effective time to complete a package.

Many growing youngsters cannot sit still or work in one place for a long time. Packages allow total mobility. A student may take the package with him, spread it out, walk away, come back, sprawl, kneel, or just sit. Since the activities themselves provide action and movement, mobility is well served by this method.

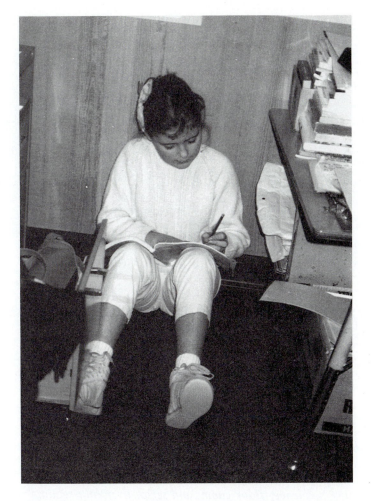

Children who enjoy working on a variety of materials anywhere in the classroom they feel most comfortable will enjoy learning through a Multisensory Instructional Package. (Photograph courtesy of Sherwood Elementary School, Edmonds, Washington.)

Case Studies Describing Students Whose Learning Styles Are Complemented by Multisensory Instructional Packages

1. Ben looked around. He couldn't seem to follow the instructions. They were printed on a sheet but they didn't make sense to him. He turned to his neighbor, Ed, and asked what he was supposed to do after finishing the

Students with tactual or kinesthetic strengths who are not succeeding in the auditory/visual mode eagerly embrace a Multisensory Instructional Package box filled with attractive instructional items. This one on New England is like a treasure chest of ways to discover answers to the objectives required for this topic. Note the Electroboard, Task Cards, Flip Chute shaped like a barn, Pic-a-Hole, Learning Circle, Programmed Learning Sequence, floor game, and script to permit reading what is provided on the tapes. (Photographs courtesy of Center for the Study of Learning and Teaching Styles, St. John's University, New York.)

second problem. Before Ed could respond, the teacher called out impatiently, "Ben, the directions are printed for you. All you have to do is read them!"

Auditory students may need to hear instructions or directions; the printed word may not be effective for them. Instructional packages provide a taped version of the written instructions.

2. Amy was very creative. She liked to put things together and often ignored the item's directions. Most of the time she was successful, but occa-

sionally she had ruined toys by not reading instruction sheets. She repeated this pattern at school, where she often plunged ahead on a test and answered questions that she had not read carefully. Her projects, too, though inspired, frequently contained many errors or were not completed because of Amy's cavalier approach to directions.

Students who require structure, concentration, concise direction, sequences, a single focus, and logical steps will benefit from the use of instructional packages.

3. John slammed his book down. The others looked at him. The teacher called John to her and asked what was wrong. ''It's the kids, I guess,'' explained John. ''Every time I start to do my work, the others ask questions or talk to me. I can't stand the interruptions when I'm working.''

Students who work best alone may find instructional packages to their liking.

4. Susie smiled. She played the tape again; her fingers traced the words in the written script as she listened. She understood perfectly! For the first time, reading had become fun. After she finished the touching and feeling game with ease, she began to build the map with the pieces in the package. She told the teacher that she wanted a new package tomorrow.

Instructional packages are ideal for those who need to learn through a perceptual strength that is not usually appealed to in the classroom and for those who require reinforcement through more than one perceptual strength.

How Multisensory Instructional Packages Facilitate Academic Achievement

Multisensory instructional packages are self-contained teaching units that appeal to students who learn slowly or whose learning style characteristics respond to this method. All packages have certain basic elements in common:

1. *Each package focuses on a single concept.*
Whether the package deals with learning how to tell time, identifying adverbs and using them correctly, the division of fractions, or war as a human atrocity, students know precisely what the focus is and can decide if it is appealing as a new topic or useful in reinforcing a previously learned skill. The cover and title always reveal what the package contains.

2. *At least four senses are used to learn the contents.*
A typewritten script that is repeated by the taped voice of the teacher gives clear directions to students to construct, manipulate, piece together, write, draw, complete, play, and in several ways use their sense of touch and their entire bodies in kinesthetic activities related to the package's objectives.

3. *Feedback and evaluation are built in.*
Tests are included in the package, and students may respond by writing, taping, or showing results. Correct answers and responses may be checked as the items to be learned are completed. The directions allow for immediate feedback and self-evaluation. Mistakes can be corrected through repetition of the taped and printed directions and by comparing the students' answers with ones prepared for the games and activities.

4. *Learning is private and aimed at individual learning styles.*
Only the teacher and student know how well the youngster is doing. Self-image and success are enhanced for the slower students as progress increases without peer competition. The multisensory approach; colorful materials and packaging; working alone; motivating choices; selection of when, where, and how; and the ability to move about and to eat if necessary make the instructional package an effective teaching aid for many students.

A Step-by-Step Guide to Designing a Multisensory Instructional Package

Step 1 Identify the topic. For example, you may want your students to understand concepts or acquire skills related to parts of speech, a specific country, fractions, magnetism, or solving math problems.

Step 2 List the things you want the student to learn about the topic.

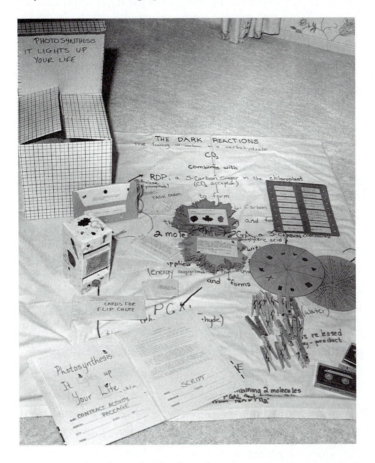

Some very bright and gifted students may gravitate toward a Multisensory Instructional Package (MIP) if it is challenging and offers sophisticated options for creating additional games, Electroboards, puzzles, and other manipulative resources. This MIP on "Photosynthesis" provides the "greening" of that type of student. (Photograph courtesy of Center for the Study of Learning and Teaching Styles, St. John's University, New York.)

Step 3   Plan to tape record simple learning objectives for your students. Use such words as *explain, describe, list,* and *identify.* For example, if you were constructing a package on nouns, the taped objective might be: "By the time you finish this package, you will be able to explain what a noun is and to recognize one in a sentence." (For specific instructions, see the section of this chapter on "How to Tape Directions for Instructional Packages.")

Step 4   Pretend you are teaching your class the most important aspects of the selected topic. Write out exactly what you would say to the children. Plan to tape record this explanation.

Step 5   Develop a visual, a tactual, and a kinesthetic activity that emphasizes these aspects in different ways. Write the directions for each of the activities as they will be taped. See Chapter 6 for directions for making Pic-A-Holes, Electroboards, Flip Chutes, Task Cards, and Floor Games.

Step 6   Make up a short test that will reveal whether the student has learned the skills and concepts after using the package. This may be recorded as well as written.

Step 7   Decorate and label a cardboard box in a manner that reveals the topic and contents. Cover the box with patterned Contact paper to ensure longevity and enhance attractiveness. Multisensory Instructional Package materials should be covered with clear Contact paper as well.

Examples of Appropriate Multisensory Instructional Packages

Language Arts: Parts of speech, correct grammar, selected skills such as:

Recognizing and using adjectives	How to write a friendly letter
How to write a friendly letter	How to develop complete sentences
What does an adverb do?	
Knowing nouns	When to use the possessive form
When to use capital letters	How to follow directions
How to solve problems	The _____
How to write an original ending	word family
	Quotation marks: Where do they go?

Social Studies: Map skills, geographical locations, community workers, common interests, such as:

East and west

Locating capital cities

Estimating mileage

Games children play

How climate affects industrial growth

Reading maps

The Canadian pipeline

A different kind of "key"

A visit to Paris

The Third World nations

Customs of the Algonquins

Say "hello!" in many languages

The energy crisis: How does it affect you?

How to cope with divorce in the family

Mathematics: Fractions, decimals, long division, calculations such as:

Let's multiply

What is the point?

What is your time worth?

All about triangles

Stop and go

Going in circles

How many ways can you form a group of _____ ?

Which package costs more?

The long and the short of it.

Take "Part" in things

Getting set

Recognizing danger signs

Science: Explaining sources of power, food, growth, and health:

What can a magnet do for you?

Making a bulb light

What is a good breakfast?

Let's have a party

Static electricity.

Who is taller than whom?

Are YOU a mammal?

What can marijuana do to you?

The water cycle preserves life

How wind works for us

Would you like to make a bell ring?

How many ways does a tree grow?

How to plant seeds

Are your teeth falling out? They will

Which drugs can kill you?

You can have beautiful skin

How to Tape Directions for Multisensory Instructional Packages

The cassette tape is, perhaps, the most important part of a multisensory package. To be effective, the tape must provide simple, concise directions and explanations so that students can use the package without your assistance. The following suggestions can help you develop a good tape:

1. State the objectives clearly and simply.
2. Speak slowly and vary your speech pattern, tone, and inflection to add listening interest. Be dramatic, but not overly so.
3. Avoid picking up background noises or taping where electrical appliances can cause interference.
4. Use explicit directions for each action that the child must do. For example, request that the package's cover be placed on the table, that items be taken out carefully, that each envelope be returned to the box, and so on.
5. Pause after giving directions so that the listener has time to consider them and carry them out. Or, to allow longer periods of time, you could say, "Turn off the tape recorder while you are putting these materials away. but remember to turn the recorder back on when you are ready to continue."
6. Don't ask questions that require only "yes" or "no" responses. Avoid saying, "Are you ready to begin the next activity?" or "Did you know the answer to that riddle?" Instead say, "I hope you are ready for the next activity! Please take out the blue box with the cotton cloud on it." Or, "I hope you knew that the answer to that riddle was 'a clock.' A clock has 'hands' but never washes them!"
7. Be certain that the tape is completely self-instructional. Put yourself in the student's place and see if you can work alone without assistance or additional resources and without having to leave the area.
8. Repeat important directions or difficult passages in a slightly different way to reinforce in an interesting manner.
9. Use good grammar and appropriate vocabulary.
10. Be certain that the tape and the materials are self-corrective. If you ask questions, pause sufficiently and then provide answers.
11. Use supplementary sounds (music, bells, animals, other people's voices).
12. Use a good tape recorder and fresh batteries; place the microphone in a comfortable position for you; place a "Taping" sign on your door to avoid bells and other intrusions; take the telephone off the hook; leave enough footage at the beginning of the tape so that your introduction is recorded in its entirety; watch that the tape does not run out while you are still speaking; check the volume; and test as you are recording to be certain the pickup is clear.
13. Identify each student's learning style and direct usage of the activities in the package in the same sequence as the individual's perceptual

strengths—strongest modality first, followed by next strongest, followed by next, and then *least* strong.

Sample Multisensory Instructional Packages

Elementary Level: Subtraction*

The following package (Figure 9–1), though designed for elementary youngsters, would be equally appropriate for other students in need of mastering the concept of subtraction. The tape; the visual, tactual, and kinesthetic activities; and the privacy in which the students may develop this skill all serve to enhance their potential for achievement and to diminish their self-consciousness about learning slowly when others appear to succeed easily. The materials for this package are housed in a gift box covered with bright red plastic and three dimensional letters that read: SUBTRACTION.

Tape and Script

Hello!
I'm very glad you chose this package on SUBTRACTION.
I hope you enjoy working with it.
By the time you finish this package, you will be able to explain what is meant by SUBTRACTION, and when and how to use it. Please look into the box and take out the pretty red booklet that has SUBTRACTION across its top. Open the booklet and let's read it together.
To SUBTRACT means to *take away*.
The sign that represents SUBTRACTION is called a "minus" sign.
A MINUS sign looks like this: −
When you see this example, it means:

$$4 \quad - \quad 1$$
Four   minus   One

Four minus One, 4 − 1, means that you have four (4) things and are now going to SUBTRACT (or take away) one (1).
Whenever you SUBTRACT, you always have less than you started with.
What is this sign called?   −
A minus sign. It looks like this   −

FIGURE 9–1   Sample Elementary-Level Instructional Package: Subtraction

*This instructional package on "Subtraction" was designed by Denise D'Acunto Johnet, St. John's University, New York.

If I SUBTRACTED, (or took away), three (3) apples from five (5) apples, how many apples would I have left?

Two (2) apples

Above you will see the five (5) apples, each one numbered. Point to each apple. Now, if you subtract three (3) apples, you can plainly see that you have two (2) left.

5 apples		If you have	5 apples
− 3 apples	OR	and take away	3 apples
2 apples		You then have	2 apples

Let's try to work together on another SUBTRACTION problem. If you are lucky enough to have three (3) candy bars, and you decide to give one to your friend, how many would you have left?

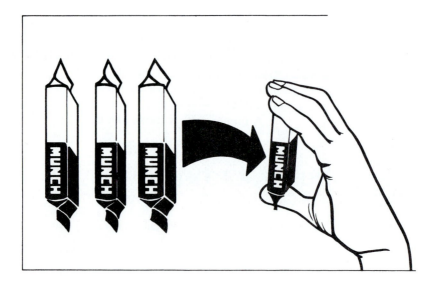

You would have 2 candy bars left.

If you had three (3) candy bars to begin with and you SUBTRACTED one (1) candy bar, you would have two (2) candy bars left.

I hope you are beginning to see from these examples that when we SUBTRACT, we are really taking away. When we take away, we have less than we started with.

Another way to say SUBTRACT is: DEDUCT
You can SUBTRACT three (3) apples from five (5) *or*
You can DEDUCT three (3) apples from five (5).

The two words mean the same thing. You can also TAKE AWAY three (3) apples if you have five (5) apples.

I have another problem I would like you to work on.

If I had two (2) kittens and gave them both away, how many kittens would I have left?

(Here is a hint for you. If you *give them away,* you are really SUBTRACTING.)

Zero (0)

If you subtract all that you have, you will have nothing left.

If you had two (2) kittens to begin with, and you gave them both away, you would have none left.

Now, if I were to ask you, "What is meant by SUBTRACTION?," what would you say?

When you speak of SUBTRACTION, you are talking about taking away a part of the original amount you started with. When you *take away,* your answer is always *less* than the amount you first started with. Whenever you SUBTRACT you will have less.

The End

TASK CARDS

Please put the book that we have been reading aside and look into the big box once more. You will see a yellow envelope with the words TASK CARDS on it. Please take the envelope out of the box and open it.

Take out the cards that are inside the envelope. Place them in front of you. These Task Cards are a game that will help you to remember the things that we just read.

There should be eight (8) different cards in front of you. Spread them out. You really have eight (8) halves of Task Cards because the parts you see must fit together to form a question part and an answer part. (See Figure 9–2.)

The question parts say: When you subtract you are
When you subtract you always
A minus sign looks like this
and

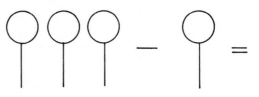

You need to find the answers to the question parts and join the answers and the questions together into whole Task Cards. See if you can correctly match each question part with its correct answer part. Turn off the tape recorder while you are trying. (Pause)

Since you've turned the tape on again, I guess you've matched the Task Card parts. When did you realize that you could only match the correct question with the correct answer? Of course!

The cards are "shape-coded" and only will fit together when they are right for each other!

FIGURE 9–2 The Eight Task Cards for the "Subtraction" Instructional Package

Kinesthetic Activity

Now you are ready for the last activity in this package. Put the Task Cards back into their envelope and then put the envelope on the table near you. (Pause)

Next, find the large plastic sheet that is inside the box and take it out carefully. Spread the large plastic sheet on the floor. You will see Mickey Mouse on the sheet, but he is divided into four (4) SUBTRACTION problems. If you can SUBTRACT correctly and find the right answers to the problems on him, the pieces of the puzzle will fit exactly onto the picture of Mickey. You may turn the tape recorder off until after you have completed the puzzle. Remember to turn it back on! (Pause)

I'm glad you came back to this tape!

If you were able to piece Mickey Mouse together, you were able to find the answers to the SUBTRACTION problems. Tomorrow we will try a different set of problems, and we'll see how much you remember about SUBTRACTION. I think you'll remember a lot!

For now, please take the large plastic sheet and fold it carefully so that it can fit back into the box. (Pause) Then place all the SUBTRACTION puzzle pieces of Mickey Mouse back into their envelope. When you have done that, put the envelope into the box on top of the large plastic sheet.

Put the Task Cards into the box, too. Now place the book about SUBTRACTION on top. The last thing that you will need to do is to rewind this tape and then put it, too, into the box. Then you are finished with this package and need only carry it back to the Learning Station where it belongs.

You must feel proud of yourself today. After all, you learned something new about SUBTRACTION: You should feel proud. I am proud of you, too!

Good-bye!

Sample Scripts

Sample scripts for "Folktales" and "Magnetism: The Power of Attraction" are included here to present script variations for Multisensory Instructional Packages (MIPs). You may select your own set of tactual/kinesthetic resources to teach any topic (see Chapter 6)

Upper Elementary: Folktales*

Hello! I'm very glad you chose this package on Analyzing Folktales. I do hope you enjoy working with it. By the time you finish this package, you will be able to identify certain characteristics of folktales.

*This Multisensory Instructional Package on "Folktales" was designed by Jeannette Bauer and Mary Dawber, graduate students, St. John's University, New York, and New York City teachers.

Most folktales use at least two (2) of the following:

a. A typical opening line
b. A heroic figure
c. Animal characteristics that have human traits, which is called *personification*
d. The technique of cleverness to outwit another character
e. An ending with a moral
f. The use of exaggerated qualities for their characters

Now, open your reading text to page 103 and let's read one folktale together.

A long time ago, on the west side of Oahu, there was a cornfield that a grasshopper had grown. A coyote lived at the south side, and she was an old coyote. One day she went outside, and she saw the cornfield and the grasshopper who sat and watched it. There were lots of corn, melon, and all kinds of vegetables. As the old lady coyote came close to the grasshopper, she heard the grasshopper singing.

"Oh, that is such a beautiful song. I could learn it and sing it to my grandchildren when they are ready for bed. I think I will go ask him to teach me the song," she said to herself and then went down to the cornfield. When she came upon the cornfield, she saw the grasshopper sitting in the shade. "Whose vegetables and fruits are these?" she asked.

"They are mine," the grasshopper answered.

"What were you singing about?" she asked.

"I was praying for the vegetables to grow quickly," he told her.

"I heard you singing. That is why I came," she said. "You sing your song for me, and I will learn it. I would like to sing it to my grandchildren," the coyote told him.

The grasshopper said, "You sit down here and listen so you will learn." Then the grasshopper sang. After he finished, he asked, "Did you learn it?"

"Yes," she said, "I will go now and sing it to my grandchildren." She started running as soon as she left the cornfield. When she was halfway home, a flock of pigeons in the cornfield flew in front of her. She fell backward. When she got up, she tried to remember the song, but had forgotten it. "I think I will go back and ask the grasshopper to sing again. I am sure he stays there all the time. He'll probably sing it for me again." She turned around and went back. When she arrived, he was still sitting in the same place as when she had left him.

"Why have you come back?" he asked her.

"A flock of no-good pigeons scared me on my way, and I forgot the song. So I came back to ask you to sing for me again." After he sang for her, she said, "Now I will go sing for my grandchildren." She ran down the hill, but a rodent scurried in front of her. The old coyote got frightened and forgot the song again. She started off by singing, "Tu-Wee, Tu-Wee," but she forgot the rest of the song.

The grasshopper saw the old coyote coming in the distance. He said to himself, "This time I am getting tired. I won't sing to her." He curled up in a ball and just sat there.

When the coyote got close, she said, "You help me again. That rodent ran in front of me, and I forgot my song again." She waited for him to sing for her, but he didn't sing anything. "Aren't you going to sing for me again?" the grasshopper sat there without saying a word. "If you won't sing for me after I have asked you four times, I am going to eat you!" the coyote threatened him. She asked once, then twice, then the third time and the fourth. Then she threatened him again by saying, "I am going to eat you up if you won't sing for me." The grasshopper didn't move an inch. He just sat there all curled up. Then the coyote put the grasshopper in her mouth. Just before she ate him, he turned into a rock. When she took a bite, to her surprise, the rock caused her front teeth to break. That is why coyotes have teeth that are short in front and long in the back.

If you would like to read the other tales in this book, rewind this tape, replace it into its plastic holder, and turn off the tape recorder. When you have read as much as you care to, look into the "Learning about Folktales" box and find the tape that says "Activity 1." Insert that tape into the recorder, and we will be ready to work a bit more on identifying the characteristics of folktales. If you are going to read the book now, get comfortable and enjoy the reading. Remember to find the second tape when you have finished the stories that interest you!

Activity 1

Hello, again! I hope you enjoyed the tale! Now let's have some fun in identifying the characteristics of folktales. Look inside the "Learning about Folktales" box and take out the folder labeled "Task Cards." Take out the cards that are inside the folder. Place them in front of you. These Task Cards are a game that will help you to remember the characteristics of folktales. There should be 12 different cards in front of you. Spread them out. What you really have are 12 halves of Task Cards. The parts must fit together to form 6 examples of the folktale's characteristics. The examples were taken directly from the reading. You will need to match the characteristic to the example to form the whole Task Card.

Turn off the tape while you are working. Here's a hint for the Task Cards. Once properly joined together, each will form a picture of a characteristic found in the folktales. Good luck! Remember, turn the tape back on when you are finished. (Pause)

I hope you liked working with the Task Cards. I'm sure you put them all together correctly. Notice that only correct examples can be matched. Hold up the cards. The cards are shape-coded, and they will fit together when they are right for each other. Just to be on the safe side, you should have pictures of a castle, a coyote, a frog, a hero, a grasshopper, and a goat on the backs of the cards when matched correctly.

Activity 2

Now you are ready for the next activity. Put the Task Cards back into their folder and set them aside. Next, find the folder labeled "Learning Circle." Take out the wheel and place it onto the table with the different colored writing facing you. Now take the eight clothespins and place them in front of you so that the words *riddle, moral, exaggerated, typical opening line, folktales, cleverness, personification,* and *heroic figure* can be seen. The object of the game is to match the folktale characteristic on it. While you turn the wheel, read each word or set of words with the correct definition. Sit back and relax while you work. Please remember to turn the tape back on when you are through. Good luck! (Pause)

Here we go again. How did you do? To check your work in defining the characteristics of a folktale, simply turn the Learning Circle over. If the symbols on the back of each clothespin match the symbol to which it is clipped, your answer is correct. Take some time to check. (Pause)

How many did you get right? This wasn't difficult at all! I'm quite certain that you are doing well. I hope you are ready for the next game! First put the Learning Circle back into the folder, and clip the clothespins to the outside of the folder. Place the folder onto the table or desk near you.

Activity 3

Now look into the large box again and find a small box labeled "Scrambled Word Game." There is a game board that goes with it. It is in a folder marked "Scrambled Word Game," which is also inside the large box. Put the game board in front of you. Now look at the 68 alphabet letters in the small box. When correctly placed together, they will form the words for the characteristics of most folktales. Look at the game board. See how it is divided into sections for each answer. The first and last letter of each word are written in front of you. I will give you additional clues as you go on. As you work to solve each word, be certain to turn off the tape. When you believe you have solved each word scramble, turn the tape on to receive your next clue. Get ready, get set, go! Here is your first clue:

1. This word means the lesson taught by a story. (Pause) I hope you remember what that word is! (Pause)
2. This word means to give human qualities to an object or an animal. (Pause) That is a long word. It has 15 letters in it! (Pause)
3. This word means to overstate an idea beyond the truth. (Pause)
4. This word means to come up with an ingenious action to overcome an opponent. (Pause)

5. This word means a puzzling question. (Pause)

6. This word is a brief story told throughout history. (Pause)

7. These words mean a person identified for courage, strength, and valor. (Pause)

Since you turned the tape back on, you must be finished. Go back to the box labeled "Scrambled Word Game." Look at the inside of the boxtop. You will see a secret compartment. Take the card labeled Answer Key and compare your answers to the key. When you are ready, stop the tape, but turn it back on when you have completed checking. Good luck! Remember to turn the tape back on when you are finished. (Pause)

How did you do? Did you have the correct answers, but some spelling errors? Those were difficult words, so it is not bad if you did. Since you have finished the Scrambled Word Game, return all the alphabet letters to the small box and be certain to place the Answer Key back into its secret compartment. Now that you have completed the three activities, you are ready to take a short quiz to see if you have mastered the characteristics of folktales.

Activity 4

Go back into the "Learning about Folktales" box. Look inside and take out the folder labeled "Folktale Characteristics Quiz." You should see a sheet with 10 questions on it. You also should see a pencil. Take the pencil and read each question on the sheet with me. At the end of each question you will see a "T" and an "F." The "T" stands for True, and the "F" stands for False. After you read and listen to each question, decide if the statement is True or False. Then circle either the "T" or the "F" depending on which answer is correct.

I hope you are ready! Follow me by referring to the quiz sheet. After you have finished, you may turn the tape off to review your answers, but remember to turn the tape back on when you have finished checking your answers. (Pause)

1. The lesson that is learned at the end of the story is called a moral.
    T   F

2. A heroic figure is a disliked character.   T   F

3. A riddle is a puzzling question.   T   F

4. Folktales have only been around for two (2) years.   T   F

5. "Once upon a time" is a typical opening line for a folktale.   T   F

6. Ingenious actions or cleverness may be present in a folktale.   T   F

7. To describe a character truthfully is known as exaggeration.   T   F

8. Personification is when an object or animal has human qualities.
   T   F

9. An animal talking is an example of personification.   T   F

10. "And they lived happily ever after" is a typical opening line for a folk-tale. T   F

Please bring your paper to the teacher's desk after you have finished listening to this tape. Would you please be kind enough to place each folder and game back into the large box? Then rewind the tape and place it back into its pocket in the box. When you have done all that, put the cover back onto the box and put the box back into its place in the Learning Center.

I hope you have enjoyed this package, because I enjoyed making it for you. Remember to put your quiz sheet into the bin for completed work and to return the package. I will read and score your quiz as soon as I can. Then we will talk about what you have learned from this package.

Thank you and goodbye for now!

Magnetism: The Power of Attraction*

The directions that follow are on tape and appear here as the written script.

> Hi! I'm happy that you chose this package to work with today. This box is filled with many interesting things for you to do. The things that you will do will teach you about magnetism.
>
> I think that you are going to enjoy learning about magnetism with this package, but if you get tired and want to stop or take a rest, just turn off the tape and relax. When you finish using this package, or want to stop for the day, please turn off the tape, rewind it, and carefully return it and the other materials to the box.
>
> I am ready to begin; I hope that you are too! Open the box and place the cover away from you.
>
> Look into the box and find a red booklet that is shaped like a magnet. Go ahead; I'll wait for you! (Pause) I'm glad you found it. I hope that you like the cover, because I made it! Let's read "Magnetism: The Power of Attraction" together.

Visual-Auditory Activities

Open the book to the first page. Imagine what it would be like if you had one very special magical power. This magical power is called MAGNETISM. With

*By Maria Turane Giresi, Teacher, The Growing Tree, Ridgefield, Connecticut.

This Magnetism MIP includes a Flip Chute, Pic-a-Hole, Electroboard, set of Task Cards, floor game, Programmed Learning Sequence, and tape that provides direction for each. Note the global subtitle: "Magnetism: The Power of Attraction." (Photograph courtesy of Center for the Study of Learning and Teaching Styles, St. John's University, New York.)

this special power of MAGNETISM you would only have to raise your hand and certain things would magically float through the air and land right in your hand. Imagine how you could amaze your friends, the tricks you could play, how easy it would be to clean your room!

IMAGINE . . . how much fun you could have if only you had the magical power of MAGNETISM!

On the next page, our friend says, "I wonder what all this is about? What's magnetism?" I hope you are wondering too!

At the bottom of this page is our pronunciation card. I will pronounce each word. Say the word after me.

magnetism
lodestone

magnetic
attraction
nickel
cobalt
iron

Turn the page. On this page our friend is dancing for joy because he's going to tell you all the fascinating things you are going to learn. He says, "I am so glad that you are going to work with this package because it will teach you to:

- Identify and describe an object that attracts iron, nickel, or cobalt.
- Describe the space around an object that attracts iron, nickel, or cobalt.
- Compare the results of bringing like and unlike ends together.

Frame 1   Long ago shepherds carried wooden staffs with iron tips. Sometimes the iron tips seemed to stick to the ground and sometimes pieces of stone stuck to the iron tips of their staffs.

Pieces   of   _____   sometimes   stuck   to   the _____ tips of shepherds' staffs.

Turn the page. Shepherds had no use for these marvelous STONES that stuck to the IRON tips of their staffs.

Frame 2   The sheep is asking, "I wonder what these marvelous stones could be?" These marvelous stones are called LODESTONES. LODESTONES make strange things happen. They can pick up pins, paper clips, and nails.

Turn the page. Our friend is asking, "What does a lodestone remind you of?" Even today LODESTONES can pick up pins, paper clips, and nails.

Frame 3   "I hope you thought of me! Hi! My name is Magnet. I have the same pulling power as the lodestone. I can make a nail jump into the air and stick to me like glue."

A lodestone acts just like a:
PAPERCLIP   MAGNET   CAN OPENER.

Turn the page. A MAGNET has pick-up power just like a lodestone.

Frame 4   This is my friend Nail. Take him out of his pocket and see if you can make Nail jump in the air and stick to me like glue. My assistant, Magnetic Wand, is just hanging around to help you. Turn off the tape. When you are finished experimenting, turn the tape back on. Be sure to put Nail back into his pocket.

Turn the page. I hope Nail behaved himself and jumped into the air and stuck like glue to Magnetic Wand.

Frame 5   Our friend nail says, "This is so embarrassing!" My pick-up or pulling power is called ATTRACTION. That is why the metal tips of the shepherd's staff could pick up lodestones, and I can pull nails to me.

_____ is my pick up or pulling power.

Turn the page. ATTRACTION is my special pulling or pick-up power.

Frame 6   These are my neighbors, the Circle family. Use my assistant Magnetic Wand to see which members fall under my magical power of attraction. Draw a circle around them.

Turn the page. Mr. Iron Circle and his son Nickel Button are my friends.

Frame 7   As you have already seen, not everything falls under my power of attraction. That's because they are not made of:

plastic (caps)   rubber   metal

Turn the page. I have lots of friends, but they all must be made of METAL to fall under my power of attraction.

Frame 8   To be my friend, metals must have NICKEL, COBALT, or IRON in them.

Place Magnetic Wand near metal objects to see if they contain:

_____ _____ _____

You may turn off the tape while you search for these objects. Please don't disturb your friends!

Turn the page. Magnets are only attracted to things made of NICKEL, COBALT, or IRON.

Our next page says, "Circle the objects that fall under Magnet's magical power of attraction."

PAPER CLIP
GLASS
BALLOON
NAIL
RUBBER BALL
HANDKERCHIEF
CAR

Turn the page. These objects are all made of metals that contain nickel, cobalt, or iron.

paper clip   nail   car

These objects are not made of metal and should not be attracted to Magnets.

glass   balloon   rubber ball   handkerchief

Frame 9 MAGNETISM is a very special part of my power of attraction. MAGNETISM means that some of my attracting power can pass through metal objects to other metal objects. Circle:

attraction   magnetism

_____ means that my magical power to attract can pass through to other metals.

Turn the page. MAGNETISM is my magical power of passing attraction along to my other metal friends.

Frame 10 Here are my friends the Paper Clip Brothers. Arnold is holding onto my foot. My MAGNETISM passes through Arnold to Wilbur, then through Wilbur to Gary. Each can hold on because MAGNETISM can pass through each clip to the next.

MAGNETISM means that my magical power of attraction can _____ through other metal objects.

A magnet's attraction can PASS through to other metal objects.

Frame 11 You can't see my MAGNETISM but you can see what it does. Take the Paper Clip Brothers out of the envelope and experiment to discover my magical power of MAGNETISM. Turn off the tape to do this experiment. When you are finished, circle the correct answer.

Magnetism can

BE SEEN   NOT BE SEEN

Then turn the tape back on. Turn the page. We say that magnetism is *invisible,* because it cannot be seen.

Frame 11 I have a big family, and we do not always look the same. My brother Bar Magnet is very straight and long. I am a HORSESHOE-shaped magnet. MAGNETIC WAND is a CIRCLE MAGNET. Not all magnets have the same _____.

Turn the page. There are many different types of magnets. They do not always look the same or have the same shape.

Frame 12 My brother Bar Magnet is a very helpful person. You can sometimes find him in the most peculiar places. Bar can hold doors and cabinets closed. Your refrigerator door probably has my brother Bar Magnet around its edges to keep it tightly closed.

Name three (3) places where my strong brother Bar Magnet might be hiding in your home.

Turn the page. Cabinets, doors, and refrigerators are some places. If you listed other places, give yourself a pat on the back!

Frame 13   Around my magnet family and me are special places where our attraction or "pulling power" works best. These places are called our POLES. They are found at each end.

Magnets have _____ or "pulling power" ends called _____.

Turn the page. A magnet's pulling places are called POLES. There are two . . . one at each end.

Frame 14   No matter what our shape is, each member of my magnet family calls his poles either NORTH POLE or SOUTH POLE.

Our poles are called the _____ POLE and the _____ POLE.

Turn the page. A magnet's poles are called the NORTH POLE and the SOUTH POLE.

Frame 15   Our poles are attracted to each other, but in a very special way. My north pole is always attracted to a south pole. My south pole is always attracted to a north pole.

A north pole is attracted to a _____ pole. A south pole is always attracted to a _____ pole.

Turn the page. That's right! OPPOSITE poles always attract. North poles always attract south poles. South poles always attract north poles.

Frame 16   Never, never, ever can a north pole attract another north pole, or a south pole attract another south pole. Magnets will always push away if their like poles are near each other. We say like poles REPEL each other.

Magnets will always _____ each other if like poles are put near each other.

Turn the page. Like poles REPEL or "push away" from each other.

Task Card   For more magnet fun, put these puzzles together! Turn off the tape now. (Pause) When you are finished putting them together, we will read your puzzles. (Pause)

I think you must be finished. Let's read the cards now.

Your puzzles can be in any order. Find the one that says:

1. Metals having *nickel, cobalt,* or *iron* are attracted to magnets.
2. *Lodestones* are nature's magnets.
3. *Attraction* is a magnet's pulling power.
4. *Magnetism* is the power to pass attraction from a magnet.
5. *Like* poles repel.

Turn the page. Our next page is even more fun. Take the continuity tester out of the box and have fun using the Electroboard! (Pause)

We hope you have enjoyed our story. Magnets are one of nature's greatest mysteries. Without us the world would be a very different place. Goodbye!

Tactual Activities

Task Cards

Please put aside the book that we have been reading and look into the big box once more. You will see yellow cards with a big red plastic paper clip on them. Please take them out of the box and place them in front of you. These Task Cards are a game that will help you to remember the things that we just read.

There should be ten (10) cards in front of you. Spread them out. You really have ten (10) halves of Task Cards because the parts you see must fit together to form one sentence. See if you can correctly match each sentence. Turn off the tape recorder while you are trying. (Pause)

Since you've turned the tape on again, I guess you've matched the Task Card parts. When did you realize that you could match only the correct sentence parts? Of course! The cards are "shape-coded" and will fit together only when they are right for each other.

Flip Chute

Now you are ready for the next activity in this package. Put the big red paper clip around the Task Cards and then put them on the table near you. (Pause)

Next, find the yellow box that has two openings and says "Magnetism: The Power of Attraction" on its top. On the Flip Chute's right side is a pocket filled with cards. Take the cards out of the pocket. Make sure that you read the side of the card with the happy face sticker first. Look at the first card and try to think of a word or words that tell about this word. Put the card into the top opening. Magically, the card will come out of the bottom opening and will tell you the answer. Turn off the tape and try the other cards. When you are finished, turn the tape back on. (Pause)

Since you've turned the tape on again, I guess you've finished using the Flip Chute. Wasn't that fun? Maybe someday you would like to make one for yourself. Meanwhile, place the cards back in the pocket and put the Flip Chute on the table away from you. (Pause)

Electroboard

Now you are ready for our next activity. Look into the box again and find the big black card. It says MAGNETISM on it. Also take out the continuity tester. Go ahead, I'll wait. (Pause)

The left column on the card contains words that you are probably becoming very familiar with. Clip one wire to the silver circle next to the word *magnetism.* Look at the choices in the right column. When you think you know which words describe the word *magnetism,* touch the other wire to that circle. If you are correct a bulb will light up.

If nothing happens, look at the choices in the right column again to discover a phrase that would be a better match. Find all the matching answers! Turn off the tape, and when you are finished don't forget to turn it back on. (Pause)

Hello again! How did you do? I hope you're becoming an authority on magnetism! Electroboards are lots of fun to use and easy to make. When you are finished with this Electroboard, put it on the table near the other materials that you have already used. Soon I'd like to show you and some of your friends how to make an Electroboard.

Pic-A-Hole

Let's go back to our box now. Look into the box and find a small yellow folder that contains cards and has a string hanging from it. Put the Pic-a-Hole on the table in front of you. Read the top of the first card. it says: "A magnet uses pushing power to:"

Now look at the three choices listed below:

ATTRACT   MAGNETISM   REPEL

Study the drawing at the top of the card. Use the wooden peg that is hanging on the string. Put the wooden peg into the hole that tells about a magnet's pushing power. Try to take the card out of the folder. If it does not come out easily, then make another choice. When your answer is right, the card should easily slide out of the folder.

You may turn off the tape while you use the Pic-A-Hole. Try to find the answer for each card! When you are finished, put the cards back in the folder and turn the tape back on.

Kinesthetic Activity

Magnet Mania

Now you are ready for the last activity in this package. Look into the box and find the large white plastic sheet and carefully take it out. Spread the sheet on the floor. You will see that there are cards attached to the back. Take the cards out and remove the rubber band. On the front you will find the magnet you need to play this game. Every card is numbered. Each card matches a square on your game board. Place your magnet in the first square. Follow the directions on each card. See if you can become our newest MAGNET MA-NIAC. When you are finished, you may turn the tape back on.

I hope you had lots of fun! I'm glad you came back to this tape! I'd like to congratulate you for being the newest MAGNET MANIAC! Tomorrow we'll see how much you remember about MAGNETISM. I know you'll remember a lot!

For now, please put away the Magnet Maniac Game. Put a rubber band around the cards. Please make sure the cards are in the correct order. Then place them back into their pocket. Place the magnet on its special magnetic pad. Carefully fold the game and put it back into the box. (Pause) Now place the Electroboard, Flip Chute, Pic-a-Hole, Task Cards, and red booklet called "Magnetism: The Power of Attraction" back into the box.

The last thing you will need to do is to rewind the tape. When it stops, put it into the box too. Then you will be finished with this package and will need to carry it back to the Learning Station where it belongs.

You must feel proud of yourself today. After all, you learned something new about MAGNETISM. You should feel proud. I am proud of you, also.

Good-bye!

A Final Word on Instructional Packages

Teachers often do not have the time or patience to teach and reteach each student who needs individualized attention. Instructional packages can do both and offer a variety of other benefits too. They develop listening skills, encourage independent work, and teach students to follow directions. They make students aware of their own growth and, gradually, build positive self-image and confidence. They provide a new teaching method when all else has failed.

Instructional packages may be used anywhere in the classroom and, thus, respond to individual preferences for sound versus quiet, soft or bright light, temperature, and design. They permit students who wish to work by themselves to do so while simultaneously allowing peer-oriented students to work

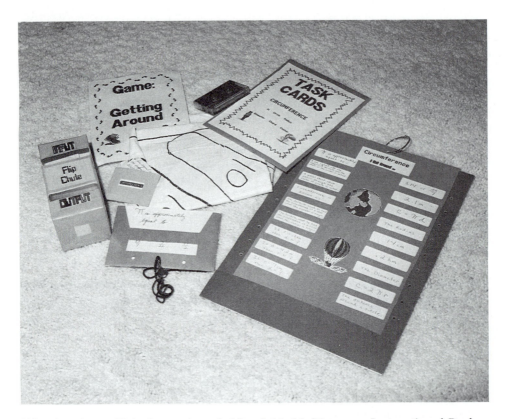

"Getting Around" is the catchy subtitle of this Multisensory Instructional Package (MIP) on the "Circumference of a Circle." Like most MIPs, it includes a Flip Chute, Programmed Learning Sequence, Electroboard, floor game, Pic-a-Hole, and the direction-giving tape. If you please, you may add a copy of the related Contract Activity Package for a final review for students who invariably wish to use the instructional methods their friend uses. However, the style-responsive, most matching method should be used first; *the less appropriate method may be used to* review. *(Photographs courtesy of Center for the Study of Learning and Teaching Styles, St. John's University, New York.)*

cooperatively with one or two classmates. They minimize direct interaction between the learner and the teacher when a poor or negative relationship exists. However, when students are teacher-oriented, the teacher's voice on the tape or directions for use provide a temporary substitute for direct personal proximity. They provide alternative activities for youngsters who enjoy variety and insure a specific pattern for those who feel secure with familiar strategies.

Instructional Packages are multisensory and thus respond to all perceptual modalities. Their activities can be sequenced so that each student learns *initially* through his or her strengths and then is *reinforced* through two differ-

"Breaking the Map Code" also contains a Programmed Learning Sequence, a Flip Chute, a Pic-A-Hole, a board game (rather than a floor game), a Learning Circle (with clothes pins), a Contract Activity Package for review if desired, and tapes to permit students who wish to hear the material read to them. (Photograph courtesy of Center for the Study of Learning and Teaching Styles, St. John's University, New York.)

ent senses. They are private; no one except the learner and the teacher knows who is learning what and how. This resource permits students to move while learning, be directly involved in their own instruction, and proceed at a pace with which they can cope—and succeed.

This resource provides structure; youngsters who are extremely self-structured (low LSI scores on structure) will not enjoy instructional packages as a routine unless the content is challenging to them. Conforming students will find them interesting; nonconformists will enjoy the choices and variety of activities.

Gifted students can *make* instructional packages for use by others, thus capitalizing on their special creativity and talents. Parents can be involved by designing and developing packages, too. Once completed, these resources can

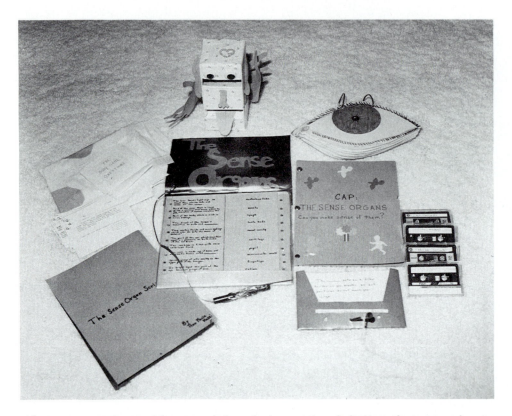

Almost any topic provides material set in instructional designs that may win students away from the television screen. Youngsters who succeed through direct involvement with tactual/kinesthetic learning materials then can score well on class, grade-level, or standardized tests. This Multisensory Instructional Package on "Sense Organs" reaches students who experience difficulty with the topic when it is taught initially *through lectures or required readings. (Photograph courtesy of Center for the Study of Learning and Teaching Styles, St. John's University, New York.)*

be used year after year by students who enjoy learning through multisensory materials. In effect, Multisensory Instructional Packages produce a pleasant, nonconfrontational, constructive environment, in which teachers who previously could not individualize instruction can do so. And, in addition to all these benefits, instructional packages are fun!

10

Teaching Style: Expanding Your Strengths—Your Way!

Matching Learning and Teaching Styles

A growing body of research addresses the question of how matching learning and teaching styles affects cognitive outcomes. If instructional resources can be considered as having a *style* of their own, then several studies verified the increased academic achievement and improved attitudes toward learning evidenced when students' learning styles were matched with complementary methods or materials (Douglas, 1979; Gardiner, 1986; Ingham, 1989; Kroon, 1985; Trautman, 1979; White, 1980)—in the absence of any teacher's presence.

However, when addressing teaching style, dependent on the instrument used to identify the instructor's procedures, different outcomes were realized. For example, Adams (1983), Copenhaver (1979), and Mehdikhani (1980) all found a positive relationship between how each teacher taught and how well that teacher's students achieved. In each case, the closer the match between the teacher's teaching style and the student's learning style, the higher the student's grade-point average. However, each of those studies used single-dimension matches—for example, independent, self-paced; independent, teacher paced; lecture; or lecture/laboratory. With our concept of learning style, which includes 21 different variables, it is not easy to determine with which single or dual elements to match or mismatch teachers and their students. In addition, when examining teachers or multidimension variables, Gould (1987) reported that most teachers in her national sample had essentially similar teaching styles, Buell and Buell (1987) matched adult students with instructors whose perceptual strengths were similar and different from theirs and, indeed, obtained both increased achievement and improved attitudes in the complementary treatments.

But how does one match children's perceptual strengths with those of their teachers when young children often are only tactual/kinesthetic (Crino, 1984; LeClair, 1986)? Apparently, the visual strengths develop among most youngsters by third or fourth grade *at the earliest,* and auditory memory does not begin to be strong for many children much before sixth grade. Indeed, many male high school students are not auditory (Kroon, 1985). How do we match time-of-day preferences of children and their teachers when the majority of elementary school students are most alert in the late morning or early afternoon, whereas their teachers are either early-morning or night preferents?

Because there are so many elements of learning style that may influence individual students, it would seem that rather than try to match their styles with similar teaching styles, it is better to address practical ways of responding to students' diverse characteristics in a series of step-by-step procedures that gradually (1) increase the number of elements to which teachers respond; (2) demonstrate how to teach to each student's perceptual strength when we must lecture; (3) help teachers identify *their* current teaching styles so that they are aware of why certain students do or do not learn easily in their classes; (4) show teachers how to expand their current styles so that they become responsive to more students' styles; and ultimately, (5) teach those students who are capable of doing so to teach themselves new and difficult information by capitalizing on methods that best respond to their individual strengths. Let's examine the steps in this process.

Which Elements of Learning Style Can Be Addressed by Redesigning the Classroom Environment?

Redesigning the conventional classroom should take no more than one period once each semester. Yet, consider the number of elements that are addressed by that single effort. The varied sections will permit soft music for those who need sound, quiet for those who function best without it, bright or soft lighting, formal or informal seating arrangements, and the ability to move purposefully for those who need mobility. Students who are aware of their own style can wear more or less clothing to respond to their temperature preferences and, if the teacher is willing, can eat healthful vegetable snacks to resolve their intake needs. Thus, six elements of style can be dealt with merely by creating a few varied instructional areas, establishing rules and regulations for using them, and then permitting students to experiment with learning in ways that are both responsive to and dissonant from their styles so that each can find the right combination.

How Can Teachers Respond to the Emotional Elements?

Motivation will increase almost automatically as students' different styles are acknowledged, given credence, and responded to. It is particularly important to read *Two-of-a-Kind Learning Styles* (Pena, 1989) to sixth-grade students and to read *Mission from No-Style* to third- through fifth-graders so that they become secure in the realization that there is no good or bad style—that all styles are equally appropriate *as long as learning becomes easier and is retained longer.*

Students who score low on Persistence on the LSI usually are global and process information differently than persistent analytics do. Most teachers expect such youngsters to stay on task and work diligently until each item is completed; they do not understand that global children function better when permitted to work on several tasks simultaneously and begin anywhere in the sequence they wish—as long as they do complete their assignments. It also is easy to misunderstand the student who scores low on Responsibility. Such a youngster responds best to (1) knowing why the thing you want him or her to learn or do is important to *you;* (2) collegial rather than authoritative or directive vocal tones; and (3) being given a choice of how he or she can demonstrate that the assignment *was* done. We encourage you to experiment with the following:

1. Every time you want to give your class an assignment, make it slightly longer than you ordinarily would. Thus, if you usually write 10 examples on the board, instead write 12; if you usually assign 20 vocabulary words, instead assign 22.

2. Divide the lengthened assignment into three parts by writing each part on one-third of the chalkboard. Tell the students that there are 12 examples on the board but that they are to complete ''any 10 of the 12.'' (You usually only ask for 10, but the choice will be well received by those who need options.)

3. Tell the students that they may work on this assignment anywhere in the environment that they feel comfortable (on the floor, at the desk, in the rear or the front, in the bright or soft light, and so forth)—as long as you can see them.

4. Too, tell the students that they may work on this assignment alone, if that is what they prefer; they also may work with a classmate. If they choose that alternative. Establish rules for choosing a co-worker—for example, they may pantomime their interest in working together but may not verbalize the request, or classmates have a right to refuse to work with someone if they wish to function alone or with another whose style is more like their own. Also tell the youngsters that, if they wish, they may bring their chairs to a specific section of the room where you will be, and that they may work with you. When students choose to work with you, know that they *need* to do that and be as nurturing as possible. You may leave the group that is working with you periodically to supervise the others, but you will see that, for the most part, the ones with you will gradually become increasingly independent, and the ones working with classmates will tend to function collaboratively.

5. When certain students ask additional questions about the assignment, understand that they may need more structure or direction than others do and that they will not be able to function securely without it. When the same students pose questions frequently, offer them the option of sitting near you; that may help. When students do not do *exactly* what you directed, consider that they may be (1) low on Responsibility/Conformity and may need to do things their own way; (2) low on Auditory and unable to remember two or more directives when told in sequence; (3) unable, though willing, to follow external directives; (4) confused, not unwilling; and/or (5) under internal pressure and temporarily blocking. Place the directions on the chalk board or on a sheet of paper and allow the youngsters to read them and refer to them repeatedly. Also illustrate them or draw symbols to help the visual/global child comprehend procedures more easily.

How Can Teachers Respond to the Sociological Elements?

It takes very little effort to permit students to complete all assignments, including homework, either alone, in a pair, or with an adult—provided that the youngster assumes the responsibility for learning everything that must be mastered and doing well on the test for each unit, theme, or lesson. Remember, however, that adult-oriented students may be unable to learn either alone *or* with a classmate, and that the option of sitting near you and obtaining guidance, reinforcement, or assistance may be a necessary alternative. If you allow *these* choices, you are responding to four more elements—the need to learn alone, in a pair, as part of a team or group, and/or with an adult.

Students who need variety should be able to opt to do some things *their* way. If you provide alternatives as part of your assignments, that should help ease the boredom that some experience with routines and patterns. Students who do not choose to do things differently may very well prefer routines.

How Can Teachers Respond to Students' Varied Perceptual Strengths?

When trying to put together one of those multipart toys that their children begged for during the holidays, some parents begin by reading the accompanying directions and following from step 1 through to the last detail when the item is ready to be used. Such people tend to be analytic/visuals; they make sense out of printed words. Global visuals don't pay much attention to written or printed *words;* instead, they look at diagrams, pictures, and/or illustrations.

Some parents rarely look at directions. They take the parts out of the box; place them into a classification determined by size, shape, sequence, or color; and then sequentially analyze what to do first, pick things up as seems appropriate, and begin to experiment through a hands-on approach. Those are likely to be analytic/tactuals. Their counterparts, the global/tactuals, merely empty the box, let every piece fall where it may, and then proceed to pick up each interesting part, one by one—and sometimes several at a time—and push, pull, jab, alter, cajole, threaten, and eventually make each piece fit somewhere. When they are finished, leftover parts may still be lying on the floor or on the table, but the "mechanic" views them as not really necessary because the gadget works without them.

Not all parents fall neatly into one of these categories. Some reach for the directions, hand them to someone else and say, "Read them to me." As the partner reads, the first person follows the verbal guidelines and puts the mechanism together. That is probably the easiest way for an analytic/auditory adult to accomplish the task. The global/auditory parent, however, will ask for the directions from the back forward, have the reader skip around, repeat, synthesize, and so forth.

All these adults will get the job done. *How* they do it depends on their *processing style* and *perceptual strengths.*

Varied instructional resources to teach the identical material through different perceptual strengths increase students' ability to succeed. Thus, some students read their texts independently while others hear the written information being read to them by their teacher on a tape. In the second photo, a youngster uses manipulative materials to understand the problem he has been assigned, whereas his teacher observes a classmate responding to her highly structured directions. (Photographs courtesy of Northwest Elementary School, Amityville, New York.)

Perceptual Strengths

Auditory learners remember 75 percent of what they *hear* in a normal 40 or 50 minute lecture. Only 30 percent of the school-aged population appears to be auditory. It is the most difficult way for many people to remember new and demanding information. Visual learners remember 75 percent of what they *read* or *see*. Approximately 40 percent of the population is visual, but that number is divided into analytics and globals, with different percentages existing at different age levels.

Tactual learners remember what they *write* (if analytic) or *draw* or *doodle* (if global). Kinesthetic learners remember best the things they experience. Kinesthetics must be *actively involved* in going, doing, traveling, acting, and on-the-job training. Young children tend to be highly tactual and/or kinesthetic, but many people remain that way into adulthood. Some add visual and auditory strengths as they grow older; others do not.

Figure 10–1 provides information on 13 experimental studies wherein students were taught through matched and mismatched perceptual strengths. In each case, at the primary (Carbo, 1980; Urbschat, 1977), elementary (Hill,

FIGURE 10–1 Experimental Research on Perceptual Learning Styles

Researcher and Date	Sample	Subject Examined	Perceptual Preference Examined	Significant Achievement
Bauer (1991)	Learning-disabled and emotionally handicapped junior high school underachievers	Mathematics	Auditory, visual, tactual	+
Buell & Buell (1987)	Adults	Continuing education	Auditory, visual, tactual	+
Carbo (1980)	Kindergartners	Vocabulary	Auditory, visual, "other" (tactual)	+
Hill (1987)	Elementary	Spelling	Auditory, visual, tactual	+
Ingham (1989)	Adults	Driver safety	Auditory/visual, tactual/visual	+
Jarsonbeck (1984)	4th-grade under-achievers	Mathematics	Auditory, visual, tactual	+
Kroon (1985)	9th-, and 10th-graders	Industrial arts	Auditory, visual, tactual, sequenced	+
Martini (1986)	7th-graders	Science	Auditory, visual, tactual	+
Thorpe-Garrett	9th-, 10th-, 11th-, 12-graders	Vocabulary	Auditory, visual, tactual	+
Urbschat (1977)	1st-graders	CVC trigram recall	Auditory, visual	+
Weinberg (1983)	3rd-grade under-achievers	Mathematics	Auditory, visual, tactual	+
Wheeler (1980)	Learning-disabled 2nd-graders	Reading	Auditory, visual, tactual, sequenced	+
Wheeler (1983)	Learning-disabled 2nd-graders	Reading	Auditory, visual, tactual	+

Source: Adapted by permission from "Survey of Research on Learning Styles" by R. Dunn, J. S. Beaudry, and A. Klavas, March, 1989, *Educational Leadership,* Vol. 46, No. 6, p. 52. Copyright © 1989 by the Association for Supervision and Curriculum Development.
Note: + represents significant positive findings.

1987; Jarsonbeck, 1984; Weinberg, 1983; Wheeler, 1980, 1983), secondary (Bauer, 1991; Kroon, 1985; Martini, 1986; Thorpe-Garrett, 1991) and adult (Buell & Buell, 1987; Ingham, 1989) levels, statistically higher test scores resulted when students were taught new and difficult information through their preferred, rather than their nonpreferred, modalities. Kroon (1985) obtained significantly higher (.01) test scores for students in matched rather than mismatched treatments, and an additional .05 significance when those same students were *reinforced* through their secondary or tertiary modality.

Applications to Lecturing

Teaching students by lecture is likely to be effective only for auditory or auditory/tactual students who listen and then take good notes. However, note-taking requires that students understand the "most important things" the teacher is saying, and many students do not have that insight. Regardless, lecturing is a well-established, convenient method (for the teacher and for auditory students) and will undoubtedly continue in most classrooms. Thus, if a teacher is going to lecture, the following method for (1) *introducing* new and difficult material through each student's perceptual strength; (2) *reinforcing* through a secondary or tertiary strength; and (3) having the students then *use* the newly acquired knowledge in a *creative* way (to ensure application) is likely to increase the effectiveness of lecturing.

Step 1   Choose a topic or lesson where test scores will not be based on previously taught concepts or skills (Dunn, 1988). For example, begin a social studies or science unit, introduce a new artist or composer, or develop a new focus in current events. Any topic in your curriculum will do, as long as everything the students need to learn is included in the lecture. In other words, be certain that the test you later use to measure their knowledge gained through this lecture sequence includes only the information being taught in this lesson (or series of lessons) and is not dependent on prior knowledge.

Step 2   Be certain that you have at least two weeks' pretest and posttest scores on similarly difficult topics or lessons before you begin working with perceptual strengths. Keep the amount of time you spend on each lesson, the methods you normally use, and the youngsters' participation essentially similar throughout all the lessons—pre-experimental and experimental.

Step 3   Develop at least one set of Task Cards, one Flip Chute, one Pic-A-Hole, and one Electroboard to teach the important information (objectives of the lesson) you will introduce during the experimental period. For easy-to-follow guidelines for making those tactual resources, see Chapter 6. Also, develop a concise list of the objectives that should be mastered during the experimental lesson or unit and typed or printed material that actually teaches that information. The latter material may be taken from a textbook but should be brief and should respond directly to what the objectives indicate must be learned.

Step 4   Obtain one copy of the *Learning Style Inventory* (LSI) by Dunn, Dunn, and Price) and Answer Sheets (the test itself) for each student in your class.[1] Different forms of the test are available for different grade levels, so specify how many Answers Sheets you need at each level. Also obtain a copy of either *Mission from No Style* for grades 2 through 6 or *Two-of-a-Kind Learning Styles* for grades 6 through 7 and *Coloring Book Explaining Global/*

Analytic Styles to Children for elementary youngsters.[2] Read the appropriate booklet to students who do not read well; others may read by themselves or in a pair or small group. Then discuss the contents so that students realize that (1) everyone has a learning style; (2) we are never too old to begin capitalizing on our style; (3) all styles are good—we all have strengths, albeit different ones; and (4) you are going to show them how to use their perceptual strengths to their best advantage.

Before administering the LSI, explain that students should answer its questions as if describing how they concentrate when they are trying to master difficult, new material. Administer the inventory and read the questions, even interpret them, for students who want or need assistance. Have the LSI Answer Sheets processed by Price Systems, Box 1818, Lawrence, KS 66046-0067.

Step 5 When the individual printouts have been processed, teach the students how to interpret them. A score of 60 or higher on auditory, visual, tactual, or kinesthetic means that that modality is strong; youngsters should be taught how to capitalize on those strengths. Conversely, students with a modality score below 40 should be cautioned to avoid beginning to learn difficult new material through that channel *initially,* although it can be used for reinforcement. Scores of 40 to 59 indicate that, if really interested in the material, the student can learn it through that modality; however, interest is a predetermining condition to concentration when scores are only in this middle range.

Step 6 Encourage the students to share, discuss, and compare their LSI data with each other and with their families and friends, and to explore similarities and differences. Then explain the need for each student to be introduced to difficult, new material through his or her strongest modality; to have the information reinforced in a secondary and tertiary modality; and then to use the information in a creative project or activity. Emphasize the need for all students to do assignments as directed by their sequenced perceptual strengths— strongest first, followed by a combined secondary and tertiary teamed modality, and then followed by making something creative that includes all the (correct) information they need to learn. If you would like to post large wall charts that provide for class information so that each student can merely look at the chart and follow his or her own perceptual sequence, those are available from the Center for the Study of Learning and Teaching Styles at St. John's University.[3] (See Figure 10–2).

Request the students' cooperation for a two-week period. Tell them that if they really study in accordance with the sequence you suggest, each should learn more, more easily, and remember it better than ever before.

Step 7 When students' auditory scores on the LSI are highest, they should hear the teacher's lecture or discussion first, before they read or take notes. Thus, auditory learners should listen in class, go home and read the succinct material the teacher developed to teach the objectives, and then simulta-

FIGURE 10-2 Capitalizing on Students' Perceptual Strengths

Students' perceptual strength:	Day One in School	Day One at Home	Day Two in School	Day Two at Home	Day Three at School	Day Three at Home
Auditory			First exposure: Teacher's lecture. No notes need be taken.	Second exposure: Read and write answers to the hand-out* while reading.[a]		Third exposure: Make a creative activity; make up a story or game from lesson content or ideas.
Visual		First exposure: Read text	Second exposure: Teacher's lecture and write answers to the handout during lecture.[a]			Third exposure: Make a creative activity.
Tactual	First exposure: Tactual materials geared to learning material; hands-on for short time period.	Second exposure: Read text or hear a tape of the reading material if available and write answers to the handout at some time.[a]	Third exposure: Teacher's lecture.			Fourth exposure: Make a creative activity.
Kines-thetic		First exposure: Read text while walking	Second exposure: Teacher's lecture; may stand to take notes; write answers to the handout during the lecture.			Third exposure: Make a creative activity.

Source: Adapted from "Capitalizing on Students' Perceptual Strengths to Ensure Literacy While Engaging in Conventional Lecture/Discussion" by R. Dunn, 1988, *Reading Psychology: An International Quarterly,* vol. 9, No. 4, pp. 431–453. Copyright © 1988 by Hemisphere Publishing Corporation.

[a]Teacher prints what must be learned (objectives) onto a handout or a wall chart. Student *begins* instruction through strongest modality, *reinforces* (second exposure) through next two strongest modalities (as revealed by the LSI), and then (third or fourth exposure) *uses* the new information in a creative application (by making a Flip Chute, Electroboard, Pic-A-Hole, Task Cards, poem, puzzle, and so forth) to ensure transfer and retention.

neously take notes and answer specific questions. The next day, such young-sters should make something creative with the information.

For example, if the lesson were on idiomatic expressions, auditory students would listen to the explanation of idiomatic expressions in class. That night they would read a short description of idiomatic expressions and answer specific questions concerning the construct in writing. The next night, they would have a choice of completing any one of the following three activities:

1. Write a rhyming poem that explains what idiomatic expressions are and how to recognize them in literature. Include at least ten (10) different idiomatic expressions in your poem.
2. Illustrate at least ten (10) idiomatic expressions and explain what they actually mean.
3. Make up a crossword puzzle with at least ten (10) idiomatic expressions and an explanation of what they mean.

When students' visual scores on the LSI are highest, they first should read the material the teacher developed to teach what idiomatic expressions are. The next day, they should hear the teacher's lecture and, simultaneously, answer the questions posed for that lesson or unit *during* the lecture as they hear the teacher give the information. The next day, the visual student should complete a creative activity chosen from among the teacher's listed alternatives.

When students' tactual scores on the LSI are highest, they first should be exposed to the new information through tactual materials such as multipart Task Cards, Flip Chutes, Pic-A-Holes, or Electroboards. After a short exposure to such materials (either alone, in pairs, or in a small group based on individuals' sociological preferences as revealed by their LSI printouts), tactual students should read the succinct material their teacher developed, take notes and answer questions, and then hear their teacher's lecture-explanation of idiomatic expressions. The next night, those youngsters should complete a creative activity chosen from among the teacher's listed alternatives.

When students' kinesthetic scores on the LSI are highest, they should stand and quietly move in place while they are listening to the teacher's introduction. However, a combined kinesthetic/auditory strength is not common. It is more likely that a kinesthetic student's next highest strength would be visual, in which case the introduction to the difficult new material should include reading at home while walking back and forth in a section of a room. The youngster then will be present on the next day to hear the teacher's presentation, during which he or she will take notes and answer the questions posed on the teacher-prepared material. The following day, the creative activity should be completed. However, if the student's strongest modalities are combined kinesthetic/tactual, the first exposure should be by using the tactual materials while standing, then reading and answering the questions by writing, followed by the teacher's lecture and, subsequently, by completion of the creative activity. Students may work in a rocking chair as opposed to pacing while learning.

Thus, every student will be present at the same time for the teacher's lecture, but each will have been introduced to the difficult new material through his or her perceptual strength, reinforced with a multisensory dual exposure, followed by application through the development of a creative resource.

Step 8 If students' early morning scores on the LSI are 60 or above, they should be advised to get up an hour earlier than usual and do their homework before they come to school. If their evening scores are 40 or below, they should do their homework in the evening. High-energy-level youngsters in the late morning or afternoon (scores of 60 or above on those LSI categories) should study or do their homework at those peak times. Explain to parents that their children's chronobiological levels are biologically imposed and that the youngsters should learn more, more easily if they concentrate on the material at the time of their best energy high.

Step 9 Encourage the students to follow this prescribed perceptual/time-of-day pattern for at least two weeks. Pre- and posttest them in each of the two weeks. Compare the students' grades on the tests you give in each of these two weeks, while they follow this suggested study/homework/lecture sequence, with the grades they achieved during the first two weeks' pre-experimental period's grades. Notice the differences (if any) in the amount of gain between the two sets of pretest and posttest scores. Share the achievement results with the students, their parents, and a colleague.

How Many Elements Can Be Responded to Easily?

We've just described how to respond to sound (#1), light (#2), design (#3), and mobility (#4) needs merely by redesigning a section or two or three of the conventional classroom. Sociological preferences can be handled just as easily by giving students options as to whom they are permitted to complete assignments with—alone (#5), with one classmate (#6), in a small cooperative group (#7), or with you nearby (#8). If you will remember to look at your classroom Wall Charts (see Chapter 11) and to be firm (but caring) with authority-oriented students and collegial with collegial or nonconforming students, you will be responding to the kind of adult each youngster needs (#9, #10). When you diversify the instruction and use various options, those who need variety will benefit (#11). Remember not to require that *everyone* try everything new; those who feel secure with patterns and routines need time to get used to the innovation or new method *before* they are ready to experience it.

When you recognize that some children need to wear a sweater but others will be warm in the same environment at the same time, *and you permit each to dress appropriately,* you will have mastered temperature requirements for individuals (#12).

Options in assignments respond to nonconformists who score low on Responsibility. If you speak to such youngsters collegially and also explain why whatever you want them to do is important to *you,* you will make headway with this usually off-the-main-track group (#13). Dealing with structure also is not difficult (#14) if you are willing to provide more or fewer directions on the basis of individuals' requests. In fact, just being *aware* of these learning style differences will help you work better than previously with many youngsters.

The foregoing list includes 14 elements of style. Add to that the understanding that nonpersistent children should be allowed to work on several items or tasks simultaneously and should be permitted a moment's breather when necessary, and we also will be addressing persistence (#15). If you can permit students to move from section to section of the room as they complete designated parts of their assignment, a combination of mobility, kinesthesia, design, responsibility, and sociological needs will be accommodated (#16).

If you permit youngsters to bring raw vegetables or fruit juice (within whatever restrictions *you* establish), intake can be addressed (#17). *You do not need to do everything;* whatever you try will yield positive results. Decide exactly what you will experiment with and what you choose *not* to try. Whatever you try, you should observe better student grades, behavior, *and* attitudes in your classroom within *six* weeks. If that does not happen, *stop!*

If you can get yourself sufficiently organized so that you can show your students how to read either before *or* after your classroom lecture or discussion and then how to reinforce with their own secondary or tertiary modalities, you will have made a big move forward and dealt efficiently with students' perceptual strengths (#18). For many, that is a certain way of improving test scores!

What Is Another Easy Way to Move into Learning Styles?

Using Team Learning to *introduce* new and difficult material and Circle of Knowledge to *reinforce* what you introduced through Team learning will (1) begin to organize instruction so that both structure and options are provided simultaneously; (2) permit low auditory or low visual students to learn through a multisensory approach; (3) show students who cannot learn alone how to achieve with classmates (or with you!); (4) provide opportunities for developing higher level cognitive skills *and* creativity; (5) reduce tension in the environment and permit youngsters to enjoy learning; (6) teach students how to work with objectives and begin to demonstrate that they *have* learned; and (7) help students internalize what they are learning and, therefore, remember it better (because of the application through creative projects).

How Difficult Is It to Teach Globally and Analytically?

If you are an analytic processor, you never concentrated on how to teach reading, math, or science globally, and you never took a required course in how to teach basic skills through the use of humor or drawings, so this is a brand new area for you. On the other hand, if you are a global processor, you rarely stay on task without deviating from a structured lesson plan. In fact, although you may be required to develop lesson plans, you rarely take them seriously. To you, the thrill of teaching is to get the students' interests responding and to help them become creatively involved in the subject.

Both approaches are correct; it is important to teach children the entire required curriculum *and* it is important to teach it through their interests and frames of reference, and to help them relate it to their own lives. Thus, both analytic and global teachers can profit from understanding how to reach both types of student processors. However, having tested thousands of teachers during the past 20 years, we find that the majority seem to be fairly strong analytic processors, whereas the majority of elementary school students are strong global processors. Thus, this is one extremely important element of style, particularly for math teachers, who tend to be very analytic. For example, it is not uncommon for math teachers to say, "I don't care if your answer is correct. You must show me every step of the process." Many globals cannot do that. They *intuit* the answers.

Thus, although this *is* a difficult element to confront, it is important. Read Chapter 4 and experiment with *planning* one lesson to include both styles. Then, two weeks later, plan for a second. As you become more and more adept at using the opposite style, you gradually will begin to incorporate it into major lessons. When you do, you will have mastered the nineteenth (19th) element!

What Can We Do with Time-of-Day?

Time-of-day energy levels are easier to respond to than initially seems feasible. For example, with a bit of organization, why wouldn't it be possible to experiment with some of these suggestions"

1. Teach a given subject at the same time of day for two months and note which students are most alert and which are least alert at that time of day. Then change the time that subject is taught *drastically*—for example, from early morning to late afternoon or from just after lunch to first thing in the morning. Note changes in individuals' attitudes, behavior, achievement, attention spans, tensions, and/or attendance. Only those students with strong preferences (LSI scores below 31 or above 69) will reveal obvious differences; but for those youngsters, time of day can be a critical factor.

2. Use a computer to match the children's best time of day and then teach their most important basic skills subject at their preferred time. You also might videotape lessons or tape record lectures at *your* best time of day and instruct students to use them at *their* highest energy level.

3. Move the entire school onto a flexible scheduling system that allows all youngsters to learn at times when they function best. Give those with extreme preferences priority in selecting the schedule for their most difficult classes. Expect about 15 or 20 percent to indicate *no* time preference; they are the lucky ones who can perform well at any time of day, provided they are interested in what they are being taught.

4. Assign morning students to morning teachers and afternoon students to afternoon teachers (if the school has any!). If there are more of one type than another, consider the extras as mismatches and compare their performances with those of their matched classmates and *their* matched teachers.

If you take even one or two steps in this direction, you will have begun to respond to the twentieth (20th) element of learning style. Now let's see if you are ready and willing to identify your own current teaching style so that you can recognize which students' styles are advantaged—or disadvantaged—by the strength of your teaching style.

Can You Identify Your Own Teaching Style Strengths?

If you are interested in appraising your teaching style, read the next few paragraphs that explain the various components of the construct. Then answer the questions honestly. You can self-score the instrument and have a fairly clear understanding of the students who are most, and least, complemented by the strengths of how you instruct. The next step will be to decide whether you are willing to try to expand at least one component of your style so that it becomes more responsive to mismatched students' styles. Let's take one step at a time.

What *Is* Teaching Style?

There are many ways of teaching the same content; some people do it verbally, others do it visually, others experientially, and others tactually. All approaches are effective—but not for the same students. Just as with learning style, perceptual communication is only *one* part of teaching style. There are nine major components of style, including each of the following:

1. *Instructional planning* (Dunn & Dunn, 1977, pp. 75–87): Instructional planning encompasses the diagnosis, learning prescriptions, and evaluations completed for each student or group of students. Knowledge of each student's ability, learning style, interests, skill development, ability to retain information, concept formation, and so forth is essential to the diagnosis. The prescription includes the design and/or use of objectives, materials, techniques, and multisensory learning activities at various levels. Evaluation en-

Note that some students stand whereas other sit; some migrate toward windows and others avoid bright light. A few work in teams, some prefer completing assignments by themselves, and others seek direct interaction with their teacher. All are learning. (Photograph courtesy of Public School #220, Queens, New York City.)

compasses pretesting, student self-assessment, and teacher assessment based on the original objectives established for each student.

2. *Teaching methods:* Teaching methods usually refer to the instructor's behavior in the learning environment—the way he or she groups students for learning, designs and/or assigns resources, uses interaction techniques with students, and employs basic approaches to the teaching and learning of each student. Since the advent of individualization strategies, teaching methods also include the specific materials through which youngsters may achieve independently, such as Contract Activity Packages, Multisensory Instructional Packages, and Programmed Learning Sequences.

3.1. *Student groupings:* Student grouping is defined as the way a teacher assigns or permits learning to occur through small groups, pairs, individuals, large groups, varied groupings, or one-to-one tutoring. Because different youngsters respond to varied sociological interactions, a teacher should have at his or her fingertips a series of alternative grouping strategies that provide a wide range of interesting activities.

3.2. *Room design:* Room design reflects the ways in which the teacher divides, decorates, and designs instructional spaces or areas to match the characteristics of his or her students. The various types of furniture arrangements, alcoves, "offices," work areas, and the like, and how they make up the instructional environment, are included in this element.

3.3. *Teaching environment:* The teaching environment includes time schedules; the different types of instructional stations and centers; the optional learning activities that are available; and the provisions that are made for mobility, multilevel resources, and nutritional intake.

Teachers who try to respond to their students' learning styles recognize that, in the same class, some students need direct assistance whereas others need only to be within reach of an adult. Some require a formal design while their classmates profit from relaxed seating. Some need quiet and others work best while listening to classical music. (Photograph courtesy of Longwood College, Virginia.)

Lamps, tables, colorful signs, and specific work corners are designed by the teacher and students to meet varied learning style strengths. (Photograph courtesy of Northwest Elementary School, Amityville, New York.)

4. *Evaluation techniques:* Evaluation techniques encompass the methods the teacher uses to assess the programs of individual students. Testing, observations, performance assessments, and self-evaluation are part of the assessment of each student.

5. *Educational philosophy:* Educational philosophy refers to the attitudes a teacher holds toward key program descriptions, such as open education, a theme-centered curriculum, or a basic skills approach.

6. *Teaching characteristics:* Teaching characteristics are the values and standards a teacher holds and the operational approaches used to transmit those values and standards. The degree of flexibility, the importance of what is learned, and the amount of direction given to students are examples of teaching characteristics.

7. *Student preference:* Student preference describes the types of youngsters the teacher prefers to have as students. Characteristics of students are itemized—the gifted, the learning-impaired, the motivated, the nonachieving, and so on—to permit easy identification.

Teaching Style Inventory

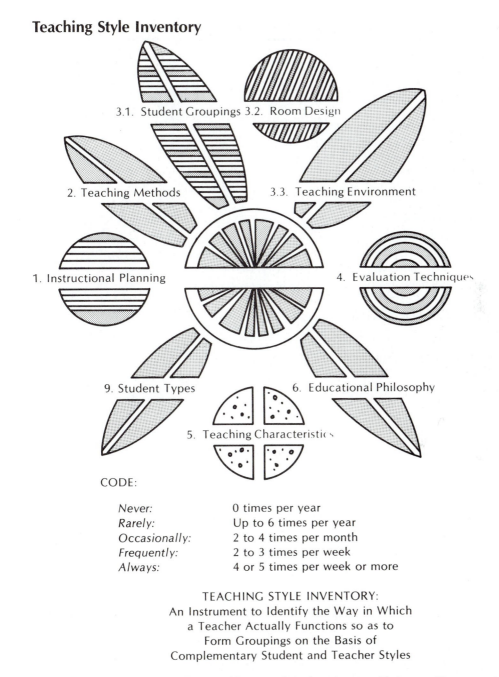

3.1. Student Groupings 3.2. Room Design

2. Teaching Methods

3.3. Teaching Environment

1. Instructional Planning

4. Evaluation Techniques

9. Student Types

6. Educational Philosophy

5. Teaching Characteristics

CODE:

Never:	0 times per year
Rarely:	Up to 6 times per year
Occasionally:	2 to 4 times per month
Frequently:	2 to 3 times per week
Always:	4 or 5 times per week or more

TEACHING STYLE INVENTORY:
An Instrument to Identify the Way in Which
a Teacher Actually Functions so as to
Form Groupings on the Basis of
Complementary Student and Teacher Styles

FIGURE 10–3 This figure, illustrated by Dr. Edward J. Manetta, Chairman, Department of Fine Arts, St. John's University, represents the eight elements of Teaching Style and a code to follow in the self-examination of how individuals communicate information to others. The number of times used from 0 times per year ("Never") to four or five times per week or more ("Always") aid in identifying teaching characteristics.

FIGURE 10–4 The Teaching Style Inventory

Question 1: *Instructional Planning*
   Directions:
   Circle the number that best describes how often you use each of the following planning techniques.

	Never	Rarely	Occasionally	Frequently	Always
a) Diagnosis and prescription for each student.................	1	2	3	4	5
b) Whole-class lessons	5	4	3	2	1
c) Contracts, Programmed Learning Sequences, or Multisensory Instructional Packages	1	2	3	4	5
d) Creative activities with student options	1	2	3	4	5
e) Programmed materials or drill assignments..................	1	2	3	4	5
f) Small-group assignments	1	2	3	4	5
g) Task Cards or games	1	2	3	4	5
h) Objectives, varied for individuals..........................	1	2	3	4	5
i) Peer tutoring or Team Learning	1	2	3	4	5
j) Role playing or Simulations................................	1	2	3	4	5
k) Brainstorming or Circles of Knowledge	1	2	3	4	5
l) Students design their own studies	1	2	3	4	5

Question II: *Teaching Methods*
   Directions:
   Circle the number that best describes how often you use each of the following teaching methods.

	Never	Rarely	Occasionally	Frequently	Always
a) Lecture (whole class)	5	4	3	2	1
b) Teacher demonstration	5	4	3	2	1
c) Small groups (3–8)	1	2	3	4	5
d) Media (films, tapes, etc.)	1	2	3	4	5
e) Class discussion (question–answer)	5	4	3	2	1
f) Individualized diagnosis and prescription for each student	1	2	3	4	5

Question III: *Teaching Environment*
   Question 3.1: *Student Groupings*
   Directions:
   Circle the number that best describes how often you use each of the following types of groupings.

	Never	Rarely	Occasionally	Frequently	Always
a) Several small groups (3–8 students)	1	2	3	4	5
b) Pairs (2 students)...	1	2	3	4	5
c) Independent study assignments (student works alone)	1	2	3	4	5
d) One-to-one interactions with the teacher	1	2	3	4	5
e) Two or more of the above groupings at one time	1	2	3	4	5
f) One large group (entire class).............................	5	4	3	2	1

FIGURE 10–4 *Continued*

Question 3.2: *Room Design*
   Directions:
   Circle the number that best describes how often you use each
   of the following classroom designs.

		Never	Rarely	Occasionally	Frequently	Always
a)	Rows of desks	5	4	3	2	1
b)	Small groups of 3–8 students	1	2	3	4	5
c)	Learning Stations or Interest Centers	1	2	3	4	5
d)	A variety of areas	1	2	3	4	5
e)	Individual and small-group (2–4) alcoves, dens, "offices"	1	2	3	4	5
f)	Three or more of the above arrangements at the same time	1	2	3	4	5

Question 3.3: *Teaching Environment*
   Directions:
   Circle the number that best describes your present instructional
   environment.

		Never	Rarely	Occasionally	Frequently	Always
a)	Varied instructional areas are provided in the classroom for different, simultaneous activities	1	2	3	4	5
b)	Nutritional intake is available for all students as needed	1	2	3	4	5
c)	Instructional areas are designed for different groups that need to talk and interact	1	2	3	4	5
d)	Varied time schedules are in use for individuals	1	2	3	4	5
e)	Students are permitted to choose where they will sit and/or work	1	2	3	4	5
f)	Many multisensory resources are available in the classroom for use by individuals and groups	1	2	3	4	5
g)	Alternative arrangements are made for mobile, active, or overly talkative students	1	2	3	4	5

Question IV: *Evaluation Techniques*
   Directions:
   Circle the number that best describes how often you use each
   of the following evaluation techniques.

		Never	Rarely	Occasionally	Frequently	Always
a)	Observation by moving from group to group and among individuals	1	2	3	4	5
b)	Teacher-made tests	1	2	3	4	5
c)	Student self-assessment tests	1	2	3	4	5
d)	Performance tests (demonstrations rather than written responses)	1	2	3	4	5
e)	Criterion-referenced achievement tests[a] based on student self-selected, individual objectives	1	2	3	4	5

Continued

FIGURE 10–4 *Continued*

	Never	Rarely	Occasionally	Frequently	Always
f) Criterion-referenced achievement tests[a] based on small-group objects	1	2	3	4	5
g) Standardized achievement tests based on grade-level objectives	1	2	3	4	5
h) Criterion-referenced achievement tests[a] based on the individual student's potential	1	2	3	4	5

Question V: *Teaching Characteristics*[a]
  Directions:
  Circle the number that best describes you as a teacher.
  I tend to be:

	Not At All	Not Very	Somewhat	Very	Extremely
a) Concerned with *how* students learn (learning style)	1	2	3	4	5
b) Prescriptive (with student options)	1	2	3	4	5
c) Demanding—with high expectations based on *individual* ability	1	2	3	4	5
d) Evaluative of students as they work	1	2	3	4	5
e) Concerned with *how much* students learn (grade-level standards)	5	4	3	2	1
f) Concerned with *what* students learn (grade-level curriculum) . .	5	4	3	2	1
g) Lesson plan–oriented	5	4	3	2	1
h) Authoritative to reach group objectives	5	4	3	2	1

Question VI: *Educational Philosophy*
  Directions:
  Circle the number that best describes your attitude toward each
  of the following approaches and concepts.

	Strongly Disagree	Disagree	Undecided	Support	Strongly Support
a) Open education	1	2	3	4	5
b) Diagnostic-prescriptive teaching	1	2	3	4	5
c) Multiage groupings	1	2	3	4	5
d) Matched teaching and learning styles	1	2	3	4	5
e) Alternative education	1	2	3	4	5
f) Student-centered curriculum	1	2	3	4	5
g) Behavioral or performance objectives	1	2	3	4	5
h) Humanistic education	1	2	3	4	5
i) Independent study	1	2	3	4	5
j) Individualized instruction	1	2	3	4	5

FIGURE 10–4 *Continued*

	Strongly Disagree	Disagree	Undecided	Support	Strongly Support
k) Traditional education..................................	5	4	3	2	1
l) Whole-group achievement	5	4	3	2	1
m) Grade-level standards	5	4	3	2	1
n) Teacher-dominated instruction..........................	5	4	3	2	1

[a]When teachers respond that they are "concerned with *how* students learn," the inference is that they permit options in the learning environment because of their awareness of individual differences. An observer should, thus, be able to see students working alone, with a peer or two, or with the teacher; sitting on chairs or on carpeting; using self-selected resources of a multisensory nature (if available); mobile (if necessary and without disturbing others), etc.

When a teacher indicates that he or she tends to be "prescriptive" but permits some student options, observers should be able to locate written objectives that include selected choices.

"Evaluative . . . as (students) work" suggests that observers will be able to see the teacher moving among the students while checking their progress and questioning them.

"Concerned with . . . grade-level curriculum" suggests that observers will see that objectives, lessons, and/or assignments tend to respond to a suggested or required grade-level curriculum.

"Authoritative to reach group objectives" suggests that observers will see the identical objectives, lessons, and/or assignments for every student in the same class.

SCORING KEY

Questions I through VIII are weighted according to the relative importance of each item. Simply multiply the weight assigned to the technique by the number selected for the frequency.

Example:

1 a) Diagnosis and prescription for each student—3—Occasionally

Item	Weight		Frequency		Score
a	5	×	3	=	15

Complete each item and the total for each question. Then chart the totals on the Teaching Style Profile. This analysis and the predictor profile will aid you in matching students and teachers.

WEIGHT KEY

5. Highly individualized
4. Somewhat individualized
3. Transitional
2. Somewhat traditional
1. Traditional

Place the total score that you obtained for each of the previous categories on the line pertaining to the item by making a dot on the line closest to the appropriate numeral (see Figure 10–5). After you have placed a dot on each line indicating your total score for each category, link each dot in succession.

Continued

FIGURE 10-4 *Continued*

1. Instructional Planning			
Item	Weight	× Frequency	= Score
a	5		
b	1		
c	5		
d	3		
e	4		
f	3		
g	3		
h	4		
i	3		
j	3		
k	3		
l	5	I: Total Score _____	

2. Teaching Methods			
Item	Weight	× Frequency	= Score
a	1		
b	2		
c	3		
d	3		
e	2		
f	5		
		II: Total Score _____	

3.1. Student Groupings			
Item	Weight	× Frequency	= Score
a	3		
b	3		
c	5		
d	2		
e	4		
f	1		
		III: Total Score: _____	

3.2. Room Design			
Item	Weight	× Frequency	= Score
a	1		
b	3		
c	4		
d	5		
e	4		
f	5		
		IV: Total Score: _____	

3.3. Teaching Environment			
Item	Weight	× Frequency	= Score
a	5		
b	4		
c	4		
d	5		
e	4		
f	4		
g	4		
		V: Total Score: _____	

4. Evaluation Techniques			
Item	Weight	× Frequency	= Score
a	4		
b	2		
c	4		
d	4		
e	5		
f	4		
g	1		
h	4		
		VI: Total Score: _____	

5. Teaching Characteristics			
Item	Weight	× Frequency	= Score
a	4		
b	5		
c	4		
d	3		
e	1		
f	1		
g	1		
h	1		
		VIII: Total Score: _____	

6. Educational Philosophy			
Item	Weight	× Frequency	= Score
a	4		
b	5		
c	3		
d	5		
e	4		
f	3		
g	4		
h	3		
i	4		
j	5		
k	1		
l	1		
m	1		
n	1		
		VII: Total Score: _____	

FIGURE 10–5   Teaching Style Profile

	Individ- ualized	Somewhat Individualized	Transi- tional	Somewhat Traditional	Tradi- tional
I: Instructional planning					
	210	168	126	84	42
II: Teaching methods					
	80	64	48	32	16
III: Student groupings					
	90	72	54	36	18
IV: Room design					
	110	88	66	44	22
V: Teaching environment					
	150	120	90	60	30
VI: Evaluation techniques					
	140	112	84	56	28
VII: Educational philosophy					
	220	176	132	88	44
VIII: Teaching characteristics					
	100	80	60	40	20

This profile should provide you with a graphic representation of your current teaching style. After linking the dots in succession and examining your teaching style, draw a perpendicular line from top to bottom through your philosophy score, as shown in Figure 10–6. *Most* teachers' philosophy is far more individualized than their methods—but that is why they recognize the need for at least some expansion of their style.

How to Select Objectives and Reach Them

If your philosophy suggests that you believe in either individualized or somewhat individualized teaching, you may wish to consider expanding your current teaching style in one area; for example, you may decide to do a little redesigning of your classroom, as the teacher in Figure 10–7 did. She thought she could do a few things with the desk and seats that might allow for at least one section where some youngsters could work informally. She also thought she could tolerate youngsters sitting in either bright or soft lighting, so she arranged for that alternative. She decided to establish an Interest Center and a Learning Station (see Chapter 3) to permit some mobility for a few boys she always had thought of as hyperactive. The more she experimented, the more she realized that the youngsters were really ''good kids'' who had just been

	Individualized	Somewhat Individualized	Transitional	Somewhat Traditional	Traditional
1. Instructional planning					
2. Teaching methods	210	168	126	84	
3.1 Student groupings	80	64	48	32	
3.2 Room design	90	72	54	36	
3.3 Teaching environment	110	88	66	44	
4. Evaluation techniques	150	120	90	60	
5. Teaching characteristics	140	112	84	56	
6. Educational philosophy	100	80	60	40	
	220	176	132	88	

FIGURE 10–6   Sample Teaching Style Profile
After completing your Teaching Style Profile, draw a perpendicular line from top to bottom
through your philosophy score as shown in Figure 10–3—a typical profile.

unable to conform to the formality of the seating and the restrictiveness of passive attention. As her teaching style changed rapidly in this one area, she found that she enjoyed teaching more than she had before.

The teacher said "No" to rows of desks and gained 3 points; increased small-group work from occasionally to frequently and gained 3 points; established Learning Stations and Centers frequently instead of rarely and gained 8 points; created a variety of areas frequently as opposed to rarely and gained 10 points; designed alcoves, dens, "offices" frequently instead of never and gained 12 points; and established three or more of these arrangements frequently instead of rarely and gained 10 points—thus elevating her score from 43 to 89 to reach her objective. Her actual practice now is consistent with her philosophy (see Figure 10–8).

	Individualized	Somewhat Individualized	Transitional	Somewhat Traditional	Traditional
1. Instructional planning					
2. Teaching methods	210	168	126	84	
3.1 Student groupings	80	64	48	32	
3.2 Room design	90	72	54	36	
3.3 Teaching environment	110	88	66	44	
4. Evaluation techniques	150	120	90	60	
5. Teaching characteristics	140	112	84	56	
6. Educational philosophy	100	80	60	40	
	220	176	132	88	

FIGURE 10–7   Sample Teaching Style Profile (Year One)

FIGURE 10–8   How One Teacher Expanded Her Teaching Style through Increased Frequency of Selected Items in Room Design

	Last Year			Now		
	Weight	Frequency	Total	Weight	Frequency	Total
a) Rows of desks	1 ×	2	= 2	1 ×	5	= 5
b) Small groups	3 ×	3	= 9	3 ×	4	= 12
c) Learning stations	4 ×	2	= 8	4 ×	4	= 16
d) Variety of areas	5 ×	2	= 10	5 ×	4	= 20
e) Alcoves, "offices"	4 ×	1	= 4	4 ×	4	= 16
f) Three or more of the above at the same time	5 ×	2	= 10	5 ×	4	= 20
	Total		43			89

As this teacher gained success and confidence through redesigning her room to match learning style needs, she elected to improve her planning and methods the following year (see Figure 10–9).

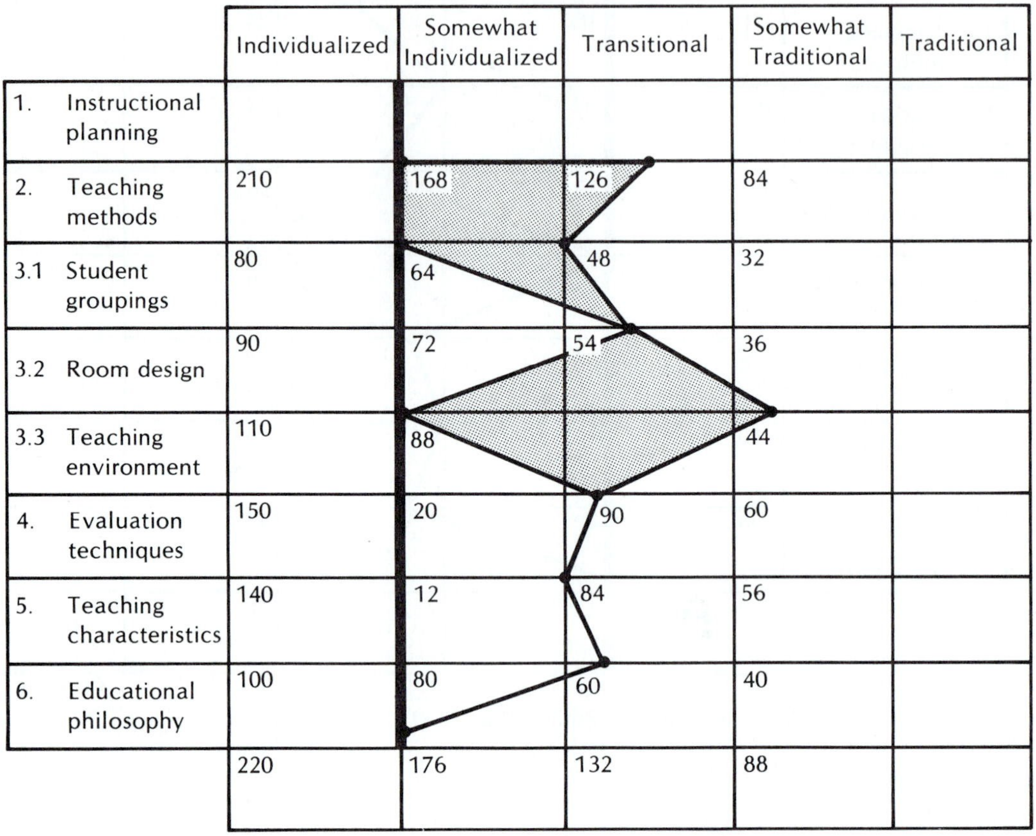

	Individualized	Somewhat Individualized	Transitional	Somewhat Traditional	Traditional
1. Instructional planning					
2. Teaching methods	210	168	126	84	
3.1 Student groupings	80	64	48	32	
3.2 Room design	90	72	54	36	
3.3 Teaching environment	110	88		44	
4. Evaluation techniques	150	20	90	60	
5. Teaching characteristics	140	12	84	56	
6. Educational philosophy	100	80	60	40	
	220	176	132	88	

Note: 1 = First year—Room design
2 = Second year—Planning and methods

FIGURE 10-9 (Year Two) Gradual Expansion of One Teacher's Teaching Style as She Began to Experiment with Increased Frequency of Items with Which She Felt Comfortable

Should you wish to consider expanding your teaching style in the same way, review the items under "Room Design" in the *Teaching Style Inventory*. Choose those items with which you feel fairly comfortable and decide to use them more frequently than you have heretofore. You will see your style expand to become increasingly responsive to students' multiple styles. If you *do* try this, retake that portion of the inventory in one month and note the difference in your score!

If you prefer to expand your teaching style in another area, choose one that interests you and, again, examine the section of the inventory related to that component. Choose the items with which you feel relatively comfortable and increase the frequency with which you do those things. Go slowly. You will enjoy the gradually developing appreciation of the differences your expanding style makes to your students.

As each area gradually expanded toward her philosophy, this teacher discovered that several other areas (Student Grouping, Learning Environment, and Characteristics) also began to move toward the left on her Teaching Style Profile. The *Teaching Style Inventory* offers an objective, self-determined approach to improved teaching and learning. If you would like to use this profile to focus on helping some youngsters you may not have been able to reach effectively in the past, experiment. If the process isn't working, obviously you will stop. But if you enjoy each change, you may find a very special delight in being able to use the right methods for the right students, instead of the same method for everyone.

The following questionnaire is related to student types with which you are most successful. It offers another dimension of matching teaching style to types of learners.

Question 7: Student Types

Directions:
Rate the degree of success you tend to have with each type of student.

CODE:

5. Almost always successful
4. Frequently successful
3. Occasionally successful
2. Rarely successful
1. Almost never successful

A. Learning Rate

_____ Quickly achieving   _____ Slowly achieving

_____ Average achieving   _____ Nonachieving

B. Motivation Scale

_____ Motivated   _____ Unmotivated

_____ Conforming   _____ Nonconforming

_____ Persistent   _____ Not persistent

_____ Responsible   _____ Not responsible

_____ Apathetic

C. *Emotional Stability*

_____ Emotionally stable   _____ Quiet-passive

_____ Active-mobile   _____ Emotionally troubled

D. *Learning Potential*

_____ Gifted   _____ Average IQ

_____ Creative   _____ Below-average IQ

_____ Far above-average IQ   _____ Learning-impaired

E. *Verbal Communication Ability*

_____ Articulate   _____ Bilingual

_____ Average verbal ability   _____ Non-English-speaking

_____ Below-average verbal ability

F. *Independence Level*

_____ Peer-oriented   _____ Independent

_____ Adult-oriented   _____ Authority-oriented

List all the types of students that received 5s under Question 7 for each of the categories A through F. You now know how to identify faculty teaching styles and the students with whom individuals believe they are successful.

TEACHER SUCCESS WITH STUDENT TYPES/PREDICTOR PROFILE

A: Learning rate _____

B: Motivation scale _____

C: Emotional stability _____

D: Learning potential _____

E: Verbal communications ability _____

F: Independence level _____

The next step is to identify individual youngsters' learning styles and then to match the right student with the right teacher—for him or her.

What Are the Next Steps?

Once you feel comfortable responding to at least some of the elements of learning style that are important to your students, you will want to share what you are doing with their parents. See Chapter 11 for resources that may assist you in this vein—for example, a booklet explaining the concept of learning styles specifically designed for parents, or a cartoon-like filmstrip and accompanying cassette explaining the concept. You may be able to solicit parental assistance in developing Contract Activity Packages (CAPs), Programmed Learning Sequences (PLSs), tactual/kinesthetic manipulatives (T/K), and/or Multisensory Instructional Packages (MIPs) for use with your students. You surely will want parents to see that their children do their homework according to their learning style strengths, so before you send home the Homework Disc prescriptions (see Chapter 11), explain to both the students *and* their parents how these should be used.

Next decide on which group of students you most wish to concentrate. Is it the gifted or nonconforming? Try a CAP. Is it the ones who need structure? Begin with a PLS. Are you most concerned with children who do not seem to remember much of what you discuss in class? Introduce them to the tactual materials in Chapter 6 and then have them reinforce what they were exposed to with a follow-up PLS. If your greatest concern is with the at-risk, underachievers, and potential dropouts, begin with MIPs.

Figure 10–10a illustrates graphically different departure points for moving into a learning styles instructional program. It is necessary to begin with identification of individuals' learning style strengths with the *Learning Style Inventory* and to share the results with students and their parents, but after that you may choose any path toward your objective of working with students through their strengths rather than through hit-or-miss approaches. Figure 10–10b presents an analytic diagram of steps and specific strategies on the path to responding to individual learning style characteristics.

What Are the Ultimate Steps?

Students will learn more, more easily, and retain it longer when they are taught through resources that complement their learning styles, but it is not always necessary to continually design new tactual resources, Programmed Learning Sequences, and Contract Activity Packages *for* them. After students have had at least three or four experiences *using* these methods, many of them will be able to begin designing their own, particularly when encouraged to work with peers. (On the other hand, remember that some children prefer to work alone, so do not mandate that they work with others.) Teaching young people to translate their textbooks into resources that respond to how they, as individuals, learn, is the biggest step we can take toward helping them to become independent learners. Eventually they will be able to teach themselves anything by using their knowledge of style and translating printed matter into the method that best matches their strengths.

Teaching students to create their own materials is easy with some and difficult with others, but *often we anticipate problems where they never emerge* and vice versa. Thus, after youngsters have had experience using a specific method, assign the development of the appropriate resource either for homework or as a unit project.

Helping Students to Create Tactual Materials

Make a transparency of the directions for creating multipart Task Cards, Flip Chutes, Pic-A-Holes, or Electroboards and their pictorial representations. Project each transparency, one at a time, onto a blank classroom wall and—keeping the overhead far away from the wall so that you project a very big image onto a large sheet of either oaktag or colored tagboard—trace the graphic and printed directions for each. Number the oaktag sections in sequence so that youngsters know with which to begin and when the manipulative has been completed. If you prefer to have these devices made at home, either photocopy the directions in Chapter 6, or have them copied from the large posters you will make for classroom display.

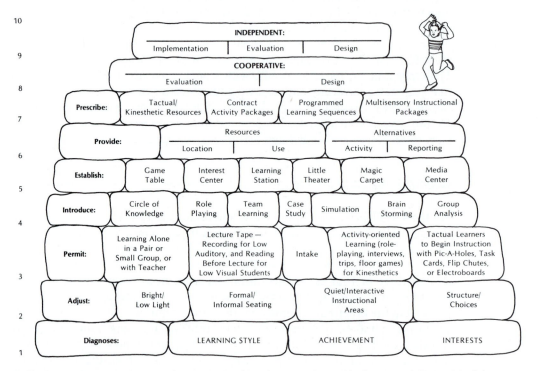

FIGURE 10–10a Learning Styles Process of Implementation with Dunn and Dunn Model

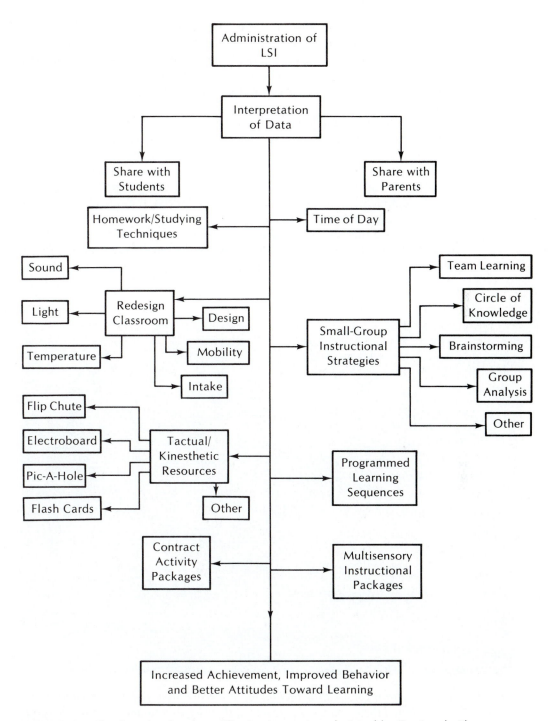

FIGURE 10-10b Stepping-Stones to Effective Instruction, designed by Dr. Angela Klavas.

An alternative is to make it a class project to create one of the tactuals as part of a class or unit lesson. You will see that many tactual students will complete that assignment easily and with confidence; they also will help their auditory and visual classmates with an aplomb rarely evidenced by these children in school! After all, *that* (using their hands skillfully) is what they are best at!

After the manipulatives have been completed, have each child be responsible for having at least two classmates *use* their original manipulative and then either sign their name on a sheet of paper indicating that they checked the device and its information is totally correct *or* refuse to sign their names until the material has been corrected. Explain that they are not helping classmates by signing when information is *incorrect;* indeed, they are harming them by not showing where the errors are.

Recognize that, by using each other's materials, all students are having the difficult material required for that topic reinforced through varied instructional resources—which may be motivating.

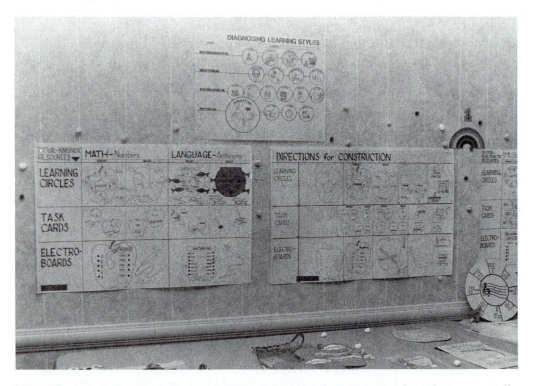

When illustrated directions for creating tactual materials are mounted on classroom walls, students often can design the resources for teaching themselves new and difficult material. (Photographs courtesy of Dr. Angela Bruno, Lamtex Incorporated, Canton, Ohio.)

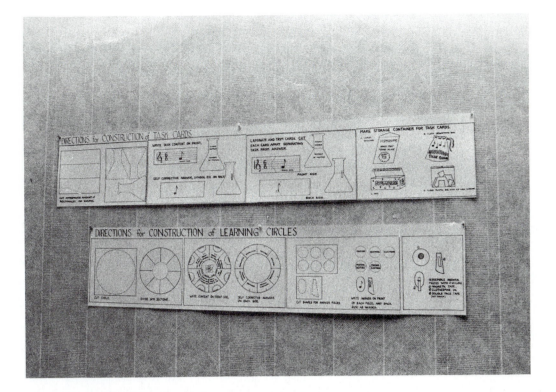

Helping Students to Create Programmed Learning Sequences

Once students have used Programmed Learning Sequences (PLSs) three or four times, many will be able to create their own either together with a classmate or, perhaps, working with a parent. Tell them to follow these steps and to use one of the PLSs you have in the classroom as a guide.

PLS Guidelines for Students

1. If you want to design a PLS to teach yourself difficult information in the curriculum, adopt the straight analytic title of the chapter in the book as your major title. Thus, if the title is **"Graphing,"** that becomes the title of your developing PLS.

2. Make up a funny subtitle to appeal to global classmates. Use a play on words or funny idea. Being corny is acceptable, but good grammar and decorum must be adhered to. Examples of funny subtitles might be:

- "Graphing: Get the Point"
- "The Mind and the Brain: Or Getting Your Head Together!"

- "Vowel Sounds: The Long and Short of It"
- "Adjectives: Words that Defy Description"
- "Figurative Language: Say What You Mean and Mean What You Say"
- "Fractions: Dividing Problems into Parts We Can Handle"
- "Descriptive Research": Tell It Like It IS!"

3. Think of a shape that represents the topic. If no shape is at all related, then use any shape that is different from an 8 × 10 rectangle.

4. Think of a way to get someone interested in this topic. How might it be helpful to know this information? Is there something practical that others can do with it? Is there a special reason that someone would find it interesting?

5. Develop a short story (one or two paragraphs) to show why this information might be important or interesting to someone studying this topic. For example, to learn about how to predict weather, you might write:

> Timmy was soaked through and through. He had walked four miles to the gym because his mom was busy and, halfway there, it had begun to thunder and rain. He had been so engrossed thinking about basketball practice this morning, that he had not even glanced at the sky. Had he just looked skyward, he probably would have noticed the huge, black nimbus clouds that dominated the horizon. He might have remembered that nimbus clouds bring rain.

6. Then write clearly what the PLS you are developing will teach. For example, "This program will show you how to recognize different weather signs so that you probably will be prepared for rain when it happens—unlike poor Timmy!" Decide what the PLS will teach by reading the questions at the end of the chapter. Those questions pertain to what the author believes are the most important things in this chapter. The most important things are what you must learn. Those are called your *objectives*. Thus, *objectives* are what must be learned in each chapter and in each PLS.

7. Clearly write the objectives for your developing PLS. For example:

> By the time you complete this PLS, you should be able to do all the following things:
>
> **1.** Name at least five (5) different cloud types and explain the kind of weather each cloud type predicts.
>
> **2.** Explain each of the following words and phrases and use them correctly when writing a story about how to predict weather: (a) precipitation, (b) predicting, (c) atmosphere, (d) wind-chill factor, (e) high/low pressure area, and (f) weather alert.

8. Copy the objectives you wrote and keep them near you as you begin to read the book chapter, beginning with the first paragraph. Keep the first two objectives in mind and *read to find the answers* to those objectives. When you find them, neatly copy the sentence or paragraph that explains the information required by the objective and the answer onto a 5 × 7 index card in the shape that you decided to use for this PLS. After you either have printed or typed the information, add a question related directly to that information at the bottom of the index card (same side). Require that whoever uses this PLS after it has been completed provides an answer to that question. Clearly state how the question must be answered. For example:

Read the following question and circle the correct answer. (In that case, you might have given three choices of answers).

or

Read the following questions and then write your answer on the dotted line.

or

Read the following question and then look at the questions in the column on the left. Then find the answer to each question and draw a line across to its correct answer in the right-hand column.

or

Fill in the missing letters and form the correct answer. You might do this: What is the name of the black cloud that predicts rain?

n _ _ b _ _

or

Open the small envelope attached to the back of this frame, carefully take the miniature Task Card pieces out, and put together the letters so that they form the answer.

9. Turn the index card over *as if you were turning a page in your textbook*. Neatly print the answer to the question on the reverse side of the index card.

10. After you print the answer on the back of the index card, draw a straight horizontal line halfway across the card and add either an illustration to further explain the answer (for example, a drawing of a nimbus cloud), a humorous or interesting comment about the answer, or additional information.

For example:

Index card:

Answer: nimbus
I hope you never have nimbus clouds in your life!—except when we need rain to make the crops and flowers grow!

11. Continue reading the textbook until you find every answer to each of the questions that were listed in the back of the chapter (your objectives). On each subsequent frame, write the important information to teach those answers. Continue to ask about the information on each frame and require answers to the questions *you* develop for each frame. Write the answers on the rear of each frame and add illustrations throughout and additional statements on the rear. Think of, and add, humorous statements related to the information—but be polite and use good spelling and grammar.

12. Every seven or eight frames, *review* everything you taught to that point. You may design a miniature tactual resource to reteach the information. If you do, glue it onto a new frame whenever you want to reinforce what has already been presented. For example, make a Pic-A-Hole or an Electroboard to reteach what the frames included. Give directions for using the resource you design.

13. After all the questions have been answered—meaning that all the information for each objective has been printed or typed onto the index cards—begin a new frame with:

You have read all the information in this PLS to this point. See how much you remember. Answer all the following questions. IF you are not *certain* that you know all the answers, either turn back to the frames that explain the information and reread them *or* use the tactual resources in your classroom and find the correct answers in the Flip Chute, the Electroboard, the multipart Task Cards, or the Pic-A-Hole related to this topic. You need to know all the answers, so be certain that you do.

14. On the next frame, write:

Please go back and wipe all your answers off this PLS so that the next person may use it. I hope you liked using it. It was a lot of work to make!

15. Go back through all the frames and be certain that you have illustrations related to the information wherever possible. Check the answers you printed on the back of the frames to be certain they are all there—and correct! Add funny comments if you can, but be certain they are in good taste.

16. Ask someone older than you to check your PLS for spelling and grammar. Make all necessary corrections. Then show it to your teacher. After he or she corrects it, make it perfect by doing whatever needs to be done (as your teacher suggests). Then laminate the PLS or cover it with clear Contact paper to keep it in good shape. Before you laminate the back cover, neatly print or type your name, class, grade, and the date. Students who use your PLS to learn this information will always know that *you* were the author!

Helping Students to Create Contract Activity Packages (CAPs)

Before you begin to use CAPs with students, print colored oaktag lists of Activity Alternatives and Reporting Alternatives side by side and mount them in the classroom (see Chapter 8). Give the students choices of Activity Alternatives and matched Reporting Alternatives as a way of doing their homework. Applying new and difficult information in making something original and creative is one of the best ways to ensure retention. In addition, the use of these alternative activities will familiarize students with the concept and practice. When they need to design similar activities for CAPs later on, they will understand what to write.

CAPs are designed for motivated students who enjoy working independently and for nonconformists who need to work alone. Both groups will *want* to design additional CAPS once they have exhausted your supply. They also will be enticed into creating their own when they become interested in a topic for which you do not have a CAP available.

If you are willing to list the objectives for a unit, CAP children will find it relatively easy to decide on Activity Alternatives and Reporting Alternatives they would enjoy for each. Remind them to create activities that respond to diverse perceptual strengths—auditory, visual, tactual, and/or kinesthetic.

Playing detective in a library or media center to see how many Alternative Resources they are able to locate will interest most CAP enthusiasts. Remind them that using multimedia is appropriate (videotapes, filmstrips, tapes, "talking books," and so forth). They can list or illustrate all the resources they find and mount them on charts somewhere in the classroom so that others may benefit from their pioneering efforts.

A Circle of Knowledge is easy for most students to develop after they have been exposed to and participated in several. Even a Team Learning is not difficult to design once the students have been made aware of the specifically stated objectives. If you are willing to experiment, encourage students either to convert questions found at the end of the their textbook chapter into objectives for the next unit *or* to develop their own with a classmate or two or in a small group. The CAP student enjoys challenges, competes willingly, and sometimes designs more interesting objectives and/or activities than we adults devise.

Having worked with CAPs, motivated auditory or visual students and nonconformists will thrive as they develop them. After those have been submitted and corrected, ask the youngsters to make them attractive and to sign their name, class, grade, age, and the date on the rear cover. They will enjoy having their CAPs duplicated and distributed among other students who have become interested in using this instructional system.

Once students can be helped to become independent learners by learning how to translate new and difficult textbook materials into instructional resources responsive to their learning styles, there is no limit to their ability to eventually teach themselves information and skills that they become interested in learning or that become important to them. Figure 10–10b describes the process as a series of stepping-stones. Take whichever steps you feel most comfortable with in the beginning. As you begin to find your way, you may alter the path and go as far as you successfully can. We've suggested a road map; chart your own course!

Helping Students to Redesign Their Classroom on the Basis of Their Individual Learning Styles

When encouraged to experiment with redesigning their conventional classroom to respond to the learning styles of their classmates and themselves, students often suggest creative, attractive alternatives. We recommend that the strengths of each youngster in the class (as diagnosed by the *Learning Style Inventory*) be recorded on a large Wall Chart (see Chapter 11). Then discuss the differences that exist among members and why it is important that each learn through strengths. Finally, distribute copies of Figure 10–11 to individuals, pairs, or groups—depending on how youngsters care to work—and ask them to create their own representations of a learning style classroom. The illustrated items can be cut out, shaded, pasted onto large colored pieces of oaktag, and then considered for adoption. Given this opportunity to engage in a bit of classroom interior decorating, many students develop both practical and artistic possibilities. Why not experiment with one or more of their suggestions? Because *they* revised the room, they will consider the privilege soberly and consciously appreciate your concern for their comfort. At the same time, they will take care not to take advantage of the privilege.

Whether or not you adopt one or more of the student-redesigned possibilities, mount and label them, giving their designers credit (in writing) for their interesting creations. Carolyn Brunner, director of the Erie 1 Board of Cooperative Educational Services' Instructional Development Center in Depew, New York, designed Figure 10–11, used it as described previously and reported, "mind-boggling" successes as perceived by *both* the students and their teachers!

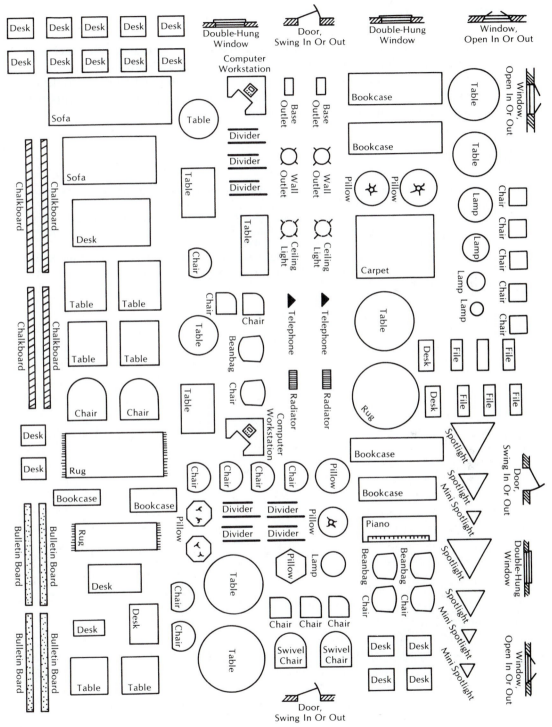

FIGURE 10-11

483

A Final Word on Teaching Style

Begin slowly. Use new strategies that make sense to you and with which *you* feel comfortable. Expand your teaching strengths gradually over a period of three to five years. As you expand your style to respond to more students' diverse styles, you will experience increasing success and your students will achieve better and enjoy learning more.

Notes

1. The *Learning Style Inventory* is available from Price Systems, Box 1818, Lawrence, KS 66046–0067.
2. *Mission from No Style* and *One-Of-A-Kind Learning Style,* are obtainable from the Center for the Study of Learning and Teaching Styles, St. John's University, Utopia Parkway, Jamaica, NY. 11439.
3. Perceptual Sequencing Wall Charts are available from the Center for the Study of Learning and Teaching Styles, St. John's University, Utopia Parkway, Jamaica, New York 11439.

11

Resources for Getting Started with Learning Styles Instruction

You believe in the concept that students learn differently from one another. You also see merit in the idea that, when taught with complementary methods or materials, students are likely to achieve better and like school more than when they are taught incorrectly (for them).

Chapter 10 explains that you do not need to do everything at once; you can choose where you want to start and take a step or two at a time—as long as you keep walking forward! But do you have to create all the resources you want to use? Are there ways of learning more procedures than were available in this solely visual book? Are there other existing materials that can help you and your students experiment with learning style practices?

Since 1979, the staff of the Center for the Study of Learning and Teaching Styles at St. John's University have been designing and testing hands-on resources to help teachers, administrators, and staff development supervisors move into learning styles instruction. They also developed materials for students so that they might master required curriculum through their different styles. This chapter outlines a series of steps you might want to consider, and resources you may wish to use, when beginning with learning style practices in your class or school.

Background Information

Your first step is to become thoroughly acquainted with the Dunn and Dunn model by reading this book. To get an overview of the model and directions

This chapter was written by Dr. Angela Klavas, Assistant Director, Center for the Study of Learning and Teaching Styles, St. John's University, New York.

on how to assess for learning style and interpret a learning style profile, you may want to do one or more of the following:

- Attend or sponsor a workshop on learning style with the Dunn and Dunn model.
- Attend a weekend or eight-day conference sponsored by the Center for the Study of Learning and Teaching Styles.
- Do an ERIC search for journal articles on learning style with the Dunn and Dunn approach (there is an excellent article on synthesis of research in *Educational Leadership,* Volume 46, Number 6, March 1989).
- Join the National Network on Learning Styles, a nonprofit organization sponsored by the National Association of Secondary School Principals and St. John's University. For a nominal yearly subscription, you receive information about developments in the field of learning style and teaching style. Services include three newsletters annually providing summaries of the latest research, practical applications, and experimental programs; information about conferences, institutes, and inservice workshops for teachers and administrators; descriptions of publications and dissertations in the field; identification of resource personnel and exemplary school sites; an updated bibliography of publications and films; and responses to written or telephone requests for information.

Publications for Adults

The following are publications available from the Center for the Study of Learning and Teaching Styles that provide background information to teachers, administrators, and trainers interested in implementing learning styles.

- *Teaching Secondary Students through Their Individual Learning Styles* by Doctors Rita and Kenneth Dunn is a practical, hands-on guide to implementing learning styles.
- *Teaching Students to Read through Their Individual Learning Styles* by Dr. Marie Carbo and Doctors Rita and Kenneth Dunn provides a diagnostic-prescriptive approach for teaching children to read. It involves the identification of individual learning styles and the subsequent matching of complementary reading strategies, resources, and environments.
- *Learning Styles: Quiet Revolution in American Secondary Schools* by Dr. Rita Dunn and Dr. Shirley Griggs contains descriptions of the achievement and attitude gains of urban, suburban, and rural middle and high schools' learning style programs.
- *A Review of Articles and Books* is a compilation of articles and research studies and their implications for gifted, special education, and regular instruction. Administrators and trainers can duplicate the journal articles for distribution to teachers. This publication also provides the docu-

mentation needed for term papers, theses, and dissertations on learning styles and hemisphericity.

Administrators, teachers, and doctoral students interested in the research behind various learning style models will find the following resources informative and valuable.

- *The Curry Report* is a psychometric review of the major instructional preference, information-processing, and cognitive personality instruments that bear on individuals' learning styles.
- *The DeBello Report* compares learning style models and the psychometric analyses of their instruments. It contains an audiotape, script, extensive reference list, and diagram comparing eleven models, with variables, appropriate populations, validity of instrumentation, and the research behind each.
- *Annotated Bibliography* is an updated review of articles, books, dissertations, and research on learning style. This is an invaluable resource for anyone involved in writing term papers, theses, proposals for funding, or manuscripts.

Videotapes

Videotapes are excellent resources for training administrators, trainers, and teachers by providing an overview of the Dunn and Dunn model, the research, and the step-by-step strategies and techniques in its implementation process. Each of these tapes provides a complete inservice course for introducing faculty to beginning steps for teaching students through their individual learning styles.

- *Videotapes: Teaching Students through Their Individual Learning Styles* is a six-hour complete training program narrated by Dr. Rita Dunn. It introduces the Dunn and Dunn learning style model by explaining the environmental, emotional, sociological, physical, and psychological elements of style. It describes how to identify individual strengths, redesign classrooms to respond to diverse styles, and teach students to do their homework through their learning style strengths.
- *Teaching At-Risk Students through Their Individual Learning Styles* is a complete training program narrated by Doctors Rita and Kenneth Dunn. It is a six-hour, hands-on, how-to description that provides the research and the methods for teaching at-risk students through their individual learning styles.
- *Videotape: Personal Learning Power,* a ten-minute rap videotape. Written by Dr. Kenneth Dunn to explain learning styles to students in grades 3–12.

The following videotapes are excellent resources for everyone interested in observing learning style techniques and strategies in classrooms. They can be used either as an introduction to the concept or as a culminating workshop activity.

- *Videotapes: The Look of Learning Styles* presents learning style programs in either four different elementary schools or four secondary schools throughout the United States, demonstrating how students' unique characteristics are matched with appropriate environments, resources, and methods in the classroom. This is also an excellent resource for students as an explanation of learning style.

Instrumentation

Before assessing the learning styles of students, teachers and administrators should have their own learning styles identified with the *Productivity Environmental Preference Survey* (PEPS). They will discover how they prefer to function, learn, concentrate, and perform in their own educational settings. Analyzing their personal style allows them to understand the process, thus making them better able to interpret the learning styles of students. More important, when they realize that they themselves have unique learning styles, they will better understand and accept the diversity in their students' styles. Administrators and trainers find that their staff development sessions become more effective after they administer and interpret the PEPS to the participants.

- The *Productivity Environmental Preference Survey* (PEPS) by Dunn, Dunn, and Price is available in a specimen set, a computerized program, and a Scan-and-Score packet.
- The *Learning Style Inventory* (LSI) is the instrument used to identify learning style for students in grades 3 through 12. It is available in a specimen set, a computerized program, and a Scan-and-Score packet. There is a special questionnaire for grades 3–4 and another for grades 5–12. Before the test is administered, students need to understand the concept of learning style and that, regardless of intelligence, age or gender, everyone has a unique learning style. Students should be informed that the LSI is not an IQ test or a reading test and that there are no "right" or "wrong" answers.
- *Learning Style Inventory: Primary Version* is the only instrument of its kind that can identify the learning style of primary (K–2) students and is available at the Center for the Study of Learning and Teaching Styles. This learning style instrument, designed by Dr. Janet Perrin, is a pictorial questionnaire with a manual that provides (1) information concerning the development of the instrument, (2) directions for administration, and (3) instructional strategies for responding to specific learning style char-

acteristics. This package includes reproducible answer forms (for assessing the learning style of an entire class) and research information that provides reliability and validity data. Before administering the LSI-P, the learning style concept should be explained to K–2 students. The following storybook is an excellent resource with which to prepare primary youngsters to take the assessment instrument.

- *Elephant Style* by Stephanie Santora and Dr. Janet Perrin explains the concept of learning style to young children by describing the various ways two elephants learn and remember new and difficult information.

Publications for Students

The following storybooks, especially written for students at different grade levels, are available to assist teachers in preparing students to take the LSI:

- *Mission from Nostyle* by Ann Braio is a storybook explaining the concept of learning style to students in grades 2–6. It describes the search of space children for information concerning how to learn new and difficult information. Earthlings join them and eventually unravel how to achieve well in school. This high-interest storybook should be read prior to diagnosing learning style, so that students can understand that everyone has strengths—only different ones.
- *Two-of-a-Kind* by Rosy Pena is a storybook that explains learning style to middle school students. In a high-interest story, GLOBAL Myrna and ANALYTIC Victor are close friends who respect their differences and study difficult material through their own unique learning styles.
- *Guide Explaining Learning Style to High School Students* by Connie Bouwman was written specifically for secondary school students.
- *Coloring Book Explaining Global/Analytic Styles to Children* by Sr. Mary Lenahan. This delightful storybook describes a sister and brother who are so different from each other that it becomes important to understand why they behave so uniquely.

Doing Homework

Research indicates that improved academic achievement occurs when students do their homework through their individual learning style. Available at the Center for the Study of Learning and Teaching Styles are resources relating to homework and learning style for teachers, parents, and students.

- *Learning How to Learn* is a programmed Learning Sequence (PLS) on how to learn, study, and do homework through one's own perceptual strengths. In 36 frames, it explains how to learn more easily and remember better by introducing new information or skills through each person's strongest modality and then reinforcing through others. This PLS can be duplicated and then colored and laminated by students who read on a fourth-grade level or above.

- *How to Do Homework through Learning Style* is a colorful and animated filmstrip with cassette tape, which shows students in grades 3–12 how to do their homework. This resource can be also shown to individual parents or PTA groups so that they provide their children with the proper home environment when studying and doing homework.
- *Perceptual Strength Homework Charts* are two inexpensive posterboard charts that are an aid to both teachers and students. The *Learning Style Instructional Chart* lists the correct sequence of instruction for the tactual, visual, auditory, or kinesthetic student and for teacher-directed lessons. The *Learning Style Class Chart* cites the six-step perceptual sequence of instruction for student, teacher-directed, and whole-group lectures. Using the primary perceptual strength from the LSI, the student is given his or her own personal sequence of self-instruction for homework assignments.
- *Homework Disk* is a software package that provides students (individually) in grades 3–12 with individual prescriptions for doing homework and studying in ways that complement their personal learning styles. Because they work through their strengths, students find doing homework more enjoyable and productive. This computer disk (available in IBM and Apple) works only with LSI data.

Teacher Inservice Packages

The four Teacher Inservice Packages (TIPs) available at the Center for the Study of Learning and Teaching Styles are designed to provide staff development through teachers' learning style preferences.

- The *Teacher Inservice Package (TIP) on Contract Activity Packages (CAPs)* demonstrates alternative methods of instructing gifted students in ways that many research studies suggest high-IQ, creative youngsters enjoy. The TIP includes: (1) a series of colored slides instructing teachers explicitly on how to design Contract Activity Packages on the elementary, middle, and high school levels, with a cassette tape that explains the slides; (2) a Programmed Learning Sequence on how to develop and use CAPs to accommodate selected learning style characteristics; and (3) three reproducible CAPs.
- *Teacher Inservice Packages (TIPs) on Programmed Learning Sequences (PLSs)* are designed for teaching motivated, persistent, visual students who need structure and like to work alone or in a pair. Environmental

preferences, time of day, and intake also can be accommodated. The package includes a Programmed Learning Sequence on the design and use of a PLS, a cassette tape, overhead transparencies, and a script.

- The *Teacher Inservice Package (TIP) on Alternatives to Lecture* is designed to show teachers better ways to teach than talking and discussing. Four small-group instructional strategies (Team Learning, Circle of Knowledge, Brainstorming, and Group Analysis) are taught through three activities accommodating teachers' learning style preferences. The activities include: (1) scripts, worksheets, and samples; (2) transparencies and an audiotape; and (3) a Programmed Learning Sequence (PLS) that can be reproduced.
- The *Teacher Inservice Package (TIP) on Conducting Staff Development Workshops* contains tips and materials for conducting inservice with the Dunn and Dunn model with suggested resources, techniques, and strategies. The package includes transparencies, a research list, an audiotape on overview, and other material to assist teachers in implementing the Dunn and Dunn model.

Instructional Resources for Students

Stimulating resources for students include *Contract Activity Packages* (CAPs) on the primary, elementary, intermediate, and secondary levels. These CAPs are self-contained units of study for motivated, persistent students. They include (1) clearly stated Behavioral Objectives; (2) suggested multisensory Resources through which students may learn the information required in the objectives; (3) Activity Alternatives offering creative ways for students to apply the information acquired through the Resources; (4) Reporting Alternatives or ways in which the Activity Alternatives are shared; (5) at least three small-group techniques such as Circle of Knowledge, Team Learning, and Brainstorming; and (6) pre- and posttests. Contract Activity Packages are an excellent resource for gifted students. They are reproducible.

The Mind and the Brain—or Getting Your Head Together is available in both a Contract Activity Package (CAP) for the motivated and a Programmed Learning Sequence (PLS) for those who need structure. It teaches (1) parts and functions of the brain and (2) careers related to the brain and mind.

Additional resources specifically designed to teach students through their individual learning styles include:

- *Comics in the Classroom: A Learning Style Approach* by Pat McCoubrey is a 175-page kit that uses comics as a practical and enjoyable resource for teaching basic skills to underachievers. It spans all grade levels (K–12) and covers a range of subject areas that include language arts, mathematics, creative arts, dramatic arts, social studies, and others. It also introduces and explains the concept of individual learning style, which greatly enhances its value as a unique and comprehensive resource. It contains 150 suggested activities and a teacher's manual.

- The *Touch and Learn Alphabet* is a kit that meets the sensory stimulation needs of the preschool, K–2 tactual learner. It contains upper- and lower-case alphabet letters, a set of numerals, a teacher's guide, and ten suggested hands-on activities.
- The *Thinking Network (TN) Software Kit* for reading and writing is an Apple microcomputer software program for improving thinking, reading, and writing skills. The TN combines computer technology with high-interest, grade-appropriate reading selections through a variety of hands-on, global reading activities not available in other software programs. Narrative Writing (grades 3–6), and Theme Writing (grades 6–9) are the two kits available from the Center.

Resources for Parents

To implement learning style fully, it is important to inform parents of their childrens' styles. The following resources are designed specifically for parents to help them understand the concept of learning style.

- *Learning Style—an Explanation for Parents* contains a filmstrip and audiotape explaining the concept of learning style. If followed by a discussion of learning style, it is an excellent resource to use at parent–teacher conferences.
- *Learning Styles: A Guide for Parents* explains learning style as it relates to parents and provides a written account of how they can accommodate their children's learning style at home.
- *The Giftedness in Every Child: A Guide for Parents,* written by Drs. Rita and Kenneth Dunn and Donald Treffinger explains learning style and how to tap into each youngster's strengths.

Resource for Counselors

The Center for the Study of Learning and Teaching Styles also has an excellent resource specifically designed for school counselors. *Learning Styles Counseling* by Dr. Shirley Griggs is a monograph that enables counselors (K–12) to diagnose learning styles, use compatible interventions, and consult with teachers about accommodating diverse styles in the classroom. This book should be read *before* troubled and difficult-to-teach students are assigned to alternative programs, psychologists, or county agencies. Though written specifically for counselors, it also should be read by teachers and parents.

Where to Obtain Resources for Getting Started

If you are interested in obtaining any of the resources listed, please write to the Center for the Study of Learning and Teaching Styles, St. John's University, Utopia Parkway, New York, NY 11439, for a free resource brochure.

A Final Word on Implementing the Dunn and Dunn Learning Style Model

Extensive and often prize-winning research has shown that improving instruction relies on teaching each student through is or her learning style strengths. Each chapter in this book has suggested strategies for gradually changing conventional teaching into instructional approaches and resources that better match *individuals'* unique characteristics.

Dr. Angela Klavas, Assistant Director, Center for the Study of Learning and Teaching Styles, St. John's University, visited elementary schools that had implemented the Dunn and Dunn Learning Styles Model in geographical locations throughout the United States. Her report (Klavas, 1991) describes those factors that both helped and hindered the development of their successful learning styles programs. Hindering factors revolved around Central Office mandates and intrusions, supervisors with a different agenda, and, in some cases, lack of financial resources for staff development. Helpful factors revolved around the understanding and insight that both staff and students developed once they became familiar with the research and theory concerned with this model and the statistically higher achievement and attitude scores that resulted from implementation.

Figure 11–1 is a graph Dr. Klavas designed to represent the four stages of implementation of the Dunn and Dunn model. Although many of the schools had been involved in learning styles instruction for five or more years, few had moved into in-depth evaluation as indicated in the fourth stage. All had completed stages 1 and 2 to varying degrees; many had moved into stage 3. *All had obtained increased test achievement.* Of those that had tested for attitudinal improvement, all had obtained significantly higher attitude test scores based on how the students felt about learning in this type of program. *All* reported improved behavior and fewer incidences (if any) of the need for referrals because of discipline problems.

Thus, follow the Klavas design as closely as possible (see Figure 11–1). Begin with the administration of the appropriate instrument to identify each student's learning style; see Appendix B for a listing of learning style instruments and the grade levels for which each is recommended. Share the children's learning style strengths with the youngsters and their parents. Interpret the results in terms of how you will alter the classroom, resources, and/or instruction to respond better to students' identified strengths. Use the St.

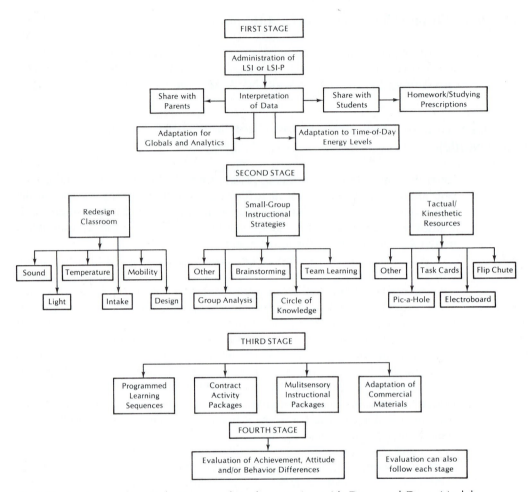

FIGURE 11–1 Learning Style Process of Implementation with Dunn and Dunn Model
Designed by Angela Klavas, Ed.D.

John's University Homework Disc to give each child and parent a prescription
for how the youngster should study and do assignments based on individual
learning style strengths. Be certain to explain that (1) in each family, parents
and their siblings often have styles that are dramatically different from each
other and (2) all styles are equally valuable. Do what you can to teach globals
globally and analytics analytically (see Chapter 4), and remind students to do
their most demanding cognitive work at the time of day that best matches their
energy highs.

Next consider with which elements in Stage 2 you feel most comfortable.
If redesigning the room does not appear overwhelming, choose those aspects
that make sense to you and begin improving the instructional environment. If

you are willing to experiment with introducing new and difficult material through Team Learning and then reinforcing through Circle of Knowledge, begin with those. If you are concerned about underachievers or bored students, begin with tactual/kinesthetic (T/K.) instructional resources—the Flip Chute, Pic-A-Hole, Task Cards, Electroboards, Learning Circles, and so forth. Permit intake (water, juice, vegetables) if you are so inclined. You do *not* need to adopt all facets of learning styles instruction; do what you can!

The third stage entails translating your objectives—what you want the students to master—into appropriate methods—CAPs, PLSs, or MIPs. You also can adapt commercial materials to reflect similar approaches. At each stage, determine the effectiveness of the approach you are implementing with each child. Thus, compare individuals' grades during a three-week interval immediately *before* and *after* you begin each phase of the learning styles approach. Youngsters should perform better with learning styles methods and resources than they did previously. Share your comparison of the students' before-and-after test scores with them. Discuss how to change instruction to better appeal to each. The final stage should be teaching students to develop their own materials (T/K, CAP, PLS, MIP) by translating their textbook into resources that benefit them most.

Move into learning styles instruction slowly; take only one step at a time into those stages you believe you can manage. Do not undertake too much, but *do* keep trying new things. You will be amazed at how well certain methods "work" for certain youngsters and not for others. With each new stage you move into, your students will (1) achieve better, (2) like school more, and (3) behave better than before. In addition, they will develop a healthy appreciation of their own—and others'—styles, and will feel better about themselves, their classmates, and their teachers than they have for a long, long time! And they will owe it all to you.

REFERENCES

Adams, J. F. (1983). The effects of the satisfaction of learning style preferences on achievement, attention and attitudes of Palm Beach junior college students. Doctoral dissertation, Florida Atlantic University. *Dissertation Abstracts International, 83,* 15060.

Andrews, R. H. (1990, July–September). The development of a learning styles program in a low socioeconomic, underachieving North Carolina elementary school. *Journal of Reading, Writing, and Learning Disabilities International, 6*(3), 307–313. New York: Hemisphere.

Annotated Bibliography. (1990). New York: St. John's University's Center for the Study of Learning and Teaching Styles, Utopia Parkway, Jamaica, NY 11439.

Bass, B. M. (1965). *Organization psychology.* Boston: Allyn and Bacon, p. 13.

Bauer, E. (1991). The relationships between and among learning styles perceptual preferences, instructional strategies, mathematics achievement, and attitude toward mathematics of learning disabled and emotionally handicapped students in a suburban junior high school. Doctoral dissertation, St. John's University, New York.

Beaty, S. A. (1986). The effect of inservice training on the ability of teachers to observe learning styles of students. Doctoral dissertation, Oregon State University, 1986. *Dissertation Abstracts International, 47,* 1998A.

Biggers, J. L. (1980). Body rhythms, the school day, and academic achievement. *Journal of Experimental Education, 49*(1), 45–47.

Braio, A. (1988). *Mission from no-style.* New York: Center for the Study of Learning and Teaching Styles, St. John's University.

Branton, P. (1966). The comfort of easy chairs. *FIRA Technical Report 22.* Hertfordshire, England: Furniture Industry Research Association.

Brennan, P. K. (1984). An analysis of the relationships among hemispheric preference and analytic/global cognitive style, two elements of learning style, method of instruction, gender, and mathematics achievement of tenth-grade geometry students. Doctoral dissertation, St. John's University, 1984. *Dissertation Abstracts International, 45,* 3271A.

Brunner, C. E., & Majewski, W. S. (1990, October). Mildly handicapped students can succeed with learning styles. *Educational Leadership, 48,* 21–23. Alexandria, VA: Association for Supervision and Curriculum Development.

Bruno, A. P., & Jessie, K. (1983). *Hands-on activities for children's writing.* Englewood Cliffs, NJ: Prentice Hall.

Buell, B. G., & Buell, N. A. (1987). Perceptual modality preference as a variable in the effectiveness of continuing education for professionals. Doctoral dissertation, University of Southern California, 1987. *Dissertation Abstracts International, 48,* 283A.

Cafferty, E. (1980). An analysis of student performance based upon the degree of match between the educational cognitive style of the teachers and the educational cognitive style of the students. Doctoral dissertation, University of Nebraska, 1980. *Dissertation Abstracts International, 41,* 07A, p. 2908.

Carbo, M. (1980). An analysis of the relationship between the modality preferences of kindergartners and selected reading treatments as they affect the learning of a basic sight-word vocabulary. Doctoral dissertation, St. John's University, 1980. *Dissertation Abstracts International, 41,* 1389A. (Recipient of the Association for Supervision and Curriculum Development National Award for Best Doctoral Research, 1980.)

Carbo, M., Dunn, R., & Dunn, K. (1986). Teaching students to read through their individual learning styles. Englewood Cliffs, NJ: Prentice Hall.

Carruthers, S. A., & Young, A. L. (1979). Do time preferences affect achievement or discipline? *Learning Styles Network Newsletter, 1*(2), 1. New York: St. John's University and the National Association of Secondary School Principals.

Carruthers, S., & Young, A. (1980). Preference of condition concerning time in learning environments of rural versus city, eighth-grade students. *Learning Styles Network Newsletter, 1*(2), 1.

Center for the Study of Learning and Teaching Styles, St. John's University, Utopia Parkway, Jamaica, NY 11439.

Cholakis, M. M. (1986). An experimental investigation of the relationships between and among sociological preferences, vocabulary instruction and achievement, and the attitudes of New York, urban, seventh, and eighth grade underachievers. Doctoral dissertation, St. John's University, 1986. *Dissertation Abstracts International, 47,* 4046A.

Clark-Thayer, S. (1987). The relationship of the knowledge of students' perceived learning style preferences and study habits and attitudes to achievement of college freshmen in a small urban university. Doctoral dissertation, Boston University, 1987. *Dissertation Abstracts International, 48,* 872A.

Clark-Thayer, S. (1988). Designing study-skills programs based on individual learning styles. *Learning Styles Network Newsletter, 9*(3), 1. New York: St. John's University and the National Association of Secondary School Principals.

Cody, C. (1983). Learning styles, including hemispheric dominance: A comparative study of average, gifted, and highly gifted students in grades five through twelve. Doctoral dissertation, Temple University, 1983. *Dissertation Abstracts International, 44,* 1631A.

Copenhaver, R. W. (1979). The consistency of student learning styles as students move from English to mathematics. Doctoral dissertation, Indiana University, 1979. *Dissertation Abstracts International, 80,* 0610.

Crino, E. M. (1984). An analysis of the preferred learning styles of kindergarten children and the relationship of these preferred learning styles to curriculum planning for kindergarten children. Doctoral dissertation, State University of New York at Buffalo, 1984. *Dissertation Abstracts International, 45,* 1282A.

Cross, J. A., Jr. (1982). Internal locus of control governs talented students (9–12). *Learning Styles Network Newsletters, 3*(3), 3. St. John's University and the National Association of Secondary School Principals.

Curry, L. (1987). *Integrating concepts of cognitive learning style: A review with attention to psychometric standards.* Ontario, Canada: Canadian College of Health Service Executives.

DeBello, T. (1985). A critical analysis of the achievement and attitude effects of administrative assignments to social studies writing instruction based on identified, eighth grade students' learning style preferences for learning alone, with peers, or with teachers. Doctoral dissertation, St. John's University, 1985. *Dissertation Abstracts International, 47,* 68A.

DeBello, T. (1990). Comparison of eleven major learning style models: Variables, appropriate populations, validity of instrumentation, and the research behind them. *Journal of Reading, Writing, and Learning Disabilities International, 6*(3), 315–322. New York: Hemisphere.

DeGregoris, C. N. (1986). Reading comprehension and the interaction of individual sound preferences and varied auditory distractions. Doctoral dissertation, Hofstra University, 1986. *Dissertation Abstracts International, 47,* 3380A.

DellaValle, J. (1984). An experimental investigation of the word recognition scores of seventh grade students to provide supervisory and administrative guidelines for the organization of effective instructional environments. Doctoral dissertation, St. John's University, 1984. *Dissertation Abstracts International, 45,* 359A. Recipient of the Phi Delta Kappa National Award for Outstanding Doctoral Research, 1984; National Association of Secondary School Principals' Middle School Research Finalist Citation, 1984; and Association for Supervision and Curriculum Development Citation for National Research (Supervision), 1984.

DellaValle, J. (1990, July–September). The development of a learning styles program in an affluent, suburban New York elementary school. New York: Hemisphere Publishing Corporation, *6*(3), 315–322.

Douglas, C. B. (1979). Making biology easier to understand. *The Biology Teacher, 4*(50), 277–299.

Dunn, K. (1985, January). Small-group techniques for the middle school. *Early Years, 15*(5), 41–43. Darien, Connecticut: Allen Raymond, Inc.

Dunn, K., & Frazier, E. R. (1990). Teaching styles. Reston, VA: National Association of Secondary School Principals.

Dunn, R. (1984, December). How should students do their homework? Research vs. Opinion. *Early Years, 15*(8), 43–45. Darien, Connecticut: Allen Raymond, Inc.

Dunn, R. (1987, Spring). Research on instructional environments: Implications for student achievement and attitudes. *Professional School Psychology, 2*(1), 43–52.

Dunn, R. (1989). Capitalizing on students' perceptual strengths to ensure literacy while engaged in conventional lecture/discussion. *Reading Psychology: An International Quarterly, 9,* 431–453. New York: Hemisphere Publishing Corporation.

Dunn, R. (1989a, May–June). Can schools overcome the impact of societal ills on students' achievement? The research indicates—yes! *The Principal, 34,*(5), 1–15. New York: Board of Jewish Education of Greater New York.

Dunn, R. (1989b, Summer). Do students from different cultures have different learning styles? *International Education, 16*(50), 3–7. New Wilmington, PA: Association for the Advancement of International Education.

Dunn, R. (1989c, Fall). Teaching gifted students through their learning style strengths. *International Education, 16*(51), 6–8. New Wilmington, PA: Association for the Advancement of International Education.

Dunn, R. (1990a, January). Bias over substance: A critical analysis of Kavale and Forness's report on modality-based instruction. *Exceptional Children, 56*(4), 354–356. Reston, VA: Council for Exceptional Children.

Dunn, R. (1990b, October). Rita Dunn answers questions on learning styles. *Educational Leadership, 48*(15), 15–19. Alexandria, VA: Association for Supervision and Curriculum Development.

Dunn, R. (1990c, Winter). Teaching underachievers through their learning style strengths. *International Education, 16*(52), 5–7. New Wilmington, PA: Association for the Advancement of International Education.

Dunn, R., Beaudry, J. A., & Klavas, A. (1989). Survey of research on learning styles. *Educational Leadership, 46*(6), 50–58.

Dunn, R., Bruno, J., Sklar, R., & Beaudry, J. (1990, May–June). Effects of matching and mismatching minority developmental college students' hemispheric preferences on mathematics test scores. *Journal of Educational Research, 83*(5), 283–288. Washington, DC: Heldref.

Dunn, R., Cavanaugh, D., Eberle, B., & Zenhausern, R. (1982). Hemispheric preference: The newest element of learning style. *The American Biology Teacher, 44*(5), 291–294.

Dunn, R., DeBello, T., Brennan, P., Krimsky, J., & Murrain, P. (1981, February). Learning style researchers define differences differently. *Educational Leadership, 38*(5), 372–375. Alexandria, VA: Association for Supervision and Curriculum Development.

Dunn, R., Deckinger, L., Withers, P., & Katzenstein, H. (1990). Should College Students Be Taught How to Do Homework? *Illinois Research and Development Journal, 26*(2), 96–113.

Dunn, R., DellaValle, J., Dunn, K., Geisert, G., Sinatra, R., & Zenhausern, R. (1986). The effects of matching and mismatching students' mobility preferences on recognition and memory tasks. *Journal of Educational Research, 79*(5), 267–272.

Dunn, R., & Dunn, K. (1972). *Practical approaches to individualizing instructional programs: Contracts and other effective teaching strategies.* Nyack, NY: Parker Publishing Company, Division of Prentice Hall.

Dunn, R., & Dunn, K. (1975). *Educator's self-teaching guide to individualizing instructional programs.* Nyack, NY: Parker Publishing Company, Division of Prentice Hall.

Dunn, R., & Dunn, K. (1977). *Administrator's guide to new programs for faculty management and evaluation.* New York: Parker Publishing Company, Subsidiary of Prentice Hall.

Dunn, R., & Dunn, K. (1978). *Teaching students through their individual learning styles: A practical approach.* Englewood Cliffs, NJ: Prentice-Hall.

Dunn, R., & Dunn, K. (1988). Presenting forwards backwards. *Teaching K–8, 19*(2), 71–73. Norwalk, CT: Early Years, Inc.

Dunn, R., & Dunn, K. *Teaching secondary students through their individual learning styles.* Boston: Allyn and Bacon.

Dunn, R., Dunn, K., & Freeley, M. E. (1984). Practical applications of the research: Responding to students' learning styles—step one. *Illinois State Research and Development Journal, 21*(1), 1–21.

Dunn, R., Dunn, K., & Price, G. E. (1975, 1977, 1978, 1979, 1985, 1987, 1989). *Learning Style Inventory.* Obtainable from Price Systems, Box 1818, Lawrence, KS 66044. $12.00.

Dunn, R., Dunn, K., & Price, G. E. (1979, 1980, 1990). *Productivity Environmental Preference Survey.* Obtainable from Price Systems, Box 1818, Lawrence, KS 66044. $12.00.

Dunn, R., Dunn, K., & Price, G. E. (1977). Diagnosing learning styles: A prescription for avoiding malpractice suits against school systems. *Phi Delta Kappan, 58*(5), 418–420.

Dunn, R., Dunn, K., Primavera, L., Sinatra, R., & Virostko, J. (1987). A timely solution: A review of research on the effects of chronobiology on children's achievement and behavior. *The Clearing House, 61*(1), 5–8.

Dunn, R., Dunn, K., & Treffinger, D. (1992). *The giftedness in every child: A guide for parents.* New York: Wiley.

Dunn, R., Gemake, J., Jalali, F., & Zenhausern, R. (1989). Cross-cultural differences in learning styles. *Journal of the Missouri Association for Supervision and Curriculum Development Journal, 1*(2), 9–15.

Dunn, R., Gemake, J., Jalali, F., Zenhausern, R., Quinn, P., & Spiridakis, J. (1990, April). Cross-cultural differences in the learning styles of fourth-, fifth-, and sixth-grade students of Afro, Chinese, Greek, and Mexican heritage. *Journal of Multicultural Counseling and Development, 18*(2), 68–93. Alexandria, VA: American Association for Multicultural Counseling and Development.

Dunn, R., Giannitti, M. C., Murray, J. B., Geisert, G., Rossi, I., & Quinn, P. (1990). Grouping students for instruction: Effects of individual vs. group learning style on achievement and attitudes. *Journal of Social Psychology, 130*(4), 485–494. Washington, DC: Heldref Publications.

Dunn, R., & Griggs, S. A. (1988a). High school dropouts: Do they learn differently from those who remain in school? *The Principal, 34*(1), 1–7.

Dunn, R., & Griggs, S. A. (1988b). *Learning styles: Quiet revolution in American secondary schools.* Reston, VA; National Association of Secondary School Principals.

Dunn, R., & Griggs, S. A. (1989a, September). Learning styles: Quiet revolution in American secondary schools. *The Clearing House, 63*(1), 40–42. Washington, DC: Heldref.

Dunn, R., & Griggs, S. A. (1989b, April). A matter of style. *Momentum, 20*(2), 66–70. Washington, DC: National Catholic Education Association.

Dunn, R., & Griggs, S. A. (1989c, January), A quiet revolution in Hempstead. *Teaching K–8, 19*(4), 55–57. Norwalk, CT: Early Years, Inc.

Dunn, R., & Griggs, S. A. (1989d, Winter). A quiet revolution: Learning styles and their application to secondary schools. *Holistic Education, 2*(4), 14–19. Greenfield, MA: Holistic Education Review, Association of Secondary School Principals.

Dunn, R., & Griggs, S. A. (1989e, February). A small private school in Minnesota. *Teaching K–8. 19*(5), 54–57. Norwalk, CR: Early Years, Inc.

Dunn, R., & Griggs, S. A. (1990). A comparative analysis of the learning styles of multicultural subgroups. *Journal of Reading, Writing, and Learning Disabilities International, 6*(3). New York: Hemisphere.

Dunn, R., Krimsky, J., Murray, J., & Quinn, P. (1985). Light up their lives: A review of research on the effects of lighting on children's achievement. *The Reading Teacher, 38*(9), 863–869.

Dunn, R., White, R. M., & Zenhausern, R. (1982). An investigation of responsible versus less responsible students. *Illinois School Research and Development, 19*(1), 19–24.

Fadley, J. L., & Hosler, V. N. (1979). *Understanding the alpha child at home and at school.* Springfield, IL: Charles C Thomas.

Fitt, S. (1975). The individual and his environment. In T. G. David & B. D. Wright (Eds.), *Learning environments.* Chicago: University of Chicago Press.

Freeley, M. E. (1984). An experimental investigation of the relationships among teachers' individual time preferences, inservice workshop schedules, and instructional techniques and the subsequent implementation of learning style strategies in participants' classrooms. Doctoral dissertation, St. John's University, 1984. *Dissertation Abstracts International, 46,* 403A.

Gadwa, K., & Griggs, S. A. (1985). The school dropout: Implications for counselors. *The School Counselor, 33,* 9–17.

Gardiner, B. (1986). An experimental analysis of selected teaching strategies implemented at specific times of the school day and their effects on the social studies achievement test scores and attitudes of fourth grade, low achieving students in an urban school setting. Doctoral dissertation, St. John's University, 1986. *Dissertation Abstracts International, 47,* 3307A.

Garrett, S. L. (1991). The effects of perceptual preference and motivation on vocabulary and attitude scores among high school students. Doctoral dissertation, University of LaVerne.

Geisert, G., Dunn, R., & Sinatra, R. (1990). Reading, learning styles, and computers. *Journal of Reading, Writing, and Learning Disabilities, 6*(3), 297–306. Washington, DC: Hemisphere.

Giannitti, M. C. (1988). An experimental investigation of the relationships among the learning style sociological preferences of middle-school students (grades 6, 7, 8), their attitudes and achievement in social studies, and selected instructional strategies. Doctoral dissertation, St. John's University, 1988. *Dissertation Abstracts International, 49,* 2911A.

Gotkin, L. (1963, December–1964, January). Individual differences, boredom, and styles of programming. *Programmed Instruction.*

Gould, B. J. (1987). An investigation of the relationships between supervisors' and supervisees' sociological productivity styles on teacher evaluations and interpersonal attraction ratings. Doctoral dissertation, St. John's University, 1987. *Dissertation Abstracts International, 48,* 18A.

Griggs, S. A. (1990). Counseling students toward effective study skills using their learning style strengths. *Journal of Reading, Writing, and Learning Disabilities: International,6*(3) 223–247. New York: Hemisphere.

Griggs, S. A., & Dunn, R. (1988, September–October). High school dropouts: Do they learn differently from those students who remain in school? *The Principal, 34*(1), 1–8. New York: Board of Jewish Education of Greater New York.

Griggs, S. A., & Price G. E. (1980). Learning styles of the gifted versus average junior high school students. *Phi Delta Kappan, 62,* 604.

Guzzo, R. S. (1987). Dificuldades de apprenddizagem: Modalidade de atencao e analise de tarefas em materisla didaticos. Doctoral dissertation, University of Sao Paulo, Institute of Pyschology, Brazil, 1987.

Hankins, N. E. (1973). *Psychology for contemporary education.* Columbus, OH: Charles E. Merrill, Chapter 7.

Hart, L. A. (1983). *Human brain and human learning.* New York: Longman.

Hill, G. D. (1987). An experimental investigation into the interaction between modality preference and instructional mode in the learning of spelling words by upper-elementary learning disabled students. Doctoral dissertation, North Texas State University, 1987. *Dissertation Abstracts International, 48,* 2536A.

Hodges, H. (1985). An analysis of the relationships among preferences for a formal/informal design, one element of learning style, academic achievement, and attitudes of seventh and eighth grade students in remedial mathematics classes in a New York City junior high school. Doctoral dissertation, St. John's University, 1985. *Dissertation Abstracts International, 45,* 2791A. Recipient of the Phi Delta Kappa National Finalist Award for Outstanding Doctoral Research, 1986.

Homans, G. (1950). *The human group.* New York: Harcourt Brace.

Homework Disc. (1990). New York: Center for the Study of Learning and Teaching Styles, St. John's University.

Ingham, J. (1989). An experimental investigation of the relationships among learning style perceptual preference, instructional strategies, training achievement, and attitudes of corporate employees. Doctoral dissertation, St. John's University, 1989. *Dissertation Abstracts International, 51,* 02A. Recipient, American Society for Training and Development (ASTD) National Research Award (1990).

Ingham, J. (1991). Matching instruction with employee perceptual preference significantly increases training effectiveness. *Human Resource Development Quarterly, 2*(1), 53–64. CA: Jossey-Bass.

Interpreting Adults' Productivity Style. (1991). New York: Center for the Study of Learning and Teaching Styles, St. John's University.

Jacobs, R. L. (1987). An investigation of the learning style differences among Afro-American and Euro-American high, average, and low achievers. Doctoral dissertation, Peabody University, 1987. *Dissertation Abstracts International.*

Jalali, F. (1988). A cross cultural comparative analysis of the learning styles and field dependence/independence characteristics of selected fourth-, fifth-, and sixth-grade students of Afro, Chinese, Greek and Mexican heritage. Doctoral dissertation, St. John's University, 1988. *Dissertation Abstracts International 50*(62), 344A.

Jarsonbeck, S. (1984). The effects of a right-brain mathematics curriculum of low achieving, fourth grade students. Doctoral dissertation, University of South Florida, 1984. *Dissertation Abstracts International, 45,* 2791A.

Johnson, C. D. (1984). Identifying potential school dropouts. Doctoral dissertation, United States International University. *Dissertation Abstracts International, 45,* 2397A.

Johnson, D. W., & Johnson, R. T. (1975). *Learning together and alone: Cooperation, competition, and individualization.* Englewood Cliffs, NJ: Prentice Hall.

Keefe, J. W. (1982). Assessing student learning styles: An overview of learning style and cognitive style inquiry. *Student Learning Styles and Brain Behavior.* Reston: Virginia National: Association of Secondary School Principals.

Kirby, P. (1979). *Cognitive style, learning style and transfer skill acquisition.* Columbus: National Center for Research in Vocational Education, The Ohio State University.

Klavas, A. (1991). Implementation of the Dunn and Dunn learning styles model in United States' elementary schools: Principals' and teachers' perceptions of factors that facilitated or impeded the process. Doctoral dissertation, St. John's University, New York.

Knapp, B. (1991). An investigation of the impact on learning styles factors upon college students' retention and achievement. Doctoral dissertation, St. John's University.

Koester, L. S., & Farley, F. H. (1977). *Arousal and hyperactivity in open and traditional education.* Paper presented at the Annual Convention of the American Psychological Association, San Francisco. ERIC Document Reproduction Service No. ED 155 543.

Kreitner, K. R. (1981). Modality strengths and learning styles of musically talented high school students. Master's dissertation, The Ohio State University.

Kress, G. C., Jr. (1966). *The effects of pacing on programmed learning under several administrative conditions.* Pittsburgh: American Institute for Research.

Kimsky, J. (1982). A comparative analysis of the effects of matching and mismatching fourth grade students with their learning style preference for the environmental element of light and their subsequent reading speed and accuracy scores. Doctoral dissertation, St. John's University, 1982. *Dissertation Abstracts International, 43,* 66A. Recipient of the Association for Supervision and Curriculum Development First Alternate National Recognition for Best Doctoral Research (Curriculum), 1982.

Kroon, D. (1985). An experimental investigation of the effects on academic achievement and the resultant administrative implications of instruction congruent and incongruent with secondary, industrial arts students' learning style perceptual preference. Doctoral dissertation, St. John's University, 1985. *Dissertation Abstracts International, 46,* 3247A.

Lam-Phoon, S. (1986). A comparative study of the learning styles of southeast Asian and American Caucasian college students of two Seventh-Day Adventist campuses. Doctoral dissertation, Andrews University, 1986. *Dissertation Abstracts International, 48*(09), 2234A.

Learning Styles Network Newsletter. (1980–1992). New York: St. John's University and the National Association of Secondary School Principals.

LeClair, T. J. (1986). The preferred perceptual modality of kindergarten aged children. Master's thesis, California State University, 1986. *Master's Abstracts, 24,* 324.

Lemmon, P. (1985). A school where learning styles make a difference. *Principal, 64*(4), 26–29.

Levy, J. (1979, September). Human cognition and lateralization of cerebral functions. *Trends in neurosciences,* 220–224.

Levy, J. (1982, Autumn). What do brain scientists know about education? *Learning Styles Network Newsletter, 3*(3), 4.

Lorge, I., Fox, D., Davitz, J., & Brenner, M. (1958). A survey of studies contrasting the quality of group performance and individual performance, 1920–1957. *Psychological Bulletin, 55,* 337–372.

Lynch, P. K. (1981). An analysis of the relationships among academic achievement, attendance, and the learning style time preferences of eleventh- and twelfth-grade students identified as initial or chronic truants in a suburban New York school district. Doctoral dissertation, St. John's University, 1981. *Dissertation Abstracts International, 42,* 1880A. Recipient of the Association for Supervision and Curriculum Development, First Alternate National Recognition for Best Doctoral Research (Supervision), 1981.

MacMurren, H. (1985). A comparative study of the effects of matching and mismatching sixth-grade students with their learning style preferences for the physical element of intake and their subsequent reading speed and accuracy scores and attitudes. Doctoral dissertation, St. John's University, 1985. *Dissertation Abstracts International, 46,* 3247A.

Mager, R. F. (1962). *Preparing instructional objectives.* Palo Alto, CA: Fearon, pp. 1–2, 53.

Mager, R. F., & McCann, J. (1963). *Learner-controlled instruction.* Palo Alto, CA: Varian.

Marcus, L. (1977). How teachers view learning styles. *NASSP Bulletin, 61,* (408), 112–114.

Mariash, L. J. (1983). *Identification of characteristics of learning styles existent among students attending school in selected northeastern Manitoba communities.* Unpublished master's dissertation, University of Manitoba, Winnipeg.

Martini, M. (1986). An analysis of the relationships between and among computer-assisted instruction, learning style perceptual preferences, attitudes, and the science achievement of seventh grade students in a suburban New York school district. Doctoral dissertation, St. John's University, 1986. *Dissertation Abstracts International, 47,* 87A. Recipient of the American Association of School Administrators (AASA) First Prize, National Research, 1986.

Mehdikani, N. (1980). The relative effects of teacher teaching style, teacher learning style, and student learning style upon academic achievement. Doctoral dissertation, Catholic University of America, 1980. *Dissertation Abstracts International.*

Miles, B. (1987). An investigation of the relationships among the learning style sociological preferences of fifth and sixth grade students, selected interactive classroom patterns and achievement in career awareness and career decision-making concepts. Doctoral dissertation, St. John's University, 1987. *Dissertation Abstracts International, 48,* 2527A. Recipient of the Phi Delta Kappan Eastern Regional Research Award, 1988.

Miller, L. M. (1985). *Mobility as an element of learning style: The effect its inclusion or exclusion has on student performance in the standardized testing environment.* Unpublished master's dissertation, University of North Florida.

Miller, M., & Zippert, C. (1987). Teaching strategies based on learning styles of adult students. *Community/Junior College Quarterly, 11,* 33–37.

Murrain, P. G. (1983). Administrative determinations concerning facilities utilization and instructional grouping: An analysis of the relationships between selected thermal environments and preferences for temperature, an element of learning style, as they affect word recognition scores of secondary students. Doctoral dissertation, St. John's University, 1983. *Dissertation Abstracts International, 44,* 1749A.

Nganwa-Baguma, M. J. (1986). Learning style: The effects of matching and mismatching pupils' design preferences on reading comprehension tests. Bachelor's dissertation, University of Transkei, South Africa.

Orsak, L. (1990, October). Learning styles versus the Rip Van Winkle syndrome. *Educational Leadership, 48*(2), 19–20. Alexandria, VA: Association for Supervision and Curriculum Development.

Pena, R. (1989). Two-of-a-kind learning styles. New York: St. John's University. Obtainable from Center for the Study of Learning and Teaching Styles, Utopia Parkway, Jamaica, NY 11439.

Perrin, J. (1984). An experimental investigation of the relationships among the learning style sociological selected instructional strategies, attitudes, and achievement in problem solving and rote memorization. Doctoral dissertation, St. John's University, 1984. *Dissertation Abstracts International, 46,* 342A. Recipient of the American Association of School Administrators (AASA) National Research Finalist Award, 1984.

Perrin, J. (1990, October). The learning styles project for potential dropouts. *Educational Leadership, 48*(2), 23–24. Alexandria, VA: Association for Supervision and Curriculum Development.

Pizzo, J. (1981). An investigation of the relationships between selected acoustic environments and sound, an element of learning style, as they affect sixth grade students' reading achievement and attitudes. Doctoral dissertation, St. John's University, 1981. *Dissertation Abstracts International, 42,* 2475A. Recipient of the Association for Supervision and Curriculum Development First Alternate National Recognition for Best Doctoral Research (Curriculum), 1981.

Pizzo, J. (1982). Breaking the sound barrier: Classroom noise and learning style. *Orbit, 64, 13*(4), 21–22.P. Ontario: Ontario Institute for Studies in Education.

Pizzo, J., Dunn, R., & Dunn, K. (1990, July–September). A sound approach to reading: Responding to students' learning styles. *Journal of Reading, Writing, and Learning Disabilities, 6*(3), 249–260. New York: Hemisphere.

Poirier, G. A. (1970). *Students as partners in team learning.* Berkeley, CA: Center of Team Learning, Chapter 2.

Price, G. E. (1980). Which learning style elements are stable and which tend to change over time? *Learning Styles Network Newsletter, 1*(3), 1.

Price, G. E., Dunn, K., Dunn, R., & Griggs, S. A. (1981). Studies in students' learning styles. *Roeper Review, 4*(2), 223–226.

Restak, R. (1979). *The brain: The last frontier.* New York: Doubleday.

The Rise Report: Report on the California commission for reform of intermediate and secondary education. (1975). Sacramento: California State Department of Education.

Roberts, O. A. (1984). Investigation of the relationship between learning style and temperament of senior high students in the Bahamas and Jamaica. Graduate dissertation, Andrews University, 1984.

Roderick, M., & Anderson, R. C. (1968). Programmed instruction in psychology versus textbook style summary of the same lesson. *Journal of Educational Psychology, 59,* 383–387.

Shea, T. C. (1983). An investigation of the relationship among preferences for the learning style element of design, selected instructional environments, and reading achievement with ninth grade students to improve administrative determinations concerning effective educational facilities. Doctoral dissertation, St. John's University, 1983. *Dissertation Abstracts International, 44,* 2004A. Recipient of the National Association of Secondary School Principals' Middle School Research Finalist Citation, 1984.

Sims, J. E. (1988). Learning styles: A comparative analysis of the learning styles of Black-American, Mexican-American, and White-American third and fourth grade students in traditional public schools. Doctoral dissertation, University of Santa Barbara, 1988. *Dissertation Abstracts International, 47,* 02, 650A.

Sinatra, C. (1990, July-September). Five diverse secondary schools where learning style instruction works. (1990, July-September). *Journal of Reading, Writing, and Learning Disabilities International.* NY: Hemisphere Publishing Corporation, 6*(3), 323–334.

Slavin, R. E. (1983). *Cooperative learning.* New York: Longman.

Slavin, R. E. (1988). Synthesis of research on cooperative learning. *Educational Lead-*

ership, 38(8), 655–660. Alexandria, Virginia: Association for Supervision and Curriculum Development.

Sykes, S., Jones, B., & Phillips, J. (1990, October). Partners in learning styles at a private school. *Educational Leadership, 48*(2), 24–26. Alexandria, VA: Association for Supervision and Curriculum Development.

Tanenbaum, R. (1982). An investigation of the relationships between selected instructional techniques and identified field dependent and field independent cognitive styles as evidenced among high school students enrolled in studies of nutrition. Doctoral dissertation, St. John's University, 1982. *Dissertation Abstracts International, 43,* 68A.

Tappenden, V. J. (1983). Analysis of the learning styles of vocational education and nonvocational education students in eleventh and twelfth grades from rural, urban, and suburban locations in Ohio. Doctoral dissertation, Kent State University, 1983. *Dissertation Abstracts International, 44,* 1326A.

Thies, A. P. (1979). A brain behavior analysis of learning style. In *Student learning styles: Diagnosing and prescribing programs.* Reston, VA: National Association of Secondary School Principals, pp. 5–61.

Thrasher, R. (1984). *A study of the learning style preferences of at-risk sixth and ninth graders.* Pompano Beach: Florida Association of Alternative School Educators.

Tingley-Michaelis, C. (1983). Make room for movement. *Early Years, 13*(6), 26–29.

Trautman, P. (1979). An investigation of the relationship between selected instructional techniques and identified cognitive style. Doctoral dissertation, St. John's University, 1979. *Dissertation Abstracts International, 40,* 1428A.

Urbschat, K. S. (1977). A study of preferred learning modes and their relationship to the amount of recall of CVC trigrams. Doctoral dissertation, Wayne State University, 1977. *Dissertation Abstracts International, 38,* 2536–5A.

Vazquez, A. W. (1985). Description of learning styles of high risk adult students taking courses in urban community colleges in Puerto Rico. Doctoral dissertation, Union for Experimenting Colleges and Universities, San Juan, Puerto Rico, 1985. *Dissertation Abstracts International, 47,* 1157A.

Virostko, J. (1983). An analysis of the relationships among academic achievement in mathematics and reading, assigned instructional schedules, and the learning style time preferences of third, fourth, fifth, and sixth grade students. Doctoral dissertation, St. John's University, 1983. *Dissertation Abstracts International, 44,* 1683A. Recipient of the Kappa Delta Pi International Award for Best Doctoral Research, 1983.

Weinberg, F. (1983). An experimental investigation of the interaction between sensory modality preference and mode of presentation in the instruction of arithmetic concepts to third grade underachievers. Doctoral dissertation, St. John's University, 1983. *Dissertation Abstracts International, 44,* 1740A.

Wheeler, R. (1980). An alternative to failure: Teaching reading according to students' perceptual strengths. *Kappa Delta Pi Record, 17*(2), 59–63.

Wheeler, R. (1983). An investigation of the degree of academic achievement evidenced when second grade, learning disabled students' perceptual preferences are matched and mismatched with complementary sensory approaches to beginning reading instruction. Doctoral dissertation, St. John's University, 1983. *Dissertation Abstracts International, 44,* 2039A.

White, R. (1981). An investigation of the relationship between selected instructional methods and selected elements of emotional learning style upon student achievement in seventh grade social studies. Doctoral dissertation, St. John's University, 1980. *Dissertation Abstracts International, 42,* 995A. Recipient of the Kappa Delta Gamma International Award for Best Doctoral Research Prospectus, 1980.

Zenhausern, R. (1980). Hemispheric dominance. *Learning Styles Network Newsletter 1*(2), 3. New York: St. John's University and the National Association of Secondary School Principals.

APPENDIX A

Research Based on the Dunn and Dunn Learning Styles Model

Andrews, R. H. (1990, July–September). The development of a learning styles program in a low socioeconomic, underachieving North Carolina elementary school. *Journal of Reading, Writing, and Learning Disabilities International, 6*(3), 307–313. New York: Hemisphere Press.

Avise, M. J. (1982). The relationship between learning styles and grades of Dexfield junior and senior high school students in Redfield, Iowa. Doctoral dissertation, Drake University, 1982. *Dissertation Abstracts International, 43,* 09A, 2953.

Bauer, E. (1991). The relationships between and among learning styles perceptual preferences, instructional strategies, mathematics achievement, and attitude toward mathematics of learning disabled and emotionally handicapped students in a suburban junior high school. Doctoral dissertation, St. John's University, New York.

Beaty, S. A. (1986). The effect of inservice training on the ability of teachers to observe learning styles of students. Doctoral dissertation, Oregon State University, 1986. *Dissertation Abstracts International, 47,* 1998A.

Bonham, L. A. (1987). Theoretical and practical differences and similarities among selected cognitive and learning styles of adults: An analysis of the literature, Volumes I and II. Doctoral dissertation, University of Georgia, 1987. *Dissertation Abstracts International, 48,* 2530A.

Brennan, P. K. (1984). An analysis of the relationships among hemispheric preference and analytic/global cognitive style, two elements of learning style, method of instruction, gender, and mathematics achievement of tenth-grade geometry students. Doctoral dissertation, St. John's University, 1984. *Dissertation Abstracts International, 45,* 3271A.

Brunner, C. E., & Majewski, W. S. (1990, October). Mildly handicapped students can succeed with learning styles. *Educational Leadership,* Alexandria, VA: Association for Supervision and Curriculum Development. *48,* 21–23.

Bruno, J. (1988). An experimental investigation of the relationships between and among hemispheric processing, learning style preferences, instructional strategies, academic achievement, and attitudes of developmental mathematics students in an urban technical college. Doctoral dissertation, St. John's University, 1988. *Dissertation Abstracts International, 48*(5), 1066A.

Buell, B. G., & Buell, N. A. (1987). Perceptual modality preference as a variable in the

507

effectiveness of continuing education for professionals. Doctoral dissertation, University of Southern California, 1987. *Dissertation Abstracts International, 48,* 283A.

Calvano, E. J. (1985). The influence of student learning styles on the mathematics achievement of middle school students. Doctoral dissertation, East Texas State University, 1985. *Dissertation Abstracts International, 46,* 10A.

Carbo, M. (1980). An analysis of the relationship between the modality preferences of kindergartners and selected reading treatments as they affect the learning of a basic sight-word vocabulary. Doctoral dissertation, St. John's University, 1980. *Dissertation Abstracts International, 41,* 1389A. Recipient of the Association for Supervision and Curriculum Development National Award for Best Doctoral Research, 1980.

Carns, A. W., & Carns, M. R. (1991, May). Teaching study skills, cognitive strategies, and metacognitive skills through self-diagnosed learning styles. *The School Counselor, 38,* 341–346.

Cholakis, M. M. (1986). An experimental investigation of the relationships between and among sociological preferences, vocabulary instruction and achievement, and the attitudes of New York, urban, seventh, and eighth grade underachievers. Doctoral dissertation, St. John's University, 1986. *Dissertation Abstracts International, 47,* 4046A.

Clark-Thayer, S. (1987). The relationship of the knowledge of student-perceived learning style preferences and study habits and attitudes to achievement of college freshmen in a small urban university. Doctoral dissertation, Boston University, 1987. *Dissertation Abstracts International, 48,* 872A.

Clay, J. E. (1984). A correlational analysis of the learning characteristics of highly achieving and poorly achieving freshmen at A & M University as revealed through performance on standardized tests. Normal: Alabama A & M University.

Cody, C. (1983). Learning styles, including hemispheric dominance: A comparative study of average, gifted, and highly gifted students in grades five through twelve. Doctoral dissertation, Temple University, 1983. *Dissertation Abstracts International, 44,* 1631A.

Cohen, L. (1986). Birth order and learning styles: An examination of the relationships between birth order and middle school students' preferred learning style profiles. Doctoral dissertation, University of Minnesota's Graduate Department of Educational Psychology, 1986. *Dissertation Abstracts International, 47,* 2084A.

Coleman, S. J. (1988). An investigation of the relationships among physical and emotional learning style preferences and perceptual modality strengths of gifted first-grade students. Doctoral dissertation, Virginia Polytechnic Institute and State University, 1988.

Cook, L. (1989). Relationships among learning style awareness, academic achievement, and locus of control among community college students. Doctoral dissertation, University of Florida. *Dissertation Abstracts International, 49*(03), 217A.

Cooper, T. J. D. (1991). An investigation of the learning styles of students at two contemporary alternative high schools in the District of Columbia. Doctoral dissertation, George Washington University, School of Education and Human Development.

Cramp, D. C. (1990). A study of the effects on student achievement of fourth- and fifth-grade students' instructional times being matched and mismatched with their particular time preference. Doctoral dissertation, University of Mississippi.

Crino, E. M. (1984). An analysis of the preferred learning styles of kindergarten children and the relationship of these preferred learning styles to curriculum planning for kindergarten children. Doctoral dissertation, State University of New York at Buffalo, 1984. *Dissertation Abstracts International, 45,* 1282A.

Davis, M. A. (1985). An investigation of the relationship of personality types and learning style preferences of high school students (Myers-Briggs type indicator, inventory). Doctoral dissertation, George Peabody College for Teachers of Vanderbilt University, 1985.

Dean, W. L. (1982). A comparison of the learning styles of educable mentally retarded students and learning disabled students. Doctoral dissertation, University of Mississippi, 1982. *Dissertation Abstracts International, 43,* 1923A.

DeBello, T. (1985). A critical analysis of the achievement and attitude effects of administrative assignments to social studies writing instruction based on identified, eighth grade students' learning style preferences for learning alone, with peers, or with teachers. Doctoral dissertation, St. John's University, 1985. *Dissertation Abstracts International, 47,* 68A.

DeBello, T. (1990, July–September). Comparison of eleven major learning style models: Variables, appropriate populations, validity of instrumentation, and the research behind them. *Journal of Reading, Writing, and Learning Disabilities International, 6*(3), 203–222. New York: Hemisphere.

DeGregoris, C. N. (1986). Reading comprehension and the interaction of individual sound preferences and varied auditory distractions. Doctoral dissertation, Hofstra University, 1986. *Dissertation Abstracts International, 47,* 3380A.

Delbrey, A. (1987, August). The relationship between the *Learning Style Inventory* and the *Gregorc Style Delineator.* (Doctoral dissertation, The University of Alabama, 1987). *Dissertation Abstracts International. 49*(2).

DellaValle, J. (1984). An experimental investigation of the word recognition scores of seventh grade students to provide supervisory and administrative guidelines for the organization of effective instructional environments. Doctoral dissertation, St. John's University, 1984. *Dissertation Abstracts International, 45,* 359A. Recipient of the Phi Delta Kappa National Award for Outstanding Doctoral Research, 1984; National Association of Secondary School Principals' Middle School Research Finalist Citation, 1984; and Association for Supervision and Curriculum Development Finalist for Best National Research (Supervision), 1984.

Della Valle, J. (1990, July–September). The development of a learning styles program in an affluent, suburban New York elementary school. New York: Hemisphere, *6*(3), 315–322.

Dunn, R. (1984). How should students do their homework? Research vs. Opinion. *Early Years, 14*(4), 43–45.

Dunn, R. (1985). A research-based plan for doing homework. *The Education Digest, 9,* 40–42.

Dunn, R. (1987, Spring). Research on instructional environments: Implications for student achievement and attitudes. *Professional School Psychology, 2*(1), 43–52.

Dunn, R. (1988). Commentary: Teaching students through their perceptual strengths or preferences. *Journal of Reading, 31*(4), 304–309.

Dunn, R. (1989a, May–June). Can schools overcome the impact to societal ills on student achievement? The research indicates—yes! *The Principal.* NY: Board of Jewish Education of Greater New York, *XXXIV (5), 1–15.*

Dunn, R. (1989b). Capitalizing on students' perceptual strengths to ensure literacy while engaging in conventional lecture/discussion. *Reading Psychology: An International Quarterly, 9,* 431–453.

Dunn, R. (1989c, Summer). Do students from different cultures have different learning styles? *International Education, 16*(50), 40–42. New Wilmington, PA: Association for the Advancement of International Education.

Dunn, R. (1989d). Individualizing instruction for mainstreamed gifted children. In R. R. Milgram (Ed.), *Teaching gifted and talented learners in regular classrooms.* Springfield, IL: Charles C Thomas, Chapter 3, pp. 63–111.

Dunn R. (1989e). Recent research on learning and seven applications to teaching young children to read. *The Oregon Elementary Principal, 50*(2), 29–32.

Dunn, R. (1989f, February). A small private school in Minnesota. *Teaching K-8, 18*(5), 54–57. Norwalk, CT: Early Years, Inc.

Dunn, R. (1989g, Fall). Teaching gifted students through their learning style strengths. *International Education, 16*(51), 6–8. New Wilmington, PA: Association for the Advancement of International Education.

Dunn, R. (1990a, January). Bias over substance: A critical analysis of Kavale and Forness' report on modality-based instruction. *Exceptional Children, 56*(4), 354–356. Reston, VA: Council for Exceptional Children.

Dunn, R. (1990b, October). Rita Dunn answers questions on learning styles. *Educational Leadership, 48*(15), 15–19. Alexandria, VA: Association for Supervision and Curriculum Development.

Dunn, R. (1990c, Winter). Teaching underachievers through their learning style strengths. *International Education, 16*(52), 5–7. New Wilmington, PA: Association for the Advancement of International Education.

Dunn, R. (1990d, Summer). Teaching young children to *read:* Matching methods of learning style perceptual processing strengths, Part One. *International Education, 17*(54), 3–4. New Wilmington, PA: Association for the Advancement of International Education.

Dunn, R. (1990e, July–September). Understanding the Dunn and Dunn learning styles model and the need for individual diagnosis and prescription. *Journal of Reading, Writing, and Learning Disabilities International, 6*(3), 223–247. New York: Hemisphere.

Dunn, R. (1991a). Are you willing to experiment with a tactual/visual/auditory global approach to reading? *International Education.* New Wilmington, PA: Association for the Advancement of International Education, *18*(56), 6–8.

Dunn, R. (1991b). Teaching young children to read: Matching methods of learning styles perceptual processing strengths, part two. *International Education, 17*(55), 5–7. New Wilmington, PA: Association for the Advancement of International Education.

Dunn, R., Beaudry, J. A., & Klavas, A. (1989). Survey of research on learning styles. *Educational Leadership, 46*(6), 50–58.

Dunn, R., & Bruno, A. (1985). What does the research on learning styles have to do with Mario? *The Clearing House, 59*(1), 9–11.

Dunn, R., Bruno, J., Sklar, R. I., Zenhausern, R., & Beaudry, J. (1990, May–June). Effects of matching and mismatching minority development college students' hemispheric preferences on mathematics scores. *Journal of Educational Research, 83*(5), 283–288. Washington, DC: Heldref Publications.

Dunn, R., Cavanaugh, D., Eberle, B., & Zenhausern, R. (1982). Hemispheric preference: The newest element of learning style. *The American Biology Teacher, 44*(5), 291–294.

Dunn, R., Deckinger, E. L., Withers, P., & Katzenstein, H. (1990, Winter). Should college students be taught how to do homework? The effects of studying marketing through individual perceptual strengths. *Illinois School Research and Development Journal, 26*(2), 96–113. Normal, Illinois Association for Supervision and Curriculum Development.

Dunn, R., Della Valle, J., Dunn, K., Geisert, G., Sinatra, R., & Zenhausern, R. (1986). The effects of matching and mismatching students' mobility preferences on recognition and memory tasks. *Journal of Educational Research, 79*(5), 267–272.

Dunn, R., Dunn, K., & Freeley, M. E. (1984). Practical applications of the research: Responding to students' learning styles—step one. *Illinois State Research and Development Journal, 21*(1), 1–21.

Dunn, R., Dunn, K., & Price, G. E. (1977). Diagnosing learning styles: Avoiding malpractice suits against school systems. *Phi Delta Kappan, 58*(5), 418–420.

Dunn, R., Dunn, K., Primavera, L., Sinatra, R., & Virsotko, J. (1987). A timely solution: A review of research on the effects of chronobiology on children's achievement and behavior. *The Clearing House, 612*(1), 5–8.

Dunn, R., Gemake, J., Jalali, F., Zenhausern, R., Quinn, P., & Spiridakis, J. (1990, April). Cross-cultural differences in the learning styles of elementary-grade students from four ethnic backgrounds. *Journal of Multicultural Counseling and Development, 18*(2), 68–93.

Dunn, R., Gemake, J., & Zenhausern, R. (1990, January). Cross-cultural differences in learning styles. *Missouri Association For Supervision and Curriculum Development Journal, 1*(2), 9–15.

Dunn, R., Giannitti, M. C., Murray, J. B., Geisert, G., Rossi, I., & Quinn, P. (1990, August). Grouping students for instruction: Effects of individual vs. group learning style on achievement and attitudes. *Journal of Social Psychology, 130*(4), 485–494.

Dunn, R., & Griggs, S. A. (1988a). High school dropouts: Do they learn differently from those who remain in school? *The Principal, 34,* 1–8.

Dunn, R., & Griggs, S. A. (1988b). *Learning styles: Quiet revolution in American secondary schools.* Reston, VA; National Association of Secondary School Principals.

Dunn, R., & Griggs, S. A. (1989a, January). Learning styles: Key to improving schools and student achievement. *Curriculum Report.* Reston, VA: National Association of Secondary School Principals, 4 pp.

Dunn, R., & Griggs, S. A. (1989b, October). The learning styles of multicultural groups and counseling implications. *Journal of Multicultural Counseling and Development, 7*(4), 146–155. Alexandria, VA: American Association for Multicultural Counseling and Development.

Dunn, R., & Griggs, S. A. (1989c). Learning styles: Quiet revolution in American secondary schools. *Momentum.* Washington, D.C.: Heldref Publications, *63*(1), 40–42.

Dunn, R., & Griggs, S. A. (1989d, April). A matter of style. *Momentum, 20*(2), 66–70. Washington, DC: National Catholic Education Association.

Dunn, R., Griggs, S. A. (1989e, January). A quiet revolution in Hempstead. Teaching K–8, *18*(5), 54–57. Norwalk, CT: Early Years, Inc.

Dunn, R., & Griggs, S. A. (1989f). A quiet revolution: Learning styles and their application to secondary schools. *Holistic Education, 2*(4), 14–19. Greenfield, MA: Holistic Education Review.

Dunn, R., & Griggs, S. A. (1990). Research on the learning style characteristics of selected racial and ethnic groups. *Journal of Reading, Writing, and Learning Disabilities, 6*(3), 261–280 Washington, DC: Hemisphere.

Dunn, R., Krimsky, J., Murray, J., & Quinn, P. (1985). Light up their lives: A review of research on the effects of lighting on children's achievement. *The Reading Teacher, 38*(9), 863–869.

Dunn, R, Pizzo, J., Sinatra, R., & Barretto, R. A. (1983, Winter). Can it be too quiet to learn? *Focus: Teaching English Language Arts, 9*(2), 92.

Dunn, R., & Price, G. (1980). The learning style characteristics of gifted children. Gifted Child Quarterly, *24*(1), 33–36.

Dunn, R., Price, G. E., Dunn, K., & Griggs, S. A. (1981). Studies in students' learning styles. *Roeper Review, 4*(2), 38–40.

Dunn, R., and Smith, J. B. (1990). Chapter Four: Learning styles and library media programs, In J. B. Smith (Ed.), *School Library Media Annual* pp. 32–49. Englewood, CO: Libraries Unlimited, Inc.

Dunn, R., White, R. M., & Zenhausern, R. (1982). An investigation of responsible versus less responsible students. *Illinois School Research and Development, 19*(1), 19–24.

Fleming, V. J. (1989, August). Vocational classrooms with style. *Vocational Education Journal, 10*(1), 36–39. Alexandria, VA: American Vocational Association.

Freeley, M. E. (1984). An experimental investigation of the relationships among teachers' individual time preferences, inservice workshop schedules, and instructional techniques and the subsequent implementation of learning style strategies in participants' classrooms. Doctoral dissertation, St. John's University, 1984. *Dissertation Abstracts International, 46,* 403A.

Gadwa, K., & Griggs, S. A. (1985). The school dropout: Implications for counselors. *The School Counselor, 33,* 9–17.

Gardiner, B. (1983). Stepping into a learning styles program. *Roeper Review, 6*(2), 90–92.

Gardiner, B. (1986). An experimental analysis of selected teaching strategies implemented at specific times of the school day and their effects on the social studies achievement test scores and attitudes of fourth grade, low achieving students in an urban school setting. Doctoral dissertation, St. John's University, 1986. *Dissertation Abstracts International, 47,* 3307A.

Garger, S. (1990, October). Is there a link between learning style and neurophysiology? *Educational Leadership, 48*(2), 63–65. Alexandria, VA: Association for Supervision and Curriculum Development.

Garrett, S. L. (1991). The effects of perceptual preference and motivation on vocabulary and attitude scores among high school students. Doctoral dissertation, University of LaVerne.

Geisert, G., Dunn, R. (1991, March). Computers and learning styles. *Principal.* Reston, VA. National Association of Elementary School Principals, *70*(4), 47–49.

Geisert, G., and Dunn, R. (1991, March/April). Effective use of computers: Assignments based on individual learning style. *The Clearing House.* Washington, DC: Heldref Publications, *64*(4), 219–224.

Geisert, G., Dunn, R., & Sinatra, R. (1990). Combining learning styles and computer education to improve reading. *Journal of Reading, Writing, and Learning Disabilities, 6*(3), 297–305. Washington, DC: Hemisphere.

Giannitti, M. C. (1988). An experimental investigation of the relationships among the learning style sociological preferences of middle-school students (grades 6, 7, 8), their attitudes and achievement in social studies, and selected instructional strategies. Doctoral dissertation, St. John's University, 1988. *Dissertation Abstracts International, 49,* 2911A.

Gould, B. J. (1987). An investigation of the relationships between supervisors' and supervisees' sociological productivity styles on teacher evaluations and interpersonal attraction ratings. Doctoral dissertation, St. John's University, 1987. *Dissertation Abstracts International, 48,* 18A.

Griggs, S. A., & Dunn, R., (1990, September). Is this a counselor's responsibility? *School Counselor, 38*(1), 24–51. Alexandria, VA: American Association for Counseling and Development.

Griggs, S. A. (1991). Learning style counseling. Ann Arbor: University of Michigan. Available from Center for the Study of Learning and Teaching Style, St. John's University, New York 11439.

Griggs, S. A. (1990). Counseling students toward effective study skills using their learning style strengths. *Journal of Reading, Writing, and Learning Disabilities: International, 6*(3) 223–247. New York: Hemisphere.

Griggs, S. A. (1985). *Counseling students through their individual learning styles.* Ann Arbor: University of Michigan. Obtainable from Center for the Study of Learning and Teaching Styles, St. John's University, Jamaica, NY 11439.

Griggs, S. A. (1989, November). Students' sociological grouping preferences of learning styles. *The Clearing House, 63*(3) 135–139. Washington, DC: Heldref. Publications.

Griggs, S. A. & Price, G. E., (1981). Self-concept relates to learning styles in the junior high school. *Phi Delta Kappan, 62,* 604.

Griggs, S. A., & Price, G. E. (1982). A comparison between the learning styles of gifted versus average junior high school students. *Creative and Gifted Child Quarterly, 7,* 39–42.

Griggs, S. A., Price, G. E., Kopel, S., & Swaine, W. (1984). The effects of group counseling with sixth-grade students using approaches that are compatible versus incompatible with selected learning style elements. *California Personnel and Guidance Journal, 5*(1), 28–35.

Guinta, S. F. (1984). Administrative considerations concerning learning style and the influence of instructor/student congruence on high schoolers' achievement and educators' perceived stress. Doctoral dissertation, St. John's University, 1984. *Dissertation Abstracts International, 45,* 32A.

Guzzo, R. S. (1987). Dificuldades de apprenddizagem: Modalidade de attencao e analise de tarefas em materials didaticos. Doctoral dissertation, University of Sao Paulo, Institute of Pyschology, Brazil, 1987.

Hanna, S. J. (1989). An investigation of the effects on achievement test scores of individual time preferences and time of training in a corporate setting. Doctoral dissertation, St. John's University, 1989.

Harp, T. Y., & Orsak, L. (1990, July–September). One administrator's challenge: Implementing a learning style program at the secondary level. *Journal of Reading, Writing, and Learning Disabilities International, 6*(3), 335–342. New York: Hemisphere.

Harty, P. M. (1982). *Learning styles: A matter of difference in the foreign language classroom.* Unpublished master's dissertation, Wright State University.

Hawk, T. D. (1983). A comparison of teachers' preference for specific inservice activity approaches and their measured learning styles. Doctoral dissertation, Kansas State University, 1983. *Dissertation Abstracts International, 44,* 12-A, 3557.

Hill, G. D. (1987). An experimental investigation into the interaction between modality preference and instructional mode in the learning of spelling words by upper-elementary learning disabled students. Doctoral dissertation, North Texas State University, 1987. *Dissertation Abstracts International, 48,* 2536A.

Hodges, H. (1985). An analysis of the relationships among preferences for a formal/informal design, one element of learning style, academic achievement, and attitudes of seventh and eighth grade students in remedial mathematics classes in a New York City junior high school. Doctoral dissertation, St. John's University, 1985. *Dissertation Abstracts International, 45,* 2791A. Recipient: Phi Delta Kappa National Finalist Award for Outstanding Doctoral Research, 1986.

Ignelzi-Ferraro, D. M. (1989). Identification of the preferred conditions for learning among three groups of mildly handicapped high school students using the *Learning Style Inventory.* Doctoral dissertation, University of Pittsburgh, 1989. *Dissertation Abstracts International, 51*(3), 796A.

Ingham, J. (1989). An experimental investigation of the relationships among learning style perceptual preference, instructional strategies, training achievement, and attitudes of corporate employees. Doctoral dissertation, St. John's University, 1989. *Dissertation Abstracts International, 51,* 02A. Recipient: American Society for Training and Development (ASTD) National Research Award, 1990.

Ingham, J. (1991). Matching instruction with employee perceptual preference significantly increases training effectiveness. *Human Resource Development Quarterly, 2*(1), 53–64. San Francisco: Jossey-Bass.

Jacobs, R. L. (1987). An investigation of the learning style differences among Afro-

American and Euro-American high, average, and low achievers. Doctoral dissertation, Peabody University, 1987.

Jalali, F. (1988). A cross cultural comparative analysis of the learning styles and field dependence/independence characteristics of selected fourth-, fifth-, and sixth-grade students of Afro, Chinese, Greek, and Mexican heritage. Doctoral dissertation, St. John's University, 1988.

Jarsonbeck, S. (1984). The effects of a right-brain and mathematics curriculum on low achieving, fourth grade students. Doctoral dissertation, University of South Florida, 1984. *Dissertation Abstracts International, 45,* 2791A.

Johnson, C. D. (1984). Identifying potential school dropouts. Doctoral dissertation, United States International University. *Dissertation Abstracts International, 45,* 2397A.

Kahre, C. J. (1985). Relationships between learning styles of student teachers, cooperating teachers, and final evaluations. Doctoral dissertation, Arizona State University, 1984. *Dissertation Abstracts International, 45,* 2493A.

Kaley, S. B. (1977). Field dependence/independence and learning styles in sixth graders. Doctoral dissertation, Hofstra University, 1977. *Dissertation Abstracts International, 38,* 1301A.

Kelly, A. P. (1989). Elementary principals' change-facilitating behavior as perceived by self and staff when implementing learning styles instructional programs. Doctoral dissertation, St. John's University, 1989.

Klavas, A. (1991). Implementation of the Dunn and Dunn learning styles model in United States' elementary schools: Principals' and teachers' perceptions of factors that facilitated or impeded the process. Doctoral dissertation, St. John's University, New York.

Kreitner, K. R. (1981). *Modality strengths and learning styles of musically talented high school students.* Unpublished master's dissertation, The Ohio State University.

Krimsky, J. (1982). A comparative analysis of the effects of matching and mismatching fourth grade students with their learning style preference for the environmental element of light and their subsequent reading speed and accuracy scores. Doctoral dissertation, St. John's University, 1982. *Dissertation Abstracts International, 43,* 66A. Recipient of the Association for Supervision and Curriculum Development First Alternate National Recognition for Best Doctoral Research (Curriculum), 1982.

Kroon, D. (1985). An experimental investigation of the effects on academic achievement and the resultant administrative implications of instruction congruent and incongruent with secondary, industrial arts students' learning style perceptual preference. Doctoral dissertation, St. John's University, 1985. *Dissertation Abstracts International, 46,* 3247A.

Kulp, J. J. (1982). A description of the processes used in developing and implementing a teacher training program based on the Dunns' concept of learning style. Doctoral dissertation, Temple University, 1982. *Dissertation Abstracts International, 42,* 5021A.

Lam-Phoon, S. (1986). A comparative study of the learning styles of Southeast Asian and American Caucasian college students of two Seventh-Day Adventist campuses. Doctoral dissertation, Andrews University, 1986.

Lan- Yong, F. (1989). Ethnic, gender, and grade differences in the learning style preferences of gifted minority students. Doctoral dissertation, Southern Illinois University at Carbondale.

LeClair, T. J. (1986). The preferred perceptual modality of kindergarten aged children. California State University, 1986. *Master's Abstracts, 24,* 324.

Lemmon, P. (1985). A school where learning styles make a difference. *Principal, 64*(4), 26–29.

Lengal, O. (1983). Analysis of the preferred learning styles of former adolescent psychiatric patients. Doctoral dissertation, Kansas State University, 1983. *Dissertation Abstracts International, 44,* 2344A.

Li, T. C. (1983). *The learning styles of the Filipino graduate students of the evangelical seminaries in metro Manila. Unpublished doctoral dissertation, Asia Graduate School of Theology, Phillipines.*

Lux, K. (1987). Special needs students: A qualitative study of their learning styles. Doctoral dissertation, Michigan State University, 1987. *Dissertation Abstracts International, 49*(3), 421A.

Lynch, P. K. (1981). An analysis of the relationships among academic achievement, attendance, and the learning style time references of eleventh and twelfth grade students identified as initial or chronic truants in a suburban New York school district. Doctoral dissertation, St. John's University, 1981. *Dissertation Abstracts International, 42,* 1880A. Recipient of the Association for Supervision and Curriculum Development, First Alternate National Recognition for Best Doctoral Research (Supervision), 1981.

MacMurren, H. (1985). A comparative study of the effects of matching and mismatching sixth-grade students with their learning style preferences for the physical element of intake and their subsequent reading speed and accuracy scores and attitudes. Doctoral dissertation, St. John's University, 1985. *Dissertation Abstracts International, 46,* 3247A.

Madison, M. B. (1984). A study of learning style preferences of specific learning disability students. University Microfilms Order No. ADG86–00733). *Dissertation Abstracts International, 46,* 3320A.

Marcus, L. (1977). How teachers view learning styles. *NASSP Bulletin, 61,*(408), 112–114.

Mariash, L. J. (1983). Identification of characteristics of learning styles existent among students attending school in selected northeastern Manitoba communities. Unpublished master's dissertation, University of Manitoba, Winnipeg, Canada.

Martini, M. (1986). An analysis of the relationships between and among computer-assisted instruction, learning style perceptual preferences, attitudes, and the science achievement of seventh grade students in a suburban, New York school district. Doctoral dissertation, St. John's University, 1986. *Dissertation Abstracts International, 47,* 877A. Recipient of the American Association of School Administrators (AASA) First Prize, National Research, 1986.

McEwen, P. (1985). *Learning styles, intelligence, and creativity among elementary school students.* Unpublished master's dissertation, State University of New York at Buffalo, Center for Studies on Creativity.

McFarland, M. (1989). An analysis of the relationship between learning style perceptual preferences and attitudes toward computer assisted instruction. Doctoral dissertation, Portland State University.

Mein, J. R. (1986). Cognitive and learning style characteristics high school gifted students. Doctoral dissertation, University of Florida, 1986. *Dissertation Abstracts International, 48,* 04, 880A.

Melone, R. A. (1987). The relationship between the level of cognitive development and learning styles of the emerging adolescent. Doctoral dissertation, State University of New York at Buffalo, 1987. *Dissertation Abstracts International, 38,* 607A.

Mickler, M. L., & Zippert, C. P. (1987). Teaching strategies based on learning styles of adult students. *Community/Junior College Quarterly, 11,* 33–37.

Miles, B. (1987). An investigation of the relationships among the learning style sociological preferences of fifth and sixth grade students, selected interactive classroom patterns and achievement in career awareness and career decision-making concepts. Doctoral dissertation, St. John's University, 1987. *Dissertation Abstracts International, 48,* 2527A. Recipient of the Phi Delta Kappan Eastern Regional Research Finalist, 1988.

Miller, L. M. (1985). Mobility as an element of learning style: The effect its inclusion or exclusion has on student performance in the standardized testing environment. Unpublished master's dissertation, University of North Florida.

Monheit, S. L. (1987). An analysis of learning based upon the relationship between the learning style preferences of parents and their children. Doctoral dissertation, The Fielding Institute, 1987.

Morgan, H. L. (1981). Learning styles: The relation between need for structure and preferred mode of instruction for gifted elementary students. Doctoral dissertation, University of Pittsburgh, 1981. *Dissertation Abstracts International, 43,* 2223A.

Morris, V. J. P. (1983). The design and implementation of a teaching strategy for language arts at Chipley High School that brings about predictable learning outcomes. Doctoral dissertation, Florida State University, 1983. *Dissertation Abstracts International, 44,* 3231A.

Moss, V. B. (1981). The stability of first-graders' learning styles and the relationship between selected variables and learning style. Doctoral dissertation, Mississippi State University, 1981.

Murrain, P. G. (1983). Administrative determinations concerning facilities utilization and instructional grouping: An analysis of the relationships between selected thermal environments and preferences for temperature, an element of learning style, as they affect word recognition scores of secondary students. Doctoral dissertation, St. John's University, 1983. *Dissertation Abstracts International, 44,* 1749A.

Murray, C. A. (1980). The comparison of learning styles between low and high reading achievement subjects in the seventh and eighth grades in a public middle school. Doctoral dissertation, United States International University, 1980. *Dissertation Abstracts International, 41,* 1005.

Napolitano, R. A. (1986). An experimental investigation of the relationships among achievement, attitude scores, and traditionally, marginally, and underprepared college students enrolled in an introductory psychology course when they are matched and mismatched with their learning style preferences for the element of structure. Doctoral dissertation, St. John's University, 1986. *Dissertation Abstracts International, 47,* 435A.

Nganwa-Baguma, M. J. (1986). Learning styles: The effects of matching and mismatching pupils' design preferences on reading comprehension tests. Bachelor's dissertation, University of Transkei, South Africa, 1986.

Orsak, L. (1990, October). Learning styles versus the Rip Van Winkle syndrome. *Educational Leadership, 48*(2), 19–20. Alexandria, VA: Association for Supervision and Curriculum Development.

Ostoyee, C. H. (1988). The effects of teaching style on student writing about field trips with concrete experiences. Doctoral dissertation, Columbia University, Teachers College, 1988. *Dissertation Abstracts International, 49,* 2916A.

Paskewitz, B. U. (1985). A study of the relationship between learning styles and attitudes toward computer programming of middle school gifted students. Doctoral dissertation, University of Pittsburgh, 1985. *Dissertation Abstracts International, 47*(03), 697A.

Pederson, J. K. (1984). The classification and comparison of learning disabled students and gifted students. Doctoral dissertation, Texas Tech University, 1984. *Dissertation Abstracts International, 46,* 342A.

Perrin, J. (1984). An experimental investigation of the relationships among the learning style sociological preferences of gifted and non-gifted primary children, selected instructional strategies, attitudes, and achievement in problem solving and rote memorization. Doctoral dissertation, St. John's University, 1984. *Dissertation*

Abstracts International, 46, 342A. Recipient: American Association of School Administrators (AASA) National Research Finalist, 1984.

Perrin, J. (1990, October). The learning styles project for potential dropouts. *Educational Leadership, 48*(2), 23–24. Alexandria, VA: Association for Supervision and Curriculum Development.

Pizzo, J. (1981). An investigation of the relationships between selected acoustic environments and sound, an element of learning style, as they affect sixth grade students' reading achievement and attitudes. (Doctoral dissertation, St. John's University, 1981). *Dissertation Abstracts International, 42,* 2475A. Recipient: Association for Supervision and Curriculum Development First Alternate National Recognition for Best Doctoral Research (Curriculum), 1981.

Pizzo, J. (1982, December). Breaking the sound barrier: Classroom noise and learning style. *Orbit, 64,* Ontario Canada: Ontario Institute for Studies in Education, *13*(4), 21–22.

Pizzo, J., Dunn, R., & Dunn, K. (1990, July–September). A sound approach to reading: Responding to students' learning styles. *Journal of Reading, Writing, and Learning Disabilities International.* Washington, D.C.: Hemisphere Publishing Corporation, *6*(3), 249–260.

Ponder, D. (1990). An analysis of the changes and gender differences in preferences of learning styles at adolescence and the relationship of the learning styles of adolescents and their parents when matched and mismatched according to gender. Doctoral dissertation, East Texas State University, 1990. *Dissertation Abstracts International, 64*(4), 1170A.

Price, G. E. (1980). Which learning style elements are stable and which tend to change over time? *Learning Styles Network Newsletter, 1*(3), 1.

Rahal, B. F. (1986). The effects of matching and mismatching the diagnosed learning styles of intermediate level students with their structure preferences in the learning environment. Doctoral dissertation, West Virginia University. *Dissertation Abstracts International, 47*(6), 2010A.

Ramirez, A. I. (1982). Modality and field dependence/independence: Learning components and their relationship to mathematics achievement in the elementary school. Doctoral dissertation, Florida State University, 1982. *Dissertation Abstracts International, 43,* 666.

Rea, D. C. (1980). Effects on achievement of placing students in different learning environments based upon identified learning styles. Doctoral dissertation, University of Missouri, 1989.

Reid, J. M. (1987, March). The learning style preferences of ESL students. *TESOL Quarterly, 21,* 87–105. Available to members only from TESP, 1118 22nd Street, N.W., Georgetown University, Suite 205, Washington, DC 20037.

Ricca, J. (1983). Curricular implications of learning style differences between gifted and non-gifted students. Doctoral dissertation, State University of New York at Buffalo, 1983. *Dissertation Abstracts International, 44,* 1324-A.

Roberts, O. A. (1984). Investigation of the relationship between learning style and temperament of senior high students in the Bahamas and Jamaica. Graduate dissertation, Andrews University, 1984.

Sage, C. O. (1984). The Dunn and Dunn learning style model: An analysis of its theoretical, practical, and research foundations. Doctoral dissertation, University of Denver, 1984. *Dissertation Abstracts International, 45*(12), 3537A.

Shands, R., & Brunner, C., (1989, Fall). Providing success through a powerful combination: Mastery learning and learning styles. *Perceptions, 25,*(1), 6–10. New York: New York State Educators of the Emotionally Disturbed.

Shea, T. C. (1983). An investigation of the relationship among preferences for the learning style element of design, selected instructional environments, and reading achievement with ninth grade students to improve administrative determinations concerning effective educational facilities. Doctoral dissertation, St. John's University, 1983. *Dissertation Abstracts International, 44,* 2004A. Recipient of the National Association of Secondary School Principals' Middle School Research Finalist Citation, 1984.

Siebenman, J. B. (1984). An investigation of the relationship between learning style and cognitive style in non-traditional college reading students. Doctoral dissertation, Arizona State University, 1984. *Dissertation Abstracts International, 45,* 1705A.

Sims, J. E. (1988). Learning styles: A comparative analysis of the learning styles of Black-American, Mexican-American, and White-American third and fourth grade students in traditional public schools. Doctoral dissertation, University of Santa Barbara, 1988.

Sinatra, C. (1990, July–September). Five diverse secondary schools where learning style instruction works. *Journal of Reading, Writing, and Learning Disabilities International, 6*(3), 323–342. New York: Hemisphere.

Sinatra, R., Hirshoren, A., & Primavera, L. H. (1987). Learning style, behavior ratings and achievement interactions for adjudicated adolescents. *Educational and Psychological Research, 7*(1), 21–32.

Sinatra, R., Primavera, L., & Waked, W. J. (1986). Learning style and intelligence of reading disabled students. *Perceptual and Motor Skills, 62,* 1243–1250.

Smith, S. (1987). An experimental investigation of the relationship between and among achievement, preferred time of instruction, and critical-thinking abilities of tenth- and eleventh-grade students in mathematics. Doctoral dissertation, St. John's University, 1987. *Dissertation Abstracts International, 47,* 1405A.

Smith, T. D. (1988). An assessment of the self-perceived teaching style of three ethnic groups of public school teachers in Texas. Doctoral dissertation, East Texas University, 1988. *Dissertation Abstracts International, 49* A-08, pg. 2062A.

Snider, T. D. (1988). A study of learning preferences among educable mentally impaired, emotionally impaired, learning disabled, and general education students in seventh, eighth, and ninth grades as measured by response to the *Learning Styles Inventory.* Doctoral dissertation, Michigan State University, 1985. *Dissertation Abstracts International, 46,* 1251.

Solberg, S. J. (1987). An analysis of the Learning Style Inventory, the Productivity Environmental Preference Survey, and the Iowa Test of Basic Skills. Doctoral dissertation, Northern Arizona University, 1987. *Dissertation Abstracts International, 48,* 2530A.

Spires, R. D. (1983). The effect of teacher inservice about learning styles on students' mathematics and reading achievement. Doctoral dissertation, Bowling Green State University, 1983. *Dissertation Abstracts International, 44,* 1325A.

Steinauer, M. H. (1981). Interpersonal relationships as reflected in learning style preferences: A study of eleventh grade students and their English teachers in a vocational school. Doctoral dissertation, Southern Illinois University, 1981. *Dissertation Abstracts International, 43,* 305A.

Stiles, R. (1985). Learning style preferences for design and their relationship to standardized test results. Doctoral dissertation, University of Tennessee, 1985. *Dissertation Abstracts International, 46,* 2551A.

Stokes, B. M. (1989). An analysis of the relationship between learning style, achievement, race, and gender. Doctoral dissertation, The University of Akron, 1989. *Dissertation Abstracts International, 49,* 757A.

Svreck, L. J. (1990). Perceived parental influence, accommodated learning style preferences, and students' attitudes toward learning as they relate to reading and mathematics achievement. (Doctoral dissertation, St. John's University, 1990).

Sykes, S., Jones, B., & Phillips, J. (1990, October). Partners in learning styles at a private school. *Educational Leadership, 48*(2), 24–26. Alexandria, VA: Association for Supervision and Curriculum Development.

Tanenbaum, R. (1982). An investigation of the relationships between selected instructional techniques and identified field dependent and field independent cognitive styles as evidenced among high school students enrolled in studies of nutrition. Doctoral dissertation, St. John's University, 1982. *Dissertation Abstracts International, 43,* 68A.

Tappenden, V. J. (1983). Analysis of the learning styles of vocational education and nonvocational education students in eleventh and twelfth grades from rural, urban, and suburban locations in Ohio. Doctoral dissertation, Kent State University, 1983. *Dissertation Abstracts International, 44,* 1326A.

Tenny, C. (1989). The learning styles of Filipino graduate students in the evangelical seminary in metropolitan Manila. Doctoral dissertation, Asia Graduate School of Theology, Phillipines, 1989.

Trautman, P. (1979). An investigation of the relationship between selected instructional techniques and identified cognitive style. Doctoral dissertation, St. John's University, 1979. *Dissertation Abstracts International, 40,* 1428A.

Vazquez, A. W. (1985). Description of learning styles of high risk adult students taking courses in urban community colleges in Puerto Rico. Doctoral dissertation, Union for Experimenting Colleges and Universities, Puerto Rico, 1985. *Dissertation Abstracts International, 47,* 1157A.

Vignia, R. A. (1983). An investigation of learning styles of gifted and non-gifted high school students. Doctoral dissertation, University of Houston, 1983. *Dissertation Abstracts International, 44,* 3653A.

Virostko, J. (1983). An analysis of the relationships among academic achievement in mathematics and reading, assigned instructional schedules, and the learning style time preferences of third, fourth, fifth, and sixth grade students. Doctoral dissertation, St. John's University, 1983. *Dissertation Abstracts International, 44,* 1683A. Recipient of the Kappa Delta Pi International Award for Best Doctoral Research, 1983.

Weinberg, F. (1983). An experimental investigation of the interaction between sensory modality preference and mode of presentation in the instruction of arithmetic concepts to third grade underachievers. Doctoral dissertation, St. John's University, 1983. *Dissertation Abstracts International, 44,* 1740A.

Wheeler R. (1983). An investigation of the degree of academic achievement evidenced when second grade, learning disabled students' perceptual preferences are matched and mismatched with complementary sensory approaches to beginning reading instruction. Doctoral dissertation, St. John's University, 1983. *Dissertation Abstracts International, 44,* 2039A.

White, R. (1980). An investigation of the relationship between selected instructional methods and selected elements of emotional learning style upon student achievement in seventh grade social studies. Doctoral dissertation, St. John's University, 1980. *Dissertation Abstracts International, 42,* 995A. Recipient of the Kappa Delta Gamma International Award for Best Doctoral Research Prospectus, 1980.

Wild, J. B. (1979). A study of the learning styles of learning disabled students and non-learning students at the junior high school level. Unpublished master's dissertation, University of Kansas, Lawrence.

Williams, G. L. (1984). The effectiveness of computer assisted instruction and its relationship to selected learning style elements. Doctoral dissertation, North Texas State University, 1984. *Dissertation Abstracts International, 45, 1986A.*

Wingo, L. H. (1980). Relationships among locus of motivation, sensory modality and grouping preferences of learning style to basic skills test performance in reading and mathematics. Doctoral dissertation, Memphis State University, 1980. *Dissertation Abstracts International, 41,* 2923.

Wittenberg, S. K. (1984). A comparison of diagnosed and preferred learning styles of young adults in need of remediation. Doctoral dissertation, University of Toledo, 1984. *Dissertation Abstracts International, 45,* 3539A.

Wittig, C. (1985). Learning style preferences among students high or low on divergent thinking and feeling variables. Unpublished master's dissertation, State University College of Buffalo at New York, Center for Studies on Creativity, 1985.

Wolfe, G. (1983). Learning styles and the teaching of reading. Doctoral dissertation, Akron University, 1983. *Dissertation Abstracts International, 45,* 3422A.

Yeap, L. L. (1987). Learning styles of Singapore Secondary Two students. Doctoral dissertation, University of Pittsburgh, 1987. *Dissertation Abstracts International, 48,* 936A.

Young, B. M. P. (1985). Effective conditions for learning: An analysis of learning environments and learning styles in ability-grouped classes. Doctoral dissertation, University of Massachusetts, 1985. *Dissertation Abstracts International, 46,* 708A.

Zak, F. (1989). Learning style discrimination between vocational and nonvocational students. Doctoral dissertation, University of Massachusetts.

Zikmund, A. B. (1988). The effect of grade level, gender, and learning style on responses to conservation type rhythmic and melodic patterns. Doctoral dissertation, The University of Nebraska, 1988. *Dissertation Abstracts International, 50,* 01A.

_____ APPENDIX B_____

Instruments for Identifying Learning or Teaching Styles

- *Adults' Learning Styles: Productivity Environmental Preference Survey* (PEPS). Specimen Set, Tests, and Processing. Price Systems, Box 1818, Lawrence, KS 66044–1818.
- *Students' Learning Styles (Grades 3–12): Learning Style Inventory* (LSI). Specimen Set, Tests, and Processing. Price Systems, Box 1818, Lawrence, KS 66044–1818.
- *Students' Learning Styles (Grades K–2): Learning Style Inventory: Primary Version* (LSI:P). Center for the Study of Learning and Teaching Styles, St. John's University, Utopia Parkway, Jamaica, NY 11439.
- *Teachers' Teaching Styles: Teaching Style Inventory* (TSI) (Chapter 10).

INDEX